You Name It
The Bible Has It!

Easy Quick References

Gordon Kashner

WINEPRESS WP PUBLISHING

I dedicate this work to my three dear children:
Bonnie, Ron, and Debbie.

• ACKNOWLEDGEMENTS •

Contributions to my dedicated life are: My parents, for starting us five children on the right path; Taylor University, Upland, Indiana for examples of Christ-like living today; and to all past and present true gospel messengers. PTL (Praise the Lord).

I like this definition: "Worship is bestowing worth to God", per Pastor Charles Gray.

• PREFACE •

The contents of this book provides an encouraging way of assisting the new or non-readers of the Bible to become acquainted with the precious Book, as well as being an aid to those who are studying the Scriptures.

It is made up of references regarding the use of common words, which I have found in the King James translation of the Bible. It could be continued endlessly; however, it is not intended to include all references, but one or more is listed for each word. It is a simple, easy, and quick way of finding any word, lesson, instruction, situation, prophecy, or historical fact.

Also, between the Bible covers, we can find and experience how much God loves us; His instructions for our living; strength from His word with promises, even to the end times (especially those found in the book of Revelation); and Christ's resurrection, which was offered for all.

It is my prayer that the direct and easy effort of using this book will be successful in encouraging more people to use the precious Book. By learning the names of both the Old Testament (OT) and the New Testament (NT), you will become proud of your skill in finding the references more quickly.

God loves everyone and will reward the Bible reader.
A much-used Bible is a beautiful sight.

ABBREVIATIONS

AA, BB, Etc.   End of book, double letters

AD   After Death (of Jesus Christ)

&   And

+   Another chapter in the same book

–>   Continue until next named reference

Etc.   Et cetera, or, and so forth

NT   New Testament   On an introductory page, the books are listed with

OT   Old Testament   the abbreviations.

Re   Regarding

vs   Versus, or against

READING CODE: When a comma appears after a key word, it indicates that the word or phrase following the comma is read before that key word.

Old Testament Books with Abbreviations

LAW

Gen.	Genesis
Exod.	Exodus
Lev.	Leviticus
Num.	Numbers
Deut.	Deuteronomy

HISTORY

Josh.	Joshua
Judg.	Judges
Ruth	Ruth
1 Sam.	1 Samuel
2 Sam.	2 Samuel
1 Kings	1 Kings
2 Kings	2 Kings
1 Chron.	1 Chronicles
2 Chron.	2 Chronicles
Ezra	Ezra
Neh.	Nehemiah
Esther	Esther

POETRY

Job	Job
Ps.	Psalms
Prov.	Proverbs
Eccles.	Ecclesiastes
Song of Sol.	Song of Solomon

MAJOR PROPHETS

Isa.	Isaiah
Jer.	Jeremiah
Lam.	Lamentations
Ezek.	Ezekiel
Dan.	Daniel

MINOR PROPHETS

Hos.	Hosea
Joel	Joel
Amos	Amos
Obad.	Obadiah
Jon.	Jonah
Mic.	Micah
Nah.	Nahum
Hab.	Habakkuk
Zeph.	Zephaniah
Hag.	Haggai
Zech.	Zechariah
Mal.	Malachi

New Testament Books with Abbreviations

GOSPEL WRITERS

Matt.	Matthew
Mark	Mark
Luke	Luke
John	John

PAUL'S LETTERS

Rom.	Romans
1 Cor.	1 Corinthians
2 Cor.	2 Corinthians
Gal.	Galatians
Eph.	Ephesians
Phil.	Philippians
Col.	Colossians
1 Thess.	1 Thessalonians
2 Thess.	2 Thessalonians
1 Tim.	1 Timothy
2 Tim.	2 Timothy
Titus	Titus
Philem.	Philemon

ACTS OF THE APOSTLES

Acts	Acts

OTHER BOOKS

Heb.	Hebrews
James	James
1 Pet.	1 Peter
2 Pet.	2 Peter
1 John	1 John
2 John	2 John
3 John	3 John
Jude	Jude

VISION

Rev.	Revelation

· A ·

A	Gen. 2:5–9, 10, 21, 22–24; Acts 10:26
Abase	Job 40:11; Dan. 4:37
" and exalt	Ezek. 21:26
Abased	Matt. 23:12; Luke 18:14
Abasing	2 Cor. 11:7
Abba	Rom. 8:15
Abel	Gen. 4:2–9; 1 John 3:12
Abhor	Lev. 20:23; Job 30:10, + 42:6; Ps. 78:59, + 119:163; Rom. 12:9
Abhorrest	Rom. 2:22
Abhorreth	Job 33:20
Abide	Luke 24:29; 1 Cor. 3:14
" Comforter	John 14:16
" forever	1 John 2:17
" in Him	John 14:16, + 15:4–7, 10; 2 Pet. 3:6; 1 John 2:28
" " us	1 John 2:24, 25, 27, + 3:24
Abideth	John 8:35; 1 Pet. 1:23; 1 John 2:6, 10, 14, 17, + 3:6, 14
" three	1 Cor. 13:13

11

Ability	Dan. 1:4
" to destroy earth	Rev. 11:19
" " minister each his	
own way	1 Pet. 4:11
Abjects	Ps. 35:15
Able	Num. 13:30, 31; Matt. 22:46;
	1 Cor. 10:13; 2 Cor. 3:6;
	James 4:12
" is the Lord God	Rom. 4:21, + 15:13; 2 Cor. 9:8;
	Eph. 3:20
" to withstand wrath	Rev. 6:17
Abode	Luke 21:37; John 1:32, 39, +
	14:23; Acts 12:19, + 14:28;
	Gal. 1:18
Abolished	Isa. 51:6; 2 Cor. 3:13;
	2 Tim. 1:10
Abomination	Gen. 43:32; Lev. 20:13;
	Ezek. 7:8, 9; Dan. 9:27, +
	12:11; Matt. 24:15; Mark 13:14;
	Rev. 21:27
" to the Lord	Deut. 18:10–12; Prov. 6:16
Abound in grace	2 Cor. 8:7, + 9:8; 1 Thess. 4:1
" " hope	Rom. 15:13
" " love	1 Cor. 1:9, 10; Phil. 1:9, +
	4:12, 18
" , suffering of Christ	2 Cor. 1:5
Abound to good works	1 Cor. 15:58;
	2 Cor. 9:6–8
Abounded to many, grace	Rom. 5:15; 2 Cor. 1:5;
	Eph. 1:8
Above power source	John 19:11
" things	Col. 3:2
Abraham	Gen. 17:5, 9, 15–24, 26, +
	21:2–14, 22–29, 33, 34

"	greatest faith	
	in sacrifice	Gen. 22:1–18; Luke 12:13–21;
		Heb. 11:17–19
"	led nation of Israel	Gen. 12:1, 2; Gal. 3:8, 16, 29
"	name changed	
	from Abram	Gen. 17:5
Abram name changed to		
	Abraham	Gen. 17:5
Abroad		Gen. 32:11; Ps. 77:17
Absence of teacher,		
	continue same way	Phil. 2:12, 13
Absent from body		2 Cor. 5:6, 8
"	present	1 Cor. 5:3
Abstain		Acts 15:29; 1 Thess. 4:3, +
		5:22; 1 Pet. 2:11
Abundance		2 Chron. 32:5; Ps. 37:11;
		Eccles. 5:10, 12; Luke 12:15
"	and others want	2 Cor. 8:14, 20
"	causes	
	sleeplessness	Eccles. 5:12
Abundance - heart to		
	mouth	Matt. 12:34
"	lovers - is vanity	Eccles. 5:10
"	of all things	Deut. 28:47; Isa. 60:5
"	" evil	Matt. 12:34
"	" peace & truth	Jer. 33:6
Abundant, grace		Exod. 34:6; 2 Cor. 4:14, 15;
		Phil. 1:26
"	life	John 10:10
"	mercy	1 Pet. 1:3
Abundantly		Gen. 9:7; Exod. 1:7;
		1 Cor. 15:10;
		Eph. 3:20; Titus 3:6
"	, life more	John 10:10; 2 Cor. 12:15

"	pardon	Isa. 55:7
Abuse law		1 Cor. 9:20, 21
Acasia		Exod. 25:10
Accept		Gen. 32:20; Acts 24:3; Rev. 22:17
Acceptable lives		Rev. 12:1–21; 1 Tim. 5:4
"	to God	Prov. 21:3; Rom. 14:17, 18; 1 Pet. 2:5
"	" Lord	Ps. 19:14, + 69:13; Isa 58:5; Eph. 5:10
"	year of Lord	Isa. 61:2; Luke 4:18, 19
Acceptance		Isa. 60:7
Acceptation		1 Tim. 4:9
Accepted		Acts 10:35; 2 Cor. 5:9, + 6:2
"	not at home	Luke 4:24
Access		Rom. 5:2; Eph. 2:18, + 3:12
"	to his grace	Rom. 5:2
Accompanied		Acts 11:12
Accomplish		Isa. 55:11; Jer. 44:25; Luke 9:31
Accomplished		John 19:28; 1 Pet. 5:9
Accord		Phil. 2:2
"	, all one	Acts 2:1, 44–47, + 5:12, + 8:6
According		Ps. 79:11; 2 Cor. 8:9, 12, + 9:7; Eph. 1:3–5, 7, + 3:16, 20; Phil. 1:20, + 4:19; James 2:8
"	to divine power	Col. 1:11; 2 Pet. 1:2, 3
"	" faith	Matt. 9:29; Rom. 12:6
"	" God	Hag. 2:5; 1 Cor. 3:10; 1 Pet. 4:6
"	" God's grace	1 Cor. 3:10, 11
"	" gospel	Rom. 2:16, + 12:3, 6; 1 Cor. 15:3,4; 1 Tim. 1:11; 2 Tim. 2:8

"	" His mercy	Col. 1:11; Titus 3:5, 7; 1 Pet. 1:3
"	" " purpose	Rom. 8:27, 28; 2 Tim. 1:1, 9; 1 John 5:14
"	" work	Isa. 44:13, + 62:12; Isa. 59:18; 2 Cor. 5:10
"	" works	Rev. 20:12, 13
Accordingly		Isa 59:18
Account by rulers		Heb. 13:17
"	each to God	Rom. 14:12
"	of every idle word	Matt. 12:36
Accounted		Rom. 8:36
"	worthy	Luke 21:36
Accursed		Rom. 9:3; 1 Cor. 12:3; Gal. 1:8, 9
Accusation		Mark 15:26; Luke 19:8; Jude 1:9
Accuse		Prov. 30:10; Luke 3:14; John 5:45, 46
Accused		Matt. 27:12
Accuser		John 8:6, 10; 2 Tim. 3:3; Rev. 12:10
Acknowledge him		Prov. 3:6; 1 Cor. 14:37; Phil. 1:6
"	sin (transgressions)	Ps. 32:5, + 51:3
"	them	1 Cor. 16:18
Acknowledgment of God's mystery		Eccles. 3:11; Rom. 16:25; 1 Cor. 2:7; Eph. 3:3, 4, 9; Col. 2:2
Acquaint		Job 22:21
Acquaintance		Luke 23:49
Acquit		Nah. 1:3
Activities, do heartily all		Col. 3:23

"	in name of Jesus	Col. 3:17
Activities of Satan		Eph. 6:12; Rev. 13:6, 12, 14–17
Actions to others		1 Thess. 5:12–18
Acts, Lords - to Israel		Ps. 103:6, 7
AD appearances - Jesus		John 20:14, 21, 26, + 21:1
Adam		Gen. 2:7, 15–24, + 5:1–5
"	, first & last	1 Cor. 15:44–49
"	responsible for man's sin	Rom. 5:12–19
Adamant		Zech. 7:12
Add plagues for punishment		Rev. 22:18
"	to faith & stature - etc.	Luke 12:25; 1 Pet. 1:5–7
Added		Matt. 6:33; Acts 2:41, 47
Adder		Ps. 91:13
Addicted		1 Cor. 16:15
Addictions		Prov. 23:29–32; Rom. 6:12–14; 1 Cor. 6:19, 20; Eph. 5:18; Phil. 3:18–21; 1 Thess. 5:14; 2 Thess. 3:14, 15
Adjure		Matt. 26:63; Acts 19:13
Administrations		1 Cor. 12:5
Admiration for advantage		Jude 1:16
Admonish		Eccles. 12:12; Col. 3:16; 1 Thess. 5:12
Admonition		1 Cor. 10:11; Titus 3:10
Ado		Mark 5:39
Adoption		Rom. 8:15, 23, + 9:4; Eph. 1:5
Adorner		Jer. 31:4
Adorneth		Isa. 61:10
Adorning		1 Pet. 3:3, 5
Adulterer		Isa. 57:3

Adulteress	Hos. 3:1; Rom. 7:3
Adulterous	Prov. 30:20; Mark 8:38
Adultery	Lev. 20:10–21; Deut. 5:18;
	Jer. 3:8, 9; Matt. 5:27, 28, +
	19:9; Mark 10:11, 12;
	John 8:3–11; Rom. 7:3;
	1 Cor. 6:9–20; James 2:11
" destroyeth soul	Prov. 6:32
" in eyes	Matt. 5:28; 2 Pet. 2:14
Advantage	Luke 9:25; 2 Cor. 4:17;
	Jude 1:16
Advantageth	1 Cor. 15:32
Advent, second	Dan. 8:14; Matt. 24:29–31
Adversaries	Ps. 38:20; Mic. 5:9;
	Phil. 1:27, 28
Adversary	Matt 5:25
" - the devil	1 Pet. 5:8
Adversity	1 Sam. 4:9, + 10:19;
	Prov. 17:17; Eccles. 7:14;
	Heb. 13:3
Advice summary	Eccles. 12:13, 14; 2 Cor. 8:10
" for last times	Jude 1:17–23
Advocate, we have	1 John 2:1, 2
Afar	Ps. 10:1; Luke 17:12, + 23:49;
	Acts 2:39
Affairs	Eph. 6:21, 22; 2 Tim. 2:4
Affection	Col. 3:2
Affectionate to one another	Rom. 12:10
Affections, vile	Rom. 1:26, 27
Affirmed	Acts 12:15
Afflict	Job 37:23; Ps. 44:2; Isa. 58:3, 5
Afflicted	Job 34:28; Ps. 90:15, +
	129:1, 2; Isa. 53:4, + 58:10;
	James 4:9, + 5:13

Affliction		Exod. 3:7; Mark 13:19; Acts 7:10, 11, 34; Phil. 1:16, + 4:14
"	draws one closer to the Lord	Ps. 119:71, 72
"	to our advantage	2 Cor. 4:17
Afflictions	advantage	2 Cor. 4:17
"	in brethren in the world	2 Cor. 2:4; 1 Pet. 5:9
"	of Gospel	2 Tim. 1:8
Affrighted		Deut. 7:21; Job 18:20; Rev. 11:13
Afore		Rom. 9:23
Aforehand		Mark 14:8
Aforetime		Rom. 15:4
Afraid		Gen. 3:10; Ps. 37:1, + 65:8, + 91:5; Job 3:25; John 14:27
"	not	Deut. 18:21, 22; Josh. 1:9; 2 Chron. 20:15; Matt. 14:27, 30
"	" when acquire riches	Ps. 49:16
Afterward		Neh. 6:10; Joel 2:28; John 13:36; Heb. 4:8
Again		Gen. 4:2; Prov. 3:28; John 14:3, 28
"	, born	John 3:3; 1 Pet. 1:23
Against		Matt. 10:35; Mark 3:24–26, + 11:25, + 13:8, 9, 12
"	me or with me	Matt. 12:30; Luke 11:23
"	thee	Ps. 51:4
"	ungodliness	Rom. 1:18
"	us, none	Rom. 8:31
"	, wrestle not	Eph. 6:11, 12

Age	Job 11:17; Ps 39:5
" , approach old	Eccles. 12:1–7
" , life	Ps. 90:10
Aged men & women	Titus 2:1–5
Ages, throughout	Eph. 3:5, 21
Agony	Luke 22:44
Agree, two or more	Amos 3:3; Matt. 18:19, 20
Agreed	1 Cor. 1:10
Agreement	2 Cor. 6:16
Agreeth	Luke 5:36
Aground	Acts 27:41
Aid	Phil. 4:4–16
Aim in life	Phil. 3:13–15
Air	1 Thess. 4:17
Alabaster	Matt. 26:7
Alas	Amos 5:16; Rev. 18:10, 16, 19
Albeit	Ezek. 13:7; Philem. 1:19
Alcohol	Prov. 3:4–7
Alertness of Lord	1 Pet. 3:12
Algum tree	2 Chron. 2:8
Alien	Isa. 61:5; Eph. 2:12
Alienated	Col. 1:21; Ezek. 23:29; Eph. 2:12
Alike	Ps. 139:12
Alive - Christ	Acts 1:3; 1 Cor. 15:3–8
" evermore - Jesus	Rev. 1:18
" in Christ	Col. 2:12, 13, + 3:1, 4; 1 Cor. 15:22
" with him	1 Thess. 4:17; 2 Tim. 2:11
All	Matt. 4:23, 24; Acts 24:15; Eph. 4:6; Phil. 4:9
" , do - in the name of Jesus	Phil. 4:13; Col. 3:17

"	, do - to the glory of God	1 Cor. 10:31
All donated		Mark 12:42, 44
"	for Christ	Phil. 3:8, + 4:6, 7
"	, God of	1 Pet. 5:10
"	in all	1 Cor. 15:28
"	is Christ	Col. 3:11
"	" Lord	2 Sam. 22:23
"	" the Lord's	Ps. 24:1
"	" thine O Lord	1 Chron. 29:11
"	look to God	Isa. 45:22
"	one accord	Acts 2:1
"	" in Christ Jesus	Gal. 3:28
"	power to Jesus	Matt. 28:18
"	powerful	1 Chron. 29:12; Ps. 62:11
"	same to the Lord	Rom. 10:12
"	sinned	Gen. 5:12; 1 Kings 8:46; Rom. 3:23, + 5:12, 13, 14; 1 John 1:8–10
"	the earth - world and people	Ps. 24:1
"	things	1 Pet. 4:7, 8
"	" - charity best	1 Cor. 16:14; Col. 3:14
"	" God's	Col. 1:17; 1 Pet. 4:7, 8
"	" lawful	1 Cor. 10:23
"	" new	2 Cor. 5:17; Rev. 21:5
"	" not edify or expedient	1 Cor. 10:23
"	to face deeds of body	John 5:22; Acts 24:15
"	to glorify God	1 Cor. 10:31
"	we	2 Cor. 3:18
"	your heart	Jer. 29:13

Alleging	Acts 17:3
Allow	Acts 24:15
Allure	2 Pet. 2:18
Almighty, God	Gen. 17:1, + 35:11; Rev. 11:17, + 15:3, + 16:14, + 21:22
" , the	Job 8:3, 5, + 22:17, 23, 25, 26, + 24:1, + 32:8, + 33:4; Rev. 1:8
Almond tree	Jer. 1:11
Alms	Matt. 6:1–4; Acts 3:2, 3, 10, + 10:4
Alms deeds	Acts 9:36
Aloe	Num. 24:6; Prov. 7:17; Song of Sol. 4:14; John 19:39
Alone	Ps. 83:18; Eccles. 4:8–11; Matt. 14:23; Mark 14:6; James 2:17
" , not	Gen. 2:18; John 16:32; Heb. 13:5, 6
Aloof	Ps. 38:11
Aloud, cry (speak)	Isa. 58:1
Alpha and Omega is the Lord	Rev. 1:8, 11, 17, + 21:6, + 22:13
Already	Phil. 3:16; Rev. 2:25
Also	Prov. 11:25; John 14:3; Rom. 5:3; 2 Cor. 5:5
Altar	Exod. 17:15, + 24:4, + 27:1, 5–7; Jer. 11:13, 14
Altogether	Ps. 50:21, + 139:4; Song of Sol. 5:16
Alway	Exod. 25:30; Prov. 28:14; Matt. 28:20; Phil. 4:4

Always	Ps. 90:1, 2; Acts 7:51; 2 Cor. 9:8; Phil. 1:4, 20
" pray	Luke 18:1: + 21:36; Eph. 5:20, + 6:18
Am he	John 4:26
" I	Exod. 3:14; Isa. 58:9; John 1:23, + 6:48, + 8:58, + 9:5, + 10:7, 9–11, 14, + 11:25, + 14:6; 1 Cor. 9:1 + 15:9, 10
" I?	Gen. 4:9; 1 Cor. 9:1
Amazed	Job 32:15; Mark 1:27, + 2:12, + 6:51; 9:15, + 16:8; Acts 2:12, + 9:21
Amazement	Acts 3:10; 1 Pet. 3:6
Ambassador	2 Cor. 5:20; Eph. 6:20
Ambassadors - we	2 Cor. 5:20
Ambassage	Luke 14:32
Ambushment	2 Chron. 13:13
Amen	1 Cor. 14:6; 2 Cor. 1:14, 20; Jude 1:25; Rev. 1:7, + 3:14
Amend	John 4:52
Amerce	Deut. 22:19
Amiable	Ps. 84:1
Amiss	Dan. 3:29; James 4:3
Among	Matt. 4:23; John 1:14, + 15:24; Acts 20:25; 2 Cor. 6:17
An	Gen. 2:20; 2 Cor. 5:1
A-nathema	
Maran-atha	1 Cor. 16:22
Ancestors of all	
on earth	Gen. 9:18, 19
Anchor	Rev. 22:19
" of soul	Heb. 6:18, 19

Ancient		Isa. 45:21, + 46:10; Dan. 7:22
Ancle		Acts 3:7
And		Gen. 1:1–31; Exod. 34:7;
		Josh. 22:5; 1 John 5:20;
		Rev. 7:9–15
Angel		2 Chron. 16:9; Job 38:7;
		Ps. 8:5, + 91:11, + 103:19, 20;
		Isa. 34:12; Ezek. 1:4–28;
		Dan. 8:16, + 10:2, 13, 21, +
		12:1, 25; 2 Pet. 2:11;
		Rev. 3:1, 7, 14, + 7:1, 2, + 8:3, +
		10:1, + 12:7
"	action on earth	Isa. 37:36; Heb. 13:2
"	Gabriel to	
	Virgin Mary	Luke 1:26–38
"	Gabriel to	
	Zacharias	Luke 1:11–20
"	in body form	Judg. 6:11, 12; 1 Kings 19:2–8;
		Matt. 28:2
"	smote Peter	Acts 12:7
"	spake	2 Kings 1:15; Matt. 28:5–7;
		Luke 1:13–37, + 2:10–12;
		Acts 10:3–6
Angel protection		Ps. 34:7, + 91:11; Acts 12:28
"	to John	Rev. 1:1, 2
Angel's activities		John 1:51; 1 Pet. 1:12;
		Rev. 12:7
Angels as guardians		Ps. 91:11
"	at last days	Rev. 14:6–20
"	marry not	Matt. 22:30
"	ministered to Jesus	Matt. 4:11
"	ministering spirits	Heb. 1:13, 14
"	see Father's face	Matt. 18:10

"	, seven	Rev. 8:2, 6–10, 12, 13, + 9:1, 13, 14, + 10:7, + 11:15, + 21:9
"	-seven seals	Rev. 5:1–9, + 6:1, 3, 5, 7, 9, 12, + 8:1
"	- " trumpets	Rev. 8:2, 7, 8, 10, 12, + 9:1, 13, + 10:7
"	to keep you	Ps. 91:11
"	visiting people	1 Kings 19:5–8; 2 Kings 1:15; Acts 12:7, 8; Rev. 14:6, 8, 9, 15, 17, 18
"	who deserted	Jude 1:6
"	worshipped God	Rev. 7:11
Anger		2 Chron. 25:10; Ps 30:5, + 90:7; Mark 3:5
"	not	Eph. 4:31; Col. 3:8
"	of Lord	2 Chron. 25:15; Ps. 145:8; Jonah 4:2
"	slow is good	Prov. 16:32
"	- wrath & envy	Prov. 27:4
Angry		Ps. 2:12; Jonah 4:1; Matt. 5:22
"	and sin not	Eph. 4:26
"	man	Prov. 22:24
Anguish		Job 7:11, + 15:24; Ps. 119:143; John 16:21
"	at world's end	Matt. 18:38–50
Animal and man similarity		Eccles. 3:19, 20
"	talked	Num. 22:28, 30
Animals are God's		Ps. 50:10, 11
"	in prophecy represent governments	Dan. 7:17, 18; Rev. 17:9–14
"	included in prayer	Ps. 36:5, 6
"	know - we don't	Isa. 1:3
"	provided for	Prov. 30:24–31

Animal's harmony	Isa. 11:6–9
" peace	Isa. 11:6–9
Anise	Matt. 23:23
Anoint	1 John 2:27
" and pray for the sick	James 5:14
Anoint with oil	Heb. 1:9; James 5:14
Anointed	1 Sam. 16:6, 13; Isa. 61:1; Ezek. 16:9; Luke 4:18; John 9:6
" , God - Jesus	Mark 14:8; Acts 10:38
" , Lord - Isaiah	Isa. 61:1–3
Anointing	Isa. 10:27
Anon	Matt. 13:20
Another	Rom. 12:5, 10; Col. 3:13; 1 Thess. 4:18; James 5:16
" god	Ps. 16:4
Answer advice	Prov. 26:4, 5; Matt. 5:37; 2 Cor. 5:12
" , Lord shall	Isa. 58:9
" of Jesus	John 6:29
Answered	Matt. 16:2, + 21:29, 30, + 28:5; John 3:3, + 6:29
Answering, Jesus	Mark 11:22
Answers great	Luke 2:46, 47
Ant	Prov. 6:6
Antichrist	Matt. 23:26, + 24:4–13; 1 John 2:22
" deceived by followers	Dan. 11:26
" exalted himself	2 Thess. 2:3–8
" is deceiver	2 John 1:7
" revealed	2 Thess. 2:1–4, 8–10
Antichrists, many	1 John 2:18

Anticipate Lord's coming		Luke 12:34–40, 43
Ants		Prov. 30:25
Any		Mark 11:25
Apart		Matt. 14:23; Mark 6:31
Apostasy of later times		2 Thess. 2:3, 4
Apostate angels		Jude 1:6
Apostle Christ Jesus		Heb. 3:1
"	, one - a devil	John 6:70, 71
"	Paul	Rom. 1:1; 1 Cor. 15:7–9
Apostles' activities		Acts 2:43, + 5:12
"	chosen by Jesus	John 6:70
"	commission	Mark 28:18–20; Acts 1:2, + 4:33
"	deceivers	Rev. 2:2
Apostles, false		2 Cor. 11:4, 13, 14; Rev. 2:2
"	given power & authority	Luke 9:1
"	twelve	Luke 6:13–16; Acts 1:13, 14, 21, 22, 26
Apostleship		Rom. 1:5
Apparel		Acts 1:10, + 12:21; 1 Pet. 3:3
"	of women	1 Tim. 2:9; 1 Pet. 3:3
Appear		Matt. 6:16, + 24:27–30; 1 Pet. 5:4; 1 John 3:2
"	for us	Heb. 9:24, 28, + 10:24
"	second time	Col. 3:4; Heb. 9:28; 1 John 3:1–3
"	, we must	2 Cor. 5:10
Appearance		1 Sam. 16:7; Ezek. 1:26
"	, AD	Matt. 28:9, 17, 18; Mark 16:9, 12, 14; Luke 23:52–55, + 24:15, 25, 30, 31, 36, 39–43; John 20:14, 15, 19, 26, + 21:1, 4, 5, 14, 15

"	again	Heb. 9:28; 1 John 3:2
"	, final	Rev. 19:11–21
"	foretold by Jesus	Matt. 16:28, + 17:22, 23, + 20:17–19; Mark 14:62; John 16:22
"	, inward & outward	1 Sam. 16:7
"	, Jesus'	1 John 3:2
"	not important	1 Sam. 16:7
"	of evil	1 Thess. 5:22
"	, outward	2 Cor. 10:7
"	to Cephas - the twelve & five hundred brethren	1 Cor. 15:5–8
"	to reveal the faithful	1 Pet. 1:7–9

Appearances of Jesus Christ AD

"	after resurrection	Luke 24:15–31, 36–51
"	before ascension (AD)	
"	to disciples	John 20:26–31
"	" " and others	John 21:1–23
"	" Mary, other Mary and disciples	Matt. 28:9, 10; Mark 16:9, 12; John 20:14–17
"	" eleven disciples	Mark 16:14–19; John 20:19–24
"	" " " " & Mary Magdalene	Matt. 28:16–20

Appeared, grace of God	Titus 1:1
" , Jesus	Acts 9:17
" , Lord	Gen. 17:1; Jer. 31:3
" to many, saints	Matt. 27:53
Appearing, glorious	Titus 2:13
" of Jesus Christ	2 Tim. 4:1
Apple " his eye	Deut. 32:10; Ps. 17:8

Apples" gold	Prov. 25:11
Apply God's word	2 Thess. 3:4
" hearts	Ps. 90:12
Appointed	2 Chron. 20:21; Luke 3:13; 2 Tim. 1:11
" day	Acts 17:31; Heb. 9:27
" heir	Heb. 1:2
" men once to die	Heb. 9:27
Appreciate God's work	Job 37:14
Appreciation	Ps. 92:1, 2
Apprehend	Phil. 3:12, 13
Approaching day	Heb. 10:25
" to God	Isa. 58:2
Approve excellent things	Phil. 1:10
Approving ourselves	1 Cor. 16:3; 2 Cor. 6:4–10
Apt	1 Tim. 3:2; 2 Tim. 2:24
Archangel Michael	Dan. 10:13; 1 Thess. 4:16; Jude 1:19
Archers	Gen. 49:23; 1 Sam. 31:3; Job 16:13
Architect	Ps. 127:1
Are	Rom. 8:16
Arguing	Job 9:25
Aright	Ps. 50:23; Prov. 15:3
Arise	Isa. 60:1–3; Luke 5:24; John 14:31; Acts 9:6, 8, 11
" false Christs	Matt. 24:24
" - the dead in Christ	Eph. 5:14; 1 Thess. 4:16, 17
Ariseth	1 Kings 18:44
Ark inhabitants' food	Gen. 6:18–22
" , Noah's	Gen. 6:14–22, + 7:1; John 14:14; 1 Pet. 3:20

" of covenant	Exod. 25:10, 14, 15, 21; Num. 10:33, + 14:44; Josh 3:6, 8, 17, + 4:7
" " testament	Rev. 11:19
Ark of wood	Exod. 25:10, 14–16, 21
" was a preparing	1 Pet. 3:20
Arm of Lord	Exod. 15:16
" ourselves as Christ	1 Pet. 4:1
Armed	Luke 11:21
Armour of God	Eph. 6:11
" " light	Rom. 13:12
Arms of God	Deut. 33:27
Army	Ezek. 37:1–10; Dan. 11:25, 26
Arose	Acts 9:18
" saints from grave	Matt. 27:52, 53
Array	Job 6:4, + 40:10; 1 Tim. 2:9
Arrayed	2 Chron. 5:12; Matt. 6:29; Luke 12:27; Acts 12:21
Arrogance	Prov. 8:12, + 27:2; Isa. 13:11; Jer. 9:23, 24; James 4:13–16; 1 Pet. 5:5, 6
Arrow	2 Kings 13:15–18; Ps. 91:5; Lam. 3:12, 13
Arrows	Ps. 11:1, 2, + 20:12, + 127:4; Jer. 51:11; Lam. 3:13
Art	Num. 14:14; 1 Kings 18:36; Isa. 51:9, 10; Matt. 16:16; Mark 1:24
" there - Lord	Ps. 139:8
Artificer	Gen. 4:22; 2 Chron. 34:11
As	John 1:12
" I live	Ezek. 16:48
Ascend (ascension)	Ps. 139:8

Ascend and descend	Acts 1:11; Eph. 4:9, 10
Ascended to heaven	Mark 16:19; Luke 24:51;
	Acts 1:11; Eph. 4:8–10
Ascension foretold	Matt. 16:21; Luke 18:33;
	John 7:33, 34, + 13:1, + 16:16,
	28, + 17:21; Acts 1:9
Ascribe	Deut. 32:3
Ash	Isa. 44:14
Ashamed	Ps. 25:2, 3, + 31:1 + 33:17;
	Isa. 45:11; Mark 8:38;
	Luke 9:26, + 10:19;
	Rom. 13:15
" by being ignored	2 Tim. 3:14, 15
Ashamed not	Rom. 5:5, + 9:33, + 10:11;
	Phil. 1:20; 2 Tim. 1:18
" " by truth	2 Tim. 2:15
" " of testimony	2 Tim. 1:8; 1 Pet. 4:16
Ashes	Ezek. 28:18; Isa. 58:5;
	Lam. 3:16
Aside, go not	Deut. 28:1, 2, 14
" , turn	Exod. 3:3, 4
Ask	Matt. 7:7–10, + 21:22, 24;
	Luke 11:9–13: + 12:48;
	1 John 5:14
" , believe and receive	Ps. 37:5; Matt. 7:7, 8, + 21:22;
	Luke 11:9–13, + 24:13–31;
	John 14:14, + 15:7, + 16:24;
	James 1:5
" - Father give	John 15:16, + 16:23, 24;
	Eph. 3:20; 1 John 5:14, 15
" in Jesus' name	John 14:14
Ask in unison even	
by two or three	Matt. 18:19, 20
" not - have not	James 4:2, 3

" seek - knock	Mark 11:9, 10
Asked Him	John 1:21, + 4:9
Asleep	Matt. 26:40, 43, 45; John 11:11–14; 1 Cor. 15:6, 18, 20, 51; 1 Thess. 4:13–15
Asp	Job 20:14, 16; Isa. 11:8; Rom. 3:13
Ass	Gen. 49:14; Judg. 15:15, 16; John 12:14; 2 Pet. 2:16
Assayed	Acts 16:7
Assemble	Mic. 4:5, 6; Heb. 10:24, 25
Assembled	Matt. 26:3
Assemblies	Eccles. 12:11
Assembly	James 2:2
Asses	Gen. 45:23, 27; Job 1:3, 14
Associate not with wicked one	1 Cor. 5:13
" with unbelievers	1 Cor. 10:27
Assurance	Acts 17:30, 31; 1 Thess. 1:5; Heb. 13:5
" unto the end	Heb. 4:11
Assure	1 John 3:20
Assured	2 Tim. 3:14, 15
Assuredly	Acts 2:36
Asswaged	Gen. 8:1
Astonied	Isa. 52:14
Astonished	Matt. 7:28 + 13:54, + 22:33; Mark 1:22, + 6:2 + 11:28; Luke 2:47; Acts 9:6, + 13:12
Astonishment	Jer. 25:9; Mark 5:42
Astray	Isa. 53:6; Matt. 18:12; 1 Pet. 2:25
Astrologers	Dan. 2:2, 10, 37
" , etc. to be burned	Isa. 47:13, 14

Asunder	Job 16:12; Matt. 19:6, + 24:51; Mark 10:9; Acts 1:18
At	Ps. 16:11
Ate food after coming from heaven	Luke 24:36–43
Atheist	Ps. 14:1
Athirst	Ruth 2:9; Rev. 21:6
Athletics	1 Cor. 9:24:27
Atonement	Lev. 16:17; Rom. 5:11
" for the soul	Lev. 17:11
Attain	Ps. 139:6; Phil. 3:11, 12, 16
Attend	Ps. 55:2
" to Father's words	Prov. 4:1, 20, + 5:1
" upon the Lord	1 Cor. 7:35
Attent	2 Chron. 7:15
Attention all	Josh. 22:5; Isa. 45:22
Aul	Exod. 21:6
Austere	Luke 19:21, 22
Author of our faith	Heb. 12:2
Authority	Matt. 21:23, 24, 27; Mark 1:22, 27; Luke 10:19; Rom. 13:1, 2; Eph. 6:1–3; 1 Thess. 5:12, 13; Rev. 2:26
" not women	1 Tim. 2:12, 13
" persons to live honestly	1 Tim. 2:1–4
" to Jesus	Mark 11:27–29; John 5:27, 30
" " servants	Mark 13:34–37
Automobiles predicted	Nah. 2:4
Availeth much	James 5:16
Avenge	Rom. 12:19; Rev. 6:10
" not	Rom. 12:19
" to the wicked	Luke 18:7, 8

Avenged the servants of God	Rev. 19:2
Avenger	Ps. 8:2; 1 Thess. 4:6
Avoid	Prov. 4:14, 15; Rom. 16:17; 1 Tim. 6:20
" various things	Titus 3:9
Awake	Judg. 5:12; Dan. 12:2; Luke 9:32; Rom. 13:11; 1 Cor. 15:34; Eph. 5:14
Award	1 Thess. 4:16–18
Aware	Matt. 24:50; Luke 12:46
Away	John 11:41, + 14:28; 2 Thess. 2:3; Rev. 21:4
" , fall	Heb. 6:6
Awe	Ps. 119:161
Ax	2 Kings 6:5; Matt. 3:10; Luke 3:9
Axletrees	1 Kings 7:32, 33

• B •

Babblings, avoid	1 Tim. 6:30; 2 Tim. 2:16
Babes	Matt. 11:25; Heb. 5:12, 13
Babies	1 Pet. 2:2
Baby Jesus	Luke 2:11
Babylon	Dan. 2:32, 38, + 7:3, 4; Rev. 3:11–17, + 18:5–10
" fallen	Rev. 14:8, + 18:1–19
Backslider or good man	Prov. 14:14
Backsliding	Jer. 2:19, + 3:6, 8, 11, 12, 14, 22, + 8:5, + 31:22; Hos. 4:16, + 14:4; 1 Tim. 1:6
Bad and good works judged	Eccles. 12:13, 14
" , put away all	Eph. 4:31
Bade	Num. 14:10; Acts 11:12
Badger	Ezek. 16:10
Balaam	Jude 1:11
Balance, false	Prov. 20:23
Balances	Job 37:16; Rev. 6:5
Balancing of clouds	Job 37:16
Bald head	2 Kings 2:23; Isa. 15:2; Jer. 47:5, + 48:37; Ezek. 29:18; Amos 8:10; Mic. 1:16

Bands	Isa. 58:6; Col. 2:19
Banquet	Esther 5:4–6
Baptism	Mark 1:4; Acts 10:37; Rom. 6:4
" , only one	Eph. 4:5
Baptized	Matt. 3:11; Acts 1:5; Rom. 6:3
" , be	Matt. 28:19; Mark 16:15–18; Acts 2:37, 38; Rom. 6:3, 4
" in one spirit	1 Cor. 12:13
" " water	Matt. 3:16; Mark 1:9, 10; Acts 8:36–39
" into Jesus Christ	Rom. 6:3, 4
Barbarbous	Acts 28:2
Bare grain	1 Cor. 15:37
" -naked	2 Sam. 12:15; Ezek. 16:7
" not is well with	Lord Isa. 54:1
" our sicknesses	Matt. 8:17
" " sins	1 Pet. 2:24
" record	Rev. 1:1, 2
" sins	Isa. 53:12
" witness	Luke 4:22
Barley	2 Chron. 2:10, 15; Job 31:40
Barns	Prov. 3:9, 10; Matt. 6:26, + 13:30; Luke 12:24
Barren	Isa. 54:1; Luke 23:29; Gal. 4:27
Barren to sing	Isa. 54:1
" woman	Ps. 113:9
Base things	1 Cor. 1:28
Basons	Exod. 24:6; John 13:5
Bastards	Heb. 12:8
Bat	Lev. 11:19
Baths of oil	2 Chron. 2:10

Battle against me	Ps. 55:18
" , bloody	Isa. 9:5
" is Lord's	1 Sam. 17:47; 2 Chron. 20:15
Be agreeable	Rom. 12:16
" careful	Phil. 4:6
" doers of God's word	James 1:22–27
Be filled with the spirit	Eph. 5:18
" holy	Lev. 11:44, 45, + 19:2, + 20:26; 1 Pet. 1:15, 16; 2 Pet. 3:11
" in Christ	1 Cor. 11:1; 2 Cor. 5:17
" it	Matt. 9:29
" my people & your God	Ezek. 36:28
" of same mind	Rom. 12:16
" perfect	Matt. 5:48
" ready	Matt. 24:44
" saved	Rom. 10:9
" still-know God	Ps. 46:10
" with me-Jesus	John 14:3; 1 Thess. 4:17
" ye	1 Cor. 15:58
Beam	Matt. 7:3, 4; Luke 6:41, 42
Bear a son	Is. 7:14
" fruit	John 15:8
" other's burdens	Gal. 6:2
" own burden	Gal. 6:5
" sins of many	Heb. 9:28
" sons	Ruth 1:2
" temptations	1 Cor. 10:13
Beard	Isa. 15:2; Jer. 41:5
Beareth all things	1 Cor. 13:7
Bearings - concerning dying of Jesus	2 Cor. 4:8–11
Bears	2 Kings 2:24

Beast		Gen. 1:24; Ps. 50:10, 11; Isa. 63:14; Rev. 13:1–4, 11–15, + 17:8
"	and man	Prov. 12:10
"	from pit	Rev. 11:7
"	, mark of	Rev. 13:16–18, + 14:9, + 19:20, + 20:4, 5
"	(or Satan) deceived & defeated	Rev. 19:20
"	to be worshipped or be killed	Rev. 13:15
"	worshippers not godly	Rev. 13:14–18, + 14:9–11, + 20:4
Beast's	blood & bodies	Heb. 13:11
Beasts		Gen. 45:17; Prov. 30:30; Isa. 46:1; Jer. 34:18–20; Rev. 4:6–9, + 13:1, 11
"	, four	Dan. 7:4–7
Beat		Prov. 23:14
Beaten		Lev. 2:16; Luke 12:48
Beatest		Prov. 23:13
Beatitudes		Matt. 5:2–11; Mark 6:20–22
Beautiful		Eccles. 3:11; Isa. 52:7, + 64:11; Acts 3:2
"	feet	Rom. 10:15
"	, Satan once was	Ezek. 28:12
"	things all made by God	Eccles. 3:11
Beauty		Ps. 27:4; Isa. 44:13
"	is vain	Prov. 31:30
"	of holiness	2 Chron. 20:21; Ps. 96:6
Became		Phil. 2:8; Heb. 2:10
"	man	1 Cor. 13:11

Becamest	Ezek. 16:18
Because	Isa. 26:3; John 7:39, + 14:12, 28; Rom. 5:5, + 14:23
Beckon	Luke 1:22; John 13:24; Acts 12:17, + 13:16, + 24:10
Become my salvation	Ps. 118:14
" sons of God	John 1:12
Becometh	Phil. 1:27
Bed	Job 7:13
" of languishing	Ps. 41:1–3
Beer	Deut. 14:26
Befall	Deut. 31:29
Befallen man & beast	Eccles. 3:19
Befell	Acts 20:19
Before	Matt. 1:18; Luke 21:36; John 1:15; Phil. 3:13; Col. 1:17
Beforehand	2 Cor. 9:5; 1 Tim. 5:24, 25; 1 Pet. 1:11
Beforetime	Acts 8:9
Beg when don't work in cold	Prov. 20:4
Began preaching, Jesus	Mark 6:2; Luke 4:14–19
Begat	Matt. 1:1–16; James 1:18
Begetteth	Prov. 17:21
Beggar	Mark 10:46–52; Luke 16:20, 22
Beggarly	Gal. 4:9
Beginning	Gen. 1:1; John 1:2, + 3:14; 1 John 1:1
" and ending	Rev. 1:8, 11, + 21:6, + 22:13
" anew	Titus 2:13
Begotten	John 1:14; 1 Cor. 4:15; Heb. 1:5, 6

"	of God not touched by wicked	1 John 5:18
"	son	John 1:18, + 3:16–18; Acts 13:33; 1 John 4:9; Rev. 1:5
"	us hope & protection	1 Pet. 1:3; 1 John 5:18
Beguile		2 Cor. 11:3; Col. 2:4
Beguiled		Gen. 3:13; 2 Cor. 1:3
Beguiling		2 Pet. 2:14
Begun		Esther 6:13; Phil. 1:6
Behalf		2 Chron. 16:9; Job 36:2; 1 Cor. 1:4; 2 Cor. 9:3
Behave in church of God		1 Tim. 3:15
Behaved		Ps. 35:15; 1 Thess. 2:10
Behavior of newsbearers		Luke 10:3–12
"	or abusive	2 Sam. 13–1–22
Beheaded for witness of Jesus		Rev. 20:4–6
"	heifer	Deut. 21:6
"	John the Baptist	Matt. 14:1–11; Mark 6:20–27; Luke 9:9
Behemoth		Job 40:15
Behind		Gen. 22:13; 2 Sam. 1:7; Ps. 139:5; Luke 4:8
Behold		Ps. 33:13–16, + 91:8; John 19:26, 27; 2 Cor. 5:17; James 3:3, 4; Rev. 1:7, + 3:20
"	- pleasure & love	Isa. 42:19, + 58:3, 4; 1 John 3:1
"	the lamb of God	John 1:29
"	thy mother	John 19:27
"	" son	John 19:26
Beholding		Acts 23:1; 2 Cor. 3:18

Behove		Luke 24:46
Being assembled	- many	Acts 1:4; Rom. 12:4, 5
"	- ours in Him	Acts 17:28
Belief		2 Thess. 2:13
Believe		Mark 1:15, + 9:23, 24, + 11:23, + 16:17; John 5:44–47, + 7:39, + 14:1, 11; James 2:19
"	all things possible	Mark 9:23, 24, + 11:24
"	and confess	Rom. 10:9–11
"	" not die	John 11:26
"	brings victory	1 John 5:4, 5
"	by a death	John 10:14, 15, 17, 23–26, 39–45
"	" seeing	John 20:29
"	-commit	John 2:23, 24
Believe for everlasting life		John 3:15, 16, 36, + 11:25, 26, + 20:31; 1 John 5:13
"	God for good works	Titus 3:8
"	God's word	John 6:29
"	gospel	Mark 1:15, + 16:15, 16; 1 Thess. 4:14
"	have place	John 14:1–4; 1 John 5:13
"	in Lord your God	2 Chron. 20:20; John 6:29, + 14:1; James 2:19
"	" prophets	2 Chron. 20:20
"	" son of God	John 3:36, + 8:24, + 14:1; 1 John 5:4, 5, 13
"	is forever even through death	Matt. 11:25
"	Jesus Christ is Son of God	Acts 8:37
"	" for life	John 11:25, 26, + 20:31
"	" per God	John 6:29

"	" totally to be resurrected	1 Thess. 4:14
"	not every spirit	1 John 4:1
"	" - results	Mark 16:16; John 8:24
"	" - see for salvation	1 Pet. 1:8
"	on God	John 6:29; Heb. 11:6; 1 John 1:5, + 5:13
"	only by seeing	John 14:28, 29
"	or not	John 3:36
"	- receive	Matt. 21:22; Mark 11:23, 24; John 5:24
"	- reward	John 1:12, + 12:46, 47
"	there is one God	James 2:19
"	to be made whole	Matt. 18:5; Luke 8:50; John 1:2; Acts 6:35, + 16:31
"	" " saved	John 3:16; Acts 16:31; Rom. 10:9–11, + 15:13
"	to live	John 11:25–27
"	" make possible	Mark 9:23
"	" see glory of God	John 11:31–45
"	word of God	1 Thess. 2:13
"	work of God	John 6:28, 29, + 14:10, 11
"	yet not seen	John 20:29; Acts 16:31; Rom. 5:1, + 10:9, 10
Believed		Dan. 6:23; Matt. 8:13, + 11:45; John 20:29; Acts 4:32, + 9:40–42
Believer's happiness		Isa. 55:8–13
Believers have accusers		John 8:10; 2 Tim. 3:3; Rev. 12:10
"	not surprised of Lord's coming	1 Thess. 5:1–5
"	powers	Mark 16:15–18
"	promised reward	Mal. 3:16–18

"	rewards	John 3:15–18, 36; Acts 2:41; Rom. 15:13
"	to be pitied	Ps. 103:11–13
"	yoked not and reward	2 Cor. 6:14–18
Believest		John 14:10; James 2:19
Believeth		Mark 9:23, + 16:16; John 6:47, + 7:38, + 11:25, 26, + 14:12; 1 John 5:5
Believing for joy & peace		John 20:31; Rom. 15:13
"	- receiving	Matt. 21:22
Belly		Job 40:16; Matt. 15:17; John 7:38; Rom. 16:18
Belongeth		Dan. 9:8
"	mercy to the Lord	Ps. 62:12
Beloved		1 John 3:2; Jude 1:17
"	son	Matt. 3:17, + 17:5; Mark 1:11
Bend bows		Ps. 64:3
Benediction examples		Num. 6:24–26; 2 Cor. 13:14; Eph. 3:20, 21; Phil. 4:6, 7, 23; Jude 1:24, 25; Rev. 7:12
Benefactors		Luke 22:25
Bent		Lam. 3:12
Bereave		Ezek. 36:12
Bereaved		Gen. 42:36: + 43:14; Hos. 13:8
Bereaveth		Lam. 1:20
Beseech		Ps. 118:25; Dan. 1:12; Heb. 13:19, 22
Besiege		Deut. 28:52; Eccles. 9:14; Dan. 1:1
Beset		Heb. 12:1
Beside me, none		Isa. 44:6, 8, + 45:21
Besought		Exod. 32:11; 2 Sam. 12:16; Matt. 14:36; 2 Cor. 12:8

Best work & gift	Eccles. 3:22; 1 Cor. 12:31
Bestow	Exod. 32:29; Luke 12:17, 18;
	1 Cor. 12:23, + 13:3
Bestowed on us & Paul	1 Cor. 15:10; 2 Cor. 1:11;
	1 John 3:1
Bethink	1 Kings 8:47
Betimes	Job 8:5
Betray	Matt. 26:21; John 13:11
" foretold	Matt. 17:22, 23
Betrayed Satan, followers	Dan. 11:26
" Son of God	Matt. 26:24, 26, 45
Betrayer of Jesus	Matt. 26:2, 14–16, 23, 45, 46;
	Mark 14:18–20, 30, 41;
	Luke 21, 22:48; John 6:70, 71
Betroth	Exod. 21:8, 9; Deut. 20:7, +
	22:23, 25, 27, 28, + 28:30;
	Hos. 2:19
Better	Prov. 16:32, + 21:9;
	1 Cor. 11:17; Heb. 11:39, 40
" two than one	Eccles. 4:9–12
Between God & us	Rom. 5:11
" us	Eph. 2:14; 1 Tim. 2:5
Betwixt	Gen. 26:28, + 31:50; Job 9:33;
	Phil. 1:23
Bewailed	Luke 23:27
Beware	Matt. 7:15, + 10:17;
	Luke 12:15; Acts 13:40;
	Phil. 3:2; Col. 2:8; 2 Pet. 3:17
Bewitched	Acts 8:9; Gal. 3:1
Beyond	1 Thess. 4:6
Bible Books (66) 39 in OT & 27 in NT	
" by God's Prophets	1 Pet. 1:21
" theme as motto	
(if there is such)	John 3:16

" to be read	Josh. 1:8
Bid	Matt. 14:28
Bidden	Luke 14:17
Bier	Luke 7:14
Bind	Ps. 105:22; Prov. 6:21; Isa. 61:1; Matt. 12:29, + 16:19, + 18:18
Birds, various	Lev. 11:13–19; Ps. 104:17; Eccles. 9:12
Bird's voice	Job 39:26–30; Jer. 17:11
Birth of Jesus foretold & to get throne	Jer. 31:22; Luke 1:31–33
Bishop of our souls	1 Pet. 2:25
Bishoprick	Acts 1:20
Bishop's behavior	1 Tim. 3:1–16; Titus 1:7–10
Bit & bridle	Ps. 32:9
Bite & devour	Gal. 5:15
Bits	James 3:3
Bitter	Num. 5:18, 19, 23, 24, 27; Job 23:2; Prov. 27:7; Col. 3:19; James 3:14
Bitterly	Ruth 1:20; Zeph. 1:14
Bittern	Zeph. 2:14
Bitterness	Job 7:11; Prov. 14:10, + 17:25; Lam. 1:4, + 3:15
Black	Lam. 5:10
Blacksmith	Isa. 44:12
Blade	Mark 4:28
Blame	2 Cor. 8:20
Blameless	Phil. 2:15, + 3:6; 1 Thess. 5:23; 1 Tim. 3:2, 10, + 5:7; Titus 1:6
Blaspheme	Mark 3:28, 29; James 2:7; Rev. 13:6

Blasphemer forgiven		1 Tim. 1:12, 13
Blasphemies vs God		Mark 2:7, + 3:28; Luke 5:21 + 12:10; Rev. 13:5, 6
Blasphemous		Acts 6:11
Blasphemy		Matt. 12:31; John 10:33, 36; Col. 3:8; Rev. 13:8
"	to Jesus	Luke 22:63–65
Blasting		2 Chron. 6:28
Blemish		Lev. 4:28, 32, + 5:15, + 21:17, 18; Eph. 5:27; 1 Pet. 1:19; 2 Pet. 2:13
Bless		Ps. 103:20–22
"	Abram	Gen. 12:2, 3
"	God	Eph. 1:3
"	others	Rom. 12:14
"	the Lord	Ps. 103:1, 2, 20–22, + 104:1, + 134:1–3, + 135:19–21
Blessed		Ps. 32:1, 2, + 128:1
"	are	Rev. 14:13
"	" commandment keepers	Deut. 28:1–15
"	are the faithful	Rev. 22:14
"	" " true believers	Rom. 4:7–9
"	- beatitudes	Matt. 5:3–11
"	be Lord God	Ps. 72:18, 19
"	by Jesus	Luke 24:50
"	hope	Titus 2:13
Blessed king & lord		1 Tim. 6:15
"	more to give than to receive	Acts 20:35
"	or cursed	Num. 23:8, 10, 20, 21, 23, + 24:9
"	that trust	Ps. 2:12; Eph. 1:3

"	them	Josh. 22:6
"	us	Eph. 1:3
Blessing		Exod. 34:26; Mal. 3:10
"	of the Lord makes rich	Prov. 10:22
"	promised to believers	Mal. 3:16–18
"	to the Lamb	Rev. 5:12
Blessings from God		Acts 2:17; Eph. 1:3
"	if hearken	Deut. 28:1, 2
Blind		Isa. 42:18, 19
"	-faithful rewarded	Isa. 42:13–16
"	healed	Ps. 146:8; Mark 10:51, 52
"	" by Anaias	Acts 9:17, 18
"	leaders	Matt. 15:14
"	led I	Isa. 42:16, 18, 19
"	not if have God's requirements	2 Pet. 1:5–9
"	-now see	John 9:25
Blinded minds		2 Cor. 4:4
Blindfolded		Luke 22:64
Blocks, stumbling		Zeph. 1:3
Blood and water		1 John 5:6, 8
"	for atonement	Lev. 17:11
"	" blood	Gen. 9:6
"	" redemption	Eph. 1:7; Col. 1:14; Heb. 9:12
"	" for remission of sins	Matt. 26:28; Heb. 9:22
"	is life & atonement	Lev. 17:11
"	of animals	Heb. 9:19, + 13:11
"	" Christ	John 6:53–56; Heb. 9:14, + 10:19, + 13:12; 1 John 1:7, 9
"	" covenant	Heb. 13:20
"	" cross for peace	Col. 1:20

"	" New Testament	Matt. 26:28
"	offering	Ps. 16:4
Blood, one-for all		Acts 17:26
"	redeemed us	1 Pet. 1:17–21
"	shed for us	Luke 22:20
"	upon them	Lev. 20:27
Bloody		Ps. 139:19
Bloodguiltiness		Ps. 51:14
Blot out		Exod. 32:33; Ps. 51:1, 9; Acts 3:19
Bloweth		John 3:8
Boards		Acts 27:44
Boast		Prov. 25:14; Rom. 2:2, 23 + 11:18; 2 Cor. 10:8; Eph. 2:9
Boasting, your - is evil		2 Cor. 2:9; James 4:16
Boaz (pillar)		2 Chron. 3:17
Bodies arose		Matt. 27:52, 53
"	- living sacrifice	Rom. 12:1
"	of beasts not used	Heb. 13:11
Bodily exercise &	godliness	Col. 2:9; 1 Tim. 4:8, + 6:6
Body		Rom. 12:1; 1 Cor. 15:35, 37, 38, 40, 41, 44
"	- a living sacrifice	Rom. 12:1–3
"	and life	Matt. 6:25
"	blameless	1 Thess. 5:23
"	exercise	1 Tim. 4:8
"	- eye	Matt. 6:22, 23
"	for Lord - not fornication	1 Cor. 6:13–20, + 12:12–27
"	, glorious	Phil. 3:20, 21
"	godliness	1 Tim. 4:8
"	, his - church - Jesus	Eph. 1:22, 23

"	is Lord's body	Luke 22:19; 1 Cor. 3:16, 17, + 6:15, 16; Col. 2:16, 17
"	" temple of Holy Ghost	1 Cor. 3:16, 17, + 6:19, 20; 2 Cor. 6:16; Eph. 4:6
"	, Jesus & our	2 Cor. 4:10, 11; Phil. 3:21
"	made	Ps. 139:13–16
"	mine - Christ magnified there	Phil. 1:20
"	, natural & spiritual	1 Cor. 15:44–46
"	not for fornication	1 Cor. 6:13, 19, 20
"	not subject for corruption	Ps. 16:10; Acts 2:27, 31
"	of earthly & heavenly	1 Cor. 15:49
"	of Jesus	Luke 24:3; 1 Pet. 2:24
"	" " after resurrection	See Section BB
"	of Jesus Christ	1 Cor. 12:27; Heb. 10:10–14
"	" " tended to	Luke 23:52–55
"	" man	Job 14:1–12; 2 Cor. 4:10, 11
"	, one	Rom. 12:4; 1 Cor. 12:12–20, 24, 27; Eph. 4:4; Col. 3:15
"	or spirit	Rom. 5:8–14, 26
"	" the Lord	2 Cor. 5:6–8
"	, our	Matt. 6:25; 1 Cor. 3:16, 17, 21; Eph. 4:16
"	our - collectively in Christ	Rom. 12:4–21; 1 Cor. 12:27
"	, our - made well	Ps. 139:14
"	parts	Rom. 6:12, 13; 1 Cor. 12:12–27; Eph. 4:16

" " not necessary to God	Matt. 18:8, 9; Mark 9:45
" " made	Ps. 139:13–16; Eph. 4:16
" power	1 Cor. 15:43, 44
" rewards	2 Cor. 5:10
" saviour	Eph. 5:23
" things done	2 Cor. 5:10
" to glorify God	1 Cor. 6:20
" " remember	Mark 14:22
Body - we of Christ	1 Cor. 12:27; Col. 3:15, 16
" whole	Eph. 4:6
" , whole - not important to God	Matt. 18:8, 9; Mark 9:45
Boil	Lev. 13:23
Boils (6th plague)	Exod. 9:8–12; Job 2:7
Boisterous	Matt. 14:30
Bold in Christ	Philem. 1:8
Boldly	Eph. 6:20; Heb. 4:16
Boldness	Acts 4:13; Heb. 10:19; 1 John 4:17
Bond	Col. 3:14
Bondage	Heb. 13:3; Rom. 5:1, + 8:15; John 8:33; 2 Pet. 2:19
Bondman	Deut. 24:22
Bone of my bone	Gen. 2:23
Bones to life	Ezek. 37:1–10
" , thy	Prov. 3:8
Book - Bible	John 20:30
" eaten by John	Rev. 10:9, 10
" , longest - in Bible	Psalms, with 150 chapters & 65 pages
" of life	Exod. 32:33; Rev. 5:1–8, + 13:8, + 20:12, 15, + 21:27
" " the law	Josh. 1:8

"	to be sealed	Dan. 12:4
Books		Eccles. 12:12
"	in Bible, 66: OT = 39 & NT = 27	
Books opened		Eccles. 12:14; Dan. 7:10, + 9:9, + 12:9; Luke 10:20; Phil. 4:3; Rev. 20:12, + 21:27
Booties		Hab. 2:7
Booty is goods		Zeph. 1:13
Bore		Exod. 21:6
Born		Gen. 10:1, + 21:3, 5, 7; Matt. 1:16, + 2:1, 2; Luke 1:35
"	again (or anew)	John 1:12, 13, + 3:3–8; 1 Pet. 1:22, 23; 1 John 3:9
"	" by word of God	1 Pet. 1:22, 23
"	again one does not sin	John 3:3; 1 John 3:6, 9, + 5:14
"	king	Matt. 2:2
"	not of blood - will of flesh or man	John 1:13
"	of God if believe	John 1:12, 13; 1 John 4:7, + 5:1, 4, 5, 18
"	" " " love	1 John 4:7–12
"	" " overcometh the world	1 John 5:1–5, 18
"	of the spirit	John 3:8
"	" water & spirit	John 3:6
"	" world is man	John 16:21
"	son to very old couple	Gen. 17:16–19, + 21:2, 3, 5; Rom. 4:16–21; Heb. 11:11
Borne		Lam. 3:28
"	our grief	Isa. 53:4
Borrowed		2 Kings 6:5, 6

Borroweth	Neh. 5:2–4; Prov. 22:7; Matt. 5:42
" , righteous & wicked	Ps. 37:21
Bosom	John 13:23; Luke 16:22
" of fathers	John 1:18
Both	1 Chron. 29:12
Bottle	Ps. 56:8, + 119:83; Mark 2:22
Bottomless pit	Rev. 20:1–3
Boughs	Deut. 34:20; Isa. 10:33
Bought with price , we are	1 Cor. 6:20; 1 Pet. 3:4
Bound	Ps. 104:9; Matt. 16:19, + 18:18; 2 Thess. 1:3; Heb. 13:3
" Satan	Rev. 20:1–3
Bounds of habitation	Acts 17:26
Bountifully - sparingly	Ps. 116:7; 2 Cor. 9:6
Bow	Gen. 9:13, 14, 16; 2 Kings 13:15, 16; Ps. 11:1, 2, + 37:14, 15, + 86:1, + 95:6; Isa. 45:23; Hab. 3:9; Rom. 14:11
" down	Ps. 95:6
" knees	Eph. 3:14
" to image	Lev. 26:1; Dan. 3:5, 6, 10, 12, 14–18
Bowed head, Jesus	John 19:30
" not	Lev. 26:1; 1 Kings 19:18; Esther 3:2
Bowels	Jer. 4:19, + 31:20; 2 Cor. 6:12; Philem. 1:7, 12, 20
Bowing	Ps. 17:11
Boy given (sold)	Joel 3:3
" Jesus	Luke 2:40, 46
Boys & girls	Zech. 8:5

Brake	2 Chron. 23:17; Matt. 14:19
Branch	Isa. 11:1; Zech. 3:8, + 6:12; John 15:1–6
Branches	John 15:4–6; Rom. 11:16–21
Brass	Job 28:2
Brawlers	Titus 3:2
Brawling woman	Prov. 21:9, + 25:24.
Breach	Isa. 58:12
Bread	Gen. 41:54; Mark 14:22; Luke 4:4, + 22:19; 1 Cor. 11:23, 24, 26
" for us	Num. 14:9
" of heaven & life	John 6:32, 35, 47–58
" " life is flesh	John 6:48, 51; 2 Cor. 9:10
" , one	1 Cor. 10:16, 17
" to the hungry	Isa. 58:7
" , unleavened	Luke 22:1, 7–20
Breadth	Job 37:10
Break	Isa. 55:12, + 58:6; Acts 21:13
Breastplate	Isa. 59:17; Eph. 6:14; 1 Thess. 5:8; Rev. 9:9, 17
Breasts	Gen. 49:25; Ps. 22:9; Prov. 5:19; Ezek. 16:7
Breath	Gen. 2:7, + 7:15, 22; Job 33:4, + 37:10; Isa. 42:5; Ezek. 37:9, 10; Acts 17:25
Breathed breath	Gen. 2:7
" on them	John 20:22
Breed	Gen. 8:17; Deut. 32:14
Brethren and mother same to Jesus	Luke 8:21
" , strengthen	Luke 22:32
" unity	Eph. 4:1–32; Phil. 3:17; Heb. 10:19, 20; 1 Pet. 4:8–10

Brickkiln	2 Sam. 12:31
Bricks	Exod. 5:16–19
Bride	Isa. 62:5; John 3:29; Rev. 18:23
" - church	Rev. 22:17
Bridechamber	Mark 2:19
Bridegroom	John 3:29
" - Jesus	Ps. 19:5; Matt. 22:5–14, + 25:1, 6, 10; Mark 2:19, 20; Rev. 18:23
Bridle	Ps. 39:1; Prov. 26:3
" in people's mouth	2 Kings 19:28
" the body	Rom. 6:12, 13; 1 Cor. 6:13–20; 2 Cor. 5:6–8; 1 Thess. 5:23
" " tongue	James 1:26
Brighter than the sun	Acts 26:13
Brightness as	
righteousness	Isa. 62:1
" corrupted wisdom	Ezek. 28:17
Brimstone	Rev. 19:20
Bring forth fruit	Luke 8:15
" it to pass	Gen. 28:15; Ps. 37:5
" up children	Eph. 6:4
" with him-God	1 Thess. 4:14
Bringeth forth fruit	Mark 4:28
Brightness as	
righteousness	Isa. 62:1
Broided hair	1 Tim. 2:9
Broidered work	Ezek. 16:10
Broken	Eccles. 4:12; Rom. 11:17, 19, 20
" heart drieth bones	Prov. 17:22
" spirit & heart	Ps. 51:17; Prov. 17:22
" up	Matt. 24:43
Brokenhearted	Isa. 61:1; Luke 4:18

Brook	1 Kings 17:3–7
Brother	Prov. 18:24; Matt. 12:50; Mark 3:35; Heb. 1:11; 1 John 4:20, 21; Rev. 1:9
" of Jesus	Matt. 12:50; Mark 3:35
Brotherly	2 Pet. 1:7
" love	Rom. 12:10; Heb. 13:1, 2; James 13:1, 2
Brother's keeper	Gen. 4:9
Brothers and sister of Jesus (James, Joseph, Simon, Judas, & sisters)	Matt. 12:50, + 13:55; Mark 3:31, 32, 35; Luke 8:20, 21
Brought	Matt. 13:8; Acts 6:12, + 7:36, 40, 45; 2 Pet. 2:19
" up	Luke 4:16; Heb. 13:20
Broughtest	Num. 14:13
Brow of hill	Luke 4:29
Bruise	Gen. 3:15
Bruised for our iniquities	Isa. 53:5
Brute beasts	2 Pet. 2:12; Jude 1:10
Brutish	Ps. 92:6; Jer. 10:14; Mark 12:1
Buckler is the Lord	Ps. 18:2, 30, + 91:4; Prov. 2:7
Budgeting	Prov. 13:16, + 14:15, 16; Luke 14:28–30
Buffet	2 Cor. 12:7; 1 Pet. 2:20
Build	Ps. 127:1; Acts 20:32
" on rock	Matt. 7:24, 25, + 16:1, 3, 9, 18, + 24:3, 4; Luke 14:28–30
" up by Lord	Ps. 102:16
" yourselves	Jude 1:20, 21
" us up by word of grace	Acts 20:32

Builder is God	Heb. 11:10
Buildeth	1 Cor. 3:10, 11
Building, God's	1 Cor. 3:9
Buildings	Mark 13:1, 2
Built	1 Cor. 3:10, 14; Heb. 3:3, 4
" all things, God	Heb. 3:4
" on cornerstone	
are we	Eph. 2:20
Bullock	1 Kings 18:23, 25, 26, 33;
	Ps. 50:9, + 51:19 + 69:31
Bulrush	Isa. 58:5
Bulwarks	Eccles. 9:14; Isa. 26:1
Burden	Ps. 55:22; Isa. 10:27, + 58:6
" of Jesus is light	Matt. 11:30; Acts 15:28
" " Lord	Mal. 1:1; Jer. 23:33, 34, 36, 38
" , other's	Isa. 46:1, 2; Gal. 6:2
" , own	Gal. 6:5
Burdens	Isa. 58:6
" , bear one another's	Gal. 6:2
Burdensome	2 Cor. 12:14
Buried with Him	Rom. 6:4
Burn	Matt. 3:12
Burn the wicked	Isa. 47:14; Mal. 4:1;
	Matt. 13:40–42
Burned everything	Mal. 4:1; 2 Pet. 3:10
Burning bush	Exod. 3:2–4
Burnt offering	Lev. 1:1–17; Ezra 3:3, 4;
	Mark 12:32, 33
Burst	Jer. 30:8; Acts 1:18
Bush, burning	Exod. 3:2–4
Business deals	Lev. 19:13; Prov. 16:11;
	Rom. 12:11
" , man's	Prov. 22:29
" of fathers	Luke 2:49

Busy bodies, not to be	1 Tim. 5:13
But	Ps. 37:17; Prov. 11:17; John 1:17 + 14:24, 26; James 2:10
" by me-Jesus	John 14:6
" - not	Gal. 2:16
" the wicked	Rev. 21:8
Butter	Prov. 30:33; Isa. 7:15
Buy without money	Isa. 55:1, 2
By	2 Cor. 6:6–8
" Him (Jesus)	1 Pet. 1:21
" me (Jesus) to Father	John 10:9, + 14:6
Byword	Ps. 44:14

• C •

Cain		Gen. 4:1–17; 1 John 3:12
Cake		Hos. 7:8
Calamity		Deut 32:35; Job 6:2; Ps. 57:1; Prov. 1:26, + 6:15, + 24:22
Calf		Mal. 4:2; Acts 7:41
Call	- answer - hear - shew	Isa. 58:9, + 65:24; Jer. 33:3
"	me Lord and not obey	Luke 6:46
"	none on earth Father	Matt. 23:9
"	on Lord and find him	Ps. 145:18; Jer. 29:11–13; Rom. 10:12–14
"	" one who believed	Rom. 10:13, 14
"	sinners to repentance	Mark 2:17
"	things not as were	Rom. 4:17
"	to be saved	Acts 2:21; Rom. 10:13
"	unto me	Jer. 33:3
"	upon God any time	Ps. 55:17
Called by God		Rom. 8:28, 30; 1 Cor. 1:9; Col. 3:15

"	" Lord	1 Sam. 3:4, 6, 8, 10
"	(named)	
	everything	Gen. 2:19, 20
"	to be holy	1 Cor. 6:12, 13, 19, 20;
		1 Pet. 1:15, 16, + 5:10
"	" " sons	1 John 3:1
Calling of God		Rom. 11:29; Phil. 3:14
"	prize	Phil. 3:14
Callops		Job 15:27
Calm		Luke 8:24
Came		Matt. 1:18; Luke 2:16;
		1 Cor. 15:21
"	by water &	
	blood	1 John 5:6, 8
"	Jesus to save	
	sinners	Mark 2:17; John 3:17;
		Acts 2:21, + 4:12; 1 Tim. 1:15;
		1 John 3:16
"	Jesus to save world	Luke 12:47
"	to give us life	John 10:10
"	" minister, Jesus	Matt. 20:28
Camel		Matt. 23:24; Luke 18:25
Camels		Esther 8:10; Job 1:3, 17;
		Isa. 60:6; Matt. 19:24
Camp		Heb. 13:11
Can do all things		Job 42:2; Phil. 4:13
Candle		Luke 8:16
Candlestick		Luke 8:16
Candlesticks, seven		
	golden	Rev. 1:12, 13, 20, + 2:1
Canker		2 Tim. 2:17
Cankered		James 5:3
Cannibalism		Lev. 26:29
Cannot		1 Tim. 5:25; 1 John 3:9

Canst	Prov. 5:6, + 30:4; Mark 1:40, + 9:22, 23
Capital of world will be Jerusalem	Dan. 11:45
Captain	Heb. 2:10
Captive	Isa. 49:24
Captives	Isa. 45:13; Luke 4:18
Captivity	Isa. 46:2; Jer. 49:6; 2 Cor. 10:5
Carcase	Lev. 11:24–26 + 35:40; 1 Kings 13:22, 24, 25, 28–30; Matt. 24:28
Carcases	Heb. 3:17
Care	1 Pet. 5:7
" for others	Col. 3:12–17
" " other's burdens	Hos. 11:1–4; Rom. 8:22; Gal. 6:2
" of God consistence	Ps. 37:25, + 40:1
Care of God for us	1 Pet. 5:6, 7
" " the Lord for saved people	2 Chron. 32:21, 22
" of the Lord for us rests us	Ps. 23:1, 2
leads "	Ps. 23:2, 3
feeds "	Ps. 23:4, 5
keeps "	Ps. 23:6
" of poor rewarded	Ps. 4:1–3
Careful	Luke 10:41
" for nothing	Phil. 4:6
Cares of this world	Mark 4:19
Careth for you	1 Pet. 5:7
" " world things	1 Cor. 7:33
Carnal minded not of God	Rom. 8:6–14; 1 Cor. 3:1–4
Carnally or spiritually minded	Rom. 8:6, 7

Carpenter and tools		Isa. 44:13; Mark 6:3
Carriages		Isa. 46:1
Carried our sorrows		Isa. 53:4
"	up to heaven	Luke 16:22, + 24:51
Carry		Exod. 33:15; 1 Tim. 6:7
Cars predicted		Nah. 2:4
Carved		2 Chron. 33:7
Cassia		Ps. 45:8
Cast		1 Cor. 7:35
"	abundance	Mark 12:41–44
"	alive	Rev. 19:20, + 20:10
"	away self	Ps. 42:11; Luke 9:25
"	burden on Lord	Ps. 55:22
"	care on God	1 Pet. 5:6, 7
"	devil into bottomless pit	Rev. 20:1–3
"	down	Ps. 42:5, 6, 11
"	into lake of fire	Mark 9:22; Rev. 19:20, + 20:15
"	me not away	Ps. 51:11
"	out of church	2 John 1:10
"	" prince	John 12:31
"	Satan down	Rev. 12:10–13
"	stone	2 Chron. 25:14; John 8:7
Castaway		1 Cor. 9:27
Casteth down the wicked		Ps. 147:6
Casting		2 Cor. 10:5; 1 Pet. 5:7
"	lots	Matt. 27:35
Castle		Acts 23:10
Catch men		Luke 5:10
Catcheth		Matt. 13:19; John 10:12
Caterpillars		2 Chron. 6:28; Jer. 51:27
Cattle		Exod. 9:3, 4, 6, 7; Ps. 50:10; Ezek. 34:17, 20, 22; Zech. 13:5

Caught	Matt. 14:31; Acts 6:12
" up	1 Thess. 4:17; Rev. 11:38
Cause	Ps. 25:3, + 143:8; Ezek. 36:12, 27; Matt. 19:3, 5; John 12:27, 30; 2 Cor. 4:16, + 5:13
" , commit	Job 5:8
" none of death	Acts 13:28
Causeth	2 Cor. 2:14
Cave	Gen. 49:29, 32; John 11:38
Cease from sin	2 Pet. 2:14
" not to pray & give thanks	Rom. 1:9; Eph. 1:16; 1 Thess. 5:17
Ceased work - rested	Heb. 4:3, 4, 9, 10; also see Sabbath
Ceasing , pray without - & thank God	1 Thess. 2:13, + 5:17; 2 Tim. 1:3; Philem. 1:4
Cedar	Lev. 14:49, 51, 52; Ps. 104:16; Isa. 44:14; Zech. 11:2
Celebration	Rev. 5:13
Celestial	1 Cor. 15:40
Cement one of another	1 Kings 4:9
Censer	Rev. 8:5
Centurion	Acts 10:1, 22 + 21:32, + 27:11, 31, 43, + 28:16; Mark 15:39
Certain	Luke 5:17, + 10:30, 31, 33, 38; Acts 17:28; 1 Tim. 6:7
" , house	Mark 5:35
Certainly	Exod. 3:12
Chaff	Ps. 1:4, + 35:5; Zeph. 2:2; Matt. 3:12
Chains	Isa. 45:14; Acts 12:7; Jude 1:6
Chamberlain	Esther 7:9

Chamelon	Lev. 11:30
Chance	Luke 10:31; 1 Cor. 15:37
Chanceth	Deut. 23:10
Change not at last days	Rev. 22:11
" ", Lord	Mal. 3:6
" " when Jesus comes	Rev. 22:11, 12
" our vile body	Phil. 3:20, 21
" -repent	Matt. 4:17; 1 Cor. 15:50–52
" times & law	Dan. 7:25
Changed minds	Acts 28:6
" not since creation, all things	2 Pet. 3:4
" , we will be	1 Cor. 15:50–52; 2 Cor. 3:18; Phil. 3:20, 21
Changeless is God	Mal. 3:6; Heb. 13:8
Chant	Amos 6:5
Chapter	1 Kings 7:16–20
Chapter - longest in Bible	Ps. 119
" - shortest in Bible	Ps. 117
Charge of Lord	Josh. 22:5; 1 Kings 2:3, 4; Ps. 91:11; Matt. 16:20; Luke 9:21
" thee per Paul	2 Tim. 4:1
" to rich	1 Tim. 6:17–19
Chargeable	2 Cor. 11:9
Charged disciples	Matt. 16:20; Mark 5:43
" witnesses	Mark 5:43
Chargedst	Exod. 19:23
Chariots	Nah. 2:4
Charity	1 Cor. 13:1–4, 8, 13, + 16:14; 1 Pet. 4:8, + 5:14
" above all things	Col. 3:14; 1 Pet. 4:8
Chase	Josh. 23:10; Ps. 35:5

Chaste		2 Cor. 11:2; 1 Pet. 3:2
Chasten		2 Cor. 11:2; 1 Pet. 3:2;
		Heb. 12:5–8, 10, 11
"	self	Dan. 10:12
"	son	Dan. 19:13, 18
"	you by God	Deut. 8:5; Ps. 6:1 + 38:1
Chasteneth		Deut. 8:5; Heb. 12:6, 7
Chastening of Lord to		
	accept	Heb. 12:5, 7, 11
Chastise		Luke 23:16, 22
Chastisement		Isa. 53:5; Heb. 12:8
Checker		1 Kings 7:17
Cheek		Isa. 50:6; Matt. 5:39
Cheer		Matt. 14:27; John 16:33
Cheerful giver		2 Cor. 9:7
Cheerfulness		Rom. 12:8
Cherubims		Exod. 25:18–22;
		2 Chron. 3:10, 13, 14, + 5:7, 8;
		Ezek. 10:1–9, 15–20
Cherisheth		1 Thess. 2:7
Cherub		Exod. 25:19; Ezek. 10:2, 4, 7,
		9, 14, + 28:14; Matt. 28:16
Chickens		Matt. 23:37
Chide		Ps. 103:9
Chief shepherd		1 Pet. 5:4
Chiefest		2 Cor. 12:11
Child believer		Matt. 18:6
"	Jesus	Luke 2:40
"	of God	
	requirements	Matt. 5:39–48
"	to God	Gen. 1:18; 1 Kings 3:7
"	" man	1 Cor. 13:11
"	training	Prov. 22:6, + 23:13, 14
Childbearing		1 Tim. 2:15

Childless		Lev. 20:20; Jer. 22:30
Children		Dan. 1:4; Matt. 19:14; Mark 10:13–15; Eph. 5:1; 1 Thess. 2:7
"	a joy	1 John 1:4
"	abide in him	1 John 2:28
"	blessed	Mark 10:16
Children, bring up		Eph. 6:4
"	instructions from father	Ps. 78:4; Prov. 4:1–27
"	keep from idols	1 John 5:21
"	, little-not accountable	Deut. 1:39
"	not to be provoked	Col. 3:21
"	" " perish	Matt. 18:14
"	obey parents	Eph. 6:1–3; Col. 3:20
"	of desolate & of married	Isa. 54:1
"	" God	Matt. 5:9; Rom. 8:16, 17; 2 Cor. 6:17; Gal. 3:26–28
"	provided for by parents	Ps. 128:3; Matt. 7:11; 2 Cor. 12:14
"	taught of the Lord	Isa. 54:13–17
"	, teach (importance)	Deut. 6:1, 5–8, 24
Children's children		Prov. 17:6
"	friend was Jesus	Mark 10:13, 14
"	glory is their father	Prov. 17:6
Chode		Gen. 31:36; Num. 20:3
Choice		Gen. 3:6; Deut. 32:5; Eccles. 7:29
"	- accept or reject	Gen. 2:16, 17; Eccles. 7:29
"	ours	1 Chron. 28:9
Choke		Mark 4:7, 19

Choose		Isa. 65:12; Josh. 24:15; Phil. 1:22
Chose	apostles	John 6:70; Acts 1:2
"	he you	Deut. 10:15
Chosen		Luke 10:42; John 15:16, 19; Eph. 1:4; 1 Pet. 2:4, 9
Christ		Dan. 7:13, 14; Rom. 8:34; Col. 3:1, 3, 4, 11, 13, 16, 24
"	, anti	1 John 2:22
"	before world	John 8:58, + 17:24; Col. 1:15–17; 1 Pet. 1:19–21
"	come in body	Matt. 25:40; Phil. 3:21; 1 Thess. 4:15–17; 2 Thess. 2:1
"	coming	Isa. 11:1–9; Jer. 31:22; Zech. 3:8; Matt. 24:29, 30; Luke 21:25–36; John 14:3; 1 Thess. 4:16–18; Rev. 1:7
"	" with saints	Zech. 14:5
Christ	died for our sins	Rom. 4:25, + 5:8; 1 Cor. 15:3
"	, false	Matt. 24:24–27, 31, + 25:31
"	-in Christ award	2 Cor. 5:17; 1 Thess. 4:16–18; 1 John 5:1
"	in Heaven	Rom. 8:34
"	" you	2 Cor. 10:5; Col. 1:27
"	is image of God	2 Cor. 4:4
"	" Jesus	John 1:7–17, + 17:3; Eph. 4:15; Col. 1:15–17, 27
"	" master	Matt. 23:10
"	" salvation	Heb. 9:28
"	" the head	Eph. 4:15
"	Jesus the mediator	1 Tim. 2:5, 6
"	knocking at our door	Rev. 3:20
"	lived & died for us	Rom. 4:25, + 5:8, + 11:36

Church		Matt. 16:16–18, + 18:20;
		Eph. 1:22, 23, + 5:24, 27
"	added to daily	Acts 2:41, 47
"	began	Matt. 16:17–19
Church body - His (Jesus)		Eph. 1:22, 23
"	comforted	Isa. 43:1–16
"	- common worship	Acts 4:44–47; Heb. 10:23;25;
		1 Pet. 4:8–10
"	duties position -	
	be content	1 Cor. 12:28, 29; Phil. 4:11
"	head	Eph. 1:22, 23, + 5:23, 27;
		Col. 1:18; Heb. 10:21
"	in Heaven	Rev. 7:14–17
"	- no blemish	Eph. 5:27
"	of God	1 Cor. 10:32
"	" the Living God	1 Tim. 3:15
"	promise of God	Isa. 43:2
"	to be holy per	
	Paul	Eph. 5:27; 1 Tim. 3:15
"	to be subject	
	unto Christ	Eph. 5:24
"	workers there	
	by God	1 Cor. 12:28, 29; Phil. 4:11
Churches' instructions		Rev. 1:4–6, 20, + 2:1, 7, 17,
		18, 29, + 3:1, 6, 7
"	, seven	Rev. 1:4, 11, 20, + 2:1, 8, 12,
		18, + 3:1, 7, 14, 22
Churning milk		Prov. 30:33
Cieled		Hag. 1:4
Cinnamon		Prov. 7:17
Circumcise, flesh		
	covenant	Gen. 17:10–14, 19, 21, 23–27
Circumcised		Gen. 17:10–14; Acts 7:8;
		Gal. 6:12–15

Circumcision	Acts 7:8, + 15:1, 5, 24, + 16:3; Rom. 15:8; 1 Cor. 7:18, 19; Gal. 2:7, + 5:2, 3, 6, 11, 12; + 6:12–15; Col. 2:10–12
" a seal of righteousness	Rom. 4:10, 11
Circumspectly	Eph. 5:15
City	Gen. 11:4, 5; Eccles. 9:15; Matt. 5:14 + 23:34
" , Holy	Rev. 21:2
Clap hands	Ps. 47:1; Isa. 55:12
Clapped	Job 34:37
Clay and metals	Dan. 2:45
" - potter	Rom. 9:21
" , we are formed of	Job 33:6
" , " " to the father	Job 33:6; Isa. 64:8
Clean	Ezek. 36:25; Mark 1:40–42; Luke 5:12, 13; 2 Pet. 2:18
Cleanness	Ps. 18:20, 24
Cleanse	Ezek. 36:25; Luke 4:27; 2 Cor. 7:1; 1 John 1:9
" us , blood	2 John 1:7, 9
" yourself to help others	Luke 6:41–46
Cleansed	Mark 1:42; Luke 4:27, + 5:13, + 17:14, 17, 18
Cleanseth	1 John 1:7
Clearer	Job 11:17
Clearly seen	Rom. 1:20
Cleave	Gen. 2:24; Deut. 10:20, + 11:22, + 13:4; Josh. 22:5; Matt. 19:5; Mark 10:7
Cleaveth	Lam. 4:8

Clods	Job 7:5
Cloke	Matt. 5:40; John 15:22; 1 Pet. 2:16
Closer	Prov. 18:24
Closet	Matt. 6:6; Luke 12:3
Clothe	Matt. 6:30; Luke 12:28
Clothed	Ps. 93:1; Ezek. 16:8, 10; Luke 12:28
" Adam & Eve	Gen. 3:21
" materially & spiritually	Isa. 61:10; 2 Cor. 5:1–10
Clothes of Jesus	Luke 23:34
Clothing	Deut. 22:5; Luke 12:35
" , woman's	2 Tim. 2:9
Cloud	Job 37:11, 15; Matt. 7:5; Rev. 11:12
Clouds	Job 37:16; Luke 12:54; Acts 1:9; 2 Pet. 2:17; Rev. 1:7
Clouts	Jer. 38:11, 12
Cloven	Acts 2:3
Clovenfooted	Lev. 11:7
Coals	Isa. 44:12; John 18:18; Rom. 12:20
Coat	John 19:23
Coats of skin	Gen. 3:21
Cock crow	Matt. 26:34, 75; John 13:38
Cockatrice	Job 31:40; Isa. 11:8, + 59:5
Cockcrowing	Mark 13:35
Cockle	Job 31:40
Cold	Job 37:9; Ps. 147:17
" of snow	Prov. 25:13
" or hot	Rev. 3:15, 16
Collection	1 Cor. 16:1
Collops	Job 15:27

Colt		Gen. 49:11; John 12:15
Coma		Obad. 1:16
Come		Rev. 22:17
"	again	John 14:3, 28
"	as go - Jesus	John 14:3, 28; Acts 1:11
"	" thief	1 Thess. 5:2; Rev. 3:3
"	, I - Jesus	Matt. 5:17; John 10:10, + 12:46, + 14:3, 28; 1 Cor. 16:2
"	in Father's name	John 5:43
"	- Lord per angel	Ps. 96:13; Matt. 24:27–44; Rev. 3:3
"	not surprise to believers	1 Thess. 5:1–5
"	per spirit	Rev. 22:17
"	short	Rom. 3:23
"	son of man	Matt. 25:31
"	the comforter & spirit of truth	John 16:7, 8, 13, 14; Acts 1:8
"	, time to	Isa. 42:23
"	to Christ	Matt. 11:28–30
"	" Father	John 14:6
"	" God - must believe	Heb. 11:6
"	to Jesus	John 6:65
"	" Lord's services	Ps. 96:8; Heb. 4:16
"	" me - Jesus	Matt. 11:28, + 19:14, + 24:27, 30, 39; John 6:35, 44, + 14:1–3
"	" pass	Gen. 8:6; Mark 13:29–31; John 14: 29
"	" worship Him	Matt. 2:2
"	" you	John 14:18
"	together for edifying	1 Cor. 14:26
"	when I - Jesus	1 Cor. 16:2

Comeliness		Isa. 53:2; 1 Cor. 12:23
Comely		1 Cor. 7:35
"	in going - four things	Prov. 30:29–31
"	is praise	Ps. 147:1; 1 Cor. 7:3, 5
"	to enjoy fruits of labor	Eccles. 5:18
Cometh	by me only - Jesus	John 14:6
"	joy	Ps. 30:5
"	my salvation	Ps. 62:1, 6, 7
"	the day to burn the proud & the wicked	Mal. 4:1
"	the son of man	Matt. 24:44, + 25:31; 1 Cor. 15:24; Rev. 1:7
"	to Father only by me - Jesus	John 14:6
"	with clouds, Jesus	Rev. 1:7
Conformable		Phil. 3:10
Comfort		Ps. 23:4, + 71:21, + 91:9–12, + 119:50; Isa. 40:1, + 66:13; Matt. 11:28; Acts 9:31; Rom. 15:4; Phil. 4:13; Rev. 21:3, 4
"	and torment	Luke 16:19–25
"	at last - forever	Rev. 21:1–7
"	from Lord God	Isa. 43:2; Jer. 31:13; 2 Cor. 1:3, 4, 6
"	handicapped	Deut. 24:19–22; 1 Thess. 5:14
"	one another	Isa. 40:1; John 14:1–4; 1 Thess. 4:13–18, + 5:11, 14
"	to faithful	John 14:15–21, 26, 27, + 16:7, 22–27; 1 Thess. 4:16–18

"	" mourners	Isa. 61:2
"	us	2 Cor. 1:2–6, + 13:11
Comfortably		2 Chron. 32:6; Isa. 40:2
Comforted		Ps. 119:52; Matt. 5:4; Rom. 1:11; 2 Cor. 1:3–6
Comforter		Ps. 46:1, 2, 10; Isa. 41:10; John 14:16, 17, 26, + 15:26, + 16:7, 8, 13
"	will reprove world	John 16:7–11
Comfortless		John 14:18
Coming and going		Mark 6:31
"	of Jesus Christ	Matt. 24:27–31, + 25:31; Rev. 6:16, 17
"	and going of Jesus Christ foretold	Zech. 14:5; Mark 13:1–37
"	of Lord	Matt. 25:13; Luke 12:35–40, 43, + 21:25–28; 2 Pet. 3:10–12; Rev. 1:7, + 3:3
"	" " like rain	Joel 2:23; 1 Thess. 4:16, 17; Rev. 1:7
"	" " signs	Matt. 24:29, 30; Mark 13:9–31; Luke 21:25–28
"	son of man foretold	Matt. 24:27–31, 36–44, + 25:31, + 26:64; Mark 14:24–27
"	son of man - when	Matt. 23:35–38, + 24:29, 30
Comliness		1 Cor. 12:23
Command		Ps. 42:8; Acts 16:18
"	by Jesus	Matt. 28:19, 20; John 15:14, 17; Acts 10:42; 1 Tim. 4:11–16
"	" Moses	Deut. 6:1, + 30:16
"	- teach	1 Tim. 4:11–16
Commanded		Matt. 15:4; Acts 10:42
"	by God	Acts 13:47, + 17:30, 31

"	" Jesus	Matt. 28:18–20
"	" Joshua	Josh. 1:7–18
Commandment doers		
	are blessed	Rev. 22:12, 14, 15
"	" have	
	understanding	Ps. 111:10
"	, first	Matt. 22:37, 38; Mark 12:29, 30
"	, greatest one	
	or two	Matt. 22:36–40; Mark 12:29–31
"	keepers blessed	Ps. 119:1, 2, 12, 32
"	, Lord's	Ps. 19:8
"	, Moses'	Deut. 5:1–21; Josh. 22:5
"	, new	John 13:34, + 14:15
"	, " & old	1 John 2:7, 8
"	of God	John 12:49, 50, + 14:31;
		Acts 17:30
"	, second	Matt. 22:39; Mark 12:31
Commandments		Deut. 6:1; Mark 10:19
"	doers	Deut. 28:1–15; Rev. 22:14
"	, greatest	Mark 12:29–31
"	, keep	John 14:15
"	kept - reward	Deut. 5:10; Matt. 5:19;
		John 14:15, 16
"	not grievous	1 John 5:3
"	repeated	Deut. 5:6–21
"	, ten	Exod. 20:3–17, + 34:28;
		Deut. 5:1–21; Matt. 19:17–19;
		Luke 18:20
"	to apostles	Acts 1:2; 1 Thess. 4:2
"	" heed	Josh. 22:5; Ps. 111:7–10
Commend		Acts 20:32; 2 Cor. 3:1, + 4:2, +
		5:12, + 10:18
"	my spirit - Jesus	Luke 23:46
Commendeth		Rom. 5:8

Commission from Jesus	Matt. 28:18–20; Mark 16:15, 16
Commit	Ps. 37:5; Luke 12:48 + 16:11; 1 Pet. 4:19
" - believe	John 2:23, 24; 2 Tim. 2:2
" evil things	Rom. 1:28–32
" not adultery	Deut. 5:18
" sin is transgressor, one to	Prov. 14:34; 1 John 3:4, 9
" thy way & works	Ps. 37:5; Prov. 16:3
Committed	Mark 15:7; Acts 28:17; Gal. 2:7
" self - Jesus	1 Pet. 2:23, 24
" sins	James 5:15
Common	1 Cor. 10:13; Jude 1:3
" people listened	Mark 12:37
" thing together	Acts 2:42–47, + 4:32; Rom. 15:30
Commonly	1 Cor. 5:1
Commonwealth	Eph. 2:12
Commune	Ps. 77:6
Communed	Exod. 31:18; Luke 24:15; Acts 24:26
Communication	Matt. 5:37; Luke 24:17; 2 Cor. 13:14; Eph. 4:29, + 5:4; Philem. 1:6; James 3:9–13
" not to be filthy	Col. 3:8
Communion	Luke 22:17–20; 1 Cor. 10:16, + 11:23–26, + 13:12
" , first	1 Cor. 11:23–29
" of Holy Ghost	2 Cor. 13:14
Compacted body	Eph. 4:16
Companied him	Acts 1:21
Companion	Rev. 1:9

Company, keep good	Jer. 9:25; 1 Tim. 3:2, 3; 1 Pet. 4:9, 10
Compare	Isa. 46:5; 2 Cor. 10:12
Compared to God	Dan. 4:35
Comparison	Hag. 2:3
Compass	Isa. 44:13; Jer. 31:22; Acts 28:13
Compassed	Ps. 118:10–12; Heb. 11:30
Compassion	Ps. 112:4; Matt. 14:14, + 15:32, + 20:34; Mark 8:2
" for others	Matt. 18:33; Col. 3:12–17; 1 Pet. 3:8, 9
Compel	Matt. 5:41; Luke 14:23; 2 Cor. 12:11
Complainers	Jude 1:16
Complete in Him	Col. 2:10
Comprehend	Eph. 3:18
Conceal	Ps. 41:12
Conceit	Prov. 18:11; Rom. 12:16
Conceive me in sin - David	Ps. 51:5
Conceived	Job 3:3; Rom. 9:10; James 1:15
Conception	Gen. 3:16; Ruth 4:13
Concern	Matt. 25:31–46; Rom. 12:10–13; Heb. 13:1–3; James 1:27; 1 John 3:17, 18
" in work	Luke 12:22–31
" me - crucifixion	Luke 23:39–46
Concerning	Rom. 9:5, + 11:28; 1 Cor. 16:1; 1 Thess. 5:18; 2 Pet. 3:9
Concerns - all of ours to God	Phil. 4:6

Concision		Phil. 3:2
Conclude		Rom. 3:28
Concluded		Rom. 11:32
Conclusion		Eccles. 12:13, 14; 1 Thess. 5:18
Concord		2 Cor. 6:15
Concupiscence		Rom. 7:8; Col. 3:5; 1 Thess. 4:5
Condemn		Job 9:20; Luke 6:37;
		John 3:18, 19, + 8:10, 11;
		Rom. 8:34
"	- judge - forgive	Luke 6:37
"	love to us	Rom. 5:8
"	not	Luke 6:37
"	or favor	Prov. 12:2
"	self	Rom. 2:1; 1 John 3:20
Condemnation		John 5:24; Rom. 5:16, 18, + 8:1
Condemned		Mark 16:64; John 5:24;
		Heb. 11:7; James 5:12;
		Jude 1:4
Condescend		Rom. 12:16
Conditions of prayer		Mark 11:22–26
Coney		Lev. 11:7
Confederacy		Isa. 8:12
Confer in Jesus Christ -		
not flesh		Eph. 1:16
Conferred		Gal. 1:16
Confess		Ps. 32:5; Phil. 2:11; 1 John 4:15
"	- believe - saved	Rom. 10:9, 10
"	faults to others	James 5:16
"	Lord Jesus	Rom. 10:9, 10; 1 John 4:15
"	me - I you	Matt. 10:32, 33; Luke 12:8
"	most important	1 John 4:15
"	name to father	Rev. 3:5
"	sins to be cleansed	Prov. 28:13; 1 John 1:9
"	to overcome	Rev. 3:5

"	with mouth	Rom. 10:8–10
Confesseth or		
	covereth sins	Prov. 28:13
Confession		Dan. 9:4; Rom. 10:10
Confidence		Prov. 25:19; Phil. 1:6, 25;
		Heb. 10:35
"	in flesh	Phil. 3:4
"	" Lord	Ps. 40:4, + 118:8, 9;
		Acts 28:30, 31; 1 John 5:14
"	not in friend or	
	bosom one	Mic. 7:5
Confident		Ps. 27:3; Rom. 2:9, + 8:38, 39;
		2 Cor. 5:6, 8; Phil. 1:6
Confirm		1 Cor. 1:6, 8
Confirming Lord		Mark 16:20
Conflict, final		Mark 13:22
Conflicts foretold		Matt. 24:6–13
Conform not to this world		Rom. 12:2
"	to God's image	Rom. 8:29; 2 Cor. 4:7–11
Conformable		Phil. 3:10
Conformed - transformed		Rom. 12:2
Confound		Jer. 10:14; 1 Cor. 1:27
Confounded		Ps. 35:4; Acts 2:6
Confusion		Job 10:15; 1 Cor. 14:33;
		James 3:16
Congregation		Num. 16:7; Acts 13:43
Conies		Ps. 104:18; Prov. 30:26
Conquer		Rev. 6:2
Conquerors - us		Rom. 8:37
Conscience		1 Cor. 10:29; 2 Cor. 1:12, +
		5:11; 1 Tim. 3:9; 2 Tim. 1:3
"	bearing witness	Rom. 9:1
"	good	Acts 23:1, + 24:16; Heb. 13:18
"	, man's	John 8:9; 2 Cor. 4:2

"	saves	1 Pet. 3:21
Consecrate		*Exod.* Lev. 32:29
Consecrated		Heb. 7:28, + 10:20
Consent not		Prov. 1:10
Consenting		Acts 8:1
Consider		Job 37:14; Ps. 50:22; Luke 12:24, 27; 2 Tim. 2:7; Heb. 12:3
"	and encourage one another	Heb. 10:24
"	enemies	Ps. 25:19
"	the poor & less fortunate	Deut. 24:19–22; Ps. 41:1–3
"	works of God	Job 37:14; Ps. 8:3; Matt. 6:28; Luke 12:27
Consideration of others		Phil. 2:3, 4
Considered		Ps. 31:7
Consist		Luke 12:15; Col. 1:17
Consistency of God's care		Ps. 37:25, + 40:1
Consolation		2 Cor. 1:5–7; Phil. 2:1, 2; Philem. 1:7; Heb. 6:18
"	for righteous	Ps. 16:5–11
Conspiracy		2 Kings 12:20, + 14:19; 2 Chron. 33:25; Acts 23:13
Constellations		Isa. 13:10
Constrain		Matt. 14:22; Luke 24:29; 2 Cor. 5:14
Constrained herself		Acts 16:15
Constraint		1 Pet. 5:2
Consulted		2 Chron. 20:21; Matt. 26:4
Consume		Ps. 39:10, 11; Zeph. 1:3; James 4:3
"	the wicked	Ps. 37:20; 2 Thess. 2:8
Consumed		Ps. 90:7

Consuming fire	Heb. 12:28
Consummation	Dan. 9:27
Consumption	Isa. 10:23
Contain	1 Cor. 7:9
Contempt	Job 31:34; Prov. 18:3; Dan. 12:2
Contemptible	Mal. 1:7; 2 Cor. 10:10
Contemptuously	Ps. 31:18
Contend	Job 9:3; Prov. 28:4; Isa. 50:8; Jude 1:3, 9
Content, be - as is	Luke 3:14; Phil. 4:11; Heb. 13:5
" , " - with any church office	Phil. 4:11
" , be - with necessities	1 Tim. 6:8
Contention	Acts 15:39; 1 Cor. 1:11; Phil. 1:16; 1 Thess. 2:2
Contentious	Rom. 2:8
" man	Prov. 26:21; 1 Cor. 11:16
" woman	Prov. 21:19, + 27:15
Contentment	1 Tim. 6:6
Continual	Prov. 15:15
Continue	John 15:9; 1 Tim. 4:16
" in the faith	John 8:31; Acts 14:22
Continually	Gen. 6:5; Job 1:5; Isa. 58:11; Luke 24:53; Heb. 13:15
Continuance	Deut. 28:59; Isa. 64:5
Contradiction	Heb. 12:3
Contrariwise	2 Cor. 2:7; Gal. 2:7; 1 Pet. 3:9
Contrary	Lev. 26:28; Matt. 14:24; Acts 23:3; Gal. 5:17; Col. 2:14
Contrite	Ps. 51:17 + 57:18; Isa. 66:2
Controversy	Deut. 21:5; Isa. 34:8; 1 Tim. 3:16
Convenient	Prov. 30:8

Conversation	2 Cor. 1:12; Gal. 1:13; Phil. 1:27, + 3:20; Heb. 13:5, 7; James 3:9–13; 1 Pet. 2:12, + 3:1, 2
" Holy	Phil. 3:20; 1 Pet. 1:15, 16
" to glorify Christ	Phil. 1:27
Conversion of Paul	Phil. 3:3–14
" wanted by God	Ezek. 33:11
Convert sinners reward	James 5:19, 20
Converted	Isa. 60:5; Matt. 18:3; Luke 22:32; Acts 3:19
" example	Acts 26:9–23
" to be healed	Matt. 13:15, + 18:3
Converts	Ps. 19:7
Convey	1 Kings 5:9
Convicted	John 8:9
Convictions of Jesus	Luke 2:49
Convince	John 8:46; Jude 1:15
" and exhort	Titus 1:9
Convinced	Job 32:12
Convocation	Lev. 23:2–4, 7, + 28:26
Cooperation	Josh. 22:1–4; Acts 4:31–35
Cord	Eccles. 4:12
Cords	Ps. 118:27; John 2:15
Core	Jude 1:11
Cormorant	Lev. 11:17; Zeph. 2:14
Corn	Gen. 41:9, + 42:2, 3, 19, 25, 26, + 43:2, + 44:2; Deut. 23:25
Cornerstone	Job 38:6; Ps. 118:22; Acts 4:11; Eph. 2:20; 1 Pet. 2:6, 7
Correct another	Prov. 3:11, 12, + 28:23
" son	Prov. 3:11, 12, + 29:17
Corrected us	Heb. 12:9

Correction	Job 37:13; Rom. 3:11, 12
Corrupt	Mal. 1:14 + 2:3; 2 Cor. 2:17; Eph. 4:29
" earth	Gen. 6:5, 11, 12; Acts 13:33, 34
" " with fornication	Rev. 19:2
" minds	2 Tim. 3:8
" themselves	Judg. 2:19; 1 Cor. 15:33; Jude 1:10
Corrupted riches	James 5:2
Corruptible	Rom. 1:23; 1 Cor. 15:53, 54; 1 Pet. 1:23
" not	1 Pet. 3:4
Corruption	Isa. 1:3, 4; 1 Cor. 15:50; 2 Pet. 2:12
" is earth	Acts 13:33, 34
" not for Jesus' flesh	Ps. 16:10; Acts 2:24, 31
Couch	Job 7:13; Ps. 6:6
Couched	Gen. 49:9
Couldst	John 19:11
Council	Mark 14:55; Acts 23:6
Counsel	Ps. 73:24; Matt. 27:1
Counseling is valuable	Prov. 11:14
Counsellor	Isa. 9:6
Count	Phil. 3:7, 8, 13; James 1:2
Countenance	1 Sam. 16:7; Ps. 4:6 + 21:6, + 42:11; Dan. 1:10–15
" , sad	Matt. 6:16
Country, earthly and heavenly	Heb. 11:14–16
Coupled	1 Pet. 3:2
Couples believe & not believe	1 Cor. 7:12, 13
Couplings	2 Chron. 34:11

Courage and help	Deut. 31:6; Ps. 27:14, + 31:24; Acts 28:15
Course	Eph. 2:2
" finished - reward	Acts 20:24; 2 Tim. 4:7, 8
Courteous	1 Pet. 3:8
" be	Josh. 1:7, 9, + 23:6
Courts of God	Ps. 92:13
Covenant	See Section CC
" , blood of	Heb. 13:20
" , first	Heb. 8:7, + 9:1
" - people	Ps. 50:16; Isa. 42:5, + 55:3
" , second (Jesus is mediator)	Heb. 8:6, 8, 13, + 12:24
Covenants of promise	Jer. 31:31–33; Eph. 2:12
Cover	1 Pet. 4:8
Covered, sins Ps. 32:1	
Covereth or confesseth sins	Prov. 28:13
Covering	1 Cor. 11:15
Covet	1 Cor. 12:31, + 14:39
Covetous practices	2 Pet. 2:14
Covetousness	Hab. 2:9; Luke 12:15; Heb. 13:5
" is idolatry	Col. 3:5
Craftiness	Job 5:13; 2 Cor. 4:2; James 2:14
Crafty	2 Cor. 12:16
Crashing	Zeph. 1:10
Craved	Mark 15:43
Create	Isa. 45:7 + 65:18
Created clean heart in me	Ps. 51:10
" all things	Gen. 1:27–30; Col. 1:16; Rev. 4:11, + 14:7
" animals	Gen. 1:24, 25

"	earth	Gen. 1:1; Isa. 40:28, + 45:18; Rom. 1:20; Rev. 14:7
"	fish and fowl	Gen. 1:20, 21
"	growing things	Gen. 1:11, 12
"	heaven and earth	Gen. 1:1
"	living creatures	Gen. 1:20, 21, 24–27; Col. 1:16
"	male & female	Gen. 1:27
"	(planned) man before forming him	Gen. 1:26, 27
"	man in His image	Gen. 1:26, 27
"	new man	Eph. 4:24
"	smith (blacksmith)	Isa. 54:16
"	we to good works	Eph. 2:10
"	woman for man	Gen. 1:20–24, 27; 1 Cor. 11:9
Creation - six days		Gen. 1:1–31; Isa. 42:5, + 45:12, 18, 22; Col. 1:16, 17
"	good	Gen. 1:31
"	- things later seen	Rom. 1:20; Rev. 14:7
"	revealed God	Gen. 1:1–31, + 2:1–8, 21–23; Ps. 19:1; Isa. 46:9, 10
Creations of Lord God		Ps. 104:2–32
Creator		Gen. 1:1; Isa. 40:28, + 42:5, + 43:1; Amos 4:13; Col. 1:16; Rev. 4:11
"	or creature	Rom. 1:25
Creature		Rom. 8:19–21; Col. 1:15
"	- new in Christ	2 Cor. 5:17; Rev. 5:13
"	of God is good	1 Tim. 4:4
Credit to God per Moses		Ps. 9:12
Creditor		Luke 7:41
Creeping things		Lev. 11:20; Ps. 104:25; Acts 11:6
Crept		Jude 1:14
Cried		1 Sam. 15:11; Ps. 3:4; Mark 15:34; Acts 23:6

"	answeredst with strength in my soul	Ps. 138:3
"	, Jesus	Luke 23:46
Criest		Prov. 2:3
Crimson		Isa. 1:18
Cripple		Acts 14:8
Critical spirit		Phil. 2:14, 15
Criticism		Prov. 15:32
Crooked nation		Phil. 2:15
"	to straight	Isa. 42:16
Cross blood made peace		Col. 1:20
"	effect is power of God	1 Cor. 1:17, 18
"	endured	Heb. 12:2
"	is power of God	1 Cor. 1:18
"	, our	Mark 8:34, + 10:21; Luke 9:23; Phil. 2:10–13
Cross preaching		1 Cor. 1:18
"	story	Gal. 1:4; Phil. 2:8
Crow		John 13:38
Crown for faithfulness		Rev. 2:11
"	" overcomers	Rev. 2:17
"	" the faithful	Rev. 2:10
"	incorruptable	1 Cor. 9:25
"	of glory	1 Pet. 5:4
"	" " & honour for death	Heb. 2:9, + 10:12; 1 Pet. 5:2, 4
"	of life	James 1:12; Rev. 2:10
"	" rejoicing	1 Thess. 2:19
"	" righteousness	2 Tim. 4:8
"	" thorns	Mark 15:17; John 19:5
Crucifixion		Matt. 27:35; Mark 15:20–25; Luke 23:33, 46; John 19:30

"	foretold	Dan. 9:26, 27; Matt. 20:17–19, + 26:2; Luke 9:44
Crucified and raised		Rom. 4:24, 25; 1 Cor. 15:3–8
"	flesh	Gal. 5:24
"	Jesus	Matt. 27:22, 23, 26, 35; Mark 15:15, 24, 25, 32, + 16:6; Luke 23:33, + 24:7, 20; John 19:23
"	" & Paul	John 19:18; Gal. 2:20, + 6:14
"	thieves	Matt. 27:44
Crucify Him		Matt. 27:31; Mark 15:13, 14, 20, 27; Luke 23:21
"	son of man predicted	Matt. 20:17–19
Cruel		Job 30:21; Prov. 11:17 + 12:10
"	merciful	Prov. 11:17
Cruel one troubleth self		Prov. 11:17
Cruse		2 Kings 2:20
Cry	aloud God hears	Ps. 55:17; Isa. 58:9
"	ignored to worshippers of God	Jer. 11:9–14
"	not - Lord to Ezekiel	Ezek. 24:15–23
"	out	Isa. 12:6
"	(speak) to people	Isa. 58:1; Acts 23:9
Cubits		Gen. 6:15; 1 Kings 6:2, 3, 6, 16, 17, 20, 24; Luke 12:25
Cuckow		Lev. 11:16
Cumbered		Luke 10:40
Cummin		Matt. 23:23
Cunning		2 Chron. 2:7, 14; Isa. 40:20; Dan. 1:4; James 2:14
Cunningly		2 Pet. 1:16

Cup		Matt. 26:39, 42; Mark 14:23, 24; Luke 22:17, 20, 42; 1 Cor. 10:16, 21
"	of wrath	Ps. 11:6; Prov. 11:31; Isa. 9:5, + 34:2; Mal. 4:1
Curdled		Job 10:10
Cure		Jer. 33:6
"	by believing	Matt. 17:19, 20
Cured many		Matt. 17:15–20; Luke 7:14, 15, 21
Curse		Prov. 3:33; Zech. 5:3; Mal. 3:9; Luke 6:28; Acts 23:12; James 3:9, 10
"	no more	Rev. 22:3
Cursed		Jer. 20:14; Gal. 3:13; 2 Pet. 2:14
"	for adultery	Lev. 20:10–21
"	" ignoring the poor	Prov. 28:27
"	is ground	Gen. 3:17
"	or blessed	Num. 23:8, 10, 20, 21, 23, + 24:9
"	serpent	Gen. 3:14
Curses for disobediences		Deut. 28:15–68
Curseth		Matt. 15:4
Custom		Ezra 3:4; Luke 4:16; Acts 28:17
"	, Sunday worship	Luke 4:16
Cut	down	Ps. 37:2
"	off offender	Ps. 37:9, 28; Mic. 5:9–12; Matt. 18:6–9; Mark 9:43, 45
"	timber	2 Chron. 2:8
Cymbals		2 Chron. 5:12; 1 Cor. 13:1
Cypress		Isa. 44:14

• D •

Daily		Heb. 7:27
"	added to church	Acts 2:41, 47
"	searched scriptures	Acts 17:11
Damnable		2 Pet. 2:1
Damnation		Mark 3:29; Rom. 13:2; 1 Tim. 5:12; 2 Pet. 2:3
Damned unbelievers		Mark 16:16; Rom. 14:23; 2 Thess. 2:10–12
Damsel		Deut. 22:20, 23, 25–29; Acts 16:16; Mark 5:39–42
Dandled		Isa. 66:13
Danger of judgment		Matt. 5:21, 22; Mark 3:29
Dangerous		Acts 27:9
Daniel in lion's den		Dan. 6:3–23, 27
Daniel's vision		Dan. 10:1–21
Dare		Job 41:10
Darkly		1 Cor. 13:12
Darkness		Joel 2:2; Amos 5:20; Zeph. 1:15; Matt. 4:16, + 6:23, + 27:45; John 3:19, 20, + 8:12; 1 Pet. 2:9; Luke 23:44, 45
"	and night activities	Rom. 13:11–14
"	(ninth plague)	Exod. 10:20–29
"	, no - but light	1 John 1:5

"	now light	Eph. 5:8
"	sixth to ninth hour	Mark 15:33, 34
Darts		2 Chron. 32:5; Eph. 6:16
Dash		Ps. 91:12
Daubed		Ezek. 22:28
Daughter		Jer. 31:22; Matt. 9:18,22;
		Mark 5:34, 35; 2 Cor. 6:17, 18
Daughters and sons		
	of Lord	Acts 2:17; 2 Cor. 6:18
David		1 Sam. 16:9–23
"	and Goliath	1 Sam. 17:4–58
"	honored	1 Sam. 18:1–30
David's death		1 Kings 2:10
"	generation	Ruth 4:13–32
"	promise from God	2 Sam. 7:16
"	soul	Acts 2:29, 31
Dawning		Job 7:4; Ps. 119:147
Day		Gen. 1:5, 14, 16, + 2:2–4;
		Jude 1:6; Rev. 9:15
"	approaching	Heb. 10:25
"	come , how	2 Pet. 3:10
"	" to burn	
	proud & wicked	Mal. 4:1
"	, first-of week	1 Cor. 16:2
"	, holy	Gen. 2:3; Isa. 58:13, 14
"	made by Lord	Ps. 118:24
"	not known	Matt. 25:13
"	of judgment	2 Pet. 3:7, 8, 10; Jude 1:6
"	" Lord will come	Phil. 1:6; 2 Thess. 5:2;
		2 Pet. 3:10
"	" wrath	Rev. 6:12–17
"	, seventh	Gen. 2:1–3
"	, terrible-to come	Joel 2:31, 32; Zeph. 1:15
"	, third	Matt. 20:19

"	to day show	
	salvation	Ps. 96:2
"	to work	John 9:4
"	with the Lord	2 Pet. 3:8
Days are evil		Eph. 5:14–16
"	, last	Acts 2:17; Rev. 14:7
"	, " - of wickedness	
	foretold	Isa. 66:12–24; 2 Tim. 3:1–15
"	, man - are	
	120 years	Gen. 6:2
"	numbered	Job 14:5; Ps. 90:12, + 139:16
"	of flood & lot	Matt. 24:37–39; Luke 17:26–29
"	, our - leave	
	impression	Ps. 90:9, 10, 12
"	speak	Job 32:7
"	, three - nights	Matt. 12:38–40; Rev. 11:9–12
Dayspring		Luke 1:78
Deacon		1 Tim. 3:8, 10, 12, 13
Dead - death		Rom. 6:2–11
"	body & spirit	James 2:26
"	, first from	Col. 1:18; Rev. 1:5
"	in corruption &	
	in incorruption	1 Cor. 15:42
"	" sins	Col. 2:13
"	, Jesus	Mark 15:44
"	judged	John 5:27–29; Rev. 11:18, +
		20:11–13
"	know nothing	Eccles. 9:5
"	- live	John 11:25
"	not influenced by	
	the living	1 Thess. 4:15
"	of itself not to	
	be eaten	Ezek. 44:31
"	praise not the Lord	Ps. 115:17

"	praised	1 Thess. 4:16
"	shall be raised	Isa. 26:19; Dan. 12:2; John 5:28, 29; Acts 24:15
"	" hear	John 5:25, 28
"	sleep until resurrection	Job 14:10–12, 21; 1 Thess. 4:14
"	to arise	Isa. 26:19; Dan. 12:2; John 5:28, 29; Rom. 8:10, 11; Eph. 5:14; 1 Thess. 4:14–17
"	" be raised	1 Cor. 15:52, 54, 57; Phil. 3:20, 21
"	" earth	Ps. 146:3, 4
"	" hear God	John 5:25, 28
"	" live	John 5:28, 29
"	" " unto	Gal. 2:19
"	with Him - alive with Him	2 Tim. 2:11
"	works	Heb. 9:14
Deadly		Mark 16:18
Deaf		Ps. 38:13; Isa. 42:18, 19; Mark 7:32
Deal		Isa. 58:7
Dealeth		Heb. 12:7
Dealings to be honest		Prov. 12:22; Rom. 12:11
Dealt		2 Chron. 33:6; Ruth 1:20; Ps. 116:7
Dear children		Eph. 5:1
Dearly		1 Pet. 2:11
Dearth		2 Chron. 6:28; Acts 7:11, + 11:28
Death abolished		John 8:51; 2 Tim. 1:10
"	better than birth	Eccles. 7:1
"	defeated	1 Cor. 15:52–54

"	experienced by Jesus	Heb. 2:9
"	for sins	Rom. 1:32; Heb. 9:15
"	" us	John 3:16; 1 Pet. 3:18
"	is enemy	1 Cor. 15:25, 26
"	, no	1 Cor. 15:26, 54–57
"	, " more	Rev. 21:4
"	not by keeping word	John 8:51
Death	of firstborn (then plague)	Exod. 11:1–9
"	of saints	Ps. 115:16
"	" wicked	Prov. 14:12; Ezek. 33:11
"	or life & peace	Rom. 8:6; 2 Cor. 4:10–12
"	pains loosed	Acts 2:24
"	passed away	Eccles. 9:5, 6; Rev. 21:4
"	- quickened	1 Pet. 3:18
"	reigned by one	Rom. 5:14, 17
"	, second - for wicked	Rev. 20:11–15, + 21:8
"	, " - has no power	John 5:28, 29; Rev. 20:6
"	sentence per Jesus	Luke 23:21, 24, 33, 46
"	- sin-life	Rom. 6:2–14, + 7:4–6; Col. 2:20, + 3:1–4; 2 Cor. 5:14–18; 1 Pet. 2:24
"	- " - lust	James 1:14, 15
"	sting	1 Cor. 15:55, 56
"	- time not known	Eccles. 8:8
"	to all	Rom. 5:14
"	" destroy devil	Heb. 2:14, 15
"	" everlasting life	John 11:25, 26
"	" life	John 5:24

"	" the Lord	Ps. 115:17, + 116:15; Eccles. 12:7; 1 Cor. 15:17–23, 51, 52; 1 Thess. 4:16–18
"	" victory	1 Cor. 15:52–54
"	with glory & honour	Heb. 2:9
Debate		Prov. 25:9; Isa. 58:4
Debt		Matt. 6:12; Rom. 4:4
Debtors		Matt. 6:12; Rom. 8:12
Deceit		Prov. 12:20; Col. 2:8
Deceitful		Prov. 31:30; Jer. 17:9; Mark 4:19; Eph. 4:22
Deceitfully work	- antichrist	Dan. 11:23, 24; 2 Cor. 4:2
Deceivableness		2 Thess. 2:10
Deceive		Mark 13:5, 6; 1 Cor. 3:18; 2 Thess. 2:3, 4; 1 John 1:6, 8, 10, + 2:4, 9
"	God	Ps. 16:4; Hos. 8:1, 2; Amos 5:16–20
"	nations again	Rev. 20:7–10
"	ourselves	1 John 1:8
Deceived - Adam & Eve		1 Tim. 2:14
"	by own followers - antichrist	Dan. 11:26; Gal. 6:7
"	by Satan	Gen. 3:4, 5; 2 Thess. 2:9, 10; Rev. 19:20
"	" " & false prophets	Matt. 24:24; 2 Tim. 3:13
"	Lord	Mal. 3:13
Deceiver		Matt. 7:15; Mark 13:5, 6
"	is antichrist	2 Thess. 2:3, 4; 2 John 1:7
"	" devil	Rev. 13:13, 15

"	" world political	
	leader-a man	2 Thess. 2:3, 4, 9
"	Satan has power	1 Pet. 5:8; Rev. 13:13, 14, +
		16:13, 14
Deceiver's plight		Isa. 5:20
Deceivers		Matt. 15:8, + 24:4, 5, 24–26;
		Rev. 2:2
"	foretold	Luke 21:8
"	, heed	Matt. 24:4–13; Acts 20:28–31
Deceiveth them on earth		Rev. 13:14
"	world, devil, &	
	Satan	Rev. 12:9
Deceiving		2 Tim. 3:13
"	self	James 1:22
"	while dining	2 Pet. 2:13
Decently		1 Cor. 14:40
Decision		1 Cor. 14:1–4
"	ours	1 Chron. 28:9
Decketh		Isa. 61:10
Declare		Ps. 19:1, + 96:3; Jer. 42:4;
		Acts 13:41; 1 John 1:5
Declared		Isa. 44:8; John 1:18; Rom. 1:4
Declined		Ps. 119:51
Decree		Ezra. 6:3; Dan. 3:29, + 6:26;
		Zeph. 2:2
Decreed		Job 38:10
Dedicate house		2 Chron. 2:4
"	our life to God	2 Cor. 6:1–10
Dedicated life		2 Cor. 4:11; Phil. 1:20
"	self	Phil. 1:20, 21
Dedication		Neh. 12:27; Phil. 3:7–11
"	of image	Dan. 3:3
Deed and truth important		1 John 3:18

"	for Jesus' sake	Col. 3:17
Deeds	, good	John 3:21
"	of body	Acts 24:15; 2 Cor. 5:10
"	" Lord be revealed	Ps. 105:1
"	" men	Mal. 3:16
"	rewarded	Rom. 2:5, 6, 9
"	ungodly	Jude 1:15
Deep	things of God	Ps. 92:5; 1 Cor. 2:10
Defamed		1 Cor. 4:13
Defaming		Jer. 20:10
Defence		Num. 14:9; Job 22:25; Ps. 7:10; Eccles. 7:11, 12
"	of God & gospel	Ps. 7:10, + 62:6; Phil. 1:17
Defer		Gen. 34:19; Dan. 9:19
Defile		Dan. 1:8; Matt. 15:18–20; Mark 7:15, 18, 20, 23; 1 Cor. 3:17; James 3:6; Jude 1:8; Rev. 21:27
Defiled		Num. 5:13, 20, 27–29; Isa. 59:3; John 18:28
Defraud		1 Cor. 6:7, 8; 1 Thess. 4:6
"	not	Lev. 19:13; Mark 10:19; 1 Cor. 7:5
Degree		Ps. 62:9; James 1:9
Degrees		Isa. 38:8
Delight		Job 22:26; Ps. 1:1, 2, + 112:1, + 119:16; Prov. 29:17
"	in provisions	Isa. 55:1, 2
"	" saints	Ps. 16:3
"	" the Almighty	Job 22:26
"	in the Lord	Ps. 37:4, 11; Isa. 58:2, 13, 14
"	the Lord	Num. 14:8; Jer. 9:24
Deliver me		Ps. 140:1
"	the godly	Matt. 10:17; 2 Pet. 2:7, 9

Deliverance		Luke 4:18
Delivered and raised		Rom. 4:25
"	from lion's mouth	Dan. 6:16–23, 27; 2 Tim. 4:17
"	" sleep on earth	Dan. 12:1–3
"	" wrath to come	1 Thess. 1:9, 10
"	people	Judg. 8:34; Dan. 12:1; Acts 28:17
"	son for us , God	John 3:16; Luke 24:7; Rom. 4:25, + 8:32
"	, to be	Joel 2:32
"	us	Gal. 1:4; Col. 1:13
Deliverer		Rom. 11:26
"	by the lord	Judg. 3:9, 15, 31, + 4:4, + 6:11, + 9:1, + 10:1, 2, + 11:1, + 12:8, 11, 13, + 13:24
Delusion		Isa. 66:4; 2 Thess. 2:11, 12
Demons - swine into sea		Mark 5:9
Demonstration of gospel		1 Cor. 2:1–5
Den	of lions	Dan. 6:7, 12, 16, 19–24
"	" thieves	Mark 11:17
Denied		Luke 12:9; John 13:38, + 18:25, 27
Denieth the son is antichrist		1 John 2:22, 23
Deny and follow me		Matt. 16:24; Mark 8:34–37; Luke 9:23
"	Him - deny us	Matt. 10:33; 2 Tim. 2:12, + 3:5
"	Me - Jesus	Matt. 10:32, 33; Mark 14:30, 66–72; Luke 12:9, + 22:61
"	or reign	2 Tim. 2:12, 13; Rev. 3:5
Denying		Jude 1:4
Depart		Job 21:14; Ps. 37:27; Matt. 7:23; John 13:1, + 16:7; 1 Tim. 4:1

Departing from Lord God	Dan. 9:5
Depth	Mark 4:5; Rom. 11:33
Derision	Job 30:1; Ps. 2:4 + 119:51, + 44:13; Lam. 3:14; Hos. 7:16
Derided	Luke 16:14
Descend - earthly wisdom	
not from heaven	James 3:15
" fire from heaven	Rev. 13:13, 14
" from heaven	Matt. 24:36–44; John 14:3; 1 Thess. 4:16–18, + 5:2
" " " foretold	Matt. 26:32; Mark 14:62
Descended, Jesus	Acts 13:29–34; Eph. 4:9, 10
Descending, spirit	John 1:32
Descent	Heb. 7:6
Deception	Matt. 24:23–26
Describeth	Rom. 4:6
Desert place	Mark 6:31, 32, 35
Deserve - will get	Dan. 12:8–13
Desire	Ps. 38:9, + 92:11, + 118:7; Mark 11:23, + 15:6, 8; Col. 1:9; Heb. 6:11
" and believe to receive	Ps. 145:19; Mark 11:24
" satisfieth	Ps. 145:16
" to eat	Luke 22:15
Desires of heart	Ps. 37:4, 5; 1 John 5:15
Desireth	Ps. 34:12 + 51:6
Desirous	John 16:19; Gal. 5:26
Desolate	Job 30:3; Jer. 10:25 + 12:10, 11; Zeph. 3:6; 1 Tim. 5:5
" at end times	Dan. 9:27, + 11:31, + 12:11
" land	Isa. 13:9; Lam 5:18
" - no	Ps. 34:22

Desolation	Jer. 25:9; Zeph. 1:15, 17, +
	2:15; Matt. 24:15; Mark 13:14;
	Luke 11:17
Desolations	Ps. 46:8; Isa. 61:4
Despair	2 Cor. 4:8
" not at morning -	
to Ezekiel	Ezek. 42:15–17
" to wicked ones	Jer. 30:16; Nah. 2:10
Desperate is devil	Rev. 12:12
Desperately	Jer. 17:9
Despise	Luke 10:16; 1 Thess. 5:20;
	1 Tim. 4:12; Heb. 12:5
" not	Matt. 18:10
Despised	Isa. 53:3; 1 Cor. 4:10
" things	1 Cor. 1:28
Despisers	Acts 13:41
Despitefully	Matt. 5:44; Luke 6:28;
	Acts 14:5
Destitute	Ps. 102:17; James 2:15
Destroy devil	Isa. 13:14; Ezek. 28:18, 19;
	Heb. 2:14
" earth	Rev. 11:18
" Jesus	Matt. 27:20
" not	Matt. 5:17; Luke 9:56
Destroy people in	
name of peace	Dan. 8:25
" temple	John 2:19–21
" wicked	Ps. 145:20; Isa. 13:9;
	Matt. 10:28; 1 Cor. 3:17
" world	Matt. 4:1; 2 Pet. 3:10
Destroyed by devil	Heb. 2:14
" everything on earth	Gen. 7:23
" , last enemy to be	1 Cor. 15:26
" yoke - anointing	Isa. 10:27

Destroyeth own soul		Prov. 6:32
Destruction		Prov. 1:27, + 27:20; Isa. 13:6, + 16:18; Jer. 4:19, 20; Zeph. 1:15; Phil. 3:18, 19; 2 Pet. 3:16
"	by misuse of mouth	Prov. 13:3
"	for ignoring gospel	2 Thess. 1:7–9
"	of wicked	Job 31:3
"	or life	Matt. 7:13
Determination		Ps. 84:10, 11; 1 Cor. 2:1–5
"	of Christian	Ps. 84:10, 11; Phil. 1:20
Determined by Paul		1 Cor. 2:2
Device		2 Chron. 2:14; Lam. 31:62; Acts 17:29
Devices		Ps. 33:10; Prov. 1:31; Dan. 11:25
Devil a liar		John 8:44
"	active	Matt. 12:22; Eph. 6:11; 1 Pet. 5:8
"	- adversary of ours	1 Pet. 5:8
"	casts down	Rev. 12:10
"	cast into bottomless pit	Rev. 20:1–3
"	cast into lake of fire	Rev. 20:10
"	comes	Rev. 12:12
Devil devours		1 Pet. 5:8
"	has short time - deceiver	Rev. 12:12
"	is deceiver	Rev. 13:13–15
"	" one apostle	John 6:70, 71
"	" sinner	1 John 3:8
"	, lion like	1 Pet. 5:8
"	or God	Rev. 13:8
Devil's miracles		Rev. 16:13, 14
"	spirits	Matt. 8:6; Mark 1:34

Devils		Mark 16:17; Luke 10:17, 18; Rev. 9:20
"	believe and tremble	James 2:19
Deviseth		Ps. 52:2
Devoted		Lev. 27:29
"	to one another	Rom. 12:10
Devour		Isa. 42:14; Jer. 15:3 + 17:27; 1 Pet. 5:8
Devoured will be the drunkards		Nah. 1:10
Devout		Acts 2:5, + 10:2, + 17:17
Dew		Exod. 16:13, 14
Diadem		Ezek. 21:26
Dictator, greatest ever on earth		Rev. 13:4–8
"	of world blasphemes God	Rev. 13:6
"	of world gets power	Rev. 13:5, + 17:8
"	" " - strife	Dan. 11:40
"	, world - foretold	Dan. 11:21
Dictatorship		Dan. 11:21
Did		Acts 10:39
"	not	Matt. 25:45
Die	for all - us for Him	2 Cor. 5:14, 15
"	" eating fruit of knowledge tree	Gen. 2:17
"	" Lord Jesus	Acts 21:13
"	" us	Rom. 5:8
"	in faith - to rise	Dan. 12:2; Rev. 1:7
"	" Lord	Rev. 14:13
"	" sins if not believe	Ezek. 18:4; John 8:24
"	is gain	Phil. 1:20, 21
"	- live	Rom. 14:7, 8
"	not if believe	John 11:26

"	once	Heb. 9:27
"	then judgment	Heb. 9:27
"	to sin	Rom. 6:10
Died - buried & rose again		1 Cor. 15:3, 4; 1 Thess. 4:14
"	for us, Christ	Rom. 5:8; 1 Cor. 15:3; 2 Cor. 5:14, 15
Diet		Matt. 15:1, 4, 5; Heb. 12:11; Rev. 3:20
Dieth - man & animal	similar	Eccles. 3:19, 20
"	no more	Rom. 6:9
Differ		Rom. 12:16; 1 Cor. 4:7
Difference, making a		Jude 1:22
"	none with Lord God	Rom. 3:22, + 10:12, 13
Differences		1 Cor. 12:5
Differing gifts		Rom. 12:6
Dig		Job 6:27, + 11:18, + 24:16; Prov. 6:27
Diligence		Prov. 4:23; 2 Tim. 4:21; 2 Pet. 1:5, 10; Jude 1:3
"	to end	Heb. 6:11
Diligent		Ps. 77:6; Prov. 22:29; 2 Pet. 3:14
"	or hasty	Prov. 21:5
Diligently		Matt. 2:8
"	hearken	Deut. 28:1–5
"	seek him	Heb. 11:6
"	teach children	Deut. 6:7
Dim		Lam. 5:17
Dimension		Acts 23:7; Eph. 3:18
Dine together		1 Cor. 11:33
Dip hand		Matt. 26:23; Mark 14:20; Luke 16:24

Dipped	John 13:26
Direct hearts	2 Thess. 3:5
" man's steps - not by others	Jer. 10:23
" our path	Prov. 3:5, 6
Directly to atoning blood	Heb. 10:19
Director of our lives	Rom. 12:12
Disallowed	1 Pet. 2:4, 7
Disannul	Gal. 3:17
Disannuleth	Gal. 3:15
Discern	Job 6:30; Mal. 3:18; Matt. 16:3; 1 Cor. 2:14
" not right from left	Jonah 4:11
Discerner	Heb. 4:12
Disciple requirement	Luke 6:40, + 12:22–24, + 14:25–33
Disciples, make nations	Matt. 28:19
" of Jesus	Matt. 5:1; John 13:35
Discontent	Eccles. 4:4–6
Discourage not children	Col. 3:21
Discretion	Prov. 1:4, + 5:2 + 11:22
Disdained	Job 30:1
Disease	Matt. 4:23, 24
Disfigure faces	Matt. 6:16–18
Dish-wiping man	2 Kings 21:13
Dishonestly	Ps. 101:7; Jer. 17:11; Acts 5:1–5; 1 Pet. 2:1, 2, 12
Dishonesty	2 Cor. 4:2
Dishonoureth God	Mic. 7:6; Rom. 2:23
Disinherit	Num. 14:12
Dismayed	2 Chron. 20:15, + 32:7; Josh. 1:9; Isa. 41:10
Disobedience	Rom. 5:19
" punishment	Gen. 2:16, 17; Col. 3:6

Disobedient	1 Pet. 2:7
" brings wrath	Col. 3:6
Disorderly one not	
desirable	2 Thess. 3:6–14
Dispensation	1 Cor. 9:16, 17; Eph. 1:10, +
	3:1–7; Col. 1:25
Dispersed	Zeph. 3:10; 2 Cor. 9:9
Displease	Ps. 2:5; Mark 10:14
Displeasure	Ps. 38:1
Dispossessed	Judg. 11:23
Dispute not	Phil. 2:14, 15; 1 Tim. 6:5
" , settle	Matt. 18:15–17
Disputed	Mark 9:34; Jude 1:9
Disquieted	Ps. 39:6, + 42:5, 11 + 43:5;
	Prov. 30:21–23
Dissembled	Gal. 2:13
Dissension	Acts 23:7, 10
Dissimulation	Rom. 12:9; Gal. 2:13
Dissolved	2 Pet. 3:12
Distil	Deut. 32:2
Distorting truth	Acts 20:30
Distraction	1 Cor. 7:35
Distress	Ps. 4:1, + 118:5; Zeph. 1:15;
	Luke 21:25
" relieved by God's	
power in us	2 Cor. 4:6–11
Distribute	Luke 18:22; John 6:11;
	Rom. 12:13
Distribution	Acts 4:34–35
Disturb not the righteous	Prov. 24:15
Ditch	2 Kings 3:16; Ps. 8:15;
	Luke 6:39
Divers diseases	Mark 1:34; Luke 4:40
" miracles	Heb. 1:4

"	temptations	Heb. 13:9; James 1:2–4
"	weights	Prov. 20:23
Diversities		1 Cor. 12:4, 6
"	, nine - of	
	spiritual life	1 Cor. 12:8–11
Divided		Gen. 15:10; Mark 3:23–26;
		Luke 11:17, 18, 23; 1 Cor. 12:11
Dividing word of truth		2 Tim. 2:15
Divination		Acts 16:16–18
Divine		Mic. 3:11
"	nature for us not	
	world corruption	2 Pet. 1:3, 4
"	power	2 Pet. 1:3
Diviners		Mic. 3:7
Divisions		1 Cor. 1:10, + 11:18
Divorce		Deut. 24:1; Matt. 5:32;
		Mark 10:2–9; 1 Cor. 7:14, 15
Divorcement		Gen. 24:1, 3; Matt. 19:7
Do		John 13:15, 17; 1 Cor. 10:31;
		Phil. 4:9; 1 Tim. 4:11–16
"	according to Bible	Josh. 1:7, 8
"	" in the name of	
	Jesus	Phil. 4:9, 13; Col. 3:17, 23
Do according things		
	heartily	Eph. 6:7, 8; Col. 3:23
"	according things	
	through Christ	Phil. 4:13; Col. 3:17, 23
"	according things	
	with might	Eccles. 9:10
"	according to glory	
	of God	1 Cor. 10:31
"	and observe	
	commandments	Deut. 28:1–15; Josh. 22:5
"	believe	1 Pet. 1:21

"	, can - everything	Job 42:2; Isa. 43:19
"	dislike & not like	Rom. 7:15–20
"	Father's will	Luke 6:46
"	" " is important	Matt. 7:21
"	good or evil	Gal. 6:10; 3 John 1:11
"	know good & do not	James 4:17
"	my teaching is wise - Jesus	Matt. 7:24–29
"	not	Luke 18:20
"	" call me Lord, etc.	Luke 6:46
"	per Paul	Phil. 4:8, 9; 2 Thess. 3:5
"	works	John 14:12
Doctors		Luke 2:46, + 5:17
Doctrine by scripture		2 Tim. 3:10, 16, 17, + 4:2, 3
"	, each one hath a	1 Cor. 14:26
"	known	Prov. 4:1, 5, 7, + 5:1; John 7:17
"	of apostles	Acts 2:42
"	" Jesus	Matt. 7:24–28; 2 John 1:9, 10
"	" Lord	Acts 13:12
"	, teach	Titus 2:1–15
Doctrines of men		Mark 7:7; Heb. 13:9
Doers of good		John 5:29
"	" law justified	Rom. 2:13
"	" the word, be	James 1:22–27
Doest good by man		Eph. 6:8
"	well	James 2:19
Doeth good or evil		3 John 1:11
"	many miracles	John 11:47
"	will of heavenly Father - reward	Ps. 1: 2, 3; Matt. 7:21
Dog		Exod. 22:31; 1 Kings 21:23; 2 Pet. 2:22

Doing God's will, happy		John 13:17; Eph. 6:7, 8
"	good & evil	Rom. 7:18, 19
"	" or evil	1 Pet. 3:17
Doleful creatures		Isa. 13:21
Dominion		Neh. 9:37; 1 Pet. 4:11; Jude 1:8
"	, everlasting	Dan. 4:34
"	from Adam to Jesus	Gen. 1:26, + 3:17
"	of God	Dan. 4:34, + 6:26, + 7:14, 26, 27; Rev. 1:5, 6
"	" man crowned with glory & honor	Ps. 8:4–6
"	, worldly	Dan. 11:36–39; Rev. 13:5–8
Done		Gen. 28:15; Ps. 66:16; Rev. 16:17
"	- ask	Matt. 18:19
"	good	Ps. 78:4; Mark 14:8
"	in body - good or bad	2 Cor. 2:10
"	to least/me	Matt. 25:40, 45
"	well	Eccles. 3:22
Door		John 10:1, 2, 7, 9; Rev. 3:7, 8
"	is Jesus	John 10:7, 9, 11, 14–16
"	keeper	Ps. 84:10
Door	open to Jesus	Rev. 3:20
"	shut when die	Rev. 3:8
"	" " pray	Matt. 6:6
"	to be opened	Rev. 3:20
"	, waiting at	Rev. 3:20
Doorkeeper		Ps. 84:10
Doted		Ezek 23:7
Doth		Prov. 6:16; Jer. 31:10; 2 Cor. 1:10; James 2:14

Double	Isa. 40:2
" minded	James 1:8, + 4:8
Doubletongued	1 Tim. 3:8
Doubt	Job 12:2; Matt. 14:31; Acts 2:12, + 11:12; also see waver
" not	Mark 11:23; 1 Tim. 2:8
Doubteth	Rom. 14:23
Doubtless	Ps. 126:6
Dove	Hos. 7:11
Downfall by people themselves - nations	Amos 3:7
Dragon	Ps. 9:13; Rev. 12:3, 7, 9, 13, 16, 17, + 13:4
" is Satan	Rev. 12:9
Draught	Matt. 15:17; Mark 7:19; Luke 5:4, 9
Draw	Isa. 58:10; Acts 20:30
" from well	John 4:7, 11
" near (nigh)	Ps. 73:28; Matt. 15:8; James 4:8
" out soul	Isa. 58:10
Drawn	Prov. 24:11; Jer. 31:3; James 1:14
Dread	Gen. 9:2; Exod. 15:16
Dreadful	Dan. 9:4; Mal. 4:5
Dream	Gen. 37:5; 1 Kings 3:5–15; Ps. 126:2
" per king	Dan. 2:1–49
Dreamers, filthy	Jude 1:8
Dreams and visions	Dan. 1:17, + 2:1; Acts 2:17
Drew bow	1 Kings 22:34
Drewest	Lam. 3:57
Drieth bones	Prov. 17:22

Drink		Matt. 26:29; Mark 14:25, + 16:8; John 7:37
"	and drink from Jesus	John 4:7, 9–15
"	" eat my blood & flesh	John 6:53–58
"	cup	Mark 14:23–25; 1 Cor. 11:25, 26
"	, do not give	Hab. 2:15
"	fruit of vine in Kingdom	Matt. 26:29
"	not	Prov. 23:20, 21, 31, 32
"	not for rulers	Prov. 31:4, 5
"	, strong	Prov. 20:1; Isa. 24:9, + 51:39:57
"	thy pleasures	Ps. 36:8
"	to perishing	Prov. 31:6
"	- water to give	Matt. 10:42
Drive		Ps. 44:2
Dromedaries		Isa. 60:6
Drop		Deut. 32:2
Dropsy		Luke 14:2–4
Dross		Prov. 25:4
Drought		Ps. 32:4; Isa. 58:11; Jer. 2:6, + 17:8
Drove		Gen. 33:8
"	out man	Gen. 3:24
Drown		1 Tim. 6:9
Druggist		Exod. 30:35
Drugs - sorceries		Rev. 18:23
Drunk		Jer. 51:57
"	, be not	Eph. 5:18
Drunkard		Prov. 26:9; Nah. 1:10
Drunken		Jer. 51:39; Lam. 3:15; Luke 21:34; 1 Thess. 5:7

Due		Prov. 3:27
"	time	Matt. 24:45; Rom. 5:6;
		1 Cor. 15:8; 1 Pet. 5:6
Dumb		Ps. 38:13, + 39:2, 9;
		Prov. 31:8, 9; Mark 9:17;
		2 Pet. 2:16
Dung		Phil. 3:8
Dungeon		Jer. 38:6–13; Lam. 3:55
Durst		Matt. 22:46; John 21:12;
		Jude 1:9
Dust		Gen. 2:7, + 3:19; Lev. 14:41;
		Job 34:15; Eccles. 3:20, +
		12:7; Dan. 12:2
Duties, godly women's		Titus 2:3–5
Duty	now	1 Thess. 4:11, 12
"	of man	Eccles. 12:13
"	" ours	Isa. 1:16, 17; 1 Tim. 4:11–16
"	, our - to know,	
	live godly &	
	worship Him	Col. 1:9–14
Dwell	anywhere - Lord	
	God leads	Ps. 139:8–10
"	, Christ - in us	Ps. 24:4; Eph. 3:17
"	, Father - in Jesus	John 14:10, 11
"	God in us	2 Cor. 6:16; 1 John 4:15, 16
"	in land - rewarded	Ps. 37:3; Isa. 6:5; Ezek. 36:28
"	in streets of	
	Jerusalem	Zech. 8:3, 4, 5
"	in unity	Ps. 133:1
"	Jesus in us & we	
	in Him	John 6:53–58
"	not in wickedness	Ps. 84:10
"	on earth of one	
	blood	Acts 17:26

"	on earth - all to worship, him	Rev. 13:8
"	righteousness forever	Ps. 37:27; 2 Pet. 3:13
Dwelleth		Acts 7:48
"	in love & in God	1 John 4:15, 16
"	" temples - God	Acts 7:48
"	the spirit	John 14:17
"	with (in) you	John 14:17; 1 Cor. 3:16, 17; Col. 2:9
Dwelling		Ps. 52:5 + 55:15
"	of Christ in hearts	Eph. 3:16–19
Dwelt	among us	John 1:14
"	Jesus	John 1:38, 39
Dying	of Lord Jesus to feel	2 Cor. 4:10

• E •

Eagle	Lev. 11:18; Job 9:26, + 39:27–30; Prov. 30:17, 19; Mic. 1:16; Matt. 24:28; Luke 17:37
" parable	Ezek 17:1–10
Ear	Ps. 78:1, + 86:1; Mark 4:9, 28, + 7:16; Rev. 2:7, 11, + 3:6
" - eye & heart of man	1 Cor. 2:9
Earing	Gen. 45:6
Early riser - Jesus	Mark 1:35
" , seek God (David)	Ps. 63:1
Earnest	2 Cor. 5:5; Eph. 1:14; Heb. 2:1
Earnestly, contend	Jude 1:3
" pray	1 Cor. 12:31; James 5:16–18
" protested	Jer. 11:7
Earring	Exod. 32:2, 3; Prov. 25:12
Ears - hear - word - turn	Isa. 30:21
" , itching	2 Tim. 4:3
" of corn	Gen. 41:5–7, 22–24
" open but hear not	Isa. 42:20
Earth	Jer. 22:29
" a place	Matt. 6:9, 10
" and heaven to God	Acts 7:48, 49
" " heavens forever	2 Pet. 3:7

"	by God	Gen. 1:31; Ps. 102:25
"	cleaned	Dan. 8:14
"	corrupt	Gen. 6:5–11; Col. 3:2
"	created	Gen. 1:1–10
"	dwellers	Luke 21:33–36
"	, first - passed away	Rev. 21:1
"	- footstool	Matt. 5:35; Acts 5:49
"	full of Lord's mercy	Ps. 119:64
"	given to man	Ps. 115:16
"	heated	Rev. 16:8, 9
"	inherited by the meek	Ps. 37:11
"	is corruption	Acts 13:33, 34
"	" Lord's	Ps. 24:1
"	" man's - heaven is Lord's	Ps. 115:15, 16; Matt. 5:34, 35
"	, new	2 Pet. 3:10, 12, 13; Rev. 21:1
"	owned by God	Gen. 1:31; Ps. 24:1; 1 Cor. 10:26
"	quieteth by Him	Job 37:17
"	round	Isa. 40:22
"	to be destroyed	2 Pet. 3:10; Rev. 11:18
"	violence	Gen. 6:5, 11
Earthly	is of the earth	John 3:31; 1 Cor. 15:47–49
"	ones destroyed	Isa. 24:1, 3, 5, 6; Rev. 11:18
"	soul & spirit	1 Cor. 15:44
"	things not in heaven	Rev. 7:16, 17, + 21:1, 4, 22–27, + 22:1–5
"	things not to seek	Luke 12:22–34
Earthquake		Matt. 28:2; Luke 21:11; Acts 16:26; Rev. 11:13, + 16:18
Ease		Ps. 25:13
Easier	to say	Matt. 9:5; Luke 16:17

Easily		Heb. 12:1
East wind		Job 27:21; Hos. 12:1
Easy		Matt. 11:30
Eat		Isa. 1:19; Matt. 15:32, 37, 38; Luke 24:43
"	and drink	Eccles. 5:18–20; Rom. 14:17, 20, 21
"	" " my flesh & blood	John 6:53–58
"	from working	2 Thess. 3:10, 11
"	nor drink with offence	Rom. 14:20
"	nothing dead of itself	Ezek. 44:31
"	of tree of life	Gen. 3:22
"	or drink	Matt. 6:25
"	per the righteous & the wicked	Prov. 13:25
"	together	1 Cor. 10:27, 28, 31, + 11:26, 33
"	with unbelievers	1 Cor. 10:27
Eaten		Rom. 14:6
Eden		Gen. 2:8, 10, 15
Edify body		Eph. 4:16
"	" of Christ	Eph. 4:12
"	one another	Rom. 14:19; 1 Thess. 5:11
Edifying		1 Cor. 14:26
Educated was Jesus		John 7:15, 16
Effect of cross is power of God		1 Cor. 1:17, 18
Effectual		Eph. 4:6; James 5:16
Effectually		1 Thess. 2:13
Effeminate		1 Cor. 6:9
Egg		Luke 11:12
Eggs		Isa. 59:5

Ego	Prov. 25:14; Matt. 23:12; Rom. 12:3; 1 Cor. 4:6, 19; Gal. 6:3
Elder - younger	1 Pet. 5:5
Elderly to be respected	1 Tim. 5:1–4
Elders of church	1 Tim. 5:17; James 5:14; 1 Pet. 5:1, 5
Elect	Matt. 24:31; Luke 18:7; Rom. 8:33; 1 Pet. 1:2
" people	Mark 13:20, 22, 27
" responsibilities	Col. 3:12–24
Election	Rom. 11:28
Elements of heaven and earth melt	2 Pet. 3:10
Elephant	Esther 8:10
Eli, Eli Lama Sabachthani	Matt. 27:46; Mark 15:34
Elias	Matt. 17:3, 10–12
Elizabeth	Luke 1:5–7, 13, 24
Else	Ps. 51:16; Isa. 45:14, 18; 1 Cor. 14:16, + 15:29; Phil. 1:27
Embalm	Gen. 50:2, 3, 26
Emboldeneth	Job 16:3
Embrace	Eccles. 3:5
Emerald	Rev. 4:3
Emmanuel	Matt. 1:23
Empty	Luke 1:53
" tomb	John 20:13
Emulation	Rom. 11:14
Encamp	Exod. 14:9; Ps. 27:3, + 34:7, + 52:5
Enchantment	Lev. 19:26
Encourage one another	Heb. 10:25
" the less fortunate	Isa. 61:1–3

Encouragement		Phil. 2:1, 2, 13–16; 1 Thess. 5:11
End		Dan. 2:44, + 12:4, 7–13; 1 Cor. 15:20–26; Phil. 3:18, 19; Heb. 6:11
"	are ways of death	Prov. 14:12
End come		Matt. 24:6, 14, 27, 35–39, 42
"	come - Jesus' instructions	Matt. 24:4–14
"	, expected	Jer. 29:11
"	of all things	1 Pet. 4:7
"	of world	Matt. 13:37–50 + 28:20; Heb. 9:26
"	things per Jesus	Matt. 24:3–13
"	times salvation offered & witness	Matt. 25:14; 1 Pet. 1:5
Endanger		Dan. 1:10
Endeavour		Isa. 55:11; Eph. 4:3
Ending and beginning		Rev. 1:8, 11, + 21:6, + 22:13
Ending good & new	beginning	Titus 2:13
Ends of the earth		Isa. 45:22
Endued		2 Chron. 2:13; Luke 24:49; James 3:13
Endure		Mark 4:17; James 5:11
"	all	1 Cor. 13:7; 2 Tim. 2:3
"	" for salvation	2 Tim. 2:10
"	any experience	Col. 1:10–14
"	temptation & reward	Heb. 6:15; James 1:12
"	to end, ones saved	Matt. 10:22, + 24:13; Mark 13:13
"	with Christ	2 Tim. 2:12, 13

Endured persecution	2 Tim. 3:11, 12
" the cross	Heb. 12:2, 3
Endureth	Ps. 30:5, + 100:5, + 145:13; James 1:12
" for ever	2 Chron. 20:21; Ps. 117:2, + 118:1–4, 29
" truth to all	Ps. 100:5
Enemies	Deut. 12:10; Ps. 8:2
" , love & pray for	Matt. 5:44; Luke 6:35
" of Christ's cross punished	Phil. 3:18, 19
" smitten	Deut. 28:1, 2, 7; Mic. 5:9
Enemy	Prov. 25:21, 22; Isa. 59:19; Acts 13:10; Rom. 12:20
" and friend	James 4:4
" is death	1 Cor. 15:25, 26
" , last	1 Cor. 15:26
Enflaming selves	Isa. 57:5
Engage	Jer. 30:21
Engines	2 Chron. 26:15
Engrafted	James 1:21
Engraving	(see graving)
Enjoin	Philem. 1:8; Heb. 9:20
Enjoy all things	1 Tim. 6:17
" good in soul	Eccles. 2:24
Enlarge	Ps. 4:1; Isa. 54:2, + 60:5; 2 Cor. 6:11, 13
Enlightened	Eph. 1:18; Heb. 6:4
Enmity	Gen. 3:15; Rom. 8:7; Eph. 2:15, 16; James 4:4
Enough	Prov. 30:15, 16
Enquire	Deut. 12:30; Isa. 21:12; Acts 9:11

Enriched by him	1 Cor. 1:5; 2 Cor. 9:11
Ensamples	1 Cor. 10:11; 1 Pet. 5:3; 2 Pet. 2:6
Ensign	Isa. 11:12
Ensnared	Job 34:30
Ensue	1 Pet. 3:11
Entangled	Gal. 5:1; 2 Tim. 2:4; 2 Pet. 2:20
Enter kingdom of God	John 3:3, 5–7; Heb. 10:19
Entered into heaven, Jesus	Heb. 9:24
" sin into world	Rom. 5:12
Entereth hope	Rom. 6:19
Entertain strangers	Heb. 13:2
Entice	Prov. 1:10; 1 Cor. 2:4; James 1:14
Entrance	1 Thess. 2:1
" to kingdom	2 Pet. 1:10, 11
Entreat	Ruth 1:16; Job 24:21; Jer. 15:11
Envious	Ps. 3:3
" , not - to those of iniquity	Ps. 37:1; Prov. 24:1
Envy	Eccles. 4:3; Isa. 11:13; Matt. 27:18; Acts 7:9; James 3:16, + 4:5
" not	1 Sam. 18:8–13; Ps. 49:16, 17; Prov. 3:31, 32, + 14:30 + 23:17 + 27:4; Gal. 5:26
" " at wicked	Prov. 23:17, + 73:3–5
Ephod	Lev. 8:7
Epistle	1 Cor. 5:9; 2 Cor. 3:1–3, 16; 2 Thess. 5:27
Equal	Isa. 46:5
" with God	John 5:18
Equality	2 Cor. 8:14
Equity void	Isa. 59:14
Ere	Num. 14:11; John 4:49

Err	Prov. 19:27; Jer. 23:30–32;
	Mark 12:24, 27; James 1:16, +
	5:19, 20
" without God	Matt. 22:29
Erred	Ps. 119:110; 2 Tim. 2:18
Erring one to correction	2 Thess. 3:14, 15
Error and errors	Ps. 19:12; 2 Pet. 2:18
" of wicked	James 5:20: 2 Pet. 3:17;
	Jude 1:11
Escape	1 Kings 18:40; Ps. 141:10;
	Heb. 12:25
" temptation	Luke 21:36; 1 Cor. 10:13
" wrath things	Luke 21:36
Escaped	Job 1:15–17; Ps. 124:7;
	Acts 27:44; 2 Pet. 2:20
Eschewed evil	Job 1:1, 8; 1 Pet. 3:11
Especially	Gal. 6:10
Espied	Gen. 42:27
Espousals	Jer. 2:2
Espoused	Matt. 1:18; 2 Cor. 11:2
Establish	Deut. 8:18; Job 36:7; Ps. 7:9;
	Isa. 62:7
Established	Gen. 9:17; 2 Sam. 7:16;
	1 Kings 2:12; Rom. 1:11
" , be	2 Chron. 20:20; Prov. 16:3;
	Heb. 13:9
" the heavens	Prov. 3:19
Estate	Rom. 12:16
Esteem	Prov. 17:28; Isa. 53:3, 4;
	Rom. 14:5; 1 Thess. 5:13
" others better than	
ourselves	Phil. 2:3, 4
Estimation	Lev. 27:3–19, 23, 25, 27
Eternal home	2 Cor. 5:1

"	inheritance	Heb. 9:15
"	is God	Ps. 90:2
"	king	1 Tim. 1:17
"	life by Jesus only	Matt. 19:26–29; Rom. 5:21
"	" for leaving all earthly things	Mark 10:29, 30
"	life for us	1 John 2:23–25, + 5:11, 13, 20
"	" in Christ Jesus	1 John 5:11
"	" is gift of God	Rom. 6:23
"	" known	1 John 5:13
"	" not in murderer	1 John 3:15
Eternal life or everlasting punishment		Matt. 25:46
"	life ordained - believed	Acts 13:47, 48
"	life through Jesus Christ	Rom. 6:23
"	life to get	Luke 10:25–27, + 18:29, 30; John 2:25, + 5:24; Gal. 6:7, 8; Titus 1:2
"	one is God	Exod. 3:14; John 8:58
"	or temporal	2 Cor. 4:18
"	redemption	Heb. 9:12
"	spirit	Heb. 9:14
"	torment	Rev. 14:8, + 17:2
Eunuch		Isa. 56:3; Dan. 1:3, 8–11; Matt. 19:12; Acts 8:34, 38, 39
Europe		Dan. 2:41–43, + 7:7
Evangelist		2 Tim. 4:5
Eve		Gen. 3:20, + 4:1
"	disobeyed God	Gen. 3:6; 2 Cor. 11:3
Even		Matt. 5:48, + 28:20; 1 Cor. 11:1; 2 Cor. 3:18, + 11:1; Col. 1:14; 1 Pet. 1:9; 1 John 5:20

"	eternal life	1 John 2:25
"	faith for victory	1 John 5:4
"	so	1 Pet. 4:10; Rev. 1:7
"	(evening)	Matt. 20:8; Mark 4:35
Events	foretold	Rev. 1:1, 2
Ever	and ever praise	Ps. 146:10; 1 Pet. 4:11
"	" " trust	Ps. 52:8, 9
"	salvation	Isa. 51:6; Heb. 6:20
"	with Lord	Isa. 51:6; 1 Thess. 4:17
Everlasting	covenant	Heb. 13:20
"	fire	Matt. 25:41
"	God	Isa. 9:6, + 40:28
"	gospel	Rev. 14:6, 7
"	joy	Isa. 51:11
"	kingdom	Ps. 145:13; Dan. 4:34; 2 Pet. 1:10, 11
"	life	John 3:15, 16, 36, + 5:24, + 6:40, 47, 48
"	" , inherit	Matt. 19:29
"	" is God's commandment	John 12:49, 50
"	love	Jer. 31:3
"	mercy	Ps. 100:5, + 103:17
"	name	Isa. 63:12
"	punishment or life eternal	Matt. 25:46
"	to everlasting	Ps. 103:17
"	way	Ps. 139:24
Evermore		Ps. 16:11, + 92:8, + 133:3
"	alive	Ps. 16:11; Rev. 1:18
"	rejoice	1 Thess. 5:16
Every	good work, abound in	2 Cor. 9:8; 1 Thess. 5:18

"	one judged	Matt. 12:36; Rom. 14:12; Rev. 20:13
"	thing a season	Eccles. 3:1
"	" beautiful	Eccles. 3:11
"	tongue confess	Isa. 45:23; Phil. 2:11
Everything is beautiful		Eccles. 3:11
"	" a season & a time	Eccles. 3:1
	is God's	Deut. 10:14; 1 Chron. 29:11, 12; Ps. 24:1
"	" Jesus	John 14:6
"	" the Lord	Rev. 1:8
"	made by God	Gen. 1:1; John 1:3
Everywhere, God is		Ps. 62:11, + 139:1–10; Acts 17:27; Rev. 19:16
Evidence		Heb. 11:1
Evident		Job 6:28; Phil. 1:28
Evidently		Acts 10:3; Gal. 3:1
Evil		Prov. 15:15; John 3:20; Rom. 12:21
"	and good	Matt. 12:34; Luke 16:19, 25; Rom. 7:18, 19
"	- curses	2 Chron. 34:24
"	details	Rom. 1:21–32
"	doers in darkness	John 3:19–21
"	" not for God's Kingdom	Ps. 37:9, + 97:16; 1 Pet. 2:12, 14, + 3:8, 9, 16
"	for evil	1 Pet. 3:8, 9
"	from tree food	Gen. 3:1–6
"	" within man	Matt. 15:19; Mark 7:18–23
"	immunity	Luke 21:36; John 17:15
"	in hearts	Matt. 9:4
"	- Jesus none	Mark 15:14

"	of world to be punished	Isa. 13:11
"	people becoming worse	2 Tim. 3:1, 13
"	people prefer darkness	John 3:19–21
"	, root of - can be love of money	1 Tim. 6:10
"	speak of you	1 Cor. 3:16
"	spirits	Mark 9:17–27; Luke 4:33–36; Heb. 1:14
"	to Good	Rom. 12:21
"	, what - Jesus	Mark 15:14
Ewe		2 Sam. 12:3
Exact		Isa. 58:3
Exalt		Ps. 46:10; Matt. 23:12; 1 Pet. 5:6
"	and abase	Ezek. 21:26
"	God	Ps. 46:10
"	self	Ps. 140:8; Matt. 23:12; 2 Thess. 2:3, 4
"	" - antichrist	Dan. 11:36, 27; 2 Thess. 2:4
"	" or humble self	Matt. 23:12; Luke 14:11; James 4:10
Exalted		1 Chron. 29:11; Ps. 46:10, + 57:5, 11, + 118:16; 2 Cor. 12:7
"	Jesus	Isa. 52:13; Acts 5:31; Phil. 2:9
Examine		2 Cor. 13:5
Example be		1 Tim. 4:12
"	- godly life	Phil. 1:9–11, + 4:8, 9
"	- Jesus	John 13:15, + 20:29–31; 1 Pet. 2:21–25
"	- us	John 13:14–17; 1 Pet. 2:21–25

Exceeding		Num. 14:7; Eph. 3:20; 2 Pet. 1:4
"	glad	Dan. 6:23; 2 Cor. 9:14
"	joy	Jude 1:24
"	sorrowful	Mark 14:34
Exceedingly		Gen. 17:2; Matt. 15:14
Excel		Ps. 103:20; Matt. 5:20; 1 Cor. 14:12
Excellency		Job 4:21; 1 Cor. 2:1
"	of God's voice	Job 37:4; 2 Cor. 4:7; Phil. 3:8
Excellent		Ps. 8:1; Prov. 17:27; 1 Cor. 12:31; Phil. 1:10
Excellest		Prov. 31:29
Excelleth		Eccles. 2:12
Except		Ps. 127:1; Matt. 18:3, + 24:22; John 3:2, 3, 5, + 6:65, + 15:4; 1 Cor. 15:36
"	shortened days - flesh	Matt. 24:22; Mark 13:20
Excess		Eph. 5:18
Exchange		Matt. 16:26
Excuse		Rom. 1:20
Excuses		Eccles. 7:29; John 3:7
Execute judgment		Deut. 10:18; John 5:22, 27
Executeth		Joel 2:11
Executioner		Mark 6:27
Exercise		Acts 24:16; 1 Tim. 4:7, 8
"	godliness	1 Tim. 4:7, 8; Heb. 12:11
Exhort		1 Thess. 5:14; Titus 2:9–15; Jude 1:3; 1 Pet. 5:1
"	and convince	1 Tim. 2:1; Titus 1:9; Heb. 3:13
"	servants	Titus 2:9

Exhortation to Christians	2 Cor. 9:5
Exhorted	1 Thess. 2:10
Exhorting one another	Heb. 3:13, + 10:25; 1 Pet. 5:12
Exists, God - and loves us	Ps. 19:1–11
Exorcists	Acts 19:13
Expectation	Ps. 62:5; Prov. 23:18 + 24:14; Acts 12:11
Expected as received Luke 12:48	
" end	Jer. 29:11
Expecting	Heb. 10:13
Expedient	John 16:7; 1 Cor. 6:12
Expel	Judg. 11:9
Experience	Rom. 5:3, 4
" doing good together	Rom. 8:28
Exploits	Dan. 11:28, 32
Expounded	Mark 4:34; Luke 24:27; Acts 11:4
Extended	Ps. 16:2
Extinct	Isa. 43:17
Extoll	Ps. 145:1; Isa. 52:13
Extremity	Job 35:15
Eye	1 Cor. 12:17
" , all seeing	Ps. 33:18; Prov. 15:3, + 30:17
" - all shall see him	Rev. 1:7
" - body	Matt. 6:22, 23
" - ear & heart of man	1 Cor. 2:9
" is light or evil	Matt. 6:22, 23
" of the Lord	Ps. 33:18
" salve	Rev. 3:18
" tooth - life - hand - foot	Exod. 21:23, 24; Deut. 19:21
Eyelids	Job 41:18; Prov. 4:25, + 6:4

Eyes and adultery	2 Pet. 2:14
" " eyelids look straight on	Prov. 4:25, + 6:4
" fastened	Luke 4:20
" of God (Lord) on righteous	2 Chron. 16:9; Job 36:7; 1 Pet. 3:12
" open	Ps. 119:18, + 146:8
" opened	Gen. 3:7
" to hills	Ps. 121:1, 2
" , seven	Rev. 5:6
" service	Eph. 6:6; Col. 3:22

• F •

Fables	2 Tim. 4:4; 2 Pet. 1:16
Face	Acts 6:15; 1 Cor. 13:12;
	2 Cor. 3:18
" of Earth	Acts 17:26
" " father	Matt. 18:10
" to face	1 Cor. 13:12; 3 John 1:14
Faced, two	Prov. 28:9
Faces, disfigure	Matt. 6:16–18
Fade	Isa. 64:6
Fadeth not	1 Pet. 1:4, + 5:4
Fail	Ps. 73:26, + 119:82; Luke 16:9
" Grace of God	Deut. 31:6
" thee not	Deut. 31:6; Lam. 3:22
Failure for rejecting	
knowledge	Hos. 4:6
" , our - accepted	
by God	Rom. 3:23–26
Fain	Job 27:22
Faint not	2 Cor. 4:16; Gal. 6:9;
	Heb. 12:5
Fair from north	Job 37:22
Fairer	Ps. 45:2
Faith	Mark 2:5, + 11:22–24;
	2 Cor. 5:7; Eph. 2:8, + 6:16;
	Heb. 11:1–33

"	according	Matt. 9:29; Rom. 12:6
"	alone	James 2:7
"	as a grain of mustard seed	Matt. 17:20
"	chapter	Heb. 11:1–40
"	- fall away as earthly growths	Heb. 6:4–8
"	for grace	Eph. 2:8, + 4:7
"	" healing	Matt. 9:29; Eph. 2:8
"	" righteousness	Rom. 4:9–16, 22
"	" salvation	2 Tim. 3:15; 1 Pet. 1:9
"	" victory	1 John 5:4
"	great	Matt. 8:10; Luke 7:9
"	healed	Luke 18:42, 43
"	hearing God's word	Rom. 10:17
"	- hope in god	1 Pet. 1:21
"	in God - not men	Mark 11:22; 1 Cor. 2:5
"	" power of God	1 Cor. 2:5
"	, justified by	Rom. 5:1, 2
"	made daughter whole	Matt. 9:22, 29
"	" thee whole	Mark 10:52; Luke 8:43–48
"	, Moses'	2 Cor. 11:23–28
"	- must believe	Heb. 11:6
"	must have works	James 2:1, 14, 17, 18, 20, 22, 24, 26, + 4:17
"	needed to be saved	Eph. 2:8
"	not in vain	1 Cor. 15:14
"	, not of	Rom. 14:23
"	nourishes the just	Hab. 2:4
"	- obeyed	Heb. 11:4–11, 17, 20–31
"	, only	Eph. 4:5, 13
"	or law	Gal. 3:13, 25–29, + 4:4, 5
"	" works	James 2:14, 17–22, 24, 26

"	, our - is Jesus	Eph. 4:13; Heb. 12:2
"	overcometh world	1 John 5:4
"	prayer save sick	James 5:15
Faith	promises a reality in	
	the future	Heb. 10:23, + 11:13
"	results not seen	
	before death	Heb. 11:13
"	reward	2 Tim. 4:7, 8
"	- sacrifice son	Gen. 22:1–13
"	saved sinner	Luke 7:50
"	saves	Eph. 2:8
"	to believers	Rom. 3:22
"	" faith	Rom. 1:17
"	" live	Hab. 2:4
"	trial precious	1 Pet. 1:7
"	- trying	James 1:1–4
"	- unity	Eph. 4:12, 13
"	without works is	
	dead	James 2:20
Faithful		Matt. 25:21; 1 Cor. 4:2;
		Heb. 3:2
"	or unjust	Luke 16:10–13
"	is God	1 Cor. 1:9, + 10:13; Heb. 10:23
"	minister	Col. 1:7
"	ones taken by God	Rev. 20:4–6
"	recognized	Deut. 28:1, 2, 10
"	steward	Luke 12:42
"	to death	Rev. 2:10
"	" forgive	1 John 1:9
"	" masters	Eph. 6:4–7
"	" witness	Prov. 14:5
Faithfulness		Ps. 36:5
Fall		Exod. 15:16; Prov. 28:10, 14, 18;
		Luke 6:39

"	away to renew	Heb. 6:4–6
"	from grace of God	Heb. 6:6 + 12; 12:15
"	not if	2 Pet. 1:5–7, 10, + 3:17
"	, papal	Dan. 7:23–26
"	, people	Prov. 11:14
"	without good	
	foundation	Prov. 24:16; Matt. 7:26, 27
Fallen		2 Kings 13:14; Job 1:16;
		1 Cor. 15:6, 18; Gal. 5:4
Falling away before		
	Christ's coming	2 Thess. 2:3; Jude 1:6
"	into place	Acts 27:41
False accusation		Luke 19:8
"	Christs shall arise	Matt. 24:24; Mark 13:5, 6, 21–23
"	ones	2 Cor. 11:15
"	prophets & Christs	Matt. 24:23–27; Mark 13:20, 21; Rev. 19:20, + 20:10
"	" " teachers	Matt. 24:24; Mark 13:21, 22; 2 Pet. 2:1
"	spirit	1 John 4:1–3
"	witness	Deut. 5:20
"	witnesses	Prov. 14:5; Matt. 26:59, 60, 65; Acts 6:11–14
Fame		Matt. 4:24 + 9:31; Luke 4:14
Familiar		Lev. 20:27
Families		Jer. 31:1
Family of earth & heaven		Eph. 3:14, 15
"	" Jesus	Matt. 12:46–50; Mark 3:31–35
"	, peaceful	Prov. 17:1
Famine		Gen. 41:27, 30, 31; Luke 4:25
"	of the world	Amos 8:11, 12
Famines foretold		Luke 21:11

" " but in divers (different) places	Matt. 24:7
Famish	Prov. 10:3; Zeph. 2:11
Fan	Matt. 3:12; Luke 3:17
Fared	Luke 16:19
Farewell	2 Cor. 13:11
Farmers helped by the Lord	Ps. 147:8
" to rejoice	John 4:35–37
Farming	Gen. 8:22
Farther	Matt. 26:39
Farthing	Matt. 5:26, + 10:29; Mark 12:42; Luke 12:6
Fashion as a man - Jesus	Phil. 2:7, 8
Fashioned	Ps. 119:73; Phil. 3:21; 1 Pet. 1:14
Fashioneth - formed	Isa. 44:12
" hearts	Ps. 33:15
Fast	Isa. 58:3–6; Mark 8:3; Acts 13:1, 2
" for God - not men	Matt. 6:16–18; Phil. 1:27
Fastened	Eccles. 12:11; Luke 4:20
Fasting	Mark 9:28, 29
Fat	Gen. 4:4; Ps. 119:70; Prov. 11:25; Isa. 58:11
Fatfleshed	Gen. 41:2, 18
Father	Matt. 23:9, + 26:39; John 15:9–12
" and Jesus are one	John 14:10, 11
" " mother to be honoured	Deut. 5:16
" and Son Jesus only know each other	Matt. 11:27

"	glorify - Jesus	John 12:28, + 15:23, 24, 26
"	God and of things	John 8:41–44; 2 Cor. 1:3
"	" is greatest	John 14:28, 3
"	greater than Jesus	John 14:22
"	, heavenly - can do all things	John 5:19–23
"	in Heaven	Matt. 7:21, + 16:17
"	is God	Matt. 23:9; John 14:9–12; 1 Pet. 1:2, 3
"	" " or devil	John 8:41–44
"	" Lord	Isa. 64:8
"	" one to all on earth	Matt. 23:9
"	is perfect	Matt. 5:48
"	of all	John 5:17–47; Rom. 4:16, 17; Eph. 4:6
"	" Jesus Christ	1 Pet. 1:3
"	one with Jesus	John 10:30
"	only one on earth & in heaven	Matt. 23:8, 9; Eph. 4:6
"	, our	Isa. 64:8; John 10:29, 30
"	, " - is none on earth	Matt. 23:9
"	, reveal the	Matt. 11:27
"	seeketh worshippers	John 4:23
"	to us	1 Cor. 6:17, 18
"	which is in heaven	Matt. 12:50
Fatherless		Deut. 24:17, 19–21; Job 31:21; Ps. 146:9
Fathers raising children		Eph. 6:4
Father's will is important		Matt. 7:21
Fatlings		Ps. 66:5
Fatness		Ps. 35:8 + 63:5

Fats overflow		Joel 3:13
Fatted calf		Luke 15:27, 30
Fault to be corrected		Matt. 18:15–18; Gal. 6:1
Faultless		Jude 1:24
Faults		1 Pet. 2:20
"	, confess & pray for	James 5:16
"	, recognize our own	Ps. 19:12; Luke 6:41, 42
"	, share	James 5:16
Favour from God		Ps. 30:5; Acts 2:17, + 7:10
"	is deceitful	Prov. 31:30
"	or condemn	Prov. 12:2
"	with people - church	Acts 2:47
Favourable		Ps. 77:7
Fear		Ps. 66:16, + 111:10; Matt. 10:28; 1 John 4:18; Rev. 14:6, 7
"	against trust	Prov. 29:25
"	and trembling	Phil. 2:12, 13
"	came to every soul	Luke 1:65; Acts 2:43
"	filled	Luke 5:26
"	God	Eccles. 8:12, 13; Luke 12:5; 2 Cor. 7:1; Rev. 14:6, 7
"	" - reverence	Heb. 12:28
"	has torment	1 John 4:18
"	Lord all the earth	Deut. 6:24; Ps. 96:9; Matt. 10:28
"	" - delivered me per David	Ps. 34:4
"	fear - want nothing	Ps. 34:9, 10
"	none in God's love	1 John 4:16–21
"	not	Ps. 46:1, 2; Isa. 41:10, 13, 14; Matt. 28:5; Luke 2:10, + 12:5, 32; Heb. 13:6; Rev. 1:17
"	" from God	Deut. 31:6; 2 Tim. 1:7

"	" of persecutions	Rev. 2:10
"	" people	Num. 14:9
"	" the Lord are rewards	Prov. 14:26, 27, + 22:4; Isa. 59:19
"	not the Lord is not wisdom	Job 28:12–15, 23, 28; Prov. 9:10
"	of the Lord	Job 28:28; Ps. 19:8, + 111:10; Prov. 1:7, + 14:26, 27; Isa. 8:12, 13
" " " " is clean		Ps. 19:9

Feared — Job 3:25

Fearers of Lord rewarded — Mal. 4:2

Feareth Him — Acts 10:35

Fearful thing into God's hands — Heb. 10:31

Feast — Gen. 26:30; Exod. 12:14; Prov. 15:15

"	continual	Prov. 15:15
"	of Passover	Matt. 26:2; John 13:1, 2
"	" the Tabernacle	Deut. 16:16, 17; Ezra. 3:4; Neh. 8:16–18

Feathers — Lev. 1:16; Job 39:13; Ps. 68:13; Ezek. 17:3

"	of Lord cover us	Ps. 91:4
Fed	by angel	1 Kings 19:2–8
"	" ravens	1 Kings 17:4–6
"	" trusting	Ps. 37:3
"	people	Hos. 11:1–4

Feeble — Prov. 30:26; 1 Cor. 12:22

Feed from neighbors - don't take away — Deut. 23:24

Feel dying of Jesus — 2 Cor. 4:10

Feelings of Jesus — Matt. 24:45

Feet		Ps. 122:2; Mark 9:45; John 13:5–14; Rom. 10:15
"	of Jesus	Luke 7:37, 38, 45, 46
"	shod	Eph. 6:15
Feignest		Neh. 6:8; Jer. 3:10; 2 Pet. 2:3
Fell		Matt. 26:39; Acts 10:10, 44
"	from grace	Jude 1:16
Felloes		1 Kings 7:33
Fellowhelpers		2 Cor. 8:23; 3 John 1:8
Fellowlaborers		Phil. 4:3
Fellowservant		Matt. 18:33; Col. 1:7
Fellowship in Gospel		Phil. 1:3–7
"	of Jesus Christ	1 Cor. 1:9; 1 John 1:3, 7
"	with devils	1 Cor. 10:20, 21
"	" God's mystery	Eph. 3:9
"	" one another	1 John 1:7
Fellowworkers		Luke 4:11
Female		Gen. 1:27
Fence		Zeph. 1:16
Fervent charity		1 Pet. 4:8
"	heat	2 Pet. 3:10, 12
"	prayer	Rom. 12:11; James 5:16
Fervently		1 Pet. 1:22
Fetch		Deut. 24:10, 19; Job 36:3; Acts 16:37 + 28:13
Fever		Mark 1:30, 31; Luke 4:38, 39; John 4:52; Acts 28:8
Fidelity		Titus 2:10
Field		Matt. 6:30
"	is world	Matt. 13:38–48
Fields white to harvest		John 4:35
Fierce		2 Chron. 30:8; Jer. 30:24; James 3:4

Fiery furnace - three	survived	Dan. 3:6, 11, 16–18
"	trial	1 Pet. 4:12
Fig	tree	Gen. 3:7; Num. 13:23; John 1:50
Fight		Deut. 3:22; Ps. 35:1; 1 Cor. 9:26; Phil. 14:13; 1 Tim. 6:12
"	the good fight	1 Tim. 6:12
Figure		Isa. 44:13; Heb. 9:9, 24
Fill	with glory & joy	Hag. 2:9; Rom. 15:13
"	" spirit	Eph. 5:18, 19
Filled		John 6:12, 13, 26; Phil. 1:11
"	with Holy Ghost	Luke 1:67; Acts 2:5
"	" the spirit	Acts 2:4; Eph. 5:18
Filthiness		2 Cor. 7:1; James 1:21
Filthy		Ps. 14:3
"	dreamers	Jude 1:8
"	lucre	1 Tim. 3:8; Titus 1:11; 1 Pet. 5:2
"	mouth	Col. 3:8
Final day near		Heb. 10:25
Finally		2 Cor. 13:11; Eph. 6:10; Phil. 3:1, + 4:8
Find by seeking		Jer. 29:13; Matt. 7:7; John 1:43
"	grace	Heb. 4:16
"	life	Matt. 10:39
"	me not - to Pharisees	John 7:32–34
"	out God's works	Eccles. 3:11
"	rest for souls	Matt. 11:28, 29
Finer		Prov. 25:4; Luke 11:20
Finger, putting forth of the		Isa. 58:9
Fingers		Ps. 8:3

Fining pot		Prov. 17:3
Finish		2 Cor. 8:6
Finished - Jesus		John 19:30
" - reward		2 Tim. 4:7, 8
Finisher		Heb. 12:2
Fir tree		2 Chron. 2:8; Ps. 104:17; Zech. 11:2
Fire		Jer. 17:27; Mark 9:45; Luke 22:55, 56; 1 Pet. 1:7
" everlasting		Matt. 25:41
Fire is a consuming fire		Heb. 13:28
" " " tongue		James 3:5, 6
" of my jealousy - Lord		Zech. 3:8
" , Satan's		Rev. 13:13
" to destroy world		Mal. 4:1; 2 Pet. 3:10
" " earth		Luke 12:49; Rev. 13:13, + 16:8
" " get the wicked		Isa. 47:14; Ezek. 28:18; Matt. 13:40–42; Jude 1:7; Rev. 20:10
" , unquenchable		Matt. 3:12
Firm		Heb. 3:6
Firmament		Gen. 1:1, 6–8, 14; Ps. 19:1, + 50:6; Ezek. 1:26; Matt. 16:19; Rev. 6:13; November 13, 1833, in the United States (quote from history books)
First a willing mind		2 Cor. 8:12
" and last		Isa. 44:6; Matt. 19:30; Rev. 1:8, 11, 17, + 21:6, + 22:13
" commandment		Matt. 22:37–40
" covenant		Heb. 8:7, + 9:1
" " not sufficient		Heb. 8:7

"	day of week	1 Cor. 16:2
"	of all	1 Tim. 2:1
"	the kingdom	Matt. 6:33
"	to rise	1 Thess. 4:16
Firstbegotten		Heb. 1:6; Ps. 110:1, 2; Rev. 1:5
Firstborn		Mic. 6:7; Rom. 8:29; Col. 1:15, 18
"	death (10th plague)	Exod. 11:1–19, + 12:29, 30
Firstfruits		Lev. 2:12, 14, + 23:10; Prov. 3:9; Rom. 3:9; 1 Cor. 15:20, + 16:15
"	of spirit	Rom. 8:23
Firstling		Gen. 4:4; Lev. 27:26
Fish		Eccles. 9:12; Luke 5:4—9; John 21:5–13
"	- good to eat	Lev. 11:9; Num. 11:5; John 21:5–13
Fishers of men		Matt. 4:19
Fist		Isa. 58:4
Fit		Luke 9:63
Fitches		Ezek. 4:9
Fitly		Prov. 25:11; Eph. 4:16
Flagons		Hos. 3:1
Flakes		Job 41:23
Flame		Exod. 3:2; Isa. 43:2
Flatter		Prov. 26:28
Flattereth with words		Prov. 2:16
Flatteries to obtain dictatorship		Dan. 11:21
Flattering words		1 Thess. 2:5
Flax		Isa. 19:9
Fled		Heb. 6:18

Flee		Zech. 14:5; 1 Cor. 6:18, + 10:14; 1 Tim. 6:11; 2 Tim. 2:22; James 4:7
Fleece		Job 31:20
Flesh	abiding is needful	Phil. 1:24
"	against spirit	Rom. 8:5–9; Gal. 5:19, + 6:8
"	, all - on earth	Gen. 9:17; Ps. 145:21
"	and spirit	John 3:5, 6; Heb. 12:9
"	cannot inherit kingdom of God	1 Cor. 15:50
"	confidence	Phil. 3:3, 4
"	death for us	1 Pet. 3:18
"	desires	Eph. 2:3
"	, different	1 Cor. 15:39
"	for gain	Gal. 5:13, + 6:12
Flesh	from word - Jesus	John 1:1, 2, 14, + 17:5, 6
"	, his - veil	Heb. 10:19, 20
"	in likeness came Jesus	John 1:6–14; Rom. 8:1–3; 2 Cor. 10:3, 4; 1 Tim. 3:16
"	is bread	John 6:51
"	, Jesus & our	Rom. 8:1–3
"	know Christ then forget Him	2 Cor. 5:16, 17
"	not justified	Gal. 2:16; Col. 2:23
"	" saved	Matt. 24:22; Mark 13:20
"	of Jesus	John 6:48–58
"	" my flesh	Gen. 2:23
"	, one	Mark 10:8; Eph. 5:31
"	or spirit	Matt 46:21; John 3:5, 6; Rom. 8:1-16, 26
"	, our own - liveth	2 Cor. 4:10, 11; Eph. 5:29–31
"	, own - hide not from	Isa. 58:7

"	profit nothing	John 6:53–57, 63; Rom. 13:14
"	reflects Jesus	2 Cor. 4:10, 11; Phil. 1:20
"	regarding heart	Ezek. 36:26
"	saved	Matt. 24:22; Mark 13:20
"	- spirit	Gen. 6:3; Ezek. 36:26; Matt. 26:41; John 3:5, 6; Rom. 8:1, 16, 26, 27; Gal. 5:16–25; 1 Pet. 3:18
"	, strange	Jude 1:7
"	with spirit is God	1 John 4:2
"	withereth	1 Pet. 1:24
"	, works of	2 Cor. 5:9
Fleshly lusts		Rom. 13:14; Gal. 5:16, 17, + 6:12; Eph. 2:3; 1 Pet. 2:11, 12; 1 John 2:16, 17
"	works	Gal. 5:9–21, 26
Fleshy tables of heart		2 Cor. 3:3
Flies (fourth plague)		Exod. 8:21–24, 29–31
Flight		Deut. 32:30; Matt. 24:20
Floats		1 Kings 5:9; 2 Chron. 2:16
Flock of God's		Luke 12:32; 1 Pet. 5:2–4
" " " pasture are men		Ezek. 34:31
Flood		Gen. 6:7, 11–22, + 7:4, 7, 10–12, 17–24, + 8:1–13
"	days	Matt. 24:37–39; Luke 17:26, 27
"	duration predicted	Gen. 7:4
"	predicted - 120 years in advance	Gen. 6:3, 13, 17
"	saved eight people	1 Pet. 3:20
Flourish		Ps. 92:7, 12–14; Prov. 11:28; Phil. 4:10
Flourisheth		Deut. 31:20; Ps. 90:6; Dan. 4:4
Flow		Isa. 60:5; Mic. 4:1; John 7:28

Flower of age	1 Cor. 7:36
Flowers	Song of Sol. 2:12; 1 Pet. 1:24
Floweth	Num. 14:8
Flowing	Jer. 11:5
Fluttereth	Deut. 32:11
Flux	Acts 28:8
Fly	Isa. 60:8
" to widerness	Rev. 12:14
Flying as birds	
(air flight predicted)	Isa. 31:5
Foal	Zech. 9:9
Focus on God	Jude 1:24, 25
Fodder	Job 6:5
Foes	Ps. 27:2; Acts 2:35
Folds one	John 10:16
Follow	Hos. 6:3; 1 Tim. 6:11, 12
" after righteous-	
ness - etc.	Rom. 14:17, 19; 1 Tim. 6:11
" and serve	John 12:26
" me - Jesus	Matt. 4:19, 20, + 9:9;
	John 1:43, + 8:12, + 21:19, 22;
	1 Pet. 2:21
" the good	Rom. 14:19; 1 Thess. 5:15;
	3 John 1:11
Follower of crowd not	
wise	1 Pet. 4:4, 14
Followers of beast	
deceived	Rev. 19:20
" of Christ	1 Cor. 11:1
Folly	Deut. 22:21; Prov. 13:16 +
	18:13; 2 Cor. 11:1; 2 Tim. 3:9
Food for man, beast &	
bird	Gen. 1:29, 30, + 9:2–4; Ps. 147:9
" for people	Gen. 6–21 + 9:2, 3

Fool		Prov. 3:35, + 17:21, 24, 28, + 26:1–12; Eccles. 5:3, 4; Luke 12:20, 21; 1 Cor. 15:36
"	has sport in mischief	Prov. 10:23
"	or wise	Prov. 24:7; Mark 10:8–10; Eph. 5:15
"	says	Ps. 14:1; Prov. 10:18
Foolish Galatians		Gal. 3:1
"	men	Ps. 73:22; Prov. 13:1–25; 1 Pet. 2:15
"	things	1 Cor. 1:27; 1 Tim. 6:9
Foolishly		Job 1:22; 2 Cor. 11:17, 21
Foolishment		1 Cor. 1:23, 25
"	folly	Prov. 24:9; Eccles. 9:14–18, + 10:12–14; 2 Cor. 11:1
"	of God	1 Cor. 1:25
Foolishness		1 Cor. 2:14
Fools die for want of wisdom		Prov. 10:21
Fool's hope more than hasty words		Prov. 29:20
"	mouth-destruction	Prov. 10:18, + 18:7
Fools or wise		Eccles. 9:17: + 10:12–15; 1 Cor. 4:10
Foot		Matt. 14:13, + 18:8; Mark 9:45; John 11:44; Rev. 10:2
"	- life - eye-tooth - hand	Exod. 21:23, 24
"	slippeth	Ps. 38:16 + 94:18
Footstool		Ps. 99:5; Matt. 5:35, + 22:44; Acts 2:35

"	is earth	Matt. 5:35; Acts 7:49
"	of Jesus Christ	Ps. 132:7; Heb. 10:12, 13
For	ever salvation	Isa. 51:6
"	or against	Luke 9:50; Rom. 8:31
"	us	Rom. 8:34
Forasmuch		Luke 1:1; Acts 17:29, + 24:10; 1 Pet. 1:18
Forbad		Matt. 3:14
Forbear		Prov. 24:11; Jer. 40:4; 1 Thess. 3:5
"	working	1 Cor. 9:8
Forbearance		Rom. 3:25
Forbearing		Prov. 25:15; Eph. 4:2; Col. 3:13
Forbid		Matt. 19:14; Luke 9:50; 1 Cor. 6:15; Gal. 2:17; 3 John 1:10
Forbidden		Acts 16:6
Forbidding		Acts 28:31
Force		John 6:15
Forces		Isa. 60:5
Forcible		Job 6:25
Forefathers		2 Tim. 1:3
Forefront		Lev. 8:7
Forehead mark		Rev. 13:11, 16, 17, + 14:9, + 20:4
"	not marked - those to reign	Rev. 20:4
Foreknow		Rom. 8:29
Foreknowledge		1 Pet. 1:2
Foreordained		1 Pet. 1:20
Forepart		Acts 27:41
Forerunner		Heb. 6:20
Foreskin		Gen. 17:10–14
Forest		Ps. 50:10; Isa. 10:34, + 44:14

Foretold	Mark 13:23; Acts 3:24
Forever for doing God's	
will	John 8:51
" things	2 Cor. 4:16, 17
Forewarn	Luke 12:5
Forewarned	1 Thess. 4:6
Forgat	Lam. 3:17
Forgave you	Col. 3:13
Forget thee	Ps. 137:5, 6
" " not	Isa. 49:15
Forgetteth	Prov. 2:17
Forgetting	Phil. 3:13
Forgive	Matt. 6:12, 14, 15, + 18:21, 22, 35; Mark 11:25, 26; Luke 6:37; Eph. 4:31, 32
" Christians	1 John 1:9
" for effective prayer	Mark 11:24–26
" judge - condemn	Luke 6:37
" many times	Matt. 18:21, 22; Luke 17:3, 4
" one another	Col. 3:13
" them - Jesus	Luke 23:34
" " - Stephen	
when stoned	Acts 7:59, 60
" sins	2 Chron. 7:14; Isa. 43:25; Jer. 31:33, 34; Mark 2:7, + 11:25, 26; 1 John 1:9
" " - God only	Mark 2:7; Luke 5:21
Forgiven ones blessed	Ps. 32:1
" or not	Matt. 12:31, 32; Mark 3:28, 29; Luke 6:37
Forgiveness of sins	Acts 5:31; Eph. 1:7; Col. 1:14
Forgiving	Col. 3:13
Forgotten	Luke 12:6; Heb. 12:5
" sins	Ps. 130:4; Jer. 31:34; Rom. 4:7

Form	Gen. 1:2; Isa. 52:14
" of God	Phil. 2:6, 7
" " godliness but	2 Tim. 3:4
Formed first - Adam &	
everything	Gen. 1:26, 27 + 2:7, 8, 19;
	Ps. 90:2, + 95:5; Isa. 45:18;
	1 Tim. 2:13
Former of all things	Jer. 10:16
" things gone	Isa. 42:9; 1 Pet. 1:14; Rev. 21:4
Fornication	1 Cor. 5:1, + 6:9, 10, 13–20, +
	7:2 + 9:1, + 10:8; 1 Thess. 4:3;
	Jude 1:7; Rev. 17:1, 2
" , avoid	1 Cor. 7:1, 2
" brings wrath of	
God	Rev. 14:8
Fornicator	1 Cor. 5:9–11, + 6:9; Eph. 5:5;
	Rev. 19:2
Forsake for Lord's sake	Matt. 19:29
" Lord - brings wrath	2 Chron. 34:25
" " - cast off	1 Chron. 28:9
Forsake not	Deut. 31:6; Ps. 38:21;
	Isa. 33:15, 16, + 14:17
" " wisdom	Prov. 4:5–7
" sins	Prov. 28:13
" them not	Ps. 112:4; Isa. 42:16; Mic. 7:8, 9
" wicked	Prov. 28:4
Forsaken	Jer. 8:29; Matt. 27:46
Forsaketh	Prov. 2:17
Forsook	2 Chron. 7:22; Isa. 58:2;
	2 Tim. 4:16
Forswear	Matt. 5:33
Forth	Mark 4:28; Luke 22:30;
	Phil. 3:13
Forthwith	Acts 9:18

Fortress	Ps. 46:7, + 91:2
Fortunate - less to be	
cared for	Deut. 24:19–22
Forward, look	2 Cor. 8:10; Phil. 3:13, 14
Found faithful	1 Cor. 4:2
" - if seek	1 Chron. 28:9
" Lord	Jer. 29:14
" with child	Matt. 1:18
" worthy	2 Pet. 3:14
Foundation	1 Cor. 3:10–14; Eph. 2:20;
	2 Tim. 2:19; Heb. 6:1
" of Jesus Christ	1 Cor. 3:11; Eph. 2:20
" " earth	Ps. 102:25, + 104:5; Heb. 1:10
" " Lord's house	Ezra 3:11
" " world	Eph. 1:4; Heb. 4:3; 1 Pet. 1:19
" per Jesus	Matt. 7:24–29
Founded the earth	Prov. 3:19
Founder	Jer. 10:14
Fountain	James 3:11
" of life	Ps. 36:9
" " water - life	Ps. 36:9; Rev. 21:6
Fourfooted	Acts 10:12, + 11:6
Foursquare	Exod. 22:16; Rev. 21:16
Fowls	Gen. 1:28, + 15:11; Ps. 50:11;
	Matt. 6:26
Fowl's life not as good as	
disciple's life	Luke 12:24
" not to be eaten	Lev. 11:13–20, 23
" to eat all flesh	Rev. 19:17, 18, 21
Foxes	Ps. 63:10; Lam. 5:18
Fragments	John 6:12
Frail	Ps. 39:4
Frameth	Ps. 50:19 + 94:20
Frankincense	Lev. 2:16; Num. 5:15

Fraud	James 5:4
Free	1 Pet. 2:15, 16
" by son Jesus	John 8:32–36
" " truth	John 8:32
Freed from sin	Rom. 6:7
Freely justified	Rom. 3:24; 1 Cor. 2:12
" , water of life	Rev. 21:6, + 22:17
Freewill	Lev. 22:21, 23
Fret	Ps. 37:1, 7
Fretting	Lev. 13:51
Friend	Ps. 41:9; Prov. 17:17, + 18:24; Luke 11:5–8; John 15:14
" loveth	Prov. 17:17
" or enemy	James 4:4
" " guide, trust not	Mic. 7:5
Friendly be	Prov. 18:24
Friends	John 15:13–15; 3 John 1:14
Friendship of world is enmity with God	James 4:4
Frightened	Luke 24:37
Fro	Job 1:7, + 2:2
Frogs (second plague)	Exod. 9:2–14
From the beginning	1 John 1:1
Frontlets	Deut. 6:8
Frost	Job 37:10
Froward	Job 5:13; Prov. 2:15, + 17:20, + 21:8; 1 Pet. 2:18
" mouth	Prov. 2:12, + 4:24
Froward tongue	Prov. 10:30
Frowardness	Prov. 2:14
Fruit	Matt. 7:16–20, + 21:34; Luke 3:8; John 15:2–5, 8, 16; Heb. 13:15; James 5:7
" is truth of gospel	Col. 1:5–8

145

"	of body	Mic. 6:7
"	" labor	Prov. 31:31; Phil. 1:22
"	" lips	Heb. 13:15
"	" the earth	Mark 4:28
"	" " spirit	Gal. 5:22, 23
"	" " vine	Matt. 26:29; 2 Tim. 2:6
Fruitful	be	Gen. 1:28; Col. 1:10
Fruits - Father glorified		Matt. 7:16; John 15:8
"	for repentance	Matt. 3:8
"	of baptized believers	Acts 2:41
"	of good & evil men	Matt. 12:35
"	" labour	Eccles. 5:18
Fruits of neighbor to be eaten - not taken away		Deut. 23:24
"	of righteousness	2 Cor. 9:10
"	of spirit	Gal. 5:22, 23, + 6:1, 8
"	, their	Matt. 7:16
Frustrate		Gal. 2:21
Frying pan		Lev. 7:9
Fugitive		Gen. 4:14
Fulfil		Matt. 5:17; Gal. 5:16; Rev. 17:17
"	law of Christ	Gal. 6:2
Fulfilled all things		Luke 24:44; Acts 13:27, 29
"	Scripture	Matt. 4:14, + 27:9, 35; Mark 5:15, + 15:28; John 13:18, 31, + 19:28; Acts 13:33; Rev. 17:17
Fullfilling		Rom. 13:10; Eph. 2:3
Full		Mark 4:28; John 1:4
"	, joy be	John 15:11; Rom. 15:14
Fully		Num. 14:24; Acts 2:1

Fullness of Christ	Eph. 4:13
" " earth & all therein	Ps. 24:1
" of God	Eph. 3:19; Col. 1:19 + 2:9
" " His (Jesus) grace	John 1:16
" " joy	Ps. 16:11
" " times	Eph. 1:10
Furious	Dan. 2:12
Furlongs	John 6:19, + 11:18
Furnace	Prov. 17:3
" , fiery	Dan. 3:6, 11, 16–18
Furnish	Isa. 65:11
Furnished	Mark 14:15; 2 Tim. 3:17
Furrows	Job 31:38; Ps. 129:3
Furtherance	Phil. 1:3, 12, 25
Furthermore	Heb. 12:9
Fury	Isa. 59:18; Dan. 3:19
Future for God's lovers	1 Cor. 2:9

• G •

Gabriel	Dan. 9:21, + 10:13; Luke 1:11–20, 26–38
Gain and lose	Mark 8:36
" for Lord	1 Cor. 9:21
" " self	Isa. 56:11; Phil. 3:7; 1 Tim. 6:6
" world	Luke 9:25
Gains	Acts 16:19
Gainsaying	Acts 10:29; Rom. 10:21; Jude 1:11
Gall	Lam. 3:5, 19; Job 16:13
Gallant	Isa. 33:21
Galley	Isa. 33:21
Gallows	Esther 7:9, 10
Gambling	Prov. 28:20; Matt. 12:35
Gap	Ezek. 22:30
Garden	Gen. 2:8–10, 15, 16; Isa. 58:11
Garlands	Acts 14:13
Garlick	Num. 11:5
Garment	Matt. 9:20; Luke 5:36
Garments	Job 37:17; Isa. 61:10; John 19:23
Garnished	Job 26:13; Luke 11:27
Gat him up	Exod. 24:18; Num. 14:40

Gate		Gen. 28:17, + 34:20, 24; Ps. 118:19, 20; Ezek. 44:1–4, 17
"	, iron	Acts 12:10
"	, straight & narrow or wide	Matt. 7:13, 14; Luke 13:24
Gates		Ps. 24:7, 9, + 100:4; Rev. 21:12, 13
"	of hell	Matt. 16:18
Gather		Deut. 24:21; Matt. 3:12; John 6:12, 13
"	riches	Deut. 24:21; Ps. 39:6
"	the elect	Matt. 24: 31
"	thee	Isa. 43:5
"	together	Zeph. 2:1; Matt. 22:41; Eph. 1:10; 2 Thess. 2:1
"	with Jesus	Matt. 12:30
"	" two or three	Matt. 18:19, 20
Gathered		2 Cor. 8:15
"	together	Isa. 44:11; Matt. 18:20, + 22:41
Gathering together		2 Thess. 2:1; 2 Cor. 8:15
Gatherings, no - when I come (Jesus)		1 Cor. 16:2
Gave		John 1:12, + 19:30; Gal. 2:20
"	selves	2 Cor. 8:5
Gay, not to be		Lev. 20:10–21; Rom. 6:12, 13
Gaze		Exod. 19:21
Gazing		Acts 1:11
Gems, twelve		Rev. 21:19, 20
Genealogy of Jesus		Matt. 1:1–17; Luke 3:23–38
Generation		Dan. 4:34; Matt. 12:34; Mark 8:38, + 13:30
"	types	Prov. 30:11–14; Eccles. 1:4; Rev. 2:9

Generations	Isa. 58:12; Matt. 24:34; Mark 13:30; Luke 21:32
" up to Jesus	Matt. 1:1–17
Generosity rewarded	2 Cor. 9:9–14
Generous	Prov. 28:27, + 29:7
Gentiles	2 Tim. 1:11
Gentle	1 Thess. 2:7; 1 Pet. 2:18
" be servant of Lord	2 Tim. 2:24
Geometry	1 Cor. 3:9, 10
Get	Matt. 4:10: + 16:23
Getting treasures	Prov. 4:7, + 21:6
Ghost	Gen. 25:8, 17; Mark 15:37, 39; John 19:30
" , holy	Matt. 1:18, 20, + 3:11; Mark 1:8; John 14:26; Acts 5:32; 1 John 5:7
" , " - from heaven	1 Pet. 1:12
" , " - gifts	Heb. 2:4
" , " - power	Luke 1:35
Ghost's, holy - witness	Heb. 10:15
Gier eagle	Lev. 11:18
Gift, best	John 3:16; 2 Cor. 9:15
" , free	Rom. 5:15, 16
" , " - is salvation	Rom. 10:13, + 5:1, 18
" greater than altar	Matt. 23:18, 19
" is precious	Prov. 17:8
" of God	Eccles. 5:18–20; Rom. 6:23
" " " is being saved	Eph. 2:8–10
" of God not purchased with money	Acts 8:20
" of God not works	Eph. 2:8–10
" " Holy Spirit	Acts 2:38
" " spirit	Rom. 12:6–8; 1 Cor. 12:1, 8–11; Eph. 3:8, 9, 16–19, + 4:11; Rev. 5:12

"	or wage	Rom. 2:7, + 6:23
"	, perfect - from above	James 1:17
"	received - minister same	1 Pet. 4:10, 11
"	, spiritual	Rom. 1:11
"	, unspeakable	2 Cor. 9:15
Gifts differ per grace		Rom. 12:6
"	, spirit	1 Cor. 12:8–10, 28–31
Gin		Isa. 8:14
Gird (girded)		Ps. 93:1; Ezek. 16:10; John 21:18; 1 Pet. 1:13; Rev. 1:13
Girdedst		John 21:18
Girl sold		Joel 3:3
Girt		John 21:7; Eph. 6:14
Give		Prov. 3:9, 10; Eccles. 11:1; Mal. 3:8–10; 2 Cor. 9:6–10; 1 Tim. 6:17–19
"	according	2 Cor. 9:7
"	and receive	Mark 6:38, + 11:25, + 12:41–44; Luke 6:38; John 14:14, + 16:24
"	as is able	Deut. 16:16, 17
"	" received	Luke 12:48; 1 John 3:16
"	by God	Isa. 43:4; John 14:27
"	cheerfully	2 Cor. 9:7–12
"	his life a ransom	Matt. 20:28
"	knowledge	Luke 1:77, 79
"	more blessed than to receive	Acts 20:35
"	needful things	James 2:14–17
"	not my glory & praise - Lord	Isa. 42:8
"	ourselves to prayer & to ministry	Acts 6:4

"	to church	Mal. 3:10
"	" poor & needy	Prov. 19:17, + 28:27, + 29:7; Eph. 4:28
"	unto the Lord	Ps. 29:1, + 96:7, 8
"	when asked	Matt. 5:40–42
"	you	Ezek. 36:26
"	your best	Luke 6:38
Given		Matt. 13:11
"	by God	Matt. 7:7; Luke 11:13, + 12:32; Rom. 8:32; 2 Tim. 1:7
Given us the victory		1 Cor. 15:57
"	various talents	Mark 6:2; 1 Cor. 12:7–11
Giver, cheerful		2 Cor. 9:7
Giving thanks		Eph. 5:20
Glad in the Lord		Ps. 104:33, 34, + 118:24; Joel 2:23; 1 Pet. 4:13
" " " works		Ps. 92:4, 5
" is my heart		Ps. 16:9, + 122:1
Gladness		Deut. 28:47; Acts 14:17
Glass		1 Cor. 13:12; 2 Cor. 3:18
" , looking		Job 37:18
" , sea of		Rev. 15:2
Glean		Deut. 24:21; Ruth 2:2, 3, 7, 8, 15–19
Glittering		Job 20:25
Gloominess		Zeph. 1:15
Glorieth, he that - glory		Jer. 9:24
Glorified God & Son		John 13:31, 32, + 14:13, + 15:8, + 17:4
Glorified in you		1 Thess. 1:10, 12; 1 Pet. 2:12, + 4:14
Glorifieth		Ps. 50:23

Glorify God		Num. 14:21; 1 Chron. 28:11–13; Ps. 50:15; John 12:28, + 17:1, 4, 5, 10, 22, 24; Acts 15:6; 1 Cor. 6:20, + 10:31; 2 Cor. 4:15–18; Rev. 14:6, 7
"	" by being Christian	1 Pet. 4:13, 14
"	God by good works	Matt. 5:16
"	" in all things	1 Pet. 4:11
"	Jesus Christ	Phil. 1:1, 2, 10, 11
"	thou me - Christ Jesus	John 17:1, 5
"	thy name - Jesus	John 12:28
Glorious appearing		Titus 2:13
"	arm - Moses	Isa. 63:12
"	body	Phil. 3:20, 21
"	gospel	2 Cor. 4:4; 1 Tim. 1:1
"	liberty	Rom. 8:21
"	name	1 Chron. 29:13; Neh. 9:5
"	things	Ps. 87:3; Luke 13:17
Glory		2 Cor. 12:1, 5, 6; 1 Thess. 2:19, 20
"	and dominion to God	Ps. 145:11–13; 1 Pet. 4:11, + 5:11
"	and grace	Ps. 84:11
"	" peace	Hag. 2:9
"	" praise to keep - Lord	Isa. 42:8
"	- appearing of Jesus Christ	1 Pet. 1:7–9
"	- Christ & God	Acts 7:55; Phil. 2:11; Col. 1:27
"	crown	1 Pet. 5:4
"	due the Lord	Ps. 29:1–11

"	hope	Col. 1:27
"	in cross of Jesus Christ only	Gal. 6:14
"	in earthly or Lord's knowledge	Jer. 9:23, 24
"	in Him per one's riches	Eph. 3:16–19; Phil. 4:19
"	in many things	1 Cor. 15:40–43
"	" the church	Eph. 3:21
"	" " Lord	1 Cor. 1:31; 2 Cor. 3:18
"	" tribulations	Rom. 5:3
"	king	Ps. 24:7–10
"	not in men	1 Cor. 3:21
"	of children	Prov. 17:6
"	" Christ revealed	John 17:24; Col. 1:27; 1 Pet. 4:13
Glory	of God declared by heavens	Ps. 19:1; Acts 7:55
"	of God revealed in us	Rom. 8:18
"	of God seen by believers	John 11:31–45
"	of the Lord	Isa. 58:8
"	partaker	1 Pet. 5:1
"	revealed	Isa. 40:5
"	in us	Rom. 8:18
"	son of man	Matt. 25:31
"	to glory (image)	2 Cor. 3:18
"	" God	Ps. 96:8; Isa. 42:8; Luke 2:14; John 7:18; Rom. 11:36; Rev. 1:5, 6
"	" God's righteousness on earth	Jer. 9:24

"	to Jesus from God	2 Pet. 1:16, 17
"	" one on throne	Rev. 4:11, + 5:13
"	" self	Jer. 9:23; John 7:18
"	, vain	Gal. 5:26
Glorying		2 Cor. 2:11
Glutton		Deut. 21:20
Gluttonous		Luke 7:34
Gnash		Ps. 112:10; Lam. 2:16
Gnashed		Ps. 35:16; Acts 7:54
Gnashing		Matt. 8:12, + 13:42, 50, + 22:13, + 24:51, + 25:30; Luke 13:28
Gnaw		Rev. 16:10
Go		Isa. 6:9; Mark 14:13, + 16:15; Luke 7:50; Acts 28:26
"	, all - to dust	Eccles. 3:20
"	aside not	Deut. 28:1, 2, 14
"	- Jesus to the twelve apostles	Matt. 28:19, 20; Mark 16:15
"	sin no more	John 8:11
Goads		Eccles. 12:11
Goat		Prov. 30:31
God	always	Ps. 90:2
"	and love	1 John 4:7–12, 15–21
"	angry with sin	Rom. 1:8–32
"	, another	Ps. 16:4
"	Beyond our understanding	Isa. 40:28
"	, born of	1 John 5:4, 5
"	changes not	Mal. 3:6; Heb. 13:8
"	compared to men	1 Cor. 1:25
"	- creator	Gen. 1:1–31; Amos 4:13; Rev. 4:11

"	deceiver	Matt. 7:15, + 24:4, 5, 24; Mark 13:5, 6; 2 Thess. 2:3, 4; 2 John 1:7
"	dwelleth in heaven	Acts 7:48, 49
"	everywhere	Ps. 139:7, 8
"	exists & loves us	Ps. 19:1–11
"	gave us His son	John 3:16; Rom. 8:32
"	, great	Titus 2:13, 14
"	- greater than all on earth	Isa. 40:15, 17, 22
"	- greatest	2 Chron. 14:11
"	has son - Jesus	John 3:16; Col. 1:27
"	hates seven things	Prov. 6:16–20
"	- holy	Ps. 14:9; 1 Pet. 1:16
"	- " & reverend is His name	Ps. 111:9
"	in all	Eph. 4:4–6
"	inspired scriptures	2 Tim. 3:16, 17
"	is eternal	Ps. 90:2
"	" everlasting	Ps. 90:2; 1 Tim. 3:16
God	is faithful	Deut. 31:8, + 32:4
"	" God of the living	Matt. 22:32; 1 Tim. 3:16
"	" help - refuge & strength	Ps. 46:1
"	is His word - the Bible	Jer. 1:1–3
"	is I Am	Exod. 3:14
"	" invisible	John 1:18; Heb. 11:1–40
"	" jealous God	Exod. 24:1; Deut. 4:24
"	" Jesus - God's son	Heb. 11:1–3
"	" light	1 John 1:5–7
"	" living	Dan. 6:26; Heb. 9:14
"	" Lord	Deut. 7:9; Jer. 16:9

"	" love	1 John 4:8
"	" omnipotent	1 Chron. 29:12; Ps. 62:11
"	" omnipresent	Ps. 139:7–10; Acts 17:27
"	" omniscient	Job 42:2; 1 Tim. 3:16; Heb. 4:13
"	" one	Deut. 4:35; Mark 12:29; Gal. 3:20; 1 Tim. 2:5, 6
"	" " only before & after	Isa. 42:5, + 43:10, 11
"	is only one	Exod. 4:6; Deut. 4:35; Isa. 43:10, + 44:6–8, + 45:18–22, + 46:9; Dan. 4:35; John 8:28, 29; 1 Cor. 8:4, 6; James 2:19
"	" our conscience & instincts	Gen. 1:1
"	is principality head	Col. 2:10
"	" saviour	Isa. 45:22; Titus 3:4
"	" true God	Isa. 44:6, + 45:18, 22; 1 John 5:20
"	" unity	Deut. 4:35; Mark 12:29
"	" us	1 John 4:16
"	knew it all	Rom. 8:29, 30
"	knowing all things	1 Chron. 28:9; Job 42:2; Acts 15:18; Heb. 4:13; 1 John 3:20
"	- life giver	Gen. 2:7, 21, 23; Ps. 100:3; Rev. 4:11
"	- love	1 John 4:7–12, 15–21
"	, love	Mark 12:30–33
"	lovers reward	Rom. 8:28
"	made man upright	Eccles. 7:29
"	" known	Ps. 19:1–11
"	, my	Ps. 63:1

"	near	Acts 17:27
"	not seen except for Jesus	John 1:18
"	of all grace	Ezek. 36:28; Mark 12:26, 27; 1 Pet. 5:10
"	" hope	Rom. 15:13
"	" the living	Matt. 22:32
"	" world	2 Cor. 4:4
"	one & mediator	Isa. 44:6, 8; Gal. 3:20; Eph. 4:6; 1 Tim. 2:5
"	or devil	Rev. 13:8
"	pretender	2 Thess. 2:3, 4
"	reigneth	Isa. 52:7
"	revealed himself through creation	Ps. 19:1; Isa. 46:9, 10
"	speed	2 John 1:10, 11
"	tempteth not man	James 1:13
"	through Christ	2 Cor. 5:18, 19; Eph. 4:6, 7
"	to be served	Luke 4:8
"	was in Christ	2 Cor. 5:19
"	" word	John 1:1
"	wearies not	Isa. 40:28
"	with one	Isa. 41:10
"	" us	Matt. 1:23
Godhead		Rom. 1:20; Acts 17:29; Col. 2:9
Godliness and bodily	exercise	1 Tim. 4:8, + 6:6
"	for divine nature	2 Pet. 1:3, 4
"	is happiness	Ps. 1:1–3
"	mystery	1 Tim. 3:16
Godly and ungodly		Ps. 1:1–6
"	be	2 Cor. 6:1–10
"	life to be rewarded	1 Thess. 5:23
"	one persecuted	Rev. 12:17, + 13:14–18

"	or wickedness	1 John 5:19
"	reminded of God & man	Jude 1:1–25
"	reward	Ps. 92:2
"	say not "I am sick"	Isa. 33:24
God's	anger not for ever	Mic. 7:18
"	enemy is friend of world	James 4:4
"	gift	John 3:16; Eph. 2:8
"	glory revealed in us	Rom. 8:18
"	grace	Ps. 65:1–13
"	- images	Exod. 34:12–17; Deut. 4:28; Ps. 16:4; Isa. 42:17
"	- " destroy	Exod. 24:13, 14
"	, there are no	Jer. 16:20
"	kingdom	Luke 17:21; John 3:3
"	law & sacrifice	1 John 3:16
"	" known	Job 22:21–23; Isa. 59:19
"	love - four dimensions:	
	high	Ps. 103:11
	far	Ps. 103:12
	deep	Ps. 103:13
	everlasting	Ps. 103:17
"	name not in vain	Deut. 5:11
Gods	, not to serve other	Josh. 24:16
God's	people to have rest	Heb. 4:9
"	power to be denied	2 Tim. 3:1–5, 10, 11
"	promise	Matt. 28:20; 2 Tim. 3:7
"	service	Matt. 25:34–40
"	son	John 3:16; 1 John 5:5; Rev. 21:7
"	sons	1 John 3:1–3
Gods	- to have none	Deut. 5:7–9, + 28:14; Ps. 96:4, 5; Jer. 16:20
"	vs Lord	Ps. 96:5

"	will	1 Thess. 5:18
"	word	Isa. 40:8; Prov. 30:5; 1 Thess. 2:13
"	" pierces deeply	Heb. 4:12
"	work	John 6:29
"	, worldly	Judg. 2:12–19; Ps. 96:4, 5; 2 Cor. 4:4

God's worshippers punished — Deut. 8:19; Ps. 16:4; Jer. 11:9–14
" worshippers get sorrow — Ps. 16:4
Godward — 2 Cor. 3:4
Goest — Josh. 1:9
Goeth word — Isa. 55:11
Going — Mark 6:31
Goings of man — Prov. 20:24
Gold — 2 Chron. 2:14, + 3:6–10; Job 28:6; Rev. 20:18

" and silver worthless at last days — Ezek. 7:19; Zeph. 1:18
Golden rule — Matt. 7:12; Luke 6:31
Golgotha — Mark 15:22
Goliath — 2 Sam. 17:4–11, 45–51
Gomorrah — Gen. 10:19, + 13:10, + 14:8, 10, 11, + 19:24–26; Isa. 1:9, + 13:19; Zeph. 2:9

Good and bad works judged — Eccles. 12:13, 14
" and evil — Matt. 12:34, 35; Luke 6:33, 38, 45, + 16:19–25; Rom. 7:18, 19

" and loving God — Acts 14:15–17
" cheer - comfort — Matt. 14:27; John 16:33; 2 Cor. 13:11

Good deeds repaid — Eph. 6:8

"	, do - to all	Gal. 6:10
"	doers	Mark 14:8; John 5:29; Eph. 6:7, 8
"	doers are of God	3 John 1:11
"	for evil	Rom. 12:21
"	" godly ones	Rom. 8:28; 2 Cor. 9:8
"	" loving God	Rom. 8:28, 31
"	" men	Ps. 145:9, 14, 15
"	from every experience	Rom. 8:28
"	, highest - in life	Eccles. 12:13, 14
"	hope	Col. 1:23
"	in all things foretold	Rev. 21:4
"	life	John 10:10
"	, Lord is	Ps. 34:8, + 100:5
"	, only one is	Matt. 19:16, 17; Mark 10:18; Luke 18:19
"	rewarded	Luke 16:25; Eph. 6:7, 8; Jude 1:22
"	tidings of good	Isa. 52:7
"	to all	Ps. 145:9
"	" evil	Gen. 3:2–5; Matt. 12:43–45
"	" own soul	Prov. 11:17
"	" those who love God	Rom. 8:28; Gal. 6:10
"	" torment - evil to comfort	Luke 16:25
"	verses evil	Matt. 12:34, 35; Mark 12:2
"	work judgest	Eccles. 12:13, 14
"	works	Matt. 5:18; 2 Cor. 9:8; 1 Thess. 5:18; 2 Tim. 3:17
"	" by widows	1 Tim. 5:9, 10
Goodly		Matt. 13:45

"	person	Deut. 39:6
Goodman		Matt. 24:43
Goodness for us if		
	goodness to God	Rom. 11:22
"	of God	Ps. 33:5, + 52:1, + 65:9–13; Rom. 15:14
"	to saints	Ps. 16:2, 3
Gospel		Rom. 1:9 + 11:28; 1 Cor. 15:1–8; Phil. 1:3–7; 1 Pet. 4:6
"	, another	2 Cor. 11:4
"	bearers slain	Rev. 6:9–11
"	- believe & repent	Mark 1:15
"	by angel	Rev. 14:6
Gospel by word of Lord		1 Thess. 1:5, 6; 1 Pet. 1:25
Gospel - Christ suffered		
	& died for our sins	Isa. 53:1–12; John 18:28–40, + 19:1–42; Rom. 5:1–10; 1 Cor. 15:1–4
"	confidence	Phil. 1:5, 6
"	demonstration	1 Cor. 2:1–5
"	everlasting	Rev. 14:6
"	facts	Ps. 31:19; Isa. 64:4; 1 Cor. 2:1–10; 1 Thess. 1:5
"	for all	John 1:16
"	from heaven	1 Pet. 1:12
"	from Jesus	Matt. 28:18, 20; 2 Tim. 1:10, 11
"	, glorious	1 Tim. 1:11
Gospel highest - in life		Eccles. 12:13, 14
"	hope	Col. 1:23
"	is	1 Thess. 4:14; 1 Pet. 1:25
"	most important	Mark 16:15, 16; 1 Thess. 1:7–12
"	mystery	Eph. 6:19
"	of Christ - not man	Rom. 1:16; 2 Cor. 4:4; Gal. 1:10–12

"	" Jesus appearing	2 Tim. 1:10
"	, one	Gal. 1:8
"	, other	Gal. 1:6–9
"	powerful	Mark 1:1–28; Rom. 1:16
"	, preach	Isa. 61:1–3; Matt. 24:14, + 26:13; Mark 13:10, + 14:9, + 24:45–48; 1 Cor. 1:17, 18, + 9:14–17
"	preached at end	Matt. 24:14; Rev. 14:6, 7
"	- prepare ourselves	Phil. 1:9–11
"	saves	John 18:28, + 29:1–42
"	truth important to know	Col. 1:5–8; 2 Thess. 2:21–25
"	writers - Matthew, Mark, Luke & John in NT	(these books thus named in NT)
Gossip		Prov. 6:16, 17, 19, + 20:19, + 26:21–25
Gourd		Jonah 4:6, 7, 10
Government		Isa. 9:6, 7
Governments represented	by animals	Dan. 7:15–21; Rev. 17:9–14
Governor		Gen. 45:26; 1 Pet. 2:13, 14
Grace		1 Cor. 1:3; 2 Cor. 9:8, + 12:9; Titus 2:11
"	abound	2 Cor. 9:8
"	and glory	Ps. 84:11
"	" mercy when need	Acts 4:33; Heb. 4:14–16
"	and truth by Jesus Christ	John 1:17
"	as earned	Eph. 4:7
"	brings salvation	Titus 2:11
"	brought at revelation of Jesus Christ	1 Pet. 1:13

"	by angel	Rev. 14:16
"	came by Jesus Christ	John 1:16; Rom. 5:1, 2
"	for apostles	Acts 4:33
"	" inheritance & redemption	Acts 20:32; Rom. 3:24
"	of God	Ps. 65:1–13; Luke 2:40; 1 Cor. 15:10; 2 Cor. 8:1
"	" " for all	Titus 2:11
"	" " tasted death	Heb. 2:9–11, + 10:12–14
"	" " teaches us	Titus 2:11–14
"	" Jesus Christ	John 1:15, 16; 2 Cor. 8:9; 2 Tim. 2:1
"	" Lord Jesus	Acts 15:11; Phil. 4:23
"	per our faith	Rom. 5:1, 2; Eph. 2:7, 8, + 4:7
"	saves	Eph. 2:8; 2 Tim. 1:9
"	settle you	1 Pet. 5:10
"	sufficient	2 Cor. 3:24
"	through faith saves	Eph. 2:7, 8
"	to the lowly (humble)	Prov. 3:34; 1 Pet. 5:5
"	to you	1 Pet. 1:2, + 5:12; 2 Pet. 1:2
"	vs resisteth	1 Pet. 5:5
Gracious		Prov. 11:14; Mal. 3:8–10; 1 Pet. 2:3
Graff		Rom. 11:23, 24
Graffed		Rom. 11:23, 24
Grain		Matt. 17:20; Mark 4:31; 1 Cor. 15:37
Grant		Ps. 20:4; Mark 20:37; Eph. 3:16; Rev. 3:21
Grapegatherers		Jer. 49:9; Obad. 1:5
Grapes		Num. 13:20, 23, 24
Grass		Isa. 40:6–8; Zech. 10:1; Matt. 6:30; 1 Pet. 1:24

Grasshopper	Eccles. 12:5
Grave	Job 5:26; Eccles. 9:10;
	Hos. 13:14; 1 Cor. 15:55
" , be	1 Tim. 3:11
" dwellers to hear &	
come forth	John 5:28, 29
Graveclothes	John 11:44
Graved	Rom. 11:23, 24
Graven images	Exod. 20:3–5; Lev. 26:1;
	Deut. 27:15; Isa. 42:8;
	Jer. 50:38
" thee upon hands	Isa. 49:16
Graving	2 Chron. 2:14
Gravity	1 Tim. 3:4; Titus 2:7
Gray hairs	Hos. 7:9
Grayheaded	Job 15:10
Grease	Ps. 119:70
Great	Gen. 1:16; Num. 14:18;
	Deut. 29:3; Matt. 5:2, 19, 35;
	Luke 1:15, 32
" and mighty	Jer. 33:3
" commandment	Matt. 22:36, 38
" day	Jude 1:6
" from least	Matt. 5:19; Luke 9:48
" God	Ps. 95:3; Isa. 12:6; Titus 2:13
" in Kingdom of	
heaven	Matt. 5:17–19
" John foretold	Luke 1:15, 32
" King	Ps. 47:2
" Lord	Ps. 95:3
" peace	Ps. 119:1, 165
" power - Lord	Ps. 147:5; Acts 4:33
" tribulation	Matt. 24:21
" works	Rev. 15:3

Greater love	John 15:13
" than I	John 14:28; 1 John 3:20
" works by believers	John 14:12
Greatest human being on earth	Matt. 11:11
" one on earth	Luke 7:28
" -servant	Matt. 23:11; Luke 22:26
Greatly rejoice	Isa. 61:10
Greatness of God	Exod. 15:16; 1 Chron. 29:11; Joel 2:1
" " kingdom	Dan. 7:27
Greece	Dan. 2:39, + 7:6
Greed	Isa. 56:11; Luke 12:13–21
Greedy not good	Prov. 1:19, + 15:27; Luke 12:15–21; Jude 1:11
Green	Ps. 52:8; Song of Sol. 2:13
Greet	1 Cor. 16:20; 2 Cor. 13:12; 1 Thess. 5:26; 3 John 1:14
Grew	2 Sam. 12:3
Greyhound	Prov. 30:31
Grief	Ps. 31:9, 10; Prov. 17:25; Isa. 53:3; 1 Pet. 2:19
" follows wisdom	Eccles. 1:18
Griefs , borne our	Isa. 53:4
Grieve	Gen. 6:6; 1 Sam. 15:11; Eph. 4:30; Heb. 3:10
Grieved	2 Cor. 2:4; Heb. 3:10
Grievous	Prov. 15:1; Phil. 3:1; Rev. 16:2
Grind	Lam. 5:13
Groan	Matt. 11:33, 38; Rom. 8:22, 23
Groaning	Judg. 2:18; Ps. 6:6, + 38:9; Rom. 8:26
Grope	Job 12:25; Isa. 59:10

Ground	Gen. 2:7, 9, 19, + 4:23; Mark 4:5, 8; Luke 8:15
" , holy	Exod. 3:5; Josh 5:15
Grounded in love	Eph. 3:17; Col. 1:23
Groves	1 Kings 18:19
Grow	Gen. 2:9; Num. 6:5; Matt. 6:28; Luke 12:27; Eph. 4:15
" in grace	2 Pet. 3:18
" up	Eph. 4:14–16
Growth of earth's plants	Mark 4:26–32; 1 Cor. 3:6, 7
Grudge	Lev. 19:18; Col. 3:13; Heb. 12:15; James 5:9; 1 Pet. 3:8, 9
" not	Lev. 19:18; James 5:9; 1 Pet. 4:9
Grudgingly	2 Cor. 9:7
Guard	Gen. 41:12; 1 Chron. 11:25
Guardian angels	Ps. 91:11
Guest	Rev. 19:9
Guide	Ps. 25:9 + 52:9; John 16:13; Acts 1:16
" by spirit	John 16:13; Rom. 8:9
" into all truth	John 16:13
" me	Ps. 73:24
" or friend trust not	Mic. 7:5
" thee	Ps. 32:8; Prov. 3:5, 6; Isa. 58:11
Guile	Ps. 32:2, + 34:13; John 1:47; 2 Cor. 12:16
" not in Jesus' mouth	1 Pet. 2:22
Guilty	Matt. 23:18, + 26:66; Rom. 3:19, 20; 1 Cor. 11:27; James 2:10
Gushed	1 Kings 18:28

• H •

Ha	Job 39:25
Habergeons	Job 41:26; 2 Chron. 26:14
Habitation	Ps. 104:12
" , my	Ps. 91:9
" of angels	Jude 1:6
" " God	Eph. 2:22
" " Lord protects us	Ps. 91:9–11
Had	Gen. 1:31, + 2:2, 3, + 7:9; Ruth 2:17–19; Matt. 10:1, + 19:1, 22
Hail	Exod. 9:22–26; Hag. 2:17; Mark 15:18; John 19:3
" (seventh plague)	Exod. 7:13–25; Rev. 16:21
Hailstones	Josh. 10:11; Isa. 30:29, 30; Rev. 16:19, 21
Hair	Ezek. 44:20; Luke 21:17, 18; 1 Cor. 11:14, 15; 1 Tim. 2:9
" colored	Matt. 5:36
" long-shame or glory	1 Cor. 11:14, 15
" , shave	Lev. 14:9
Hairs, gray	Hos. 7:9
" numbered	Matt. 10:30
Haling	Acts 8:3

Hallow sabbath is good
    sign   Ezek. 20:20
  "   you per Lord   Lev. 22:32
Hallowed   Exod. 20:11; Lev. 22:32;
                     Num. 3:13; 2 Chron. 7:7;
                     Luke 11:2

Halt into life   Mark 9:45
Hammer   1 Kings 6:7; Isa. 41:7
Hammers   Isa. 44:12; Jer. 10:4
Hand   2 Chron. 3:17; Isa. 30:21, +
                     41:13; Acts 7:25, 35, 55, 56

  "   , at - are pleasures
    of joy   Ps. 16:11
  "   , hold - to help   Ps. 139:10; Isa. 41:13
  "   - life - eye - tooth -
    foot   Exod. 21:23, 24
  "   , Lord at   Phil. 4:5
  "   made   Job 26:13; Isa. 66:1, 2;
                     Acts 7:48, 50
  "   of God   1 Chron. 29:12, 16; Ps. 8:6, +
                     95:4, 5, 7; 1 Pet. 5:6
  "   of Lord leads   Ps. 139:5–13; Matt. 14:31
  "   , right and left   Dan. 12:7
  "   , " or left -
    unknown   Jonah 4:11
Handicapped all right with
    God   Matt. 18:8, 9
  "   , help   Deut. 24:19–22; 1 Thess. 5:14
  "   , invite - to feast Luke 14:12–27
Handiwork of God   Ps. 19:1
Handle   me - Jesus Luke 24:37–39
Handled   1 John 1:1
Handleth   Prov. 16:20

Handmaid		Ruth 3:7; Prov. 30:23
Handmaidens		Acts 2:13
Hands		Ps. 8:6; Dan. 2:34; Matt. 15:20, + 26:50; Luke 4:40
"	work - do with might	Eccles. 9:10
Handsbreath		Ps. 39:5
Handwriting		Col. 2:14
Hang		Matt. 22:40
"	on a tree	Acts 10:39; Gal. 3:13
Haply		Luke 14:29; Acts 17:27; 2 Cor. 9:4
Happened		Phil. 1:12; 2 Pet. 2:22
Happeneth		Eccles. 2:14, 15
Happenings to pagans		Rev. 20:15
Happiness of believers		Isa. 55:8–13
Happy		Ps. 144:15, + 146:5; John 13:17
"	for trusting in the Lord	Prov. 16:20
"	in the Lord	Ps. 69:30, + 98:4–6, + 104:33, 34
"	is the one in the Lord	Ps. 144:15; Prov. 16:20, + 28:14
Hard, nothing too		Jer. 32:17
Harden not your heart		Ps. 95:8; Prov. 28:14; Heb. 3:8
Hardness		2 Tim. 2:3
"	of heart	Matt. 19:8; Mark 3:5, + 10:5
Harken		Jer. 29:12
Harkened - Harkeneth		Gen. 4:17; Prov. 1:33
Harlot		Matt. 21:31; 1 Cor. 6:15, 16; Heb. 11:31
Harm - give answers to		1 Pet. 3:13–16

"	not	Hab. 1:8, + 3:8, 15; Acts 16:28; 1 Pet. 3:12, 13
"	one - Lord suffers	Matt. 25:40
Harmless		Phil. 2:15
Harmony		Rom. 15:1–7
"	in groups	1 Cor. 1:10
"	of all beings predicted to come	Isa. 11:6–9
"	of believers	Acts 2:42–47, + 4:32
"	with all	1 Thess. 5:12–28; 1 Pet. 3:8, 9
Harp		Gen. 4:21; 1 Sam. 16:23; 2 Chron. 5:12; Ps. 147:7
Harrows		2 Sam. 12:31
Harvest		Gen. 8:22; Matt. 13:30, 38–41; Luke 10:2; John 4:35–37
"	and reapers	Matt. 13:38, 39
"	is ripe	Joel 3:13; John 4:35
Harvestman		Isa. 17:5
Hast		Gen. 3:11, 13, 14, 17; Matt. 6:6, + 8:13; John 11:41, 42, + 20:15
Haste		Ps. 38:22, + 40:13, + 70:1, 5; Luke 19:5, 6
Hasten		Ps. 16:4
Hastily		Prov. 20:21
Hasting		2 Pet. 3:12
Hasty or diligent		Prov. 21:5, + 29:20
Hate		Ps. 5:5, + 118:7 + 139:21, 22; Prov. 25:17; John 15:18; 1 John 3:13
"	by Lord	Prov. 6:16–19
"	not	Luke 14:26; 1 John 3:15, + 4:20
"	seven things, Lord	Prov. 6:16–19
"	you by world	John 15:18, 19

Hated, be	Mark 13:13
" us for Lord's sake	Luke 21:17; John 24, 25
Hates not own flesh	Eph. 5:20
Hateth	John 15:19, 23; 1 John 3:15
Hath	Gen. 1:20, + 3:1, 3; 1 Cor. 14:26; 2 Cor. 8:12; Gal. 3:13, 22; Heb. 13:5
" father & the son	2 John 1:9
" - hath not	2 Cor. 8:12; 1 John 1:10
" made us	Rev. 1:6
Hatred or love	Mark 10:12
Haughtiness	Isa. 13:11
Haughty	Isa. 10:33; Zeph. 3:11
" spirit	Ps. 131:1; Prov. 16:18, + 18:12
Have	Rom. 11:30–32; 1 Tim. 2:3, 4; Heb. 13:5; James 4:2
" advocate	1 John 2:1
" faith in God	Mark 11:22
Have life	John 20:31
" not because ask not	James 4:2, 3
" sinned, all	1 Kings 8:46; Rom. 5:12, 13; 1 John 1:8, 10
Havock	Acts 8:3
Hawk	Job 39:26
He	Mark 1:8–45; John 4:26
" in you greater than he in the world	1 John 4:4
" is true	John 8:26
Head	Rom. 12:20
" is Christ	1 Cor. 11:3; Eph. 4:15
" of all	1 Chron. 29:11; 1 Cor. 11:3; Col. 2:9, 10
" " church	Eph. 1:22, 23, + 5:23, 27; Col. 1:18

"	" John the Baptist	Matt. 14:8, 11
"	" principality	Col. 2:10
"	is wife	Eph. 5:23
Headlong		Acts 1:18
Heady		2 Tim. 3:4
Heal		2 Chron. 7:14; Jer. 3:22, + 30:17; Luke 5:17, + 6:7
Heal per Jesus		Luke 4:18, + 10:9
"	power present	Luke 5:17
"	thyself	Luke 4:23
Healed - also see Miracles Section MM		
"	by confess and prayer	James 5:16
"	by his stripes	1 Pet. 2:24
"	" Lord - David	Ps. 30:2
"	many	Matt. 4:24, + 14:14, 30; Mark 1:30–34, + 3:10, 11; Luke 6:19, + 9:6
"	by Paul	Acts 28:8, 9
"	various handicaps	Matt. 15:31
Healer - Jesus		Mark 1:32–34
Healing		Mal. 4:2; Matt. 4:23, 24; James 5:13, 16
"	- first one by Jesus	Mark 1:23–28
"	- must be converted	Matt. 13:15
Health		Prov. 12:18 + 16:24; Isa. 58:8; Jer. 30:17, + 33:6; Acts 27:34
"	wish	3 John 1:2
Heapeth		Ps. 39:6
Hear		Deut. 6:4, 5; Mark 4:9, 12, 18, 23, 24; James 1:19
"	and keep	Matt. 15:10; Luke 11:28
"	better than speak	Eccles. 5:1–7
"	, dead shall	John 5:25

"	from heaven	2 Chron. 7:14
"	God's voice	Job 37:2–6; Ps. 66:16; John 8:47
"	not	Matt. 13:13; Isa. 59:1, 2
"	peoples voice	2 Chron. 7:14
"	words for knowledge & understanding	Prov. 2:1–6, + 4:1, 10, 20, + 5:1; Rom. 10:17
Heard		Matt. 8:10; Mark 4:16; John 11:41; 1 John 1:5
"	voice	2 Cor. 6:2; Rev. 1:10, + 14:13
Hearer		James 1:22, 23
Heareth not having ears		Isa. 42:20
"	the word	Matt. 13:19, 20, 22, 23
Hearing brings faith		Mark 6:2; Rom. 10:17
Hearken		Deut. 28:1, 2, 13; Judg. 3:17, + 11:28; Jer. 29:12; Mark 4:3, + 7:14
"	not - punished seven times	Lev. 26:14–39
Heart, apply - to wisdom		Ps. 90:12
"	, believe in	Rom. 10:9
"	- ear & eye of man	1 Cor. 2:9
"	faileth but	Ps. 73:26
"	good or evil	Matt. 12:35
"	hardened	Ezek. 14:4, 5; Mark 3:5
"	" not to be	Heb. 3:8
"	is as thinketh	Prov. 23:7; Ezek. 14:4, 5
"	, look at inside	1 Sam. 16:7
"	, man of the	1 Pet. 3:4
"	, merry - doeth good	Ps. 28:7; Prov. 15:13–15, + 17:22
"	, new-and spirit	Ezek. 36:26

"	not to be troubled	John 14:27
"	perfect with Lord	1 Kings 15:11, 14;
		2 Chron. 15:17, + 16:9
"	rejoice	John 16:22
"	searched by God	1 Chron. 28:9
"	so mouth speaketh	Matt. 12:34
"	, sound	Prov. 14:30
"	, take	John 14:27
"	, thankful - will	
	please God	Heb. 12:28
"	to be perfect	1 Chron. 28:9; 1 John 3:20
"	,troubled	John 14:1
"	where treasure is	Matt. 6:19–21; Luke 12:34
"	, whole	Ps. 9:1
"	with two	Eccles. 4:11
Heartily do all things		Col. 3:23
Hearts hardened		Mark 10:13, 14
"	to be ruled with	
	peace	Col. 3:15
Hearty council		Prov. 27:9
Heat to destroy earth		2 Pet. 3:10
" " " the ungodly		Rev. 16:8, 9
Heathen		Zech. 9:10; Ps. 115:2, 3;
		Gal. 1:16, + 2:9
Heathen's fate		Ps. 2:8, 9
"	vain repetitions	Matt. 6:7
Heaven		Gen. 1:1, 7
"	a place	Matt. 6:9, 10, + 8:11, + 19:14;
		Luke 15:7, + 23:42, 43;
		2 Cor. 5:1
"	and earth to God	Acts 7:48:49
"	at hand	Matt. 10:7
"	- enter righteous	Matt. 5:20; 2 Tim. 4:18
"	entry requirements	Matt. 7:21, + 18:3

"	, first - passed away	2 Cor. 3:10, 12, 13; Rev. 21:1
"	has no earthly things	Rev. 7:16, 17, + 21:1, 4, 22–27, + 22:1–5
"	is Lord's - earth is man's Ps.	115:15, 16; Matt. 5:34, 35
"	, new	Rev. 21:1–27
"	, those from - above all	John 3:31
"	voice from	Rev. 14:13
Heavenly above flesh & blood		Eph. 1:16
"	place for believers	John 14:1–4; Eph. 1:3
Heavens and earth long lived		2 Pet. 3:7
"	and earth new	2 Pet. 3:13
"	are the Lord's	Ps. 115:16
"	by God	Gen. 1:1, 7, 8, 14–18; Ps. 102:25
"	declared glory	Ps. 19:1; Acts 7:55
"	opened	Matt. 3:16
Heavens to be dissolved		2 Pet. 3:12
Heaven's kingdom		Matt. 10:7, + 13:43–45, + 18:10, + 19:14
"	kingdom to enter	Matt. 18:3
Heaviness		Prov. 14:13
Heavy		Ps. 38:4; Matt. 11:28
Hedge		Lam. 3:7; Eccles. 10:8; Rom. 1:10
Hedges		Mic. 7:4; Luke 14:23
Heed		Deut. 4:15, 23; Josh. 22:5, + 23:11; Ps. 39:1; Prov. 1:8; Matt. 24:4–14; Luke 8:18; + 12:15; Acts 3:5

"	, take - for deceivers	Matt. 24:4–14; Mark 13:5, 9, 23, 33, + 21:34
"	to self	1 Cor. 3:10; 1 Tim. 4:16
"	words of Jesus	Luke 21:33–36
Heel		Ps. 41:9
Heifer		Deut. 21:3, 4, 6; Hos. 10:11
Height		Rom. 8:39
Heir and son of God		Gal. 4:7
"	of all things	Heb. 1:2
"	" the world through faith	Rom. 4:12–16
Heirs		Rom. 8:17; 1 Pet. 3:7
"	of salvation	Heb. 1:13, 14
"	with Christ	Gal. 3:26–29; Titus 3:7
Hell and destruction		Prov. 27:20
"	- any can be candidates	2 Pet. 2:4
"	depths	Prov. 9:18
"	fire	Deut. 32:22
"	for wicked	Ps. 9:17
"	not necessary	Acts 2:27, 29, 31
Helm		James 3:4
Helmet of salvation		Isa. 59:17; Eph. 6:17
Help		Gen. 2:18, 20; Mark 9:22, 24; Heb. 4:16
"	and courage	Deut. 31:6
"	from Lord	Ps. 121:1, 2; Isa. 41:10, 13, 14
"	handicapped & unfortunate	Deut. 24:19–22; 1 Thess. 5:14
"	is God	Ps. 46:1, 2, + 121:1, 2; Rom. 8:28; Heb. 4:16
Helped by Lord		Ps. 28:7
Helper is God		Ps. 54:4; Heb. 13:6

177

Hem	Matt. 9:20
Hen	Matt. 23:37
Hence	John 14:31 + 17:20; Acts 1:5; James 4:1
Henceforth	Ps. 125:2; Isa. 9:7; John 14:7; Eph. 4:14; Heb. 10:13
Henceforward	Matt. 21:19
Her	Prov. 4:6, 8, 13
Herb	Exod. 9:22, 25; Ps. 37:2; Rom. 14:2
Herbs	Exod. 12:8; Prov. 15:17; Heb. 6:7
Here am I	Exod. 3:4; Isa. 6:8, + 58:9
Hereafter	Isa. 41:23; Matt. 26:64; John 1:51, + 13:7
Hereby	1 John 2:3, + 3:16, + 4:13
Herein	2 Cor. 8:10; 1 John 4:10
Hereon	Lev. 11:19
Heresies	1 Cor. 11:19; 2 Pet. 2:1
Heresy	Acts 24:14
Heretick	Titus 3:10
Hereunto	1 Pet. 2:21
Heritage	Isa. 54:17, + 58:14; 1 Pet. 5:3; Jer. 12:8, 9
Herods (three)	**1)** Matt. 2:1, 3, 7, 13, 15, 16, 19, 22; **2)** Matt. 14:1, 3, 6; Mark 6:14, 16–18, 20–22; Luke 3:1, 19, + 9:7, 9, + 13:31, + 23:7, 8, 11, 12, 15; Acts 4:27; **3)** Acts 12:1, 6, 11, 19–21
Hewn	Isa. 10:33; Lam. 3:9; Matt. 3:10; Mark 15:46
Hid	Gen. 3:8, 10; Exod. 2:2; Job 3:23; Matt. 5:14; Col. 2:3, + 3:3

" - gospel	2 Cor. 4:3
" , nothing is	Luke 8:17; 1 Tim. 5:25
" word in heart	Ps. 119:11
Hidden	Ps. 51:6; 1 Pet. 3:4; Rev. 2:17
" things	Isa. 48:6
Hide face from my sins	Ps. 51:9
" me	Ps 27:5 + 143:9
" not eyes	Prov. 28:27; Ezek. 39:29
" " from own flesh	Isa. 58:7
" nothing	Mark 4:21, 22
" sins	Prov. 28:12, 13
Hide thyself	Isa. 26:20
High and low things	Rom. 12:16
" calling prize	Phil. 3:14
" look	Prov. 21:4
High over all	Ps. 83:18
" priest	Heb. 3:1, + 4:15
Higher	Heb. 7:26
Highest's son	Luke 1:32, + 2:14
Highly	1 Thess. 5:13
Highminded	Rom. 11:20; 1 Tim. 6:17; 2 Tim. 3:4
Highway	Isa. 11:16, + 19:23, + 35:8, + 49:1; Matt. 22:9, 10; Luke 14:23
Hill	Deut. 11:11; Mic. 4:1; Matt. 5:14; Luke 1:65
Him	Mark 1:5–45 (30 times); John 14:17; Rom. 11:36; Col. 1:16, 17, 19, 20
Himself	Prov. 11:25, + 25:14; Isa. 45:18; Jer. 10:23; Eph. 2:20
Hinder	Neh. 4:8
Hindered by Satan	1 Thess. 2:18
Hind's feet	Ps. 18:33

Hire	Deut. 24:14, 15; James 5:4
Hired	Hos. 8:9
Hireling	Job 7:1, 2; John 10:12, 13
His - Jesus Christ	Rom. 8:9
Hiss	Jer. 25:9; Zeph. 2:15; Zech. 10:8
History repeat	Luke 17:26–30
Hither	2 Chron. 28:13; Matt. 17:17; Acts 19:37
Hitherto	Job 38:11; John 5:17 + 16:24
Hoar hairs	Isa. 46:4
Hoard	Luke 12:16–21
Hoisted	Acts 27:40
Hold	Ps. 39:12, + 139:10; Heb. 3:6, + 4:14
" faithful word	Titus 1:9
Holden	Ps. 73:23; Isa. 42:14
Holding word of life	Phil. 2:16
Holiest	Heb. 10:19
Holily	1 Thess. 2:10
Holiness	Zech. 14:20, 21; 2 Cor. 7:1; Eph. 4:24; 1 Thess. 3:13, + 4:7
" required to see the Lord	Heb. 12:14
" to Lord	Rev. 2:17
Holpen	Luke 1:54
Holy	Rev. 3:7, + 4:8
" are we to be	Eph. 1:4; 1 Pet. 1:15, 16
" , be	Lev. 11:44, 45, + 19:1, 2, + 20:26; 1 Pet. 1:15, 16; 2 Pet. 3:11
" , " - in body & in spirit	1 Cor. 7:34; 1 Pet. 1:16, 17; 2 Pet. 3:11
" , church to be - per Jesus	Eph. 5:27

"	city	Matt. 27:53; Rev. 21:2, 10, + 22:19
"	conversation	1 Pet. 1:15, 16
"	day	Neh. 8:9–11; Isa. 58:13, 14; Mark 2:28
"	Ghost	Matt. 1:18, 20, + 12:31, 32; Mark 1:8, + 3:29; Luke 1:35, + 2:26, + 3:32, + 4:1; Rom. 5:5; 1 Pet. 1:2
"	" enabled old time prophesy	2 Pet. 1:21
"	Ghost enables witnesses	Acts 1:8, + 5:32
"	Ghost fell on hearers of word	Acts 10:44
"	Ghost from heaven	1 Pet. 1:12
"	" given after Jesus to be glorified	John 7:39
"	Ghost to obeyers	Acts 5:32, + 7:55, + 10:44
"	" in God	Acts 7:55; Rom. 5:5, + 14:17
"	" " power	Luke 1:35; Rom. 15:13
"	" is comforter	John 14:26
"	Ghost shed love of God	Rom. 5:5
"	Ghost witness	Acts 5:32, + 20:23; Heb. 10:15–17
"	God	Josh. 24:19
"	ground	Exod. 3:5; Josh. 5:15
"	is God	1 Pet. 1:15, 16
"	living is essential	Rom. 12:1; Gal. 5:19–21; 1 Pet. 1:15, 16
"	one of God	Mark 1:24; Acts 2:27
"	prophets	Acts 3:21
"	Spirit	Luke 10:21

" unto the Lord	Lev. 27:30, 32
Holyday	Ps. 42:4; Col. 2:16
Home in heaven	2 Cor. 5:1
" of Christians	Rom. 8:28
Homeborn	Exod. 12:49
Homers - quails	Num. 11:32
Homosexuality	Lev. 18:22; Rom. 1:26, 27, +
	6:19–21; 1 Cor. 6:9–11
Honest heart	Luke 8:15
" in conversations	1 Pet. 2:12
" " dealings	Prov. 12:22; Rom. 12:17
Honestly, walk	Rom. 13:13
Honesty best policy	Prov. 15:27; 2 Cor. 8:21;
	1 Tim. 2:2
Honey	Ps. 19:10; Prov. 24:13, +
	25:16, 27; Isa. 7:15; Jer. 11:5
Honeycomb	Ps. 19:10; Prov. 24:13, + 27:7
Honour	1 Sam. 2:30; Prov. 26:1;
	John 5:23, 41, 44; Rom. 12:10
" and praise by all to	
god	Rev. 4:11, + 5:13
" king & men	1 Pet. 2:17
" of kings	Prov. 25:2
" thy father &	
mother	Deut. 5:16; Matt. 15:4;
	Mark 7:10
" to man fruitless	Ps. 49:12
" with substance &	
firstfuits	Prov. 3:9
Honourable	Isa. 42:21, + 43:4
" - despised	1 Cor. 4:10
Honoureth	John 5:23
Hoof	Judg. 5:22; Jer. 47:3

Hope		Jer. 17:7; Lam. 3:26; Rom. 4:18, + 5:4, 5, + 8:24, 25, + 12:12; Heb. 6:19; 1 John 3:3
"	abound in	Rom. 15:13
"	, believed in	Rom. 4:18
"	, blessed	Titus 2:13
"	by resurrection	1 Pet. 1:3
"	- faith in God	1 Pet. 1:21
"	for unseen things	Rom. 8:24, 25
"	from gospel	Col. 1:23
"	" scriptures	Rom. 15:4, 13
"	in Lord God	Ps. 39:7, + 42:11, + 146:5; Rom. 5:5, 13
"	" " - be strengthened	Job 11:18, 20; Ps. 31:23
"	is Christ in you	Col. 1:27; Titus 2:13, + 3:7
"	of Christians	Rom. 8:28, 39
"	" glory	Col. 1:29; Rom. 8:18; Titus 2:13 + 37
"	, our	Heb. 3:6, + 4:16, + 6:19
"	purifieth	1 John 3:2, 3
"	saves	Rom. 8:24–26
"	shared by all in heaven & on earth	Col. 1:20
"	through power	Rom. 15:4, 13
"	today	Rom. 15:4; Col. 1:5
Hopeth		1 Cor. 13:7
Horn		Ps. 92:10
"	of salvation	Luke 1:69
Hornet		Josh 24:12
Horns		Gen. 22:13; Deut. 33:17; 1 Kings 1:51; Rev. 5:6, + 17:3, 7, 12, 16

Horrible		Ps. 40:2; Jer. 5:30
Horse		2 Chron. 1:16, 17; Esther 6:8–11; Ps. 20:7; Prov. 21:31; Isa. 2:7; Zech. 14:20; Rev. 9:17
"	hoofs	Judg. 5:22; Isa. 5:28; Jer. 47:3
Horseback		Esther 6:8–11
Horseleach		Prov. 30:15
Horseman		Jer. 46:4; Hos. 1:7; Rev. 9:16
Horsemen		Rev. 9:16
Hospitality		Rom. 12:10–13; 1 Tim. 3:3; 1 Pet. 4:9, 10
"	, be lover of	Titus 1:8
Host - evil one		Ps. 27:2, 3
Hosts, Lord of		Amos 4:13
Hot		Ps. 39:3
Hour		Luke 22:53, 59; Rev. 3:3
"	cometh & is	Matt. 24:42–44; John 4:23
"	not known	Matt. 25:13
"	of darkness per Jesus	Luke 22:53
"	" Jesus' ascension	John 13:1
Hours, night		Ps. 127:2
House		Gen. 7:1; Matt. 12:25; John 14:2; Acts 16:15, 31, 32, 34, 40; Heb. 3:2–6
"	curtain	Mark 5:35
"	in heaven	2 Cor. 5:1
"	, Lord's	Matt. 21:13
"	, my	Josh. 24:15
"	of faith and God	Gal. 6:10; Eph. 2:18–22
"	" Lord	Ps. 92:13
"	" prayer	Mark 11:17; Luke 19:46
"	, prison	Isa. 42:22

" , spiritual	1 Pet. 2:5
Household of God is foundation of apostles & prophets	Gal. 6:10; Eph. 2:18–22
How	Luke 1:34; 1 Cor. 14:26
" Christ died	1 Cor. 15:3
How day of Lord will come	2 Pet. 3:10
" God sent his son	Rom. 8:3
Howbeit	2 Sam. 2:23, + 13:14; John 11:13, + 16:13; Acts 7:48; 2 Cor. 11:21; Heb. 3:16
Howl	Zech. 1:11; James 5:1
Howling	Deut. 32:10
Humanity of Jesus	Isa. 7:14–16; Phil. 2:5–8
Humble informed of spirit	Luke 10:20, 21
" ourselves	Phil. 2:1–8; James 4:10; 1 Pet. 5:5, 6
" " - be exalted	Luke 14:11; Phil. 2:1–9; 1 Pet. 5:6, 7
" self or exalt self	Luke 14:11; James 4:10
" spirit	Prov. 16:19
" themselves	2 Chron. 7:14
" you to know heart	Deut. 8:2
" vs proud	1 Pet. 5:5
Humbled	Isa. 10:33
" himself, Jesus	Phil. 2:7, 8
Humiliation	Acts 8:33
Humility	Acts 20:19; Phil. 2:1–30; Col. 2:18; 1 Pet. 5:5, 6
Hundred	Matt. 18:3
Hundredfold	Matt. 13:8
Hunger	Matt. 5:6; Rom. 12:20
" , never	John 6:35

Hungred	Acts 10:10; Luke 6:3
Hungry	Isa. 58:10; Phil. 4:12
Hurl	Num. 35:20; Job 27:21
Hurt	Dan. 6:22, 23; Acts 18:10
" not in second death	Rev. 2:11
" , nothing - you are power from Lord	Luke 10:19
Hurtful lusts	1 Tim. 6:9
Husband	Ruth 1:12; John 4:16–18
" love wife	Col. 3:19
" - wife	1 Cor. 7:10–16; Eph. 5:21–33; Titus 1:6
Husbands likewise	1 Pet. 3:7
Husbandman	John 15:1; James 5:7
Husbandry	1 Cor. 3:9
Hymn	Mark 14:26; Eph. 5:19; Col. 3:16
Hypocrisies	1 Pet. 2:1–3
Hypocrite	Prov. 11:9; Matt. 7:5; Mark 7:6; Luke 12:56, + 13:15
Hypocrites	Matt. 6:2, 16, + 23:13–30
Hyssop	Ps. 51:7; Heb. 9:19

I		John 10:15–18, 30, 34, 37, 38, + 14:2–6, 9–21, 25–31 + 15:1–5, 9–26 + 17:4–26; Acts 10:26, + 11:5–8, 11, 15–17
"	am	Exod. 3:14; Mark 14:62; John 6:48, + 8:58, + 9:5 + 10:7, 9–11, 14, 36, + 11:25, + 14:6, + 17:11, 24; Rev. 1:11, 17, 18, + 22:13, 16
"	am alive	Rev. 1:17
"	" come - Jesus	John 10:10
"	" God	Isa. 45:21, 22
"	" here	Isa. 58:9
"	" Lord	Gen. 15:7; Isa. 42:8, + 48:17
"	" there with two or three	Matt. 18:19, 20, + 28:20
"	live	John 14:19
"	thirst	John 19:28
"	will	Ps. 9:1, 2; Isa. 41:10
Ice		Ps. 147:17
Ideal Lifeway		Col. 3:8–17; Titus 2:11–15
"	woman	Prov. 31:10–31
Identification with Christ		Mark 8:34, + 10:21; Luke 9:23; Phil. 2:10–13

Identify - we common in
Christ — Phil. 2:10–13

Idle — Exod. 5:8, 17; Matt. 20:3, 6

" , do not be — 1 Tim. 5:13

" words judged — Matt. 12:36, 37

Idol — 2 Chron. 33:7, 15; Isa. 66:3; 1 Cor. 8:4, 7, + 10:19

" is anything — 1 Cor. 10:19; Acts 7:41

" worshippers — Exod. 32:7–9; 1 Kings 12:28–33; Isa. 65:2, 3

Idolators — 1 Cor. 10:7

Idolatry — Isa. 57:5; 1 Cor. 10:14

" includes covetousness — Col. 3:5

Idols — Ps. 115:4–8; Isa. 2:10, 12, 20, 21; Jer. 44:15, 23, 25, + 50:38; Ezek. 14:4, 5; 1 Cor. 8:4, 5, 7-10, + 10:19

Idols' pollutions — Acts 15:20, 29

Idols to be avoided — Lev. 26:1; Ps. 96:5; Hab. 2:18, 19; Acts 15:20, 29; 1 John 5:21; Rev. 9:20

If — Deut. 28:1–15; Matt. 4:3, 6, 9, + 26:39; Mark 14:21, 31, 35; John 11:40, + 14:3, 7, 23; 1 Pet. 2:3; 1 John 2:4; Rev. 14:9

" believe all things possible — Mark 9:23

Ignominy — Prov. 18:3

Ignorance — Acts 3:17 + 17:30; 1 Pet. 1:14, + 2:15

Ignorant — Acts 4:13; Rom. 10:3; 1 Cor. 10:1, + 12:1, + 14:38

" not — 2 Cor. 2:11; 2 Pet. 3:5, 8

"	worship	Acts 17:23
Ill to the wicked		Isa. 3:11
Illuminated		Heb. 10:32
Image		Dan. 3:17, 18; 1 Cor. 15:49; 2 Cor. 3:18; Col. 1:15
"	and ministry of God for us	2 Cor. 4:1–5
"	by spirit	2 Cor. 3:18
"	dedication	Dan. 3:3
"	earthly & heavenly	1 Cor. 15:49
"	, graven	Exod. 20:3–5; Lev. 26:1; Deut. 27:15; Jer. 50:38
"	- idols	Lev. 26:1; Deut. 4:23; Hab. 2:18, 19
"	is falsehood	Jer. 10:14
"	Isaiah's	Isa. 48:5
"	of beast worshippers	Rev. 19:20, + 20:4
"	of creator	Col. 3:10
"	" God is gospel	2 Cor. 3:18, + 4:4; Eph. 5:5; Col. 1:15, + 3:10
Image of His Son		Rom. 8:29
"	to the beast	Rev. 13:14, 15
"	" us in Him	Gen. 1:26, 27
Images destroy-per God		Exod. 34:13, 14
"	- not to have these gods	Deut. 5:7–9; Isa. 42:8; Jer. 50:38
Imagination		Gen. 6:5, + 8:21; Deut. 29:19; Jer. 11:8
Imaginations		1 Chron. 28:9; Lam. 3:61; 2 Cor. 10:3–5
Imagine		Job 6:26; Ps. 2:1, + 38:12, + 140:2; Acts 4:25

Imitator of God	2 Thess. 2:1–4
Immanuel	Isa. 7:14, + 9:6; Matt. 1:23
Immediately	Matt. 4:22, + 20:34;
	Mark 1:31, + 4:5, 15, 17, 29;
	Luke 4:39, + 5:25
Immersion	Matt. 3:3, 6, 13; John 1:25–28;
	Acts 2:37, 38
Immorality	Rom. 2:7; 1 Cor. 15:53, 54;
	1 Thess. 4:13–18; 1 Tim. 6:15, 16;
	2 Tim. 1:10
Immorality, sexuality	Acts 15:20
Immortal king	1 Tim. 1:17, + 6:15, 16
Immutability	Heb. 6:17
Immutable	Heb. 6:18
Impart	Rom. 1:11
Important for us	1 Chron. 28:9
Importunity	Luke 11:8
Impossible and possible	Matt. 19:26; Mark 10:27;
	Luke 18:27; Heb. 11:6
" , nothing	Matt. 17:20; Luke 1:37, + 18:27
Imposter	Rev. 13:13, 14, + 16:13, 14
Imposters	Luke 21:8
Impotent	Josh. 5:3; John 5:37;
	Acts 4:8–10, + 14:8
Impoverished	Isa. 40:20
Imputed	Rom. 4:22–24, + 5:13;
	James 2:23
Imputeth	Ps. 32:2
Imputing	2 Cor. 5:9
In	John 17:21
" Christ	Acts 17:28; Col. 1:10;
	1 Cor. 1:30; 2 Cor. 5:17
" " award	1 Thess. 4:16–18

" heaven - hell - torments - bosom - water - flame - purple	Luke 16:19, 22–24
" Him	Acts 17:28; Col. 2:6–10; 1 John 2:4–6
" me - you - us	John 17:21
" you - greater	1 John 4:4
" world	John 17:11
Inasmuch	Matt. 25:40; Heb. 3:3, + 7:20; 1 Pet. 4:13
Incense	Jer. 11:12; Rev. 8:3, 4
" burners	Num. 16:18; Isa. 65:2, 3; Jer. 44:15, 23, 25
Incensed	Isa. 41:11 + 45:24
Incest	Lev. 20:11, 12, 17, 19, 20; Rom. 6:12, 13
Incline	Ps. 17:6, + 78:4 + 102:2; Prov. 2:2, + 4:20; Jer. 11:8
Inclosed	Luke 5:6
Incontinent	2 Tim. 3:3
Incorruptible	1 Cor. 15:52, 54; 1 Pet. 1:4, 23
Incorruption	1 Cor. 15:50, 53, 54
Increase	Ps. 115:14; Prov. 3:9, 10; Isa. 29:19; John 3:30; 2 Cor. 9:10; Col. 1:10
" of God	Col. 2:19
Increased wisdom at end times	Dan. 12:4
Incurable	Job 34:6; Jer. 30:12, 15
Indebted	Luke 11:4
Indeed	Matt 3:11; John 8:31, 36; Phil. 1:15, + 2:27, + 3:1; 1 Pet. 2:4

Indignation	Job 10:17; Ps. 102:10; Isa. 26:20; 30:27, + 66:14; Matt 6:8
Inditing	Ps. 45:1
Infallible	Acts 1:3
Infamy	Prov. 25:10
Inferior	Job 13:2
Infidel	2 Cor. 6:15; 1 Tim. 5:8
Infirmities	Matt. 8:17; Luke 7:21, + 8:2; 2 Cor. 12:9, 10; Heb. 4:15
Infirmity	Ps. 17:10; Luke 13:11–13; Rom. 6:19; Heb. 7:28
Inflammation	Lev. 13:28
Inflexibility	Ps. 32:8, 9; Prov. 3:5, 7, + 18:12, + 29:1; Zech. 7:8–14
Informed	Acts 21:21
Inhabit	Prov. 10:30; Isa. 45:18, + 65:21, 22; Amos 9:14
Inhabitant	Isa. 12:6
Inhabitants of earth nothing compared to God	Isa. 40:22; Dan. 4:35
Inherit a blessing	1 Pet. 3:9
" all things	Matt. 19:29; Rev. 21:7
" kingdom	Matt. 25:34
" not	1 Cor. 6:9
" the earth	Ps. 37:11; Matt. 5:4
" " land	Gen. 15:7, 8; Ps. 37:29
" " wind	Prov. 11:29
Inheritance	Jer. 10:16; Ezek. 36:12; Acts 20:32 + 26:18; Eph. 1:18; Col. 1:12, + 3:23, 24; Heb. 11:14-16; 1 Pet. 1:4
" , eternal	Heb. 9:15

"	from on high	Job 31:2; Ps. 16:5
"	of those not in	
	kingdom	Eph. 5:5
Inherited sin		Gen. 3:19
Iniquities		Isa. 59:2–13; Ezek. 28:18;
		Heb. 10:17
"	He suffered for us	
	all	Isa. 53:5, 11
"	written	Isa. 65:6, 7
Iniquity		Num. 14:18; Ps. 32:2, 5;
		Isa. 53:6, + 59:1–13;
		Ezek. 28:18, + 33:8, 9, 13, 18;
		Hab. 2:12; 2 Thess. 2:7–10;
		Rev. 18:5
"	punished	Isa. 26:20, 21
"	workers	Matt. 7:21–23
Injustice		Job 16:17
Inkhorn		Ezek. 9:2, 3
Inn		Luke 10:34
Inner man		Eph. 1:16 + 3:16–19
Innermost		Prov. 18:8
Innocency		Dan. 6:22: 1 Peter 1:19, 20
Innocent		Deut. 21:8
Innumerable		Ps. 40:12, + 104:25; Heb. 12:22
Inordinate		Col. 3:5
Insence		Jer. 44:23, 25
Inside - outside		Matt. 23:25–29
Insomuch		Matt. 15:31; Mark 1:27 + 9:26;
		Acts 1:19, + 5:15
Inspiration of God		Job 32:8; 2 Tim. 3:16, 17
Inspired scripture by God		1 Tim. 3:16, 17
Instant		2 Tim. 4:2
"	in prayer	Rom. 12:12
Instead		Isa. 55:13

Instruct	Ps. 32:8
Instructed, be	Ps. 2:10–12
Instruction and knowledge	Prov. 1:7, 8; Mark 12:1
" from scriptures	2 Tim. 3:16, 17
" important	Prov. 1:2, 3, 7, 8, + 4:1, 13, 23, + 7:4, 7, + 8:33, + 9:9
" keepers are blessed	Ps. 119:1, 2, 12, 32
" to children	Ps. 78:4; Prov. 4:1–27
Instructions bring joy	Ps. 119:12–16
" by Jesus	Matt. 28:18–20
" " Paul	Eph. 6:1–20
" for living	Col. 1:9–12; 1 Thess. 5:11–22
" from parents	Prov. 1:8, + 4:1–27, + 13:1
" regarding wisdom to all	Prov. 1:1–10
" to churches	Rev. 1:4–6, 20, + 2:1, 7, 17, 18, 29, + 3:1, 6, 7
" " youth	Prov. 1:2–4
Instructor	Gen. 4:22; Rom. 2:20
Instruments of music	Ps. 92:3, + 98:4–6; Dan. 3:5, 7, 10, 15
Insurrection	Ps. 64:2; Mark 15:7
Integrity	Job 2:3, 9; Ps. 26:1, + 41:12; Prov. 19:1
Intensity	Mark 13:22
Intent	Dan. 4:17; John 16:15, + 13:28; Heb. 4:12
Intercession by spirit	Rom. 8:26
" , Christ's	Isa. 53:1–12; Heb. 7:25, + 9:24
" for saints	Rom. 8:27
" for us	Rom. 8:26, 27, 34; 1 Tim. 2:1; Heb. 7:25
Intercessor	Isa. 59:16
Intermeddleth	Prov. 14:10, + 18:1

Intermission	Lam. 3:49
Interpret	Prov. 14:13, 19–29, 39, 40;
	1 Cor. 14:13; John 1:41
Interpretation	Gen. 40:8; Dan. 2:6, 9, 16,
	24–26, 30, 36, 45; Acts 9:36;
	1 Cor. 14:26; Heb. 7:2
Interpreter	Job 33:23
Into	Gen. 2:7, + 6:18, 19;
	Acts 1:11, 13; 2 Thess. 3:5
Intreat (entreat)	Ruth 1:16; 2 Cor. 8:4; Phil. 4:3
Intruding	Col. 2:18
Invade	Hab. 3:16
Invent	2 Chron. 26:15; Amos 6:5
Inventions	Eccles. 7:29
Invest in sin (evil)	Isa. 30:1
Invisible God	John 1:18; Col. 1:15, 16;
	Heb. 1:40
" king	1 Tim. 1:17
" seen	Rom. 1:20
Invitation	Matt. 11:28–30; Rev. 22:17
Invite the humble (poor)	
to feast	Luke 14:12–27
Inward and outward man	1 Sam. 16:7; 2 Cor. 4:16
" parts	Ps. 51:6; Jer. 31:33; Luke 11:39
Inwards	Lev. 4:8, 11 + 7:3 + 8:16, 21,
	25 + 9:14, 19
Iron	2 Kings 6:6; Job 28:2;
	Jer. 15:12; Acts 12:10
Is	Jer. 17:7; John 4:22–25;
	2 Cor. 13:10
" as thinketh	Prov. 23:7
" the way	Isa. 30:21
" to come, Lord	Rev. 1:8
Island	Acts 28:9

Isle		Acts 28:11; Rev. 1:9
Isles		Isa. 42:10; Zeph. 2:11
Israel		Gen. 49:2, 16; Luke 2:32
Israel deserves sonship		
	& glory	Rom. 9:4, 5
"	from Jacob	Gen. 32:28, + 35:10
"	proved	Judg. 3:1, 9, 15, 31, + 4:4, + 6:11, + 9:1, + 10:1, 3, + 11:1, + 12:8, 11, 13
Issues of life		Prov. 4:23
It		Job 31:5–40
"	is finished	John 19:30
Itch		Deut. 28:27
Itching ears		2 Tim. 4:3
Itself		Rom. 8:16, 21
Ivory		Ps. 45:8; Ezek. 27:6, 15

• J •

Jachin - Pillar	2 Chron. 3:17
Jacob name to Israel	Gen. 32:28, + 35:10
Jacob's ladder	Gen. 28:12
" well	John 4:6
Jailer	Acts 16:23
Jasper stone	Rev. 4:3, + 20:18
Javelin	1 Sam. 18:10, 11
Jaw	Judg. 15:16
Jawbone	Judg. 15:17
Jealous	Exod. 20:17; 1 Sam. 18:8–12; Ps. 49:16, 17; Prov. 14:30, + 23:17 + 27:4; Zech. 3:8
" God	Exod. 34:14; Deut. 4:24; Gal. 5:26, 27; James 3:14, 16
Jealousy	Num. 5:14, 15, 18, 25, 29, 30; Isa. 42:13; 1 Cor. 10:22; Rev. 8:6
Jehovah	Ps. 83:18; Isa. 26:4
Jeopardy	Luke 8:23; 1 Cor. 18:30; Heb. 8:23
Jeremiah heard the Lord	Jer. 32:26
Jericho	Neh. 3:2, + 7:36
Jerusalem	Matt. 3:5, + 21:1–10; Luke 2:22, + 24:27
" , new	Isa. 65:17–25; Dan. 9:25

"	wall	Neh. 12:27
Jesus and Father God only		
	know each other	Matt. 11:27
"	and Father God	
	the same	John 14:9
"	' appearances	(see appearances)
"	ascended - to return	John 13:33, + 14:28, + 16:7, 28, + 17:13
"	began preaching	Luke 4:14–19
"	' birth	Luke 2:7–18
"	' " foretold	Jer. 31:22; Mic. 5:2; John 1:31
"	' brethren & mother	Luke 8:20, 21
"	' brothers & sisters	Matt. 13:54–56; Mark 6:3; John 7:3, 5, 6
"	came for judgment	John 9:37
"	" to save	Mark 6:3; Luke 9:56, + 19:10
"	" " " sinners	1 Tim. 1:15
"	Christ brought grace & truth	John 1:17
"	Christ came by water & blood	1 John 5:6
"	Christ is chief cornerstone	Isa. 53:1–12; John 1:7–17; Eph. 2:20; Col. 1:15–17
"	Christ is master	Matt. 23:10
"	" not of this world	John 17:5, 11, 16, 24
"	Christ of God	Isa. 53:1–12; 2 Cor. 5:18, 19
"	" " water & the blood	1 John 5:6
"	Christ one with God	John 17:11
"	" of our Lord	Rom. 6:23; Acts 10:36
"	" coming predicted	Jer. 31:22; John 14:18, 19
"	" convictions	Luke 2:49

"	" description	
	prophesied	Isa. 52:13, 14
"	did eat	Luke 24:43
"	died in flesh for us	Luke 23:33; Col. 1:21, 22
"	family	Matt. 12:46–50; Mark 3:31–35
"	, genealogy	Matt. 1:1–17; Luke 3:23–38
"	, God with	Acts 10:38
"	healed many	Matt. 4:24, + 14:14, 30; Mark 3:10, 11; Luke 6:19, + 9:6
"	, humanity	See Section JJ
"	in Galilee	Matt. 4:23
"	in me	Eph. 1:16
Jesus	is Christ	Acts 17:3
"	" master & lord	John 13:13, 14
"	" our faith	Heb. 12:2
"	" way - truth - life	John 14:6
"	king of Israel	John 1:49
"	, last words before ascension	Acts 1:8, 9
"	lives	John 14:18, 19
"	, love to father is great	Luke 14:30, 31
"	made famous - first healing	Mark 1:23, 27, 28
"	, mission	John 10:10; 1 John 4:10
"	, mother	Matt. 13:55; Luke 1:43, 44, 46, + 8:21
"	named by angel	Luke 2:21
"	not to stay	Matt. 26:11
"	one with us	John 17:11, 20, 21
"	peace or world tribulation	John 16:33
"	prayed also alone	Mark 1:35

"	prophesied	Ps. 2:4–10; Isa. 7:14, + 9:6, + 52:13, 14; Jer. 31:22; Zech. 3:8; Luke 1:31–33
"	, purpose in world	Gal. 1:4; John 16:33
"	resurrection & life	John 11:25, 26
"	- rose of Sharon	Song of Sol. 2:1
"	- safety no concern	Luke 22:53
"	said	John 20:21
"	seen after ascension	Acts 13:29–34; 1 Cor. 15:5–8
"	sent by God in likeness of sinful flesh	Rom. 8:3
"	suffered for us all	Isa. 53:1–12
"	, suffering predicted	Matt. 17:12
"	to appear again	1 John 3:2
"	" reign foretold	John 1:31–33
"	, true life (way to father)	Prov. 16:2; John 14:6
"	words are God's words	John 14:24
"	youth	Luke 2:40, 46–52
Jet	cars predicted	Nah. 2:4
Jew		John 4:9, + 18:35
Jewel		Gen. 24:53; Prov. 20:15; Isa. 61:10
Jews - many turned to Jesus		John 4:22, + 12:1–11
Jobs various for widows		1 Tim. 5:10
John - fisherman - author Book of John		Mark 1:19, 20; Luke 9:9; John 20:30, 31, + 21:24; Rev. 1:9
"	the Baptist foretold	Luke 1:11–13

" " " greatest	
on earth	Matt. 11:11; John 1:1, 2
John's baptism	Mark 11:30–33
" qualification	3 John 1:1, 2
Joined	Matt. 19:6; Mark 10:9;
	1 Cor. 1:10
Joint - heirs	Rom. 8:17
Jonas in belly of whale	Jonah 1:17, + 2:1–10;
	Matt. 12:38–40
Jordan River	Josh. 3:8, 11–17; 2 Kings 2:8;
	Matt. 3:6, 13, 16
Joseph	Gen. 49:22
Jot and tittle	Matt. 5:18
Journey	Mark 13:34; Acts 9:3;
	Rom. 1:10
Joy	Ps. 30:5; John 15:11; 3 John 1:4
" and pleasures	Ps. 16:11
" , Christ's - your joy	John 15:11
" everlasting	Isa. 51:11
" from mourning	
(sorrow)	Isa. 61:2, 3; Jer. 31:10–13;
	John 16:20–22
" , great	Luke 2:10
Joy great in testimonies	Ps. 119:14
" in believing	Ps. 30:5; Rom. 15:13
" " Lord God	Isa. 55:12; Rom. 5:11, + 15:13;
	1 Pet. 1:8
" " poverty	2 Cor. 8:2
" " receiving	John 16:24
" " repentance	Luke 15:10
" " temptations	James 1:2, 3
" " thy presence	Ps. 16:11; Matt. 25; 21
" " you	John 15:11
" is forever	John 16:22

"	of the Lord	Deut. 28:47
"	over you for the Lord God	Zeph. 3:17
"	to see Jesus	John 16:22
"	unspeakable	1 Pet. 1:8
Joyful		Isa. 61:10
"	noise	Ps. 95:1, 2, + 98:4, + 100:1
"	riches	Ps. 119:14
Joyfully		Luke 19:6
Joyfulness for abundance		Deut. 28:47; Col. 1:9–11
Jubilee		Lev. 25:54 + 27:23
Judas		Matt. 26:47–50, + 27:3–5
"	(apostle) replaced by Matthias	Acts 1:26
Judea		Matt. 2:1, 5, 6; Luke 1:5
Judge		Ps. 50:4, 6; James 4:11
"	- condemn - forgive	Luke 6:37
"	is God	Ps. 75:6, 7; John 12:44–48
"	" Jesus	John 5:22, 23
"	" " & God	Rom. 2:16; 2 Tim. 4:1
"	" " " Lord	1 Cor. 4:4
"	me - Jesus	John 8:15, 16
"	none	Rom. 14:3, 4, 13
"	" per Jesus	Luke 6:37; John 8:15, + 12:47; Luke 6:37; 1 Cor. 6:2, 5
"	" " Paul	Rom. 2:1
"	not	Luke 6:37; 1 Cor. 4:4, 5
"	" per appearance	John 7:24
"	nothing	Matt. 7:1–5; 1 Cor. 4:4, 5
"	ourselves	1 Cor. 11:31
"	righteous judgment	John 7:24
"	secrets of men	Rom. 2:16
"	the quick & the dead	2 Tim. 4:1

"	" spirit	Prov. 16:2
"	world by Lord	Ps. 96:11–13; Acts 17:31; Jude 1:14, 15; Rev. 11:18, + 19:11, + 20:12
"	" " saints	1 Cor. 6:2
Judged		John 16:11; 1 Cor. 11:31, 32
"	according to works	John 16:11; Rev. 20:11–15
Judges		Judg. 2:16–19
"	be instructed	Ps. 2:9–12
Judgeth me (Paul) is the	Lord	1 Cor. 4:4
Judging others		Rom. 2:1–4; James 4:11
Judgment		Ps. 37:28; Prov. 21:3; Eccles. 12:14; Dan. 7:10, 22; John 9:39, + 12:31, + 16:11; 2 Cor. 5:10; 1 John 4:17; Rev. 14:7, + 15:4, + 19:11
"	after death	Heb. 9:27; 2 Pet. 2:9
"	and justice	Prov. 21:3
"	by knowledge & love	Phil. 1:9
"	comes from the Lord	Prov. 29:26; Mic. 3:8
Judgment coming		John 5:25–30; Jude 1:14–16
"	day	2 Pet. 3:7
"	given to Jesus	John 5:27, 30
"	is reason for Jesus coming here	John 9:39
"	, Lord's	Ps. 19:9
"	of the great day	Jude 1:6
"	seat	2 Cor. 5:10
"	to be executed	John 16:11; Jude 1:14–16
"	" come	Isa. 66:12–24
"	" the soul per Jesus	John 5:22; Acts 10:42; Heb. 9:27; Rev. 20:12, 13

"	upon all men	Rom. 5:18
Judgments		Deut. 5:1; Rom. 11:33
Jumped		Ps. 18:29
Juniper		Job 30:4
Just and unjust		Prov. 24:16, + 29:37; Matt. 5:45; Acts 24:15; 1 Pet. 3:18
"	are ways of God	Rev. 15:3
"	live by faith	Hab. 2:4; Rom. 1:17
"	of the wicked	Mal. 4:1–3
"	one - Jesus	Acts 7:52
"	to forgive	1 John 1:9
"	weights etc.	Lev. 19:35, 36
Justice		Prov. 2:8, 9, + 21:3; Isa. 58:2, + 59:14
Justifications, our		Rom. 4:24, 25, + 5:16
Justified by being doers		Ps. 51:4; Rom. 2:13
"	" faith	Rom. 3:28, + 4:25, + 5:1, 2, 9; Gal. 2:16, + 3:24, 26; Heb. 10:39; James 2:21, 24
"	" " not law	Rom. 3:28; Gal. 2:16, 21; Titus 3:5
"	" God	Rom. 8:30
"	" His blood & grace	Rom. 5:9; Titus 3:7
"	by Jesus	Acts 13:39
"	" words	Matt. 12:37
"	" works	James 2:21
"	freely	Rom. 3:24
Justifier		Rom. 3:26
Justifieth by God only		Rom. 8:33
"	by spirit	1 Cor. 6:1–20
Justify		Luke 16:15; Gal. 3:8
Justle		Nah. 2:4
Justly		1 Thess. 2:10
Justus - Jesus		Col. 4:11

• K •

Keep from idols		1 John 5:21
"	glory name and praise - Lord	Isa. 42:8
"	God's commandments	Deut. 28:1, 2, 9; John 14:15, 21, 23; 1 John 2:3, 4, + 5:3
"	heart with diligence	Prov. 4:23; Phil. 4:7
"	law	James 2:10
"	me	Ps. 140:4
"	saying of Jesus	John 8:51, + 14:23
"	selves in love of God	1 John 5:18, 21; Jude 1:20, 21
"	sound wisdom	Prov. 3:21
"	thee	Gen. 28:15
"	word of God	Luke 8:15, + 11:28; Rev. 1:3
Keeper		Acts 16:27
Keepeth God's commandments		John 14:21
Kept		Luke 2:19
"	by angels	Ps. 91:9–11
"	" power of God	1 Pet. 1:5
"	not estate	Jude 1:6
Kerchief		Ezek. 13:18, 21
Kernels		Num. 6:4

Key to door of salvation	Rev. 3:7
Keys of hell & death	Rev. 1:18
" to Kingdom of Heaven	Matt. 16:19; Rev. 1:18
Kick	Acts 9:5
Kid	1 Sam. 16:20
Kidneys	Lev. 3:4, 10, 15, + 4:9 + 7:4; Isa. 34:6
Kill	Num. 11:15; Matt. 10:28; John 8:40; James 2:11; Rev. 6:8
" Jesus foretold	Matt. 17:22, 23
" not	Deut. 5:17; Matt. 5:21; Luke 18:20
" truth speaker	John 8:40
" with sword - be likewise killed	Gen. 9:6; Rev. 13:10
Killed	Rom. 8:35; 1 Thess. 2:15
Kind	Matt. 17:31; Eph. 4:32
Kindle	Jer. 17:27; Luke 22:55
Kindled	Josh. 23:16; Job 32:2, 3, 5; Lam. 4:11
" anger	Ex. 4:14
Kindly	Rom. 12:10
Kindness	Isa. 54:10; Col. 3:12, 13; 2 Pet. 1:7
Kindred	Acts 7:13, 14
Kindreds of earth	Rev. 1:7, + 13:7
Kinds of Christians	Gal. 3:28
King	Prov. 30:31
" is God	Ps. 47:7
" of all	Ps. 47:2; Zech. 14:9
" " glory	Ps. 24:7–10
" " Israel - Jesus	John 1:49

"	" Jews	Matt. 2:2; Luke 22:38; John 19:19, 21
"	" kings	Rev. 17:14, + 19:16
"	" saints	Rev. 15:3
"	" world to prosper	Dan. 11:36
Kingdom and dominion everlasting		Dan. 4:2, 3
"	, enter	Matt. 18:3
"	, everlasting	Dan. 7:22, 23, 27
"	given to saints of God	Dan. 7:27; Luke 22:29, 30
Kingdom king's dream		Dan. 2:1–49
"	know	John 3:3
"	, Lord's	Ps. 145:11–13
"	of God	Dan. 2:44, 45, + 7:14; Mark 1:15; Luke 22:16; Rom. 14:17
"	" " established	Isa. 9:6, 7; 2 Tim. 4:1, 2
"	" " forever	Dan. 2:44, + 6:26
"	" " in power	1 Cor. 4:20
"	" " is	Rom. 14:17
"	" " " power	1 Chron. 29:11; 1 Cor. 4:20
"	" " " within you	Luke 17:21
"	" " not earthly	Rom. 14:17, 18
"	" " promised	Luke 21:28, 30, 31; 2 Tim. 1:11
"	" ", see	John 3:3, 7; Rom. 14:17
"	" ", seek - not earthly things	Matt. 6:33; Luke 12:22–34
"	of heaven	Matt. 10:7, + 13:43–45
"	" " as little children	Matt. 18:10, + 19:14
"	of Jesus	John 18:36
"	preached at end times	Matt. 24:14

"	prepared	Jude 1:24
Kingdom's end - all on		
	earth	Dan. 7:14
"		Rev. 11:15
Kings	be instructed	Ps. 2:10–12
"	peaceably acting	Dan. 11:21, 24
"	prince	Rev. 1:5
"	to come from	
	Israel's land	Gen. 35:11
Kinsfolk		Luke 2:44, + 1:16
Kinsman		Ruth 2:1, + 3:9, 12, 13, + 4:1, 6, 8, 14
Kinsmen		Ruth 2:20; Rom. 9:3
Kinswomen		Lev. 18:12, 13
Kiss		Ruth 1:14; Prov. 24:26; Rom. 16:16; 1 Cor. 16:20; 2 Cor. 13:15, + 16.14; 1 Pet. 5:14
Kissed Jesus' feet		Luke 7:38, 45
Kite		Deut. 14:13
Knee shall bow		Isa. 45:23
Kneed		Ps. 95:4–7; Mark 1:40; Acts 7:60
Kneel		Ps. 95:6; Acts 20:35
Knees		Dan. 6:10, 13; Eph. 3:14
Knew	all men, Jesus	John 2:24
"	Jeremiah before he was born	Jer. 1:4, 5
"	, Lord	John 4:1
"	not Father	1 John 3:1
Knife		1 Kings 18:28; Jer. 36:23
Knit		Acts 10:11; Col. 2:2, 19
Knock - ask & seek		Matt. 7:7, 8; Luke 11:9, 10
"	by Jesus	Rev. 3:20
"	- opened	Matt. 7:7; Luke 11:9

Knops		Exod. 25:33–36
Know		Ps. 100:3, + 139:23;
		John 7:26–29, + 14:4, 5;
		James 1:3; Rev. 2:19
"	all - God omniscient	1 Chron. 28:9; Job 48:2;
		Heb. 4:13
"	and do	John 8:31, 32, + 13:15, 17
"	Bible	Job 22:21–23
"	doctrine of God	John 7:17; 1 John 5:13
"	God	Deut. 7:9; Ps. 46:10;
		Ezek. 20:20
"	good & evil	Gen. 3:5
"	have eternal life	1 John 5:13
Know Him		Jer. 31:34; John 14:7, 17;
		Phil. 3:10; 1 John 2:4
"	hope & inheritance	Eph. 1:18; 1 John 5:13
"	, I	1 Cor. 13:12
"	Lord's people	Gal. 3:7; 1 Thess. 5:12
"	spoken word	Deut. 18:21, 22
"	me	Ps. 139:24
"	mystery of God	Mark 4:11, 12
"	not	Luke 1:34
"	" time of Lord's coming	Matt. 24:42, 43, + 25:13;
		Luke 21:34–36
"	not what	Rom. 8:26
"	nothing	1 Cor. 8:2
"	" by myself	1 Cor. 4:4
"	way	John 14:4–6
"	, ye may	Matt. 9:6; 1 Cor. 3:16
Knowest		Jer. 33:3; Mark 10:19
Knoweth God		1 John 4:7
"	good & do not, is sin	James 4:17

"	his, Lord	2 Tim. 2:19
"	our needs	Matt. 6:8; 1 John 3:20
Knowing good by man		Eph. 6:8; James 1:3
"	prophesies are per	
	God only	2 Pet. 1:20, 21
Knowledge		Acts 4:13; Gal. 2:16;
		2 Pet. 1:2, 3, 5, 6, 8, + 3:18
"	and judgment by	
	love	Phil. 1:9
"	" instruction	Mark 12:1; 2 Cor. 2:14
"	brings sorrow	Eccles. 1:18; 1 Cor. 8:1
"	by love	Phil. 1:9
"	enriched by Him	1 Cor. 1:5
"	from God's light	2 Cor. 4:6
"	" Lord's mouth	Prov. 2:6
"	, holy - is	
	understanding	Prov. 9:10
"	in marriage	1 Pet. 3:7
"	increased	Dan. 12:4
"	increases strength	Prov. 24:3–7
"	, lack of	Hos. 4:6
"	, Lord's - about me	Ps. 119:1–16
"	necessary	Eph. 4:10–13
"	needed for the soul	Prov. 19:2
"	of God beyond ours	Ps. 139:6; 2 Pet. 1:2
"	" God's will	Col. 1:10
"	" Him is wise	Prov. 9:10; Eph. 1:17–21
"	" one spareth	
	words	Prov. 17:27
"	of salvation	Luke 1:77
Knowledge of Son of God		Eph. 4:13
"	, perfect	Job 37:16
"	, pleasant	Prov. 2:10
"	rejected by God	Hos. 4:6

"	second to love of Christ	Eph. 3:19
"	tree	Gen. 2:17
"	, world full of	Isa. 11:9
Known	-all from Father	John 14:7, 9, + 15:15
"	by God	Ps. 139:1–5
"	me & the Father	John 14:7, 9
"	not my ways	Heb. 3:10
"	of end times - by the faithful	1 Thess. 5:1–4
Known	self	1 Cor. 13:12
"	unto God	Acts 15:18
"	way	John 14:4–6
Knows	all, Lord	1 Chron. 28:9; Job 42:2; Acts 15:18; Heb. 4:13

• L •

Labor		Ps. 127:1, 2; Prov. 13:11, + 14:23; Matt. 11:28–31
"	as pleases soul	Eccles. 2:24
"	profiteth	Prov. 13:11
"	six days	Exod. 20:9; Deut. 5:12–14
"	to rest	Matt. 11:28–30
"	rewarded	Isa. 32:18, + 60:18, + 65:21, 22; Matt. 16:27; 1 Cor. 3:12–15
Labour		John 4:37, 38, + 6:27
"	and reward	1 Cor. 3:8
"	for soul to enjoy	Eccles. 2:24, + 3:13
"	fruits to enjoy	Eccles. 5:18
"	, in - is prophet	Prov. 14:23
"	not in vain	Matt. 11:28, 29; 1 Cor. 15:58; Col. 4:11; 1 Thess. 3:5
"	to support the weak	Acts 20:35
Labourers among us		1 Thess. 5:11–13
"	for God	Luke 10:2–5; 1 Cor. 3:8, 9
Laboureth		1 Cor. 16:16; 2 Tim. 2:6
Labouring man		Eccles. 5:12
Lack		Ps. 34:10; Matt. 19:17–21; James 1:5
"	nothing by own efforts	1 Thess. 4:11, 12

Lacking		1 Cor. 16:17
Lad		Gen. 22:12, + 48:16; John 6:9
Ladder, Jacob's		Gen. 28:12
Lade		Luke 11:46
Laded		Acts 28:10
Laden		Matt. 11:28
Lady		2 John 1:1, 5
Laid		Luke 16:20; John 11:41
"	foundation, house of Lord	Ezra 3:11, 12
"	foundation which is Jesus Christ	1 Cor. 3:10, 11; Eph. 2:20; Heb. 1:10
"	hands on	Rev. 1:17
"	it not to heart	Isa. 42:25
"	Jesus	Isa. 53:6; Mark 15:47
"	up in heaven	Col. 1:5
Lain		Num. 5:19, 20; John 20:12
Lake gets the wicked		Rev. 20:15, + 21:8
"	of fire & brimstone	Rev. 20:10, 15
Lamb		Exod. 29:39; 2 Sam. 12:3, 4, 6; Isa. 11:6; Rev. 14:1, 4, + 15:3, + 17:14
"	of God	John 1:29
"	slain	Rev. 5:12, + 13:8
"	without blemish	1 Pet. 1:18–20
"	worthy	Re. 5:12, 13
Lamb's book of life		Rev. 21:27
Lame		Isa. 33:24; Acts 3:2, 11
Lament		Dan. 6:20; Luke 23:27; John 16:20
Lamentation		2 Sam. 1:17; Lam. 2:5; Acts 8:2
Lamp		Matt. 25:1, 3, 4
"	and light is word	Ps. 119:105, 130

Lamps , seven - of fire		Rev. 4:5
Lancets		1 Kings 18:28
Land		Deut. 11:8–14, 17; Jer. 11:5
"	desolate	Isa. 13:9
"	- earth	Gen. 1:1, 10–12, + 6:12, 13, 17, + 7:12, 17, 24, + 8:3, 21, 22
"	- hills & valleys	Deut. 11:11
Landing		Acts 28:12
Language, first		Gen. 11:1
"	many - over 1,600 in Africa per religious report	
"	, one	Gen. 9:18, 19, + 11:1, 6; Acts 2:6–11
Languish		Hos. 4:3; Isa. 19:8
Languishing bed		Ps. 41:1–3
Lanterns		John 18:3
Lasciviousness		Eph. 4:19; 1 Pet. 4:3; Jude 1:4
Last and first		Isa. 44:6; Matt. 19:30; Rev. 1:8, 11, + 21:6, + 22:13
"	days	Isa. 66:12–24; Acts 2:17; 1 Tim. 3:1–5; Rev. 14:7
"	" instructions	Jude 1:17–23
"	" signs	Mark 13:9–31
"	more than first	Rev. 2:19
"	times advice	Luke 21:6–19; Jude 1:17–23
Latchet		Luke 1:7, + 3:16; John 1:27
Latter times		Heb. 4:1–11
Laugh		Gen. 17:17, + 18:13, 15; Ps. 2:4; Prov. 1:26
Laughter		Ps. 126:2; Prov. 14:13; James 4:9
Launch		Luke 5:4
Laver		1 Kings 7:38

Lavish		Isa. 46:6
Law		Ps. 19:7, + 119:18, 97, 142, 165; Rom. 4:15, 16, + 7:12; 1 Tim. 1:6–11; 1 John 3:6
"	abiders contend with wicked	Prov. 28:4, 7, 9, + 29:18
"	, all of	Matt. 22:37–40; Gal. 5:14
"	breaker	Rom. 2:23–25
"	but	John 1:17
"	by Moses	Josh. 22:5; Neh. 10:29; Luke 24:27, 44; John 1:17, + 7:19
"	, Christ's	Ps. 1:1–3, + 119:1, 97; Gal. 5:14, + 6:2; 1 John 1:9
"	commandment 1 & 2	Matt. 22:37–40
"	, daughters - in -	Ruth 1:7
"	defined	Matt. 7:12; Luke 10:27
"	doctors	Luke 5:17
"	- faith	Rom. 3:27, 28, + 4:13–16
"	for and not for	1 Tim. 1:9, 10
"	" punishment	Exod. 22:1–31, + 23:1–33
"	forsakers of keepers	Prov. 28:4
"	, God's	Ps. 119:18
"	imbedded	Jer. 13:33
"	in one word	Gal. 5:14
"	keepest	Acts 21:24
"	, Lord's - is holy & perfect	Ps. 19:7; Rom. 7:12
"	, Lord's - is the godly's peace	Ps. 1:2, + 119:1, 165
"	magnified	Isa. 42:21
"	, Moses	Josh. 1:7, 8, + 22:5; Luke 24:44

"	, not-but by faith	Rom. 3:19–21, 27, 28, + 4:13–16, + 10:4, 5; Gal. 2:16, 21; Titus 3:5
Law	not for righteous	John 1:17; 1 Tim. 1:6–11
"	, obey	Acts 21:24
"	of Christ fulfill	Gal. 6:2
"	" god & of sin	Rom. 7:25
"	" liberty	James 2:12
"	" man - not for brother	1 Cor. 6:6–8
"	of spirit vs that of sin & death	Rom. 8:2, 6
"	or faith	Gal. 3:13, 25–29, + 4:4, 5
"	to be fulfilled	Rom. 13:8–10
"	, under the	1 Cor. 9:20, 21
"	, where is - no transgression	Rom. 3:27, 28, + 4:13–16
Lawful		Matt. 12:10, 12, + 19:3; Mark 10:2; 1 Cor.. 6:12, + 10:23
Lawgiver		Isa. 33:22; James 4:12
Laws into hearts & minds		Heb. 10:16
Lawyer		Matt. 22:35
Lawyers per Jesus		Luke 11:45–52, + 14:3
Lawsuits		Prov. 25:8–10; Rom. 12:17; 1 Cor. 6:5, 6
Lay		Ruth 3:4, 8, 14; 2 Sam. 11:4, + 13:14; Prov. 10:14
"	down my life	John 10:15, 17, 18
"	in store	Matt. 6:20; 1 Cor. 16:2
"	up	1 Tim. 6:18, 19; Heb. 6:18
Laying aside		1 Pet. 2:1
"	on of hands	1 Tim. 4:14
Lead good life		1 Tim. 2:2

"	me	Ps. 25:5, + 139:10, 24
"	" by the hand	Ps. 139:5–10, 14; Isa. 11:6; Luke 11:4
Leader departs		John 16:5–16
Leaf		Ps. 1:3; Isa. 64:6
Lean		Prov. 3:5
Leaped		Ps. 18:29; Luke 1:41, 44; Acts 3:8, + 14:10
Learn		Isa. 1:17, + 2:4; 1 Tim. 1:20, + 2:11
Learned of Jesus		Acts 4:13; 2 Tim. 3:14, 15
"	of the Father	John 6:45
Least		Luke 12:26; Eph. 3:8
"	- great	Matt. 5:19; Luke 9:48
"	- much	Luke 16:10
"	of apostles	1 Cor. 15:9
Leather		2 Kings 1:8; Matt. 3:4
Leave		Matt. 18:12; Heb. 13:5
"	all for God's sake	Luke 18:29, 30
"	gift	Matt. 5:24; John 14:27
"	parents	Gen. 2:24; Matt. 19:5
"	thee not	Gen. 28:15
Leaven		Matt. 16:6; Mark 8:15; Luke 13:20, 21; 1 Cor. 5:6–8
Lebanon		Hos. 14:5–7
Led by Lord (spirit)		Isa. 55:12; Matt. 4:1; Rom. 8:14
"	by Jesus	Mark 15:20; Luke 22:54
Ledges		1 Kings 7:35, 36
Leeks		Num. 11:5
Lees		Zeph. 1:12
Left all for Jesus' sake		Mark 10:29, 30; Luke 18:28–30
"	alone	John 8:9
"	handed	Jude 20:16
"	thy first love	Rev. 2:4

Legion	Mark 5:9
Leisure	Mark 6:31
Lend to all	Luke 6:34, 35
Lending	Deut. 15:7, 8; Prov. 22:26, 27; Matt. 5:42, + 23:19, 20
Length	Rom. 1:10
Leopard	Isa. 11:6
Leper	2 Kings 5:27; Mark 1:40–42; Luke 5:12, 13, + 17:12, 13
Lepers	Luke 4:27, + 17:12–19
Leprosy	2 Kings 5:27; Mark 1:42; Luke 5:12, 13
Lesbian, not to be	Rom. 6:12, 13
Less	Eph. 3:8; Mark 15:40
Lesser things, God uses	1 Cor. 1:25–28
Lest	Mark 13:36; Eph. 2:8, 9; Heb. 2:1; James 5:12
Let	Gen. 1:3–26; Ps. 119:76–80; Matt. 5:16, + 26:39; Phil. 2:5; James 1:3, 19, + 5:12–14
Letter	Rom. 2:29; 2 Cor. 3:6; Gal. 6:11; Heb. 13:22
Letters	2 Cor. 10:9–11
Leviathan - assumed to be monster	Job 41:1–34; Ps. 104:26
Lewd	Acts 17:5
Liar	Prov. 30:5, 6; 1 John 1:9, + 2:4, 22, + 4:20
" is devil	John 8:44
Liars	Rev. 2:2
Liberal	Prov. 11:25
Liberality	1 Cor. 16:3; 2 Cor. 8:2
Liberally	James 1:5

Liberty		Isa. 61:1; 2 Cor. 3:17; Heb. 13:23; 1 Pet. 2:16
"	, glorious	Rom. 8:21
"	law	James 2:12
Liberty to flesh & love		Gal. 5:1, 13, + 6:12
"	where spirit is	2 Cor. 3:17; Gal. 5:1
Lice (third plague)		Exod. 8:16–19
Licked		Luke 16:21
Lie		1 John 1:6
"	not	Exod. 20:16; Acts 5:1–4; Col. 3:9
"	" against truth	James 3:14
"	" with	Lev. 18:6–23
"	of Satan	Gen. 3:4
"	with	Gen. 39:7, 10, 12, 14; Num. 5:13; Deut. 22:22, 23, 25, 29
Lied		Isa. 57:11
Lieth down		Job 14:12
Life a ransom		Matt. 20:28
"	abundantly	John 10:10
"	after death	John 1:25, 26
"	and atonement is blood	Lev. 17:11
"	and body	Matt. 6:25
"	and or death	Rom. 8:6; 2 Cor. 4:10–12
"	book	Rev. 21:27
"	by believing	John 3:36, + 11:25, 26, + 14:6, + 20:31
"	, Christian	Rom. 12:1–21; Col. 1:8–18; 1 Thess. 5:11–22
"	, Christian - as pleases God	Phil. 2:1–16

"	, Christ-like - rewarded	Matt. 16:25–27
"	complete	1 Tim. 2:1–4
"	dedicated	2 Cor. 4:11; Phil. 1:20
"	, disciples - worth more than fowls	Luke 12:22–24
"	eternal	Acts 13:47, 48; Rom. 5:21, + 6:23; 1 John 2:25, + 5:11, 13, 20
"	" not in murderer	1 John 3:15
Life	eternal or everlasting punishment	Matt. 25:46
"	everlasting	Matt. 18:8, 9; John 3:15, 16, + 5:24, + 17:3; Rom. 6:23; Gal. 6:7, 8
"	" is God's commandment	John 12:49, 50
"	, find or lose	Matt. 10:39; Mark 8:35; Luke 9:23–25
"	for ceasing to sin	1 John 5:16
"	" ever	1 John 2:17
"	" Father God & Son	John 5:26
"	for life	John 10:17; 2 Cor. 3:6
"	fountain	Ps. 36:9
"	from bones	Ezek. 37:1–10
"	" spirit	2 Cor. 2:6
"	" words	Matt. 4:4; John 6:63
"	, gave-for us	John 3:16
"	- give or take	John 10:17, 18; Rom. 8:6
"	giver is God	1 Chron. 29:11–13
"	, happy - pleases God	Eccles. 9:7
"	, have	John 10:10; 1 John 5:12

"	hereafter - maimed better than whole body	Matt. 18:8, 9
"	in God & in Christ Jesus	John 1:1–4; 2 Tim. 1:1
"	in Him (Jesus)	John 1:4, 5, 7–9
"	is Jesus	John 14:6
"	issues	Prov. 4:23
"	lay it down - take it again	John 10:17, 18
"	more abundantly	John 10:10
"	" than food & raiment	Luke 12:22–24
"	of righteousness by one	Rom. 5:17
"	path	Ps. 16:11
"	- tooth - eye - hand - foot	Exod. 21:23, 24
"	was light	John 1:4, 5, 7–9
"	water	Rev. 21:6
Lifetime		Luke 16:25
Lift up eyes & soul		Ps. 25:1 + 143:8; Isa. 51:6
Lifter		Ps. 3:3
Light and lamp is word		Ps. 119:105, 130
"	, burden is	Matt. 11:30
"	for the righteous	Ps. 97:11
"	" darkness	John 12:35, 35; Eph. 5:8
"	" god's light	Ps. 36:9
"	from candle to be seen	Luke 8:16
"	from darkness	Isa. 58:8; John 12:35, 36; Eph. 5:8

"	- glory of God & lamb - not sun & moon	Rev. 21:23, 24 + 22:5
"	, God is	Ps. 36:9; Isa 58:8
"	is God	1 John 1:5
"	, Lord's	Ps. 119:130; Isa. 42:6, + 60:1, 3, 19, 20; 2 Cor. 4:6
"	, marvellous	Acts 26:13; 1 Pet. 2:9
"	not in men	John 10:10
"	of gentiles	Acts 13:47
"	" God	Gen. 1:3–5; John 1:4, 5
"	" knowledge from God	2 Cor. 4:6
"	of men	John 1:4, 5
"	" world is Jesus	John 8:12, + 9:5
"	" " " us	Matt. 5:14–16; Eph. 5:8, 13–16
"	, thy	Isa. 58:8
Light	to go by	Exod. 13:21
"	" lighten	Luke 2:32; John 1:9; Rev. 21:23
"	" righteous	Ps. 97:11
"	" salvation	Acts 13:47
"	, true	John 1:9
"	, walk in	1 John 1:7
"	was life	John 1:4, 5, 7–9
"	we are	Rom. 2:19; Eph. 5:8; Phil. 2:15
"	witness	John 1:4–9
Lighten	by light	Luke 2:32
"	our eyes	Ezra 9:8
Lighteneth	every man	John 1:6–9
Lightness		2 Cor. 1:17
Lightning		Job 37:3; Jer. 10:13; Matt. 24:27
Ligure		Exod. 28:19

Like		Deut. 33:26, 29; Prov. 17:22, 29, + 23:32; Phil. 3:21
"	Him - Jesus	1 John 3:2, 3
Likeminded		Rom. 15:5, 6; Phil. 2:2, 20
Liken		Isa. 46:5; Matt. 7:24
Likeness		Ezek. 1:26; Rom. 6:5; Phil. 2:7; 1 John 4:17
"	of God made He man	Gen. 5:1
"	" sinful flesh - Jesus	Rom. 8:3
Likewise		Matt. 24:33; Rom. 8:26; Gal. 2:13; 1 Pet. 3:1, + 4:1
Lily		Song of Sol. 2:2; Hos. 14:5
Limbs of people		Matt. 18:8, 9
Line , carpenter's		Isa. 44:13
Linen		Dan. 12:7; 2 Cor. 5:12
Lingereth		2 Pet. 2:3
Lintel		Exod. 12:22, 23
Lion		Gen. 49:9; Job 4:10, 11; Ps. 91:13; Prov. 30:30; Isa. 11:6; Dan. 6:16–23, 27
"	, delivered from	2 Tim. 4:17
"	like is the devil	1 Pet. 5:8
Lip		Ps. 17:1, 4; Prov. 12:19
Lips		Prov. 4:24, + 5:3, + 10:18, 19, 21, + 12:13, 17–22, + 13:3; Matt. 15:8
"	fruit-praise God	Ps. 63:3, 5; Heb. 13:15
"	- no guile	1 Pet. 3:10
"	of righteous feed many	Prov. 10:21
"	shutteth	Prov. 17:28
"	unclean	Isa. 6:5

Liquor		Num. 6:3
Liquors OK for offering		Exod. 22:29
Listen better than talk		Eccles. 5:1–7
"	to Lord - example	1 Sam. 3:1–14
"	" parents	Prov. 4:1–27
Listeneth		John 3:8; James 3:4
Listeth		John 3:8
Little better than riches		Ps. 37:16
"	but wise	Prov. 30:24–31
"	child to God	1 Kings 3:7
"	children	Deut. 1:39; 1 John 5:21
"	" not to perish	Matt. 8:14
"	while	John 16:16–18
Live		2 Cor. 13:11; Gal. 2:20
"	and die	Phil. 1:21
"	" walk in the spirit	Gal. 5:16, 25
"	because of Jesus' suffering	1 Pet. 2:23, 24
"	by believing	John 11:25–27
"	" faith	Hab. 2:4; Gal. 2:20
"	" Jesus	John 11:25
"	" word of God	Matt. 4:4
"	for Him & ourselves	2 Cor. 5:15
"	godly & properly	Rom. 12:1–21; 1 Pet. 4:2, 6
"	God's word	2 Thess. 3:4
"	, I - Jesus	John 14:19, 20
"	in flesh	Phil. 1:21, 22
"	" Lord	Acts 17:28
"	" the spirit	Gal. 5:16, 25; Eph. 4:3, 4
"	is Christ	John 11:25; Phil. 1:20, 21
"	or die	Rom. 14:7, 8
"	peaceably	Rom. 12:18
"	per Jesus	John 14:19

"	righteously	1 Pet. 2:24
"	through Jesus	1 John 4:9
"	unto Him	2 Cor. 5:15
"	with Christ	Gal. 2:20, + 5:24, 25
"	" hope & expectations	Ps. 119:144; Titus 2:11–15
Lively hope		1 Pet. 1:3, + 2:5, 9
Lives - ours for others		1 John 3:16
Liveth and believeth		John 11:26
"	" was dead	Rev. 1:18
"	forever	1 Pet. 1:23
"	unto God	Rom. 6:10; Heb. 7:25
Living God		Dan. 6:26; Matt. 16:16; 1 Tim. 6:17; Heb. 9:14
"	", trust in	1 Tim. 6:17
"	holy is essential	Rom. 12:1; Gal. 5:19–21
"	instructions	Col. 1:9–12; 1 Thess. 5:11–22
"	know they will die	Eccles. 9:5
"	sacrifice	Rom. 12:1
"	soul	Gen. 2:7
"	unto God	Luke 21:4; Rom. 12:1
"	water	John 4:7, 9–15
"	way	Col. 3:8–17; Titus 2:11–15
Lizard		Lev. 11:30
Lo		Gen. 8:11; Matt. 3:16, 17, + 28:20; Mark 13:21, + 17:21; Heb. 10:7, 9
Loathe		Job 7:16
Loatheth		Prov. 27:7
Loathsome		Job 7:5; Ps. 38:7; Prov. 13:5
Loaves		Matt. 15:34; Mark 8:5–9
Locusts (8th plague)		Exod. 10:1–19; Prov. 30:27
Lodge		Ruth 1:16; Song of Sol. 7:12
Lodged		1 Tim. 5:10

Lodging	Philem. 1:22
Lofty	Ps. 131:1
Loins - be girded	Luke 12:35, 37; 1 Pet. 1:13
Long	Rom. 1:11
" life	Prov. 3:1, 2
Longeth	Ps. 63:1
Longing helplessly	Deut. 28:32
Longsuffering	Num. 14:18; Col. 1:11; 2 Tim. 4:2
" of God	Rom. 9:22; 1 Pet. 3:20; 2 Pet. 3:15
" to us - ward	2 Pet. 3:9
Look back - no	Luke 9:62
" for Christ - will get salvation	Heb. 9:28
" forward	Phil. 3:13, 14; Titus 2:11–15
" , high	Prov. 21:4
" not	2 Cor. 4:18
" to Jesus	Phil. 3:20: Heb. 12:1, 2
" " things of others	Phil. 2:4
" up	Luke 21:28
Looked down, God	Ps. 53:3
" , Lord & man	1 Sam. 16:7
Looketh	1 Sam. 16:7
Looking for that hope appearance	Titus 2:13, 14
" glass	Job 37:18
Loose	Matt. 16:19 + 18:18; John 11:44; Acts 24:26
Loosed	Judg. 15:14; Matt. 18:18, 27; Luke 1:64; Acts 2:24
Looseth	Ps. 146:7
Lop	Isa. 10:33

Lord be praised in worship
    service   Ps. 111:1
"   cometh with his
     saints - prophesied   1 Thess. 4:16, 17; Jude 1:14
"   coming like rain   Joel 2:23; 2 Pet. 3:10–12
"   deserves glory   Ps. 29:1–11; Prov. 96:4
"   does many various
     things   Ps. 146:5–10
"   feareth - to be
     praised   Prov. 31:30, 31
"   God Almighty   Isa. 43:10–15
"   - great king   Ps. 47:2
"   hates seven things   Prov. 6:16–19
"   is alpha & omega   Rev. 1:8
"   " everything   2 Sam. 22:23; Ps. 27:1;
                            Rev. 1:17, 18
"   " God   Lev. 7:9; Ps. 100:3; Jer. 16:9
"   " Jehovah   Isa. 6:4
"   " Jesus Christ   Matt. 22:43–45; John 9:35–39 +
                            13:15; Acts 10:36; Phil. 2:5–11
"   " light everlasting   Isa. 60:19, 20
"   " my strength -
     song - salvation   Ps. 18:2, 6, + 118:14
"   is only one Lord   Zech. 14:3–5, 9; 1 Cor. 1:9;
                            Eph. 4:5
"   " our Father   Isa. 64:8
"   " same to all   Rom. 10:12, 13
"   " spirit   2 Cor. 3:17
"   " worthy   Rev. 4:11
"   Jesus Christ   Rom. 6:23
"   Judgeth me   1 Cor. 4:4, 5
"   knoweth His   2 Tim. 2:19
"   liveth   Jer. 23:8

"	, Lord	Matt. 7:21
"	, " - call me this & do not obey	Luke 6:46
"	made heaven & earth	Ps. 115:15
"	meek & lowly in heart	Matt. 11:28–30
"	, must live peaceably to see	Heb. 12:14
"	none else	Isa. 45:18
"	of all	Acts 10:36
"	" Lords	Jer. 16:9; Rev. 17:14, + 19:16
"	or our body	2 Cor. 5:6–8
"	repented	Gen. 6:6
"	saves	Acts 2:21
"	- saviour only	Isa. 43:11
"	see - holiness required	Heb. 12:14
"	seekers not wanting	Ps. 34:10
"	to be praised	Ps. 146:1–10
"	" the living & to the dead	Rom. 14:8, 9
Lords		Ps. 24:1; 1 Pet. 5:3
Lord's	body resurrected	Luke 24:39, 40, 42, 43; John 20:19, + 21:9–13; also see Section BB
"	Care for us:	
	rests us	Ps. 23:1, 2
	leads "	Ps. 23:2, 3
	feeds "	Ps. 23:4, 5
	keeps "	Ps. 23:6
"	face not seen	Exod. 33:20, 22, 23
"	law is perfect	Ps. 19:7
"	prayer	Matt. 6:9–13; Luke 11:2–4

"	spirit	2 Cor. 3:17
"	traits are perfect	Ps. 19:7–9
"	, we are	Rom. 14:8
"	works are great	Ps. 111:2–9
Lordship		Luke 22:35
Lose all for Jesus Christ		Phil. 3:7–11, + 4:6–8
"	and find	Luke 15:3–32
"	" gain	Mark 8:36
"	or save life	Matt. 16:25; Mark 8:35; Luke 9:25, + 17:33
Loss		Phil. 3:8
Lost		Ps. 119:176; Luke 15:24, + 19:10
Lot		Gen. 13:10, + 19:14–18; Ps. 16:5; 2 Pet. 2:7
Lot's days		Luke 17:28, 29
"	wife	Gen. 19:26; Luke 17:32
Loud		Matt. 27:46, 50; John 11:43
Love		1 John 3:1, + 4:7, 8, 10–12, 16–21
"	abound	Phil. 1:9
"	and good works	Luke 6:31–38
"	brethren	1 John 3:14, 15, + 4:20, 21
"	brings knowledge & judgment	Phil. 1:9
"	, brotherly	Rom. 12:10; Heb. 13:1, 2
"	by Jesus & Father	John 14:21, 23
"	chapter - charity	1 Cor. 13:1–13
"	, Christian	1 Cor. 12:14
"	, Christ's - better than knowledge	Eph. 3:19
"	enemies	Matt. 5:44
"	" - get reward	Luke 6:31–37
"	everlasting	Jer. 31:3

"	for keeping commandments	John 14:21
"	God for good	Rom. 8:28
"	" is loving brother	1 John 4:21
"	"- love children of God	1 John 5:2
"	" rewarded	Rom. 8:28
"	, God's	Ps. 103:11–14
"	, " - toward us	Rom. 5:8; 1 John 4:16–21
"	gospel truth is important to know	2 Thess. 2:10, 11
"	, greater	John 15:12, 13
Love, greatest		John 3:15, 16
"	indeed & truth	1 John 3:18
"	is	John 3:15, 16; 1 John 4:7–12, 16, 20, 21
"	" God	1 John 4:8
"	" of God & from God	2 Tim. 1:7; 1 John 4:7
"	Jesus	John 14:21, 23, 24
"	" not then don't obey	John 14:24
"	, magnitude of	1 John 4:7–12
"	may abound	Phil. 1:9
"	me (Jesus) will obey me	John 14:15, 21, 23
"	more than offerings and sacrifices	Mark 12:32, 33
"	much	Luke 7:44–48
"	" not painless	Luke 22:39–46
"	neighbor	Matt. 22:39; James 2:8
"	not the Lord, if	1 Cor. 16:22
"	" world	John 15:19; 1 John 2:15–17
"	of Christ & God	Rom. 8:35–39

"	" God is in Christ Jesus	Rom. 8:39
"	of God is most important	Rom. 8:38, 39
"	of God (see ten commandments)	Deut. 5:1–21
"	of God toward man	Titus 3:4–7
"	" Jesus is great to the Father	John 14:30, 31
"	of God saves lives	1 Tim. 1:15
"	" world	John 15:19
"	one another	John 13:34, 35, + 15:12, 17; 1 Thess. 4:9; 1 Pet. 1:22
"	or hatred	Mark 10:12
"	, perfect	1 John 4:17–21
"	proof	Rom. 5:8; John 14:21, 23
"	, our - same as God's love	1 John 4:7–12, 16–21
"	, secret	Prov. 27:5
"	self	Prov. 25:14; Matt. 23; 12; Rom. 12:3; 1 Cor. 4:6, 19; Gal. 6:3
"	truth - saves	2 Thess. 2:10
"	- we must love God	Rom. 8:31, 38, 39
Loved us		1 John 4:10
Lover of hospitality & good people		Titus 1:8
Lovers		Hos. 8:9
"	of God have great future	1 Cor. 2:9
"	of God to be saved	Ps. 145:20
"	" pleasures or God	2 Tim. 3:4
"	" self at last time	2 Tim. 3:1–5
Loveth a friend		Prov. 17:17

" not	John 14:24; 1 John 4:8
" others is born of	
God	1 John 4:7–12
Lovingkindness	Ps. 36:7, 10, + 40:11, + 42:8, + 51:1, + 63:3; Isa. 63:7; Jer. 31:3
Low and high things	Rom. 12:16
Lowest	Ps. 139:15; Luke 14:9, 10
Lowliness	Phil. 2:3
Lowly be	Phil. 2:1–9
" gets grace	Prov. 3:34
Loyal to God or Satan	Rev. 12:12
Lucifer	Isa. 14:12–17; Ezek. 28:5–9, 15–19
Lucre	1 Tim. 3:3, 8; Titus 1:11; 1 Pet. 5:2
Luke - physician - author Book of Luke and Acts	Acts. 1:1–4; Phil. 1:23, 24; Col. 4:14
Luke's genealogy	Luke 3:38
Lukewarm	Rev. 3:16
Lump	Rom. 9:21+ 11:16; 1 Cor. 5:6, 7; Gal. 5:9
Lunatic	Matt. 17:15
Lurk	1 Sam. 23:23; Ps. 17:12; Prov. 1:11
Lust	1 Sam. 11:1–27; Matt. 5:28; Gal. 5:17–21; 1 Thess. 4:3–5; James 1:1–3; 1 Pet. 2:11; 1 John 2:15–17
" - sin - death	James 1:14, 15
" walking	Jude 1:16

Lusts of body	Rom. 6:12, + 13:14; 1 Cor. 10:6; James 4:1–5
" " flesh	Rom. 1:24–27, + 13:14; Eph. 2:3; 1 Pet. 2:11, 12; 2 Pet. 2:10, 18, + 3:3; 1 John 1:15–17
" " women	Prov. 5:3–6, + 6:24–26, 32; Rom. 1:26, 27
Lying	Prov. 6:16, 17, 19, + 7:1–27, + 12:19, 22, + 19:5, + 26:28; Eph. 4:25; Col. 3:9, 10
" tongue	Prov. 21:6

· M ·

Mad		1 Sam. 2:14, 15; Jer. 50:38; Acts 12:15 + 26:24, 25
Made		Gen. 1:7, 16 + 2:2, 3, 9
"	by God is good	Gen. 1:31
"	" Spirit of God	Job 33:4; Ps. 119:13, 14
"	day	Gen. 1:3–5, 8, 13, 16, 18, 19, 23 + 2:2, 3; Ps. 118:24
"	, everything - by God	Gen. 1:31; Ps. 146:5, 6; Eccles. 3:11; John 1:3
"	heaven & earth	Ps. 134:3
"	in likeness of men	Phil. 2:7
"	" righteousness	2 Cor. 5:21
"	known	John 15:15
"	me	Job 33:4; Ps. 119:73
"	toward	Acts 27:40
"	us - by Lord	Ps. 139:14, 17; Isa. 64:8
"	whole	Matt. 15:28; Mark 5:34; Luke 17:19
"	worlds	Heb. 1:2
Madest		Ps. 8:6
Magic - sorceries		Isa. 47:12
Magicians		Dan. 2:2, 10, 27

Magistrates	Luke 12:11, 58; Acts 16:20, 25, 38; Titus 3:1
Magnified in me is Christ	Phil. 1:20
Magnify God	Ps. 70:4; Luke 1:46
" law	Isa. 42:21
" self - king	Dan. 11:36, 37
Magnitude of Christ's love	Eph. 3:16–19
" " God's love	1 John 4:7–12
Maid	Esther 2:7; Matt. 9:24, 25
Maidservant	Jer. 34:9, 10
Maimed all right with God	Matt. 18:8, 9
" not accepted as offering	Lev. 22:22
Mainsail	Acts 27:40
Maintainest	Ps. 16:5
Majesty	Dan. 5:18, 19
Make	Gen. 1:26 + 2:18 + 6:14; Ps. 39:4, 8; 2 Pet. 1:8, 10
" a way	Isa. 43:19
" free by truth	John 8:32; Col. 1:27
" haste	Ps. 38:22
Maker	Ps. 95:6; Isa. 22:4 + 54:5
Maketh	Rom. 8:34
" by carpenter	Isa. 44:13
" from the beginning	Eccles. 3:11
Making request	Rom. 1:10
Male	Gen. 1:29
" - first is holy to the Lord	Luke 2:23
Malefactors	Luke 23:32, 33, 39
Malicious words	3 John 1:10
Maliciousness	1 Pet. 2:16
Mallows	Job 30:4
Mammon	Matt. 6:24

Man		Ps. 8:4–6; Jer. 31:22
"	am I - Peter	Acts 10:26
"	- animal similarity	Eccles. 3:19, 20
"	became	Gen. 2:7
"	created	Gen. 1:26, 27 + 2:7, 21–23 + 5:1, 2
"	days are 120 years	Gen. 6:3
"	- dominion over God's works	Ps. 8:4–8
"	- father is God	Matt. 23:8–10
"	feareth Lord to be blessed	Ps. 128:4, 5
"	, first & second	1 Cor. 15:47–50
"	first then woman	Gen. 1:27 + 2:21–23; 1 Cor. 11:7–11
"	- greatest on earth is John the Baptist	Matt. 11:11
"	- holy	2 Pet. 1:21
Man in heaven		Mark 14:62
"	, inner	Eph. 1:16 + 3:16–9; 1 Pet. 3:4
"	, inward & outward	1 Sam. 16:7; 2 Cor. 4:16
"	- living soul	Gen. 2:7
"	made in image of God	Gen. 9:6
"	most precious	Isa. 13:12
"	, natural	Rom. 1:28–32 + 8:36–39; 1 Cor. 2:14
"	nature & need	Gen. 1:26–31
"	, new & old	Rom. 7:6; Eph. 4:24, 25; Col. 3:9, 10
"	new, gets peace	Eph. 4:14–18
"	not to glory in being rich	Jer. 9:23, 24
"	of sin to be revealed	2 Thess. 2:3, 4

"	, old - died with Christ	Rom. 6:6 + 7:4–6; Col. 3:9, 10
"	perfect with tongue	James 3:2
"	, poor wise	Eccles. 9:15
"	- wife believe differently	1 Cor. 7:12, 13
"	- woman	Gen. 2:23
"	, young - enjoy wife & be true to her	Prov. 5:18–21
Mandrakes		Gen. 30:14 –16
Manger		Luke 2:7, 12, 16
Manhood from youth		1 Cor. 13:11, 12
Manifest		John 3:21; Acts 4:16; 2 Cor. 4:10, 11 + 5:11, 19; Heb. 4:13
"	by light	Eph. 5:13
"	for us	1 Pet. 1:20
"	in flesh - God	1 Tim. 3:16; 2 Tim. 1:16
"	- Jesus in our body	John 14:21; 2 Cor. 4:8–11
"	them	Eccles. 3:18
"	to saints	Col. 1:26
Manifestation		1 Cor. 12:7
Manifested		John 17:6; 1 John 1:2 + 3:8 + 4:9
"	, love of God	1 John 4:7–12
Manifold		Amos 5:12; Ps. 104:24; 1 Pet. 1:6 + 4:10
Mankind		1 Cor. 6:9; 1 Tim. 1:10
Manna		Ps. 78:24; John 6:49; Rev. 2:17
Manner		Gen. 18:11, 25; Lev. 7:23, 26, 27; Matt. 4:23; Luke 12:25
"	of love	1 John 3:1
"	" men	1 Thess. 1:5
"	" sickness	Matt. 4:23

" " sin	Matt. 12:31
Manners	1 Cor. 15:33
Man's fruit & work	Ps. 1:1–3; 1 Cor. 3:13–15
Manservant	Jer. 34:9, 10
Mansions	John 14:2
Mantle	Job 2:12
Many	Mark 6:31; John 1:2
Mar	Job 30:13
Marble	Esther 1:6
Mark - a reporter wrote	
book of Mark	Phil. 3:14; 1 Pet. 5:13
" for the arrow	Lam. 3:12
" not on foreheads	Rev. 20:4
" of the beast	Rev. 13:16–18 + 19:20 + 20:4, 5
" " " " on	
person - suffer	Rev. 14:9, 10 + 16:2
Marketh	Isa. 44:13
Marketplace	Luke 7:32
Marks - none on body	Lev. 19:28
Marred	Isa. 52:14
Marriage	Gen. 2:24; Eccles. 9:9;
	Matt. 19:4–6 + 22:2, 4, 9, 30;
	John 2:1, 2; Heb. 13:4
" again	Exod. 21:10, 11
Married but all right not	
to be married	1 Cor. 7:7–9
" not is more holy	1 Cor. 7:33
" twice	Rom. 7:3
" woman & virgin	1 Cor. 7:28, 34–40
Marrow	Job 21:24; Ps. 63:5; Prov. 3:8
Marry	Isa. 62:5; Matt. 22:30;
	Mark 12:23; 1 Cor. 7:9
" not after risen from	
dead	Mark 12:25

"	" in heaven (resurrection)	Matt. 22:30
Martyr		Acts 22:20
Martyrs		Rev. 6:9 + 20:4
"	all killed then Christ's reign	Rev. 6:9–11, 13–17 + 20:4–9
Marvel		Gal. 1:6; Acts 3:12
"	not	John 3:7 + 5:28
Marvelled		Matt. 9:8; Mark 15:44; John 4:27
Marvellous		Zech. 8:6
"	light	1 Pet. 2:9
"	things	Job 5:9
"	works	2 Chron. 26:15; Ps. 9:1 + 31:21 + 105:5; Rev. 15:1,3
"	" of God	Job 5:9; Ps. 31:21 + 105:5
Mary	among women	Luke 1:28, 42
"	- mother of Jesus	Matt. 1:16–25 + 2:11–14, 20, 21; Luke 1:27, 30, 34, 38, 39, 41, 46, 56 + 2:5, 16, 19
Masons		2 Kings 12:22; 2 Chron. 24:12
Mast		Isa. 33:23
Master		Luke 6:40
"	is Jesus Christ	Matt. 23:10; John 13:13; 1 Tim. 2:5, 6
"	, only one - and his complete care	Matt. 6:24–34 + 23:10; 1 Tim. 2:5, 6
Masterbuilder, earthly		1 Kings 7:13–32; 1 Cor. 3:10
"	of God's foundation	1 Cor. 3:9–14
Masteries		2 Tim. 2:5
Mastery		1 Cor. 9:25
Materialism		Eccles. 5:10; Matt. 6:19–21, 24; Luke 12:15–21; 1 Tim. 6:9, 10

Matter	Dan. 2:21; Eccles. 12:13; Mark 10:10
Matthew - tax collector - gospel writer - book of Matthew	Matt. 9:9
Matthias replaced Judas as Apostle	Acts 1:26
Maul	Prov. 25:18
May be perfect	2 Tim. 3:17
" give by Father	John 15:16
Mayest	Ps. 130:4; 3 John 1:2
Me	Ps. 33:4, 5; Jer. 29:12, 13; Phil. 4:13
" - made well by God	Job 33:4; Ps. 119:73
Means	Ps. 49:7; Mal. 1:9; Acts 4:9
Measure	Ps. 39:4; Mark 4:24; Luke 6:38; Rev. 6:6
Meat, eat	Gen. 9:2, 3; Ps. 69:21; John 21:5–13; Acts 27:34, 36; 1 Tim. 4:1–6
" for Jesus	John 4:32, 34
" not important	Rom. 14:17, 20, 21; Heb. 13:9
" perishes	John 6:27
" , strong	Heb. 5:12, 14
" unknown	John 4:32, 34
Meats, clean & unclean	Lev. 11:1–47
Meddle	Prov. 20:19
Meddling	Prov. 20:3 + 26:17
Mediator of New Testament	Heb. 9:15
" , one	Gal. 3:19, 20; 1 Tim. 2:5; Heb. 8:6 + 9:15, 28; 1 John 3:2
" medicine	Prov. 17:22
" for eyes	Rev. 3:18
" " good health	Prov. 3:7, 8

Mediate		Ps. 77:12 + 119:15; 1 Tim. 4:15
"	always - will prosper	Ps. 1:1–3
"	in God's law	Josh. 1:8; Ps. 1:1–3
Meditation		Ps. 49:3 + 104:34 + 119:97
Meek		Isa. 61:1; Matt. 5:5 + 11:29; Gal. 6:1
"	and lowly	Matt. 11:29
"	inherit the earth & get peace	Ps. 37:11; Matt. 5:5
"	spirit	1 Pet. 3:4
Meekness		Titus 3:2; 1 Pet. 3:15
Meet		1 Cor. 15:9; 1 Thess. 4:17; 1 Tim. 2:21
Melchizedek order		Gen. 14:18; Ps. 110:4; Heb. 5:6, 10 + 6:20 + 7:1, 10, 11, 17, 21
Melody, making		Eph. 5:18–21
Melt, elements of heaven and earth		2 Pet. 3:10
Melteth		Ps. 119:28
Member - parts of body		1 Cor. 6:15 + 12:12–26; James 3:5, 6
Members of Christ's body		1 Cor. 6:15 + 12:27–31; Eph. 4:25 + 5:30
"	one body	Rom. 12:4,5
"	" of another	Eph. 4:25
Memorial		Exod. 12:14; Matt. 26:13; Mark 14:9
Memorize word		Ps. 119:11; Prov. 4:10
Memory		Ps. 145:7; 1 Cor. 15:2
Men are flock of God		Exod. 34:31
"	compared to God	1 Cor. 1:25
"	, conduct of aged	Titus 2:2

"	, Jesus knew all	John 2:24, 25
"	pray	1 Tim. 2:8
"	, sons and daughters	Acts 2:17; 2 Cor. 6:18
"	, unmarried	Gen. 5:21, 27
"	, young	Titus 2:6
Menpleasers		Col. 3:22
Mention		Ps. 87:4; Isa. 62:6; Rom. 1:9; Philem. 1:4
Merchandise		Deut. 24:7; Isa. 45:14; 1 Pet. 2:3; Rev. 18:10–19
Merchant		Matt. 13:45
Merciful		Exod. 34:6; Ps. 41:4, 10 + 57:1; Matt. 5:7; Luke 6:36
"	cruel	Prov. 11:17
Mercy, abundant		1 Pet. 1:3; Jude 1:2
"	endureth forever	1 Chron. 20:21; Ps. 136:1–26 + 138:8
"	everlasting	Ps. 100:5 + 103:17
"	for confessing sins	Prov. 28:13
"	" God lovers	Deut. 7:9; Ps. 32:10
"	of God	Ps. 52:8 + 57:3, 9 + 103:11–17
"	" " saved us	Titus 3:5
"	" the lord on earth	Ps. 119:64; Isa. 55:7
"	to faithful	Exod. 20:6
"	" poor - reward	Dan. 4:27
"	when need	Heb. 4:14–16
Merry		Prov. 15:13, 15
"	heart is good	Prov. 13–15 + 17:22
Message		Hag. 1:13; 1 John 1:5
"	for Christian living	Col. 1:8–17
Messengers		Josh. 7:22; Mark 1:2
Messiah - Jesus		Dan. 9:25; John 1:41 + 4:5–26
Messias		John 1:41 + 4:25, 26

Metals and clay	Dan. 2:45
Mete	Matt. 7:2; Luke 6:38
Meteyard	Lev. 19:35
Methuselah - oldest person	Gen. 5:21, 22, 25–27
Michael the Archangel	Dan. 10:13, 21; Jude 1:9
Midday	1 Kings 18:29
Midnight	Acts 16:25
Midst	Exod. 3:2; Ps. 46:2; Isa. 12:5 + 58:9
Midwife	Exod. 1:15–21
Might	Num. 14:13; Deut. 6:5; Eccles. 9:10; Matt. 8:28 + 12:10; John 10:10 + 14:29 + 15:11; + 16:33 + 20:31; 1 Cor. 9:19–23
" by spirit	Mic. 3:8; Eph. 3:16; 1 Pet. 1:21
" , his (Lord Jesus)	Eph. 6:10
" not sin	Ps. 119:11
Mightier	Num. 14:12
Mightily	Jude 15:14; Col. 1:29
Mighty	Deut. 10:17; Jer. 9:23 + 3:33; 1 Pet. 5:6
" angels	2 Thess. 1:7
" are God's wonders	Dan. 4:2, 3
" God	Isa. 9:6
" is Lord God	Ps. 93:1–5 + 95:3–7; Isa. 42:13
" man	Jude 6:12
" one	Isa. 10:34 + 40:26; Mark 1:7
Mildew	2 Chron. 6:28; Hag. 2:17
Mile	Matt. 5:41
Milk	Exod. 3:8, 17; Jer. 11:5; 1 Cor. 3:2
Milk user	Heb. 5:12, 13
Millstone	Deut. 24:6; Job 41:24; Matt. 18:6; Luke 17:2

243

Mind, double		James 4:8
"	in us as in Christ	Phil. 2:2–5; 1 Pet. 4:1
"	, life or death	Rom. 8:6
Mind on God		Isa. 26:3
"	, one & pure	Rom. 15:6; Phil. 1:27; 1 Pet. 3:8
"	, own	Rom. 12:16
"	, renew	Rom. 12:2; Eph. 4:23, 24
"	, reprobate	Rom. 1:28; 2 Tim. 3:8
"	, same	Rom. 12:16; 1 Cor. 1:10
"	, sound - from God	2 Tim. 1:7
"	, willing	2 Cor. 8:12
Minded, carnally or spiritually		Rom. 8:6, 7; Phil. 3:15, 16
"	, double	James 1:8 + 4:8
Mindful		2 Tim. 1:4; 2 Pet. 3:2
Minds		Acts 14:2; 2 Cor. 3:14
"	, changed	Acts 28:6
Mingled		Lev. 7:12; Rev. 15:2
Mine		Ps. 16:5 + 50:10–12; Eccles. 3:17, 18; John 14:24
Minister by God's strength & power		Eph. 3:7
"	by us believers	Matt. 20:26, 28; 1 Tim. 4:6
"	per own ability	1 Pet. 4:11
"	same gift to another	1 Pet. 4:10
"	to remind brethren	1 Tim. 4:6
"	" saints - Paul	Rom. 15:25; 2 Cor. 9:1, 10
"	" saved	Heb. 1:13, 14
Ministered by angels		Matt. 4:11
"	" one healed	Mark 1:31
"	to us	2 Tim. 1:11
Ministering spirits		Heb. 1:13, 14
Ministers		1 Cor. 3:5 + 4:1; 2 Cor. 3:6

" of God in us	Rom. 12:7; 2 Cor. 6:4–10
" to be observed	Heb. 13:7
" , true	Prov. 9:9, 10
Ministration	2 Cor. 3:7–9 + 9:13
Ministry work	2 Cor. 6:3; Eph. 4:12
Mint	Matt. 23:23
Miracle, Jesus' first	John 2:3–11
" , " second	John 4:46–54
Miracles	John 9:16 + 12:37
" by Stephen	Acts 6:8
" , divers	Heb. 2:4
" , Jesus doeth many	John 3:2 + 11:47
" listed	See section MM
" of devil	Rev. 16:13, 14
Mire	Jer. 38:6; 2 Pet. 2:22
Miry clay	Ps. 40:2
Mirror	Job 37:18
Miscarrying	Hos. 9:14
Mischief	Exod. 21:23, 24; Ps. 38:12; Prov. 10:33; Acts 13:10
" by two kings	Dan. 11:27
" is sport to a fool	Prov. 10:23
" of wicked	Prov. 4:14–16 + 12:21 + 14:16 + 24:16 + 28:14; Mark 11:27
Miseries of rich	James 5:1–3
Misery	Job 11:16; Eccles. 8:6
Mission	Ps. 98:1, 4–6; 2 Cor. 4:15–18
" of God	Ps. 96:13
" " God's son	1 John 3:8
" " Jesus	John 3:17 + 4:34; 1 John 4:10
" " ours	Ps. 98:1–9 + 100:1–5; Eccles. 12:13, 14; 1 Cor. 6:20
Missionary verse	Gen. 12:1; Mark 16:15; Acts 7:3

" works of Jesus	Matt. 4:23
Mist	2 Pet. 2:17
Mistress	Ps. 123:2
Mites	Mark 12:42
Mitre	Lev. 8:7, 9
Mixture	John 19:39
Mock	Prov. 14:9 + 17:5; Matt. 20:19; Luke 14:29 + 23:36
Mocked	Job 12:4 + 13:9; Mark 15:20; Luke 18:32 + 23:11, 36; Gal. 6:7
Mockers in last times	Jude 1:17, 18
Mocking	Mark 15:31
Moderation	Phil. 4:5
Moisture	Ps. 32:4
Molten image	Deut. 27:15; Isa. 44:10; Jer. 10:14
Moment	Ps. 30:5; 1 Cor. 15:52
Money	Gen. 42:25, 27, 28, 35 + 43:12, 15, 23 + 44:1, 2; Job 42:11
" failed	Gen. 47:15, 16
" for good only	Ps. 15:5
" in fish mouth	Matt. 17:27
" , love of	1 Tim. 6:10
" no value at end	Ezek. 7:19; James 5:1–3
" perish	Acts 8:20
Month	Exod. 12:22, 23
Months	Exod. 2:2
" are numbered	Job 14:5
Moon	Gen. 1:14–18 + 37:9; Ps. 104:19; Isa. 60:19, 20
" , new	2 Chron. 2:4
Moral virtues	Prov. 13:1–25

Morality free from its shackles	Rom. 8:19–21
More	Gen. 17:5; Prov. 21:3; 1 Cor. 12:31
" than first	Rev. 2:19
Moreover	1 Sam. 12:23; Matt. 6:16; Acts 11:12
Morning	Gen. 1:5–31; Isa. 21:12
Morrow	Matt. 6:34; Acts 22:30; James 4:13, 14
Morsel	Prov. 23:8
Mortal	1 Cor. 15:53, 54
Mortality	2 Cor. 5:4
Mortgage	Neh. 5:2–4
Mortify	Col. 3:5
Moses	Exod. 2:1–10
" healthy to end	Deut. 34:7
" hid three months	Heb. 11:23
Moses' commandment & law	Josh. 22:5
" covenant	Gen. 9:15
" death	Deut. 34:5–12
" law	Neh. 10:29; Luke 24:27, 44
Most high - lord	Ps. 47:2
Mote in eye	Matt. 7:4, 5; Luke 6:41, 42
Moth	Matt. 6:20; James 5:2
Motheaten	James 5:2
Mother	Gen. 3:20; Prov. 1:8 + 31:27–31; Isa. 49:15 + 66:13; Mark 3:35
" and brethren same to Jesus	Luke 8:21
" " father to be honored	Deut. 5:16

"	of Jesus	Matt. 12:50; Mark 3:31, 32, 35; Luke 8:20, 21; John 2:1–5
"	" one proved	1 Kings 3:16–28
Mount of Olives		John 8:1
"	" " is a sight of last days	Zech. 14:3–5
"	, sermon on	Matt. 5:1–13 + 7:29
Mountain		Ps. 40:1–3; Mic. 4:1, 2; Matt. 18:12; John 6:3, 15
"	, sermon on	Matt. 5:1 + 7:29
Mourn		1 Sam. 16:1; Matt. 5:4; Mark 16:10
Mourning to joy		Isa. 61:2, 3; Jer. 31:13
Mouse		Lev. 11:29
Mouth		Job 4:3; Ps. 17:3 + 51:15; Prov. 8:1–9 + 18:4, 6; Eph. 4:29 + 5:4
"	confess	Rom. 10:9
"	disuse, destruction by	Prov. 13:3
"	for confession	Rom. 10:8–10
"	, froward	Prov. 4:24
"	God's word & prosper	John 1:7, 8; Isa. 33:11–13; Prov. 31:8, 9
"	not to be filthy	Col. 3:8
"	of holy prophets	Acts 3:21
"	" hypocrites	Prov. 11:9, 10
"	praise thee	Ps. 63:5
Mouth's		
	control	Prov. 13:2, 3
"	fruit	Prov. 13:2, 3 + 18:20
Moveable		Prov. 5:6
Moved by Holy Ghost		2 Pet. 1:21

" , righteous never	Ps. 55:22
Moving things meat for man	Gen. 9:3
Mower	Ps. 129:7
Much	Luke 12:48; Heb. 9:14; James 5:16
Mulberry	2 Sam. 5:23, 24
Mule	1 Kings 1:33; Esther 8:10, 14; Ps. 32:9; Ezek. 27:14
Multiplied	Ps. 16:4; Dan. 6:25; 1 Pet. 1:2; 2 Pet. 1:2
Multiply	Gen. 17:2; Deut. 30:16; Heb. 6:14
Multitude	Ps. 51:1 + 69:13, 16; Matt. 4:25 + 14:14 + 15:30 + 26:55; Mark 4:1, 36; Luke 6:18; John 21:6
" of sins	James 5:20
Multitudes	Joel 3:14; Matt. 4:25 + 5:1+ 8:1; Rev. 17:15
Murder	Hos. 6:9; Matt. 19:18
Murderer hath not eternal life	1 John 3:15
Murmer	Num. 14:2, 27, 29; John 6:41 + 7:12; 1 Cor. 10:10
Murmerers	Jude 1:16
Murrain (fifth plague)	Exod. 9:3–7
Muse	Ps. 143:5
Mused	Luke 3:15
Music	Gen. 4:21; 1 Sam. 16:23; Ps. 100:1 + 104:33, 34
" to the lord	Ps. 33:2, 3 + 92:1, 3 + 96:1, 2 + 98:4–6 + 100:1 + 104:33, 34

Musical instruments	Ps. 98:4–6 + 150:3–5; Dan. 3:5, 7, 10, 15
Musick	2 Chron. 34:12; Luke 15:25
Musing	Ps. 39:3
Must	John 3:7, 14, 30; Acts 21:22
Mustard seed	Matt. 17:20; Mark 4:31, 32
Mustered	Isa. 13:4
Mutter	Isa. 8:19
Mutual	Rom. 1:12
Muzzle	1 Cor. 9:9; 1 Tim. 5:18
My (words - truth -	Ps. 18:2
" determination -	Ps. 17:1–3
Cross - life)	John 15:7–16; Phil. 1:20
" blood	Matt. 26:28
" God - my God	Exod. 33:14; Ruth 1:16; Ps. 118:14, 28; Matt. 27:46
Myrrh	Ps. 45:8; Prov. 7:17; Matt. 2:11
Myrtle tree	Isa. 55:13
Myself - Adam	Gen. 3:10
" , comforted	Ps. 119:52; Acts 24:16
" - Jesus	Luke 24:39–43
" know nothing	1 Cor. 4:4
" - Peter	Acts 10:26
Mysteries	Matt. 13:11; 1 Cor. 4:1
Mystery fellowship preaches	Eph. 3:8, 9
" of God	Eccles. 3:11; Rom. 16:25; Col. 1:26, 27; 1 Cor. 2:7: + 4:1 + 15:51; Eph. 3:3, 4, 9
" " " acknow- ledged	Col. 2:2; Rev. 10:7
" of godliness	1 Tim. 3:16
" " gospel	Rom. 16:25; Eph. 6:19

· N ·

Nail to cross	Col. 2:14
Nails	Eccles. 12:11
Naked	Gen. 2:25 + 3:7, 10; Job 1:21; Ezek. 16:7; Matt. 25:36; 1 Tim. 6:7; Rev. 16:15
" are all creatures to God	Heb. 4:13
Nakedness	Ezek. 16:8; Gen. 9:22, 23; Lev. 20:17–21
Name	Matt. 1:21, 23, 25; Luke 1:5, 13, 27, 31, 49, 61, 63; John 1:6; 1 John 5:13
" being good is preferable	Eccles. 7:1
" , blessed be - of Lord God	Ps. 72:19
" declared earth - wise	Rom. 9:17
" is Lord	Isa. 42:8
" " word of God	Rev. 19:13
" of God saves	Ps. 54:1, 6
" " Lord is Holy - reverend & powerful	Ps. 111:9; Mark 16:17; Acts 8:12

"	on foreheads	Rev. 22:4
"	(Son of God) through faith healed one	Acts 3:16
Named among you		Eph. 5:3
"	everything	Gen. 2:19, 20
Namely		Deut. 4:43; Jude 3:3; Mark 12:31
Names blotted out		Exod. 32:33
"	in Book of Life	Rev. 21:27
"	to everything	Gen. 2:19, 20
Napkin		John 11:44
Narrow		Matt. 7:14
Nation began by God		Gen. 12:1, 2
"	, blessed is the	Ps. 33:12
"	exalted by righteousness	Prov. 14:34 + 16:12
"	should look to the Lord	Ps. 33:12–16
"	verses nation	Matt. 24:7
Nations, godly - to be blessed		Exod. 33:13; Ps. 33:12
"	manners	Lev. 20:23
"	nothing without God	Isa. 40:15, 17
"	, ten - of Europe	Dan. 7:8–10; Rev. 17:17
"	to be made	Gen. 35:11
"	" " taught	Mic. 4:2; Matt. 28:19
"	, ungodly - will perish	Isa. 60:12
Native		Jer. 22:10
Nativity		Ezek 16:3, 4
Natural man		1 Cor. 2:14
"	things - knowledge	Job 28:1–11

" use of men & women abused	Rom. 1:24–27
Naturally	Phil. 2:20
Nature	Rom. 1:26; 1 Cor. 11:14; Eph. 2:3
" and God	Ps. 65:9–13
" , divine for us not world corruption	2 Pet. 1:3, 4
Naught	2 Kings 2:19
Naughtiness	Prov. 11:6; James 1:21
Naughty	Prov. 6:12; James 1:21
Naval	Prov. 3:8
Naves	1 Kings 7:33
Navy	1 Kings 9:26, 27
Nay and yea	Matt. 5:37; Luke 13:3; Rom. 8:37; 2 Cor. 1:17–20; James 5:12
Nazareth	Matt. 21:11; Luke 1:26 + 4:16
Near to God	Ps. 73:28
" us, Lord	Zeph. 1:14, 15; Acts 17:27, 28
Necessary	Acts 15:28 + 28:10; 2 Cor. 9:5
Necessity	2 Cor. 9:7
Neck	Gen. 33:4; Ps. 75:5; Prov. 29:1; Luke 15:20
Necromancer	Deut. 18:11
Need	Luke 12:30; Acts 2:45; Heb. 4:16
" for help	Heb. 4:16
" supplied per riches in Christ	Phil. 4:19
Needful	Luke 10:42
Needle and camel	Matt. 19:24
Needlework	Ps. 45:14
Needs	Acts 17:3 + 21:22; Phil. 4:19

" known by God	Matt. 6:8
Needy need aid	Matt. 9:12, 13; Eph. 4:28
Neesings	Job 41:18
Neglect	Matt. 18:17; Acts 6:1; Heb. 2:3
" not gift in thee	1 Tim. 4:14
Neglecting of the body	Col. 2:23
Neighbor	Lev. 19:13, 18; Prov. 24:28; Matt. 22:39; Luke 10:27–37; Rom. 13:9, 10; Gal. 5:14
" , debate	Prov. 24:28 + 25:9
" deceived by sinners	Jer. 9:4, 5, 8
" , love - as thyself	Gal. 5:14
" - treat fairly	Lev. 19:13; Eph. 4:25
Neighbor's property to be respected	Deut. 5:21
Neighed	Jer. 5:8
Neither	Acts 4:12; Rom. 8:38, 39; Gal. 3:28; James 5:12
Nest	Jer. 22:23; Matt. 8:20
Net	Matt. 4:18, 20; Luke 5:5, 6
Nether	Exod. 19:17; Job 41:24
Nets	Ps. 141:10; Mark 1:18; Luke 5:4
Nettles	Job 30:7; Hos. 9:6
Never	Lev. 6:13; Ps. 31:1 + 55:22; John 6:35; Heb. 13:5
Nevertheless	Matt. 26:39; 2 Cor. 3:16; Phil. 3:16
New, all things	Isa. 42:9, 10; 2 Cor. 5:17; Rev. 21:5
" and living way	Heb. 10:20
" " old heart & spirit	Ezek. 36:26
" commandment	John 13:34
" covenant - Jesus is mediator	Heb. 8:6, 8, 13 + 12:24

"	creature	2 Cor. 5:17
"	heaven & earth	2 Pet. 3:13; Rev. 21:1–4
"	man	Eph. 4:24; Col. 3:10, 11
"	one gets peace	Eph. 4:14–18
"	, put on	Eph. 4:17–24
"	testament is the cup	Luke 22:20
"	, no - thing	Eccles. 1:9, 10
Newborn		1 Pet. 2:2
Newly		Deut. 32:17
Newness of life		Rom. 6:4, 11
" " spirit		Rom. 7:6
News , good		Luke 2:10
Newsbreaker's behavior		Luke 10:1–11
Next		John 1:29, 35
Nigh		Ps. 91:7 + 145:18; Luke 19:11 + 21:28; Phil. 2:27, 30; James 4:8
Night		Isa. 21:12
"	and darkness activities	Rom. 13:11–14
"	hours	Ps. 127:2
Ninety		Gen. 5:9
"	and nine	Gen. 17:1; Matt. 18:12
No		Gen. 16:1; Exod. 20:3; Eccles. 9:10; 1 Tim. 1:3
"	earthly things & sorrow in heaven	Rev. 7:16
Noah		Gen. 5:28, 29 + 6:7–10, 13, 14 + 7:5–15 + 8:6 + 9:29; 1 Pet. 3:20
"	- eighth person - preacher	2 Pet. 2:5
Noah's three sons are ancestors of all on earth		Gen. 9:19; Rev. 7:16 + 21:1, 4, 22, 23, 25 + 22:3, 5

Noble	Esther 6:9; Isa. 13:2
Nobleman	John 4:49
Noe	Matt. 27:37, 38; Luke 17:26, 27
Noise	1 Sam. 4:6, 14; Job 37:2;
	Matt. 9:23; 2 Cor. 3:10
" , joyful	Ps. 95:1, 2 + 98:4 + 100:1
Noised abroad	Luke 1:65
Noisome	Ps. 91:3; Rev. 16:2
None	Rom. 3:10–12; 1 Cor. 8:4
" against us	Rom. 8:31
" else	Deut. 5:7–9; Isa. 45:14, 18 + 46:9
Noon	Amos 8:9
Noonday	Ps. 37:6 + 91:6
Nor	Eccles. 9:10; Rom. 8:38, 39;
	1 Cor. 10:32; 2 Thess. 2:2
North brings fair & cold	
weather	Job 37:9; Prov. 25:23
" cometh fair weather	Job 37:22
Nose bleed	Prov. 30:33
Nostrils	Gen. 2:7; Job 41:20
Not	John 14:27; Col. 2:21 + 3:2;
	Titus 3:5; James 4:2–4 + 5:12
" - but	Gal. 2:16
" everyone	Matt. 7:21
" far from us, Lord	Acts 17:27
" seen & seen	2 Cor. 4:18
" your own, body	1 Cor. 6:19
Notable	Matt. 27:16
Note	2 Thess. 3:14
Nothing	Isa. 44:10; Dan. 4:35;
	Amos 3:7; Acts 11:12
" , be careful for	Phil. 4:6
" , do - rashly	Acts 19:36
" except from above	John 3:27

"	in or out of world	1 Cor. 4:4; 1 Tim. 6:7
"	known by myself	1 Cor. 4:4
"	too hard for Lord	
	God	Jer. 32:17
"	want if fear Lord	Ps. 34:9, 10
"	without charity	1 Cor. 13:2–4, 8, 13
"	" me - Jesus	John 15:5
Notwithstanding		Phil. 1:18 + 4:14; 1 Tim. 2:15; 2 Tim. 4:17; James 2:16
Nought		Job 1:9; Luke 23:11; Acts 5:38; 1 Cor. 1:28; Rev. 17:18
Nourish		Gen. 50:21; Isa. 44:14
Nourished		Rev. 12:14
"	by words of faith	1 Tim. 4:6
Nourisher		Ruth 4:15
Novice		1 Tim. 3:6
Now		Gen. 2:23; 1 Chron. 29:13; John 14:29 + 15:3; 1 John 3:2
Number		Isa. 65:11, 12; Acts 4:4 + 11:21
Numbered, our days		Job 14:5
"	with	Mark 15:28; Acts 1:26
Nurse		Ruth 4:16; 1 Kings 2:7
Nurture		Eph. 6:4
Nuts		Gen. 43:11

· O ·

O	Ps. 70:1, 5 + 96:1, 9; Isa. 46:8; Matt. 15:28
Oak	2 Sam. 18:9, 10; Isa. 6:13 + 44:14
Oath	Luke 1:73; Heb. 7:20
" maketh the son	Heb. 7:28
Oaths	Matt. 5:33
Obedience	Deut. 11:1–25; Ps. 95:4–7; Rom. 1:5 + 5:15, 19 + 16:26; Philem. 1:20
" be to Jesus Christ	Phil. 2:5–11; 1 Pet. 1:2
" of Christ	2 Cor. 10:5
" to righteous	Rom. 5:19
Obedient, be	Isa. 1:19; Eph. 6:5; 1 Pet. 1:14
" unto death	Phil. 2:8
Obeisance	1 Kings 1:16
Obey God	Acts 5:29–32; Phil. 2:12, 13
" " for salvation	Heb. 5:9
" " - not men	Acts 5:29, 32
" gospel	1 Pet. 4:17
" " important	2 Thess. 1:7–10
" if love Jesus	John 14:15; 1 John 5:3
" masters	Col. 3:22
" me - Jesus	John 14:15, 23
" parents	Eph. 6:1

"	rulers	Heb. 13:17; 1 John 5:3
"	- sacrifice	1 Sam. 15:22
"	truth	1 Pet. 1:22
Obeyed by spirits		Mark 1:27
"	faithfully	Phil. 2:12
Obeyedst		Jer. 22:21
Oblation		Lev. 2:13 + 3:1; Isa. 66:3; Dan. 2:24 + 9:27
Obligation, our - and reward		2 Cor. 6:16–18
Obscure		Prov. 20:20
Obscurity		Isa. 58:10
Observe		Matt. 28:20; Mark 23:3
"	all the law	Josh. 1:7, 8 + 22:5; Ps. 119:34
"	" things	Matt. 28:20
"	and do all commandments	Deut. 6:1–3 + 28:1–15 + 58–61; Josh. 22:5; Neh. 10:29
"	by reading Bible	Josh. 1:7, 8
"	to do what I command you	Deut. 11:32 + 12:28, 32
Observest not even by seeing		Isa. 42:20
Obstinate		Isa. 48:4
Obtain		Matt. 5:7; Eph. 1:11; 1 Thess. 5:9; 1 Pet. 2:10
"	favor or condemn	Prov. 12:2
"	mercy	Heb. 4:16
"	the salvation	2 Tim. 2:10
Obtained the promise		Heb. 6:15
Obtaineth favour		Prov. 18:22
Occasion		2 Cor. 5:12 + 11:12; Gal. 5:13
Occult		Deut. 18:10–13; Isa. 8:19; Acts 19:11–20; Eph. 6:12, 13

Occupation	Gen. 47:3
Odious woman	Prov. 30:23
Off	Gen. 8:3, 7, 8; Acts 2:39
" , put - disobediences	Col. 3:6–9
Offence of one man	Matt. 16:23; Rom. 5:15–17
" , their	Hos. 5:15
" to none	1 Cor. 10:32; 2 Cor. 6:3; Phil. 1:10
Offences	Matt. 18:6–9; Rom. 4:25 + 5:16
Offend	Matt. 26:31; Mark 9:45 + 14:27; Luke 7:23
" in one point	James 2:10
" not	Matt. 18:6; 1 Cor. 8:13; James 3:2
" us, nothing	Ps. 119:165; Matt. 5:29, 30
Offended	Mark 6:3
Offer spiritual sacrifices	Mal. 1:8; 1 Pet. 2:5
Offered himself	Heb. 7:27 + 9:14, 24, 25, 28 + 10:10–14
Offering	Ps. 96:8; Prov. 3:9, 10; Heb. 10:10
" him	Luke 23:36
" of body	Heb. 2:9–11 + 10:10–14
Offerings, burnt	Mark 12:32, 33
Office	1 Tim. 3:1
Offscouring of the earth	1 Cor. 4:13
Offspring	Isa. 44:3
" of David is Jesus	Rev. 22:16
" " Lord	Acts 17:28, 29
Oft	Job 21:7; Matt. 17:15 + 18:21; 1 Cor. 11:26; 2 Cor. 11:23; Heb. 6:7
Often	2 Cor. 11:26, 27; 1 Tim. 5:23
Oftener	Acts 24:26
Oftentimes	Rom. 1:13

Ofttimes	Matt. 17:15; Mark 9:22
Oil	Exod. 29:2; 2 Chron. 2:10, 15; Mic. 6:7; Mark 6:13
" , baths of	2 Chron. 2:10
Ointment	Matt. 26:12; Luke 7:37, 38; John 12:3
Old	Gen. 5:32 + 17:1; John 3:4; 2 Cor. 5:17
" time	Matt. 5:21; 2 Pet. 1:21
Oldest person	Gen. 5:21, 22, 25–27
Olive tree	Hos. 14:6; Zech. 4:3, 11, 12
Olives, Mount	John 8:1
Omegaand alpha	Is. 44:6; Matt. 19:30; Rev. 1:8, 11 + 21:6 + 22:13
" - last word in Greek alphabet	Rev. 1:8 + 21:6
Omnipotent - all powerful	1 Chron. 29:12; Ps. 62:11; Rev. 19:6
Omnipresent - everywhere	Ps. 139:1–10; Acts 17:27
Omniscient - knowing all things	1 Chron. 28:9; Job 42:2; Acts 15:18; Heb. 4:13
On	Col. 3:14
Once suffered, Jesus	1 Pet. 3:18
One	Gen. 1:9 + 2:21, 24; John 17:20, 21; Eph. 4:2–6
" accord	Acts 2:1
" and ninety nine	Luke 15:7
" another	Eph. 4:2; 1 Thess. 4:18; James 5:16
" can make sinner or righteous	Rom. 5:19
" everyone in all things	1 Cor. 1:10

"	everything	Eph. 4:4–6
"	father	John 8:41
"	flesh	Gen. 2:23
"	God	Exod. 34:14; 1 Cor. 8:4, 6; Eph. 4:6; 1 Tim. 2:5; James 2:19
"	" in Christ	John 17:11, 20–24; Gal. 3:28, 29; Eph. 2:13–16
"	" Jesus & Father in Heaven	John 8:16–19 + 10:30; Acts 4:12
"	is God - a unity	Deut. 4:35; Mark 12:29
"	" three	1 John 5:7, 8
"	mediator	1 Tim. 2:5; Heb. 8:6 + 9:15
"	mind	Rom. 15:6, 7; Phil. 1:27; 1 Pet. 3:1, 8
"	not as good as two	Eccles. 4:8–12
"	one sinner repent	Luke 15:10
"	sound from instruments & singers	2 Chron. 5:13
"	- unity	Acts 4:32; Eph. 1:10 + 4:4–7; Phil. 1:27
"	who serveth	Luke 22:27
"	with Jesus Christ & God	John 17:11–23, 26; Eph. 2:14–18
Onions		Num. 11:5
Only		Josh. 1:7; Mark 2:7; Phil. 1:27
"	begotten	John 1:14
"	God	Isa. 45:22; Mark 2:7; John 3:16; Rom. 10:9
"	" to serve	Luke 4:8
"	observe & do	Josh. 1:7
"	one good	Mark 10:18

"	son	John 3:16; 1 John 4:9, 10
"	wise God & King	1 Tim. 1:17; Jude 1:25
Onyx		Gen. 2:12; Job 28:16
Open		Gen. 1:20; Matt. 7:7; 1 Pet. 3:12
"	book - no man worthy	Rev. 5:4
"	door to Jesus	Rev. 3:20
"	eyes	2 Kings 6:17, 20; 2 Chron. 6:20; Ps. 119:18
"	face	2 Cor. 3:18
"	rebuke	Prov. 27:5
Opened		Matt. 9:30
Opening		Acts 17:3
Openly		Matt. 6:6
Operation		Isa. 5:12
Operatons - diversities		1 Cor. 12:6
Opinions		1 Kings 18:21
Opportunity		John 12:35; Gal. 6:10
Opposeth God		2 Thess. 2:3, 4
Oppress		Lev. 25:14, 17; Jude 2:18
"	the poor	Prov. 14:31
Oppressed		Ps. 146:7; Isa. 58:6; Acts 10:38
Oppression		Job 36:15; Ps. 42:9; Eccles. 4:1, 2
"	, papal	Dan. 7:25
Oppressions		Eccles. 4:1
Oppressors		Ps. 54:3
Or		Mark 2:9 + 3:4; 1 Cor. 3:22
Oracles of God		Rom. 3:2; Heb. 5:12; 1 Pet. 4:11
Oration		Acts 12:21
Orchestra		Eccles. 2:8
Ordain		Isa. 26:12; Mark 3:14; 1 Tim. 2:7
Ordained		Acts 1:22 + 10:42; 1 Cor. 2:7; Jude 1:4

"	before us	Ps. 8:3; Eph. 2:10
"	prophet before he was born	Jer. 1:5
"	to eternal life	Acts 13:47, 48
Order		Luke 1:3, 8; 1 Cor. 14:40 + 16:1
"	of Melchizedek	Heb. 6:20 + 7:1
Orderly, walk		Acts 21:24
Ordinance of man		Exod. 12:14; 2 Chron. 2:4; 1 Pet. 2:13
Ordinances		Isa. 58:2; Eph. 2:15; Col. 2:14, 20
Ordinary		Ezek. 16:27
Organ		Gen. 4:21
Ornament		Prov. 1:9; Ezek. 16:7; 1 Pet. 3:4
Orphans		Lam. 5:3
Ossifrage		Lev. 11:13
Ospray		Lev. 11:13
Ostrich		Job 39:13
Other		Deut. 5:7; Josh. 24:16; Acts 4:12
"	gospel	Gal. 1:6–9
Others to be considered		Matt. 25:45; Phil. 2:4
Otherwise		Ps. 38:16; Phil. 3:15
Ought		Matt. 5:23 + 21:3; Mark 8:23 + 11:25; Acts 24:19; James 4:15; 1 John 4:11
"	to heed things, re. God & His Son	Heb. 2:1
"	to obey God	Acts 5:29 + 20:35
"	" pray	Rom. 8:26
"	yea to be holy	2 Pet. 3:11
Oughtest to behave in church		1 Tim. 3:15
Our image (God)		Gen. 1:26
"	mission	1 Cor. 10:33

"	sufferings - and Christ's	1 Pet. 4:13
"	years	Ps. 90:10
Ourselves		2 Cor. 4:5 + 5:13; Phil. 2:4; 2 Thess. 1:4
Out, find		Eccles. 3:11
"	of Bethlehem	Matt. 2:6
"	" heart	Matt. 12:34
"	" man	Gen. 2:23
Outcast		Jer. 30:17
Outcasts		Isa. 56:8
Outlived		Jude 2:7
Outrageous		Prov. 27:4
Outrun		John 20:4
Outside and within		Matt. 23:25–28
Outward and inward man		1 Sam. 16:7; 2 Cor. 4:16
"	appearance	2 Cor. 10:7
Oven		Lev. 26:26; Mal. 4:1; Matt. 6:30
Over		Gen. 1:18, 26, 28
"	to	Jude 1:7
Overcame		Rev. 3:21
Overcharge		2 Cor. 2:5
Overcharged		Luke 21:34
Overcome		2 Pet. 2:20; Rev. 21:7
"	evil	Rom. 12:21
"	rewarded	Rev. 3:5
"	world	John 16:33; 1 John 5:4, 5; Rev. 3:21
Overcomer's crown		Rev. 2:11, 17 + 3:5
Overcometh one rewarded		Rev. 2:7, 26 + 3:5, 12, 21 + 21:7
"	the wicked one	1 John 1:14
"	" world	John 16:33; 1 John 5:4, 5
Overflow		Deut. 11:4; Isa. 43:2; Joel 3:13; Hag. 2:22

Overflowed	2 Pet. 3:6
Overflowing	Isa. 28:2 + 30:28
Overmuch	2 Cor. 2:7
Overpast	Ps. 57:1
Overseers	Acts 20:28
Overshadow	Luke 1:35
Oversight	1 Pet. 5:2
Overspreading	Dan. 9:27
Overtaken	Gal. 6:1
Overthroweth	Prov. 13:6; 2 Pet. 2:6
Overtook	Exod. 14:9
Overturn	Ezek. 21:27
Overwhelm	Job 6:27; Ps. 61:2 + 124:4
Owe	Rom. 13:8; Luke 16:5; Rom. 13:8
Owl	Lev. 11:16, 17; Deut. 14:15, 16; Isa. 13:21 + 34:11, 14, 15
Own	Gen. 1:27; Phil. 2:4; Jude 1:16, 18
" body	1 Pet. 2:24
" conceits	Rom. 12:16
" - not yours but God's	Acts 4:32; 1 Cor. 6:19, 20
" , our & others	Phil. 2:4
Owned by God	Job 1:19–22; Ps. 24:1, 2 + 50:10–12
Ox	Exod. 21:28, 29; Job 40:15; Prov. 14:4; Isa. 11:7 + 66:3; 1 Tim. 5:18
Oxen	2 Chron. 3:3; Job 1:3, 14; Prov. 14:4

· P ·

Pagan one	2 Thess. 2:3, 4; Rev. 13:5–7
Pain no more	Rom. 8:22; Rev. 21:4
Painful	Ps. 73:16; 2 Cor. 11:27
Palace	Mark 14:54, 56
Palm of hand	Isa. 49:16; Dan. 10:10; Matt. 26:67
Palsy	Luke 5:18–20; Acts 8:7 + 9:33, 34
Pant, heart	Ps. 42:1
Panteth	Ps. 42:1
Papal fall	Dan. 7:23–26
Paps	Luke 11:27 + 23:29; 2 Tim. 1:8; Rev. 1:13
Parable	Matt. 13:24 + 21:28–44 + 24:32; Mark 3:23 + 4:2, 11, 13, 33, 34
" , eagle	Ezek. 17:1–10
Parable of Jesus	Matt. 13:1–53; Mark 3:23; Luke 6:39 + 18:1, 4, 9–11
Paradise	Luke 23:43; 2 Cor. 2:4; Rev. 2:7
Paralysis	Luke 5:18
Parcel of ground	John 4:5
Pardon	Neh. 9:17; Isa. 55:7

267

Parents	2 Cor. 12:14; Col. 3:20
Part	Mark 4:38; John 19:23
" and perfect	Luke 11:36; 1 Cor. 13:9–12
" , your	2 Pet. 4:14
Partaker	1 Tim. 5:22; 2 Tim. 2:6
" of the glory	1 Cor. 9:22, 23
Partakers not of deceivers	Eph. 5:6, 7
" of Christ	Heb. 3:1, 14; 1 Pet. 4:13 + 5:1
" " divine nature	Col. 1:2; Heb. 12:10; 2 Pet. 1:4
" " one table	1 Cor. 10:21
Parted possessions	Acts 2:45
" raiment	John 19:24
" to heaven	Luke 24:51
Partial	James 2:4
Partition or wall	
between us	Eph. 2:14
Partner	Philem. 1:17
Partridge	Jer. 17:11
Parts of body	Prov. 18:18; Eph. 4:16
" " garments	John 19:23
Pass , bring to	Ps. 37:5
" , come to	Gen. 8:6; Mark 13:29–31;
	John 14:29
Passed away, old things	2 Cor. 3:10, 12, 13 + 5:17
" from death to life	John 5:24
Passeth, peace	Phil. 4:7
Passion, Christ's	Isa. 53:4–11
" , " - fortold	Isa. 53:4–12; Matt. 20:17–19
Passions	Acts 14:15
Passover	Mark 14:16; Luke 22:1, 7–20;
	John 13:1, 2
" feast	Matt. 26:2, 17
" instituted	Exod. 12:3–28
" , our - is Christ	1 Cor. 5:7

Past sins	Rom. 3:25
Pastors	Eph. 4:11
Pasture	Ps. 23:2 + 95:7 + 100:3; Isa. 30:23
" , God's	Ezek. 34:31
Pastures	Ps. 65:12, 13
Path	Prov. 4:18
" of feet	Prov. 3:6 + 4:26, 27
" " life	Ps. 16:11
Paths of Lord	Ps. 25:4, 10
" " Righteousness	Ps. 23:3
Patience	Luke 21:9; Rom. 2:7 + 5:3, 4 + 8:25; Heb. 12:1; James 1:2–4; Rev. 14:12
" for faith	Rom. 5:3, 4; James 1:2–4
Patience for hope - results	Rom. 8:25
" needed to receive promise	Heb. 6:12 + 10:36; James 1:1–4
" of Jesus Christ	Rev. 1:9 + 3:10
" " Job	James 5:11
" " saints	Rev. 14:12
" to possess soul	Luke 21:19; 2 Cor. 6:4 + 12:12
" " the end	1 Cor. 1:9, 10
Patient	Ps. 40:1; 1 Pet. 2:20
" be to all	1 Thess. 5:14; 1 Tim. 3:3; James 5:7, 8
" waiting	2 Thess. 3:5
Patiently	Ps. 40:1; 1 Pet. 2:20
Patriarchs (twelve)	Acts 7:8, 9
Patriotic	Mark 12:14–17; Luke 20:22–50
Pattern of life instructions	1 Tim. 5:1–25; Titus 2:7
" " things in heaven	Heb. 9:23
Paul	Eph. 4:1; Phil. 1:7, 8
" appointed preacher	2 Tim. 1:11

"	before conversion	Phil. 3:4–11
"	- formerly Saul	Acts 13:9
"	glorified	Acts 18:9, 10 + 19:11
"	minister of the gospel	2 Cor. 11:10, 28, 31; Eph. 6:16–20; Col. 1:23–29
"	persecuted church before conversion	Gal. 1:13
"	tells all regarding God	Acts 20:25–27; Rom. 11:22
"	the apostle	1 Cor. 9:1–27; 2 Cor. 2:9 + 10:1–8 + 12:10
Paul's commission		Acts 20:19–21; 1 Cor. 9:16, 17
"	commitment	Phil. 1:21
"	conversion	Phil. 3:3–14
"	dedication	Phil. 1:12–24
"	gospel teaching	1 Cor. 2:1–5
"	instructions	Col. 2:6, 7 + 3:17; 1 Thess. 5:14–24
"	joy	Phil. 1:21, 22 + 2:1, 2 + 4:1, 10
"	persecutions	2 Cor. 11:23–27
"	sufferings	Phil. 1:12–24
"	teachings	Acts 20:20, 21 + 28:30, 31; Eph. 6:19, 20; Phil. 1:9–11 + 3:15–21 + 4:8, 9
"	vision	Acts 16:9 + 18:9
Paver of authority		Rom. 13:1, 2
Pavilion		Ps. 27:5
Paw		1 Sam. 17:37
Paweth		Job 39:21
Pay		Ps. 50:14; Jon. 2:9; Rom. 13:6
Peace, abundance of		Ps. 37:11; John 14:27
"	among all	1 Thess. 5:12, 13
"	and glory	Hag. 2:9; Luke 2:14

"	" good cheer	John 16:33
"	" life or death	Rom. 8:6–10, 13
"	" safety	1 Thess. 5:2, 3
"	" service as guide	Rom. 14:19
"	at home important	Prov. 17:1
"	by conversion	Eph. 2:14–18
"	" God	Ps. 29:11; John 14; 27; Rom. 15:13
"	from Jesus	John 1:4–6 + 14:27 + 20:26; Col. 1:20
"	, God of	Rom. 15:33; Phil. 4:7, 9; Heb. 13:20, 21
"	, great	Ps. 119:165
"	, heavenly not worldly	John 14:27
"	in believing	Isa. 26:3; Rom. 15:13
"	" Jesus	John 16:33; 1 Pet. 5:14
"	, Lore God will speak	Ps. 85:8
"	- love	Ps. 119:165
"	makers	Matt 5:9
"	multiplied	Dan. 6:25
"	needed with all	Heb. 12:4
Peace	no end	Isa. 9:7
"	- none to wicked	Isa. 48:22 + 57:20, 21
"	not to world per Jesus	Matt. 10:32–42
"	of God for us	Phil. 4:7
"	or death	Rom. 8:6–10
"	" tribulation	John 16:33
"	perfect	Isa. 26:3
"	prayer	Num. 6:24–26
"	prince	Isa. 9:6

"	promised &	
	pretended by	
	antichrist	Dan. 8:25
"	, seek & have	Jer. 29:7
"	thoughts by Lord	Jer. 29:11–13
"	through faith	Rom. 5:1, 2
"	to Lord's people	Ps. 29:11; 1 Pet. 5:14
"	" you - Jesus'	
	second appearance	John 20:21, 26
"	with all	John 14:27; Heb. 12:14
"	" God (Jesus) or	
	world tribulation	John 16:33; Rom. 5:1
Peaceable life		2 Tim. 2:2
Peaceably come - antichrist		Dan. 11:21, 24
" live with all men		Rom. 12:18
Peacemakers		Matt. 5:9
Peacock		Job 39:13
Pearl		Matt. 13:45, 46; Rev. 17:4
Peculiar		Exod. 19:5; Titus 2:14
Pen		Ps. 45:1
Penny		Matt. 20:9, 10 + 22:19;
		Luke 20:24; Rev. 6:6
Pennysworth		Mark 6:37
Pentecost		Acts 2:1 + 20:16
People are bread for us		Num. 14:9
"	, common - listened	Mark 12:37
"	delivered	Dan. 12:1
"	destroyed in name	
	of peace	Dan. 8:25
"	for his name - God	Acts 15:14
"	, Lord's - rewarded	2 Chron. 7:14
"	, my - per God	Ruth 1:16; Ezek. 36:28
"	nothing compared	
	to God	Dan. 4:35

"	of God have rest	Heb. 4:9
"	out of Galilee	Acts 15:14
"	recover	Isa. 11:11
Peradventure		Gen. 18:24, 28–32; Jer. 20:10; Rom. 5:7
Perceive		Eccles. 2:14 + 3:22; Mark 7:18; John 4:19; Acts 10:34
Perceivest		Luke 6:41
Perch		1 Kings 7:6–8
Perdition		John 17:12; Phil. 1:28; 2 Thess. 2:3, 4; 1 Tim. 2:3 + 6:9; 2 Pet. 3:7; Rev. 17:8, 11
Perfect and upright		Job 2:3
"	" in part	1 Cor. 13:9–12
"	, be - as Father	Deut. 18:13; Matt. 5:48; Col. 1:28
"	heart with Lord	1 Kings 15:11, 14; 2 Chron. 15:17 + 16; 9
"	is God's way	2 Sam. 22:31
"	law of the Lord	Ps. 19:7
"	, made	2 Cor. 12:9; Heb. 2:10 + 13:20, 21
"	, make you	1 Pet. 5:10
"	man	Eph. 4:13
"	, man may be	2 Tim. 3:17
"	peace	Isa. 26:3
"	way	Ps. 18:30, 31
"	will of God	Rom. 12:2
Perfected praise		Matt. 21:16
"	sacrifice	Heb. 10:12–14
Perfection		Eph. 1:9, 10; Col. 3:14
Perfectionism		Ps. 119:96; Mark 14:8; 2 Cor. 12:9, 10; Eph. 2:8–10; Phil. 2:13 + 3:4–11

Perfectness	Col. 3:14
Perform	Ps. 57:2; 2 Cor. 8:11; Phil. 1:6
" as promised	Rom. 4:21
" oaths	Matt. 5:33
Performance	2 Cor. 8:11
Performed by man	Isa. 66:1–3
Perilous times	Luke 21:28; 2 Tim. 3:1–5; Rev. 13:8
Perils	2 Cor. 11:26
Perish	Job 31:19 + 34:15; Ps. 1:6 + 9:18 + 146:4; John 3:15, 16; Acts 8:20; 1 Cor. 1:18
" in own corruption	Jer. 10:15; 2 Pet. 2:12
Perished	Acts 5:37; 2 Pet. 3:6; Jude 1:11
Perishing to get strong drink	Prov. 31:6
Permit	Heb. 6:3
Pernicious	2 Pet. 2:2
Perpetual	Jer. 25:9 + 50:5
Perplexed	2 Cor. 4:8
Perplexity	Mic. 7:4; Luke 21:25
Persecute	Matt. 5:11 + 10:22, 23; Luke 21:12; John 17:20; Rom. 12:14
Persecuted	Ps. 143:3; Matt. 5:10–12 + 24:4–14, 21, 22; John 17:20; Acts 9:4, 5; Gal. 1:13; Rev. 13:5–7
" church - Paul	Gal. 1:13
" good people	Ps. 11:2
" predicted	Isa. 14:3–6; Dan. 7:25; Luke 21:12, 16, 17; Acts 26:10
" to blessed	Matt. 5:11
Persecution	Acts 11:19; 2 Cor. 4:8–10

" , fear not from	Rev. 2:10
Persecution for godly	Luke 21:12; Acts 8:1
Persecuters	Jer. 20:11
Persecutions of Paul	2 Cor. 11:23–27 + 12:10;
	2 Tim. 3:11, 12
Perseverance in prayer	Eph. 6:18; Col. 4:2
Persia	Dan. 2:39
Person, goodly	Deut. 39:6
" , vile	Dan. 11:21
Persons	Prov. 24:23; Ezek. 27:13;
	Acts 10:34; Rom. 2:11
Persuade	2 Chron. 32:11, 15; 2 Cor. 5:11
Persuaded	Prov. 25:15; Rom. 8:38, 39 +
	15:14; Acts 14:19
Persuasion	Gal. 5:8
Pertain	2 Pet. 1:3
Perverse	Prov. 4:24: + 14:2 + 19:1 +
	23:33; Matt. 17:17; 1 Tim. 6:5
" things spoken	Prov. 4:24; Acts 20:30
Perverseness	Isa. 30:12
Pervert	Deut. 24:17; Job 8:3: + 34:12;
	Prov. 17:23; Acts 13:10
Perverted	Job 33:27
Pestilence	2 Chron. 20:9; Ps. 91:3, 6;
	Ezek. 28:33; Luke 21:11
Peter	Matt. 10:2 + 14:28, 29;
	Mark 9:2, 5; Luke 9:32, 33;
	John 13:6, 8, 9; 1 Pet. 1:1;
	2 Pet. 2:1
" healed many	Matt. 8:15, 16
" - man I am	Acts 10:26
" married	Matt. 8:14
" preached	Acts 10:34–45
" rebuked Jesus	Matt. 16:22, 23

Peter's vision	Acts 10:9–17
Petition	Esther 5:6–8; 1 John 5:15
Pharisees	Matt. 5:20; John 8:3, 13
Philosophers	Acts 17:18
Philosophy good	Luke 3:13, 14
" , worldly	Col. 2:8
Phylacteries	Matt. 23:5
Physical not as important	
as God's love	Rom. 8:38:39
Physically perfect not	
required to enter	
Heaven	Mark 9:43–48
Physician	Matt. 9:12, 13, 43–48;
	Mark 2:17; Luke 5:31;
	Col. 4:14
" - Luke	Col. 4:14
Piece	Gen. 15:10; Jer. 37:21
Pierced	Jesus John 19:34, 37; Rev. 1:7
Piercings	Prov. 12:18
Pigeon	Gen. 15:9
Pilgrimage	Ps. 119:54
Pillar	Num. 14:14
" is church of living	
God	1 Tim. 3:15
" of salt	Gen. 19:26
Pillars	Gal. 2:9
Pillow	Gen. 28:18
Pine for iniquities	Ezek. 24:23
Pining	Isa. 38:12
Pinnacle	Matt. 4:5
Pisseth	1 Kings 21:21
Pit	Job 6:27
" , bottomless	Rev. 17:18 + 20:1–3
" with no water	Zech. 9:11

Pitch		Gen. 6:14
Pitcher		Gen. 24:15, 16; Mark 14:13
Pitieth		Ps. 103:13
Pitiful		James 5:11; 1 Pet. 3:8
Pity	on me	Job 19:21
"	the believers	Ps. 103:11–13
"	to the poor	Prov. 19:17
Place, give		Rom. 12:19
"	heaven and earth	Matt. 6:9, 10 + 17:20
"	, heavenly - for believers	Luke 23:43; John 14:1–4; Eph. 1:3
"	- none for the wicked	Isa. 48:22
"	of judgment	Eccles. 3:16
"	prepared	John 14:1–4
"	with Christ	Phil. 1:23
"	written	Luke 4:17
Places, heavenly		Eph. 1:3
Plague		Ps. 91:10; Mark 5:34
"	appears 39 times in Lev. 13	
Plagues		
1.	water to blood	Exod. 7:14–25
2.	frogs	Exod. 8:2–14
3.	lice	Exod. 8:16–19
4.	flies	Exod. 8:20–24, 29–31
5.	murrain - infectious disease of cattle	Exod. 9:3–7
6.	boils	Exod. 9:8–12
7.	hail	Exod. 9:13–25
8.	locusts	Exod. 10:1–19
9.	darkness	Exod. 10:20–29
10.	death of firstborn	Exod. 11:1–19 + 12:29, 30

Plagues added for punishment	Deut. 28:58–61; Rev. 22:18
Plain	Gen. 13:10–12; Prov. 15:19; Ezek. 3:22, 23; Mark 7:35
Plainly	John 16:29
Plainness	2 Cor. 3:12
Plaister	Lev. 14:42, 43; Isa. 38:21
Plant	Gen. 2:5; Eccles. 3:2
Planted	Ps. 92:13 + 104:16; Jer. 17:8
Planteth	1 Cor. 3:6–8
Plants	Matt. 15:13
" , earth's	Mark 4:26–32; 1 Cor. 3:6, 7
Platted	Matt. 27:29
Play	Ezek. 33:32
Playing, boys & girls	Zech. 8:5
Plead	Job 9:19; Ps. 35:1; Prov. 43:1
Pleasant is knowledge	Prov. 2:10
" words	Prov. 16:24
Please all men	1 Cor. 10:33
" Father	John 8:29; Col. 1:19, 20
" God by faith	Heb. 11:1, 6
" Him	Isa. 55:11; Heb. 11:6
" husband	1 Cor. 7:35
" Isaiah	Isa. 55:11
Pleased God	Matt. 3:17; Mark 1:11
Pleasing God not men	1 Thess. 2:4
Pleasure	Eccles. 2:1–23; Phil. 2:13
" , Father's	Luke 12:32
" God's - that wicked turn	Isa. 46:10, 11; Ezek. 33:11
" in Lord's works	Ps. 111:2–9
" " unrighteousness	Rom. 1:32; 1 Thess. 2:10–12
" lovers will be poor	Prov. 21:17
" to God	Rev. 4:11

"	" honour sabbath	Isa. 58:13
"	" man of own works	Eccles. 3:22
Pleasures and joy		Ps. 16:11
"	of joy at hand	Ps. 36:8; 2 Tim. 3:4
"	, worldly - at end	Matt. 24:37–44
Pledge		1 Sam. 17:18; Isa. 36:8
Plenteous		Ps. 86:5
Plenteousness or want		Prov. 21:5
Plentifully		Ps. 31:23
Plenty		Gen. 41:29–31; Job 22:25; Prov. 3:10
"	owned - want more	Eccles. 5:10
"	words	Prov. 16:24
Plight of deceiver		Isa. 5:20
Plow		Ps. 129:3; Mic. 3:12; Luke 9:62
Plowing		Job 1:14
"	of wicked is sin	Prov. 21:4
Plowmen		Isa. 61:5
Plowshares		Isa. 2:4; Mic. 4:3
Pluck		Ps. 25:15 + 52:5; Eccles. 3:2; John 10:27–29
Plummet of house		2 Kings 21:13
Plunge		Job 9:31
Poets		Acts 17:28
Point		James 2:10
Poison		Job 6:4
Pollute		2 Chron. 36:14; Ezek. 20:31, 39
Pollution		2 Pet. 2:20
Pollutions of idols		Acts 15:20, 29
Pomegranate		1 Kings 7:20; Sol. 6:7, 11; Hag. 2:19; Rev. 8:2
Ponder		Prov. 4:26 + 5:6 + 21:2 + 24:12; Luke 2:19

Pool		John 5:2, 4, 7 + 9:7, 11
Poor always here per Jesus		Matt. 26:11; Mark 14:7; John 12:6–8
"	and rich	Prov. 14:20; James 2:2, 3
"	blessed	Luke 6:20
"	chosen by God	James 2:5
"	, consider	Ps. 41:1, 2; Prov. 14:31
"	from rich	2 Cor. 8:9
"	- give to good	Prov. 19:17
"	heard	Isa. 41:17
"	" by righteous & wicked	Prov. 29:7, 27
"	heard or not heard	Prov. 21:13
"	helpers blessed	Ps. 41:1–3
"	ignored by the wicked	Prov. 29:7, 27
"	in spirit	Matt. 5:3
Poor, invite - to feast		Luke 14:12–27
"	to be pitied	Prov. 19:17
"	" riches	Prov. 13:7
"	wise man	Eccles. 9:15
"	with integrity is good	Prov. 19:1
Porch		Acts 3:11
Pork - old law		Lev. 11:7
Pornography		Job 31:1; Prov. 6:25–28
Portion		Job 31:2; Ps. 16:5 + 73:26; Eccles. 2:10, 21 + 3:22 + 5:18, 19; Lam. 3:24
Possess		Num. 13:30; Deut. 6:1; Ezek. 36:12
"	kingdom - saints	Dan. 7:22
"	land	Deut. 11:10, 11
"	soul in patience	Luke 21:19

Possesseth abundance	Luke 12:15
Possession is Lord's	Ps. 24:1; Acts 4:32
Possessions	Ps. 37:16; Luke 12:15
" shared	Acts 4:32
" sold & distributed	Acts 4:33–35
" worthless	Zeph. 1:13, 18; Luke 12:15
Possessor of heaven & earth	Gen. 14:22
Possessors shared	Acts 4:33–35
Possible	Mark 14:36; Rom. 12:18
" and impossible	Matt. 19:26; Mark 10:27; Luke 18:27
" if believe	Mark 9:23 + 11:24
" with God - not man	Matt. 26:39; Luke 18:27
Potentate	1 Tim. 6:15
Potsherd	Rom. 2:8
Potter	Isa. 64:8; Rom. 9:21
" is the Lord	Isa. 64:8
Pour blessings, etc.	Isa. 44:3
" oil in the wound	Luke 10:34
" out heart	Ps. 62:8
" " spirit	Ezek. 39:29; Prov. 1:23; Joel 2:28, 29; Acts 10:45
Poured out soul	Isa. 53:12
Poverty	Prov. 11:24, 25; Mark 11:24
Poverty ones to get wine	Prov. 31:6, 7
" - riches (joy)	2 Cor. 8:2
" to rich	2 Cor. 8:9, 12
Power, all - given to Jesus	Matt. 28:18
" , believer's	Mark 16:16–18; 2 Tim. 1:7
" by receiving God's witness	John 1:12
" by the Lord's spirit	Mic. 3:8; Acts 1:7, 8
" divine	2 Pet. 1:3, 4

"	from God	2 Tim. 1:7
"	given to the faint	Isa. 40:29
"	" " " twelve apostles	Matt. 12:11; Mark 3:15 + 6:7–9; Luke 9:1; Acts 1:8 + 4:33
"	given to the world dictator	Rev. 13:5 + 17:8
"	head is God	Col. 2:10
"	in me - Lord Jesus	Matt. 28:18; Eph. 6:10
"	is God's	Ps. 62:11; Rom. 13:1, 2
"	" in kingdom of God	1 Cor. 4:20
"	of God in us	2 Cor. 4:6–11; 2 Tim. 1:7
"	" " is cross	1 Cor. 1:18, 24, 25
"	" God to be denied	1 Tim. 3:1–5
"	is Holy Ghost	Acts 1:8; Rom. 15:13
"	" lions	Dan. 6:27
"	" lord on earth	Isa. 43:1, 2; Rom. 13:1–7; Luke 5:17 + 24:49
"	" prayer	James 5:13–16
"	" resurrection	Phil. 3:10
"	" the spirit	Luke 4:14
"	" tongue	Prov. 18:21
Power,	quickening	John 5:21
"	through Christ	Mark 6:7 + 16:15–18; John 19:11; Phil. 4:13
"	to become sons of God	John 1:12
"	to get wealth	Deut. 8:18
"	" heal was present	Luke 5:17
"	" Jesus	Matt. 28:18; Acts 10:38
"	" lay down life or take it	John 10:17:18
"	to salvation	Rom. 1:16

" , tongue	Prov. 18:21
" worketh in us	Eph. 3:20
Powerful, all	Dan. 2:20–22; Jude 1:24, 25
" God - omnipotent	1 Chron. 29:12; Ps. 62:11
Practice what preach	1 Cor. 9:14–17
Praise, all kinds of	Ps. 147:1 + 148:1–7 + 149:1–3 + 150:1–6; Rev. 7:10, 11
" all kinds to God	1 Chron. 29:11–13
" " " " keep	Isa. 42:8
" , all sing	Isa. 42:10
" by all everywhere to one on throne	Rev. 4:11 + 5:13
" continually giving thanks	Heb. 13:15
" glorifieth God	Ps. 50:23
" God per David	Ps. 63:5 + 145:1–21
" " cheerfully	Ps. 100:1–5 + 150:1–6
" " for thinking	Phil. 4:8
" " urged	Ps. 92:1, 2; Heb. 13:15
" , His - endureth forever	Ps. 111:10
" Lord God for great things	Ps. 113:1–9
" not by the dead	Ps. 115:17
" perfected	Matt. 21:16
" the Lord - PTL	2 Chron. 20:21; Ps. 134:1–3 + 135:19–21 + 147:1, 12, 20 + 148:1–14 + 150:1–6
" " " in worship services	Ps. 111:1
" to be universal	Rev. 5:13
" urged	Ps. 95:1–6 + 149:1–14; 1 Thess. 5:18; James 1:17
" " per God	Isa. 61:11

Prating		Prov. 10:8, 10
Pray		Exod. 33:13; Jude 16:28;
		Matt. 5:44 + 6:5–9; Mark 11:24;
		Luke 11:2–4; James 5:16
"	always	Luke 18:1 + 21:36
"	behind door	2 Kings 4:33; Matt. 6:6
"	, cease not to	1 Thess. 5:17
"	for enemies	Matt. 5:44
"	" one another	James 5:13–16
"	" others	Col. 1:9–18
"	" sick - faults &	
	earthly things	James 5:13–18
"	help	Rom. 8:26
"	in secret	Matt. 6:5–8
"	" the name of Jesus	Acts 3:1–13 + 4:10
"	per Solomon	2 Chron. 7:14, 15
"	without ceasing	1 Thess. 5:17, 18
Prayed all night, Jesus		Luke 6:10
"	for children	Matt. 19:13–15
Prayer - acceptable time		Ps. 69:13
"	, all	Eph. 6:18
"	and fasting - power	Mark 9:17–29
"	assisted by the spirit	Rom. 8:26
"	believing - receive	Matt. 21:22; John 15:7
"	conditions	Mark 11:22–26
"	daily	Rom. 12:12; 2 Cor. 4:16
"	- endure any	
	experience	Col. 1:9–12
"	examples	Ps. 51:9–12 + 139:23, 24;
		1 Thess. 5:23
"	heard	Ps. 102:17; James 5:17, 18
"	includes forgiving	Mark 11:24–26
"	, longest in Bible	Sol. 8:23–53

Prayer, Lord's		Matt. 6:9–13; Luke 11:2–4
"	more now near final day	Heb. 10:25
"	power	James 5:16
"	saves sick	James 5:14, 15
"	, shortest in Bible	Matt. 14:30
"	- thanks included	Phil. 4:6
"	to renew salvation	Ps. 51:1–19
"	" saviour	Jude 1:24, 25
"	with faith saves the sick	James 5:15
"	with other believers	Heb. 10:25; James 5:16
Prayerlessness		1 Sam. 12:19–23
Prayers answered		John 16:23, 24; James 5:17, 18
"	, four - and answered	Ps. 107:6, 7, 13, 14, 19, 20, 28–30
"	without ceasing	2 Tim. 1:3; Philem. 1:4
Praying - forgive		Mark 11:25
Preach Christ crucified		1 Cor. 1:23, 24; Phil. 1:15–17
"	, everyone	Phil. 2:11; Rev. 14:6
"	gospel	Luke 4:18, 19 + 24:46, 47; 1 Cor. 1:17, 18 + 15:1, 12, 14
"	" & practice same	Mark 16:15–18; 1 Cor. 9:14–17
"	- Jesus to all	Mark 1:14, 15; Luke 4:18, 19, 43, 44
"	per anointed	Luke 4:18
"	the Word	Luke 4:18, 19, 43, 44 + 24:47; 2 Tim. 4:2
"	to the end	Matt. 24:14
"	" " humble people	Luke 4:18, 19, 43
"	to the meek & the poor	Isa. 61:1; Luke 4:18

Preached		Matt. 4:23; Mark 16:20; Acts 13:5 + 28:30, 31
"	forgiveness of sins	Acts 13:38
"	gospel of end times	Rev. 24:14
Preacher		Eccles. 1:12
"	, wisdom	Eccles. 12:9–14
"	to be observed	Heb. 13:7
Preaching		Acts 20:25 + 28:30, 31
"	, Jesus began	Luke 4:14–19
"	of the cross	1 Cor. 1:17, 18
Precept		Mark 10:5
Precepts		Ps. 119:15, 27, 45, 93, 94, 100, 134, 141, 168, 173; Heb. 9:19
Precious and prospereth is		
	a gift	Prov. 17:8
"	is faith	1 Pet. 1:7
Precious, most literature		John 3:16
"	to Lord God	Ps. 116:15 + 139:17; Isa. 43:4; 1 Pet. 2:4
Predesinate - by God		Rom. 8:29, 30
Predestinated		Eph. 1:5, 11
Preeminence		Eccles. 3:19; Col. 1:18; 3 John 1:9
Prefer one another		Rom. 12:10; 1 Tim. 5:21
Preferred		Dan. 6:3
"	before me per John	John 1:15, 27, 30
Prejudice		John 7:24; Rom. 12:16; Gal. 3:26–28; Col. 3:11; James 2:1–10
Premeditate		Mark 13:11
Preparation		Mark 15:42; Eph. 6:15
Prepare		Matt. 3:3; Luke 3:4 + 21:34–36
"	heart	Job 11:13

" place	John 14:2, 3
Prepared, be - example	Matt. 24:48–51
" for us by God	Ps. 31:19; Isa. 64:4; 1 Cor. 2:9
Prepareth heart	2 Chron. 30:19
Preparing was the ark	1 Pet. 3:20
Presbytery	1 Tim. 4:14
Presence	Exod. 33:14, 15; Ps. 16:11 + 95:2; Phil. 2:12, 13
" of Lord to come	Acts 3:19–26; Heb. 9:24
Present - absent	1 Cor. 5:3
" all perfect with Christ	Col. 1:28
Present bodies	Rom. 12:1
" everywhere at same time	Ps. 139:7–10; Acts 17:27
" or absent	2 Cor. 5:6, 8
" us	2 Cor. 4:14; Jude 1:24
" was power to heal	Luke 5:17
" with the Lord God	Ps. 46:1; 2 Cor. 5:8
Presented us holy if faithful to gospel	Col. 1:21–23; Heb. 10:10
Presently	Phil. 2:23
Preserve	Ps. 121:7, 8; 1 Thess. 5:23; 2 Tim. 4:18
" God lovers	Ps. 145:20
" godly	Ps. 12:7 + 121:7, 8
" life	Luke 17:33; 1 Thess. 5:23
" me	Ps. 16:1 + 40:11 + 140:1
" us alive	Deut. 6:24
Preserved	Ps. 37:28
" in Jesus Christ	Jude 1:1
Preserver	Prov. 7:20
Preserveth	Ps. 146:9
Press	Joel 3:13; Phil. 3:14

Pressed down	Luke 6:38
Presseth	Luke 16:16
Pressfat	Hag. 2:16
Presumptious	Deut. 18:22; Ps. 19:13;
	2 Pet. 2:10
Presumptuously	Deut. 17:13
Pretence	Matt. 23:14; Mark 12:40;
	Phil. 1:18
Pretender, God	2 Thess. 2:3, 4
Prevail	2 Chron. 13:18 + 14:11;
	Eccles. 4:12; Isa. 7:1;
	Matt. 16:18 + 27:24
Prevailed vs saints	Dan. 7:21
Prevailest	Job 14:20
Prevent	1 Thess. 4:15
Prey	Ps. 17:12; Isa. 42:22 + 59:15
Price we are bought	1 Cor. 6:20; 1 Pet. 3:4
Pricked in hearts	Acts 2:37
Pricks	Acts 9:5
Pride	Ps. 10:4; Prov. 16:18;
	Zeph. 2:10; 1 John 2:16
" fruits	Prov. 16:18; 1 Tim. 3:6
Priest cannot take away	
sins	Heb. 2:10–14
" , high	Heb. 8:1–6
" no compassion	Heb. 4:15
" to glorify God	Mal. 2:1, 2, 10
Priesthood, holy - are we	1 Pet. 2:5, 9; Rev. 1:6
Priests	Acts 26:10
" of God	Rev. 20:4, 6
Priest's sacrifices never	
take away sin	Heb. 10:11
" sins	Lam. 4:16; Mal. 2:1–10

Prince of kings		Rev. 1:5
"	" life	Acts 3:15
"	" peace	Isa. 9:6
"	" this world cometh	John 14:30, 31; Acts 5:31
"	of this world judged	John 16:11
Principal		Prov. 4:7
Principalities		Titus 3:1
Principality head		Col. 2:10
Priorities		1 Cor. 11:3
Prison		Jude 16:21, 25; Acts 12:5–11
"	houses	Isa. 42:22
Prisoner of Jesus was Paul the apostle		Eph. 3:1; Philem. 1:1, 9
Prisoners		Zech. 9:11
Private		2 Pet. 1:20
Privately		Mark 6:32
Privates covered		Luke 12:35, 37
Privily		Prov. 1:11, 18; Matt. 1:19; 2 Pet. 2:1
Privy		Deut. 23:1
Prize		1 Cor. 9:24
"	of God's calling	Phil. 3:13, 14
Problem is God's - not ours		2 Chron. 20:15–25
Proceed		Isa. 29:14; John 15:26; Acts 12:3; 2 Tim. 3:9
Proclaim		Exod. 33:19; Lev. 23:4, 21, 37; Prov. 20:6; Jer. 3:12 + 7:2
"	Good tidings to the less fortunate	Isa. 61:1–3
"	Lord's death	Mark 14:55, 64; John 11:13 + 12:33 + 18:32

Proclaimed	Isa. 62:11; Luke 12:3; Acts 20:23
" unto end of world	Isa. 62:11
Proclamation	Dan. 5:29
Procrastination	Prov. 2:27, 28; Luke 9:57–62; James 4:17
Profane	Lev. 22:32; Matt. 12:5; 1 Tim. 6:20; 2 Tim. 2:16
Profanity	Exod. 20:7; Ps. 17:1–3; Mark 14:71; Eph. 4:29–31; James 3:9, 10
Profess	Matt. 7:23
Professing	Rom. 1:22
Profession	2 Tim. 6:12; Heb. 4:14 + 10:23
Profit	Mark 8:36, 37; 1 Cor. 10:33 + 12:7; James 2:14
" gain - lose soul	Matt. 16:26; Mark 8:36, 37
" in all labour	Prov. 14:23
" not self	Rom. 15:1–3; 1 Cor. 10:33
" nothing	John 6:63
" , the greatest	Luke 7:28
Profitable	Isa. 44:10; 1 Tim. 4:8
" scripture for doctrine of God	2 Tim. 3:16
Profiteth	1 Tim. 4:8
Prognosticator	Isa. 47:13
Prolong	Deut. 11:9; Eccles. 8:13
Prolonged	Deut. 5:16 + 6:2; Isa. 8:12 + 13:22; Dan. 7:12
Promise	Isa. 43:2; Luke 24:49; John 2:25; Acts 2:39
" - eternal life	1 Tim. 4:8; Heb. 9:15; 1 John 2:25
" obtained	Heb. 6:15

" to God	Ps. 51:13
Promised	Heb. 10:23
Promisedst	1 Kings 8:24, 25
Promises seen ahead by faith	Heb. 11:13
Promote	Esther 3:1
Promoted	Dan. 3:30
Promotion	Ps. 75:6, 7
Pronounce	Jude 12:6; Jer. 36:7 + 40:2
Proof	Gen. 17:13; Acts 1:3; Phil. 2:22
Property sold for tithes	Acts 4:34, 35
" taken	Dan. 11:21–24
" violation	Job 24:1–3
Prophesied	Luke 1:67; Jude 1:14
Prophesies	1 Cor. 13:8
Prophesy	Ps. 16:10; Ezek. 37:1–28; Acts 2:16–18; Rom. 12:6; 1 Cor. 14:1–40; 1 Thess. 5:20; 2 Pet. 1:21
" Better than tongues	1 Cor. 14:2–6, 14
" book - revelation not to be altered	Rev. 22:18, 19
" by young	Acts 2:17
" God inspired	1 Pet. 1:21
" , heed	1 Cor. 14:39; Rev. 1:1–3
" OK (all right)	1 Thess. 5:20
" , read - and be blessed	Rom. 12:6; Rev. 1:3
" sealed - completed	Dan. 9:24
" , second coming	Jer. 23:7, 8 + 50:4–6, 19, 20
" spirit	Rev. 19:10
Prophesyings	1 Thess. 5:20
Prophet, great	Luke 7:16

"	greater than tongue speaker	1 Cor. 14:2–6
"	no honor at home	Mark 6:4; John 4:44
"	prophesied	Acts 3:19–26
"	- to be raised up	Deut. 18:15; Acts 3:21–24 + 7:37
Prophetess		Jude 4:4
Prophetic description of Jesus		Isa. 52:13, 14
Prophets are God's servants		Amos 3:7; 2 Pet. 1:21
"	by holy men	2 Chron. 20:20; 2 Pet. 1:21
"	, false	Matt. 24:24; Mark 13:21, 22
"	get God's secrets	Amos 3:7
"	persecuted	Matt. 5:12
"	witness	Acts 10:43
"	, women	Acts 21:9
Prophet's words		2 Pet. 3:1–4
Propitiation for our sins		Rom. 3:25; 1 John 2:1, 2 + 4:10
Proportion		Rom. 12:6
Proselytes, religious		Matt. 23:15; Acts 13:43
Prospect		Ezek. 40:44–46
Prosper		Gen. 39:23; Deut. 29:9; 1 Kings 2:3; 2 Chron. 20:20 + 22:13; Isa. 55:11; Jer. 10:21
"	- body & soul	3 John 1:2
"	by meditating in law of the Lord	Ps. 1:1–3
"	by reading Bible	Josh. 1:8
"	" seeking God	2 Chron. 26:5
"	from word	Isa. 55:11
"	given by God	Deut. 8:8; Jer. 29:11; 1 Cor. 16:2
"	not if cover sin	Prov. 28:13
Prospered		2 Chron. 31:21
Prospereth by a gift		Prov. 17:8; 3 John 1:2

Prosperity	Josh. 1:7, 8
Prosperous	Josh. 1:8; Job 8:6; Rom. 1:10
Prostitute	Lev. 19:29
Protect families	Neh. 4:14; Mark 13:36, 37; Eph. 6:17, 18
Protected by God	Dan. 3:1–30
" " Lord	Deut. 33:12; Acts 18:9, 10
Protection by angels	Matt. 4:6
" for the godly	Ps. 91:1–16
" of God - Lord	Ps. 46:1–11; 1 Pet. 3:12
Protest	1 Cor. 15:31
Protested	Jer. 11:7; Zech. 3:6
Protesting	Jer. 11:7
Proud	Ps. 40:4 + 86:14; Isa. 13:11; 1 Pet. 5:5
" heart is sin	Prov. 21:4
Provocation	Ps. 95:8
Prove	Rom. 12:2; Gal. 6:4, 5
" all things	1 Thess. 5:21
Proved	Dan. 1:14
Proverb	Prov. 1:6; Luke 4:23; John 16:25, 29
Proverbs of Solomon	1 Kings 4:32; Prov. 10:1–32; 1 Cor. 16:25
Provide	2 Chron. 2:7; 1 Tim. 5:8
" for children	2 Cor. 12:14
" " less fortunate	Deut. 24:19–22
" honestly	Rom. 12:17
Provided by God	Ps. 23:1–6; 1 Cor. 3:6, 7
" for	Deut. 28:1, 2, 11, 12; Heb. 11:39, 40
Provider is God	Rom. 12:1, 2
Province	Jer. 1:1; Dan. 2:48, 49
Provision not for flesh	Rom. 13:14

Provisions, delight in	Isa. 55:1, 2
Provocation	1 Kings 21:22; Ps. 95:8; Heb. 3:8, 15
Provoke Lord	Num. 14:11; Deut. 31:29 + 32:16; 2 Chron. 33:6 + 34:25; 1 Cor. 10:22; Col. 3:21
" not children	Eph. 6:4
" one another	Gal. 5:26; Heb. 10:24
Provoked	Num. 14:23; 1 Kings 21:22; Neh. 4:5; 2 Cor. 9:2
Provoking	Deut. 32:19; 1 Kings 14:15; Gal. 5:26
Prudence	Eph. 1:8
Prudent	Prov. 14:8, 15, 18 + 15:5 + 18:15; Luke 10:21; 1 Cor. 1:19
Pruninghooks	Isa. 2:4; Mic. 4:3
Psalm	Acts 13:33, 35
" of David	Ps. (most of this book)
Psalms and hymns	Ps. 95:2; Eph. 5:19; Col. 3:16; James 5:13
Psalteries	2 Chron. 5:12; Ps. 108:2
Psaltry	Ps. 92:3
Publican	Matt. 5:47 + 18:17 + 21:31
Publick	Matt. 1:19; Acts 20:20
Publish	Deut. 32:3; Ps. 26:7
" against instructions	Mark 1:44, 45
" gospel	Mark 13:10; Acts 10:37
Publisheth	Isa. 52:7
Puffed up	1 Cor. 4:6, 19, 20 + 5:2; Col. 2:18
Pulse to eat	Dan. 1:11–20
Punish	Isa. 26:20, 21; Zeph. 1:9
" for evil	Isa. 13:11

"	seven times more for sins	Lev. 26:18, 21, 24, 28
"	son while there is hope	Prov. 19:18
"	wicked	Isa. 13:9–11
Punishment everlasting or life eternal		Matt. 25:46
"	for evil doers	Job 31:3; 1 Pet. 2:14
"	" our failure	John 3:16
"	" the wicked	Rev. 21:8
Purchase		Jer. 32:11, 12
Pure		1 John 3:2, 3
"	conscience	1 Tim. 3:9
"	" in degrees	Luke 47:12
"	in heart	Matt. 5:8
"	, Jesus was	1 Pet. 2:21, 22
"	, keep	1 Tim. 5:22
"	minds	2 Pet. 3:1
"	religion	James 1:27
"	words	Ps. 12:6
Purge		Ps. 51:7 + 65:3; Isa. 6:7; Matt. 3:12; Mark 7:19; 1 Cor. 5:7; Heb. 9:14
Purged with blood		Heb. 9:22
Purification		Luke 2:21, 22
Purified, many		Jer. 12:30; Dan. 12:10
"	souls	1 Pet. 1:22
"	things in heaven	Heb. 9:23
"	words	Ps. 12:6
Purify me - prayer		Ps. 139:23, 24
"	self by hope	1 John 3:3
"	souls	1 Pet. 1:22
"	themselves	John 11:55
"	us to Himself	Titus 2:14

Purity	1 Tim. 4:12
Purloining	Titus 2:10
Purpose	Eccles. 3:1, 17 + 12:13, 14
" , life's	1 Cor. 6:20; 2 Cor. 4:15–18; Phil. 1:20
" of Christ	Eph. 1:10
" " God	Rom. 8:28
" " Lord's coming	Isa. 61:11; Luke 19:10; John 4:34; Gal. 1:4; Eph. 3:11
Purposefully, walk wise	Eph. 5:15
Purposeth	2 Cor. 9:7
Push	Ps. 44:5; Dan. 11:40
Pursue	Ps. 18:37 + 34:14
Pursuing	1 Kings 18:27
Put	Gen. 2:8, 15; Ezek. 36:27; Matt. 8:3; Rom. 13:12, 14
" away wives	Matt. 19:8, 9
" off	Col. 3:8, 9
" on	Rom. 13:14; Eph. 4:24; Col. 3:10, 12, 14
" trust in Him	Ps. 2:12
Putting away	Eph. 4:25
" forth of the finger	Isa. 58:9
" on apparel	1 Pet. 5:3

⁜ Q ⁜

Quails to eat	Num. 11:32; Ps. 105:40
Qualifications to see Lord	Heb. 12:14–16
Quarrel	Lev. 26:25; Col. 3:13
Queen	Lev. 18:22 + 20:13
Quench	Matt. 12:20; Mark 9:45, 46, 48
" darts of wicked	Eph. 6:16
" not the spirit	1 Thess. 5:19
Quenched	2 Chron. 34:25; Isa. 43:17
Question the Lord's	
words - reprisal	Luke 1:5–22, 57–64
Questioned	Mark 1:27
Questions	Matt. 22:46
Quick	Acts 10:42; Heb. 4:12;
	1 Pet. 4:5
" and dead	Acts 10:42; 2 Tim. 4:1;
	1 Pet. 4:5
Quicken me	Ps. 119:107 + 143:11
" our bodies	Rom. 8:11; Phil. 3:20, 21;
	1 Thess. 4:14–18; 1 John 3:2, 3
Quickened	1 Cor. 15:36; Eph. 2:5;
	Col. 2:13; 1 Pet. 3:18
Quickeneth	John 5:21 + 6:63 + 15:21;
	1 Tim. 6:13

Quickly	Jude 2:17; Eccles. 4:12; Acts 12:7
" come the Lord	Rev. 22:12
Quiet *Judges*	~~Jude~~ 18:7; 1 Thess. 4:11; 1 Pet. 3:4
Quieteth the earth	Job 37:17
Quit	1 Cor. 16:13
Quiver	Ps. 127:4, 5; Isa. 49:2; Lam. 3:12

• R •

Rabbi	John 1:49
Raca (not translated into English)	Matt. 5:22
Race, run	1 Cor. 9:24, 26; Heb. 12:1
" unpredictable	Eccles. 9:11
Radio predicted	Job 38:34, 35; Luke 12:3
Rage	2 Kings 5:12; 2 Chron. 28:9; Ps. 2:1; Acts 4:25
Rail	Deut. 22:8
Railed	Luke 23:39
Railing	1 Pet. 3:8, 9; 2 Pet. 2:11; Jude 1:9
Raiment	Matt. 3:4 + 6:28; 1 Tim. 6:8
Rain	Job 37:6; Joel 2:23; Zech. 10:1; Matt. 5:45; James 5:17, 18
" - way of Lord's coming	Hos. 6:3; Joel 2:23
Rainbow	Gen. 9:13, 14, 16; Rev. 4:3
Raise us up	2 Cor. 4:14; John 6:44
Raised	Acts 12:7 + 13:23, 30, 33, 37
" again	Rom. 4:25
" for our justification	Rom. 4:24, 25

" from dead	Acts 13:30–34; Rom. 4:24 + 6:4 + 10:9; 1 Cor. 15:51, 52; 1 Thess. 4:16
Raising children	Eph. 6:4
Raisins	1 Sam. 30:12
Ram	Gen. 15:9 + 22:13; Mic. 6:7
Ranks	Mark 6:40
Ransom	1 Tim. 2:3–6; Titus 2:14
Ransomed	Isa. 35:10
Rape	2 Sam. 13:1–14
Rapture	Eph. 4:8
Rash not with mouth	Eccles. 5:2
Rashly	Acts 19:36
Rather	Ps. 84:10; Mark 15:11, 15; Luke 10:20 + 12:31
Raven	Gen. 8:7; 1 Kings 17:4–6; Prov. 30:17; Luke 12:24
Ravished	Prov. 5:19; Lam. 5:11
Raw	Exod. 12:9
Razor	Jude 16:17; Isa. 7:20; Ezek. 5:1
Reaching forth	Phil. 3:13
Read	2 Chron. 34:30; Luke 4:16
" Bible for God's guidance	Deut. 17:18–20; Eph. 3:4
" Bible for success	Josh. 1:8; John 7:15; Rev. 1:3
" prophesy	Rev. 1:3
Readiness of mind	Acts 17:11; 2 Cor. 8:11
Ready	Luke 22:12, 13; 2 Cor. 9:3; 1 Pet. 1:5 + 4:5
" , be	Matt. 24:36–44; Titus 3:1
" mind	1 Pet. 5:2
Reap	Matt. 6:26; John 4:35–37; Gal. 6:8, 9

" as sown	John 4:36–38; 2 Cor. 9:6, 7; Gal. 6:7, 8
Reaped	James 5:4
Reapers are angels	Matt. 13:39
Reason	2 Chron. 20:15; Mark 2:8; Luke 5:21, 22; 2 Cor. 3:10
" together	Isa. 1:18
Reasonable service	Rom. 12:1
Rebel	Num. 14:9; 1 Sam. 12:14, 15
Rebelled	Gen. 14:4; Lam. 1:18, 20
Rebellion is sign of witchcraft	1 Sam. 15:23
Rebellious	Isa. 30:1; Ezek. 2:3 + 12:9 + 17:12
Rebuke	Ps. 6:1; Prov. 27:5 + 28:23; Isa. 25:8; Matt. 16:22; Mark 1:25; Jude 1:9
" and chasten ones to repent	Rev. 3:19
Rebuked	Matt. 17:18 + 20:31; Mark 1:25 + 9:25 + 10:13; Luke 4:39 + 8:24 + 18:15, 39; + 23:40; 2 Pet. 2:16
Rebuking	Luke 4:41
Recall	Lam. 3:21
Receive abundance of grace	Rom. 5:17
" and give	1 John 3:16
Receive another - did not receive Jesus	John 5:43
" as done	2 Cor. 5:10
" " given	Luke 6:38
" by asking - etc.	Matt. 7:7; John 14:14 + 16:24
" " believing	Matt. 18:5 + 21:22; Mark 11:22

"	child	Matt. 18:5
"	" & Jesus & God	Luke 9:48
"	- get power	John 1:12
"	- give accordingly	Luke 12:48; 1 Pet. 4:10
"	God & Jesus	John 13:20
"	Jesus & God	Matt. 10:40; John 13:20
"	" when receive a child	Matt. 18:5; Luke 9:48
"	kingdom	Luke 18:17
"	law	Job 22:22
"	not as blessed as in giving	Acts 20:35
"	one another	Rom. 15:7
"	others	Matt. 10:40, 41; John 5:40–43; Rom. 15:7
"	prophet	Matt. 10:41; Phil. 1:17
"	remission of sins	Acts 10:43
"	us	2 Cor. 6:17, 18
"	you, will	John 14:3
Received Him		John 1:12
"	in heaven, Jesus	Mark 16:19
Receiveth		Matt. 7:8 + 10:40, 41; Mark 9:37; John 13:20
Reckon		Matt. 18:24; Rom. 4:4 + 8:18
Reckoneth		Matt. 25:19
Recognize God & His	greatness	Rev. 4:11 + 14:7
"	Lord not enough	Matt. 7:21
"	the faithful	Deut. 28:1, 2, 10
Recompense		Ruth 2:12; Prov. 11:31; Isa. 35:4; Luke 14:14; Rom. 12:17; Heb. 10:35
"	for one's work	Ps. 62:12; Isa. 59:18; 2 Cor. 5:10
"	honestly	Rom. 12:17

Recompensed on earth	Prov. 11:31
Reconciled to Him	Matt. 5:24; 2 Cor. 5:18–20; Col. 1:20, 21
Reconciliation for iniquity	Dan. 9:24; 2 Cor. 5:18–20
Record	John 8:14 + 19:35; Phil. 1:8; 1 John 5:7; Rev. 1:1, 2
Recover Lord's people	Isa. 11:11
" strength	Ps. 39:13; Luke 4:18
Red	Num. 19:2; Ps. 136:13; Isa. 1:18; Matt. 16:2, 3
Redeem	Gal. 4:4, 5
" me	Ps. 49:15
" us	Titus 2:14
Redeemed by blood of Christ	1 Pet. 1:18, 19
" of servants	Ps. 34:22
" the way of holiness per God	Isa. 35:8; Mal. 4:2
" us	Gal. 3:13
" with blood	1 Pet. 1:17–21
Redeemer is Lord	Isa. 41:14 + 48:17 + 49:26 + 59:20
" liveth	Job 19:25; Prov. 23:11; Isa. 59:20
Redeeming time	Eph. 5:16; Col. 4:5
Redemption	Luke 21:25–28; Eph. 1:7; Heb. 9:15
" by Jesus' blood	Heb. 9:11, 12
" in Christ Jesus	Rom. 3:24
" of our body	Rom. 8:23
" purchased at Calvary	Col. 21–23; Heb. 10:12
" through His blood	Col. 1:14; Heb. 9:15
" time coming	Luke 21:28; Eph. 4:30
" to grace	Rom. 3:24

Redound	2 Cor. 4:15
Reed	Mark 15:19, 36
Reformed shall live	Ezek. 18:27, 28
Refrain from sorrow & evil	Jer. 31:16, 17; 1 Pet. 3:10
Refraineth	Prov. 10:19
Refresh	Prov. 25:13; Acts 3:19; Philem. 1:20
Refuge is God	Ps. 46:1, 7 + 62:7, 8 + 91:2–10 + 121:5–7
" " Lord	Ps. 9:9 + 91:9
Refuse not speaker from heaven	Heb. 12:25
Refused	Heb. 11:24
Regard	1 Kings 18:29; Lam. 4:16; Rom. 14:6
Regeneration	Titus 3:5
Region	Matt. 3:5; Luke 4:14
Reign	Rom. 5:21
" forever - Christ	Luke 1:33; Rom. 5:17, 21; Rev. 11:15
" with Christ a thousand years	Rev. 20:4, 6
" with Christ first resurrection	Rev. 20:5
" with Christ or deny Him	2 Tim. 2:12, 13
Reigned for witness of Jesus	Rev. 20:4, 5
Reigneth God	Isa. 52:7; Rev. 19:6
" Lord God over all	1 Chron. 29:11–13
Reins	Ps. 7:9 + 139:13
Reject	Mark 7:9

Rejoice		Ps. 65:8 + 118:24; Isa. 62:5; Luke 15:6 + 16:23; Phil. 2:17, 18 + 4:4, 10
"	always	Luke 10:20; Phil. 4:4; 1 Thess. 5:16–18
"	at Jesus going to Father	John 14:28
"	at last days	Rev. 12:10–12
"	because the day is holy to the Lord	Jer. 8:9–11
"	evermore	1 Thess. 5:16
"	from sorrow	Jer. 31:10–13
"	- God over us	Isa. 62:5
"	, heart - in Lord	Prov. 23:15, 16, 24; Zech. 10:7
"	in boasting is evil	James 4:16
"	" farming	John 4:35–37
"	" gospel	Phil. 1:18
"	" hope & prayer	Rom. 12:12, 15
"	" the Lord	Ps. 33:1; Isa. 61:10; Luke 1:46; Phil. 3:1 + 4:4
"	" " truth	1 Cor. 13:7; 1 Pet. 4:13; 3 John 1:3
"	- Jesus	Luke 10:21
"	not when enemy falleth	Prov. 24:17
"	seekers of Lord	Ps. 105:3
"	some is evil	James 4:16
"	to see Jesus	John 16:22
"	- weep	Rom. 12:15
"	, why	Neh. 8:10
Rejoiceth		Isa. 64:5
Rejoicing		1 Cor. 1:12
Release		Matt. 27:15, 17, 20, 21; Mark 15:6, 9, 11, 15

Religion not necessarily Christian	James 1:26, 27
" , pure - duties	James 1:27
Religious	James 1:26
" , not to be	Rom. 16:17, 18; Eph. 2:13–16
Remain	John 6:12; 1 Thess. 4:15, 17
" , joy in you	John 15:11
Remaineth, day	2 Cor. 3:14
Remedy	Prov. 29:1
Remember	Luke 17:32; 1 Cor. 11:2; 2 Thess. 2:5; Jude 1:17
" Lord's works & judgments	Ps. 25:6, 7 + 105:5–7
" prisoners	Heb. 13:3
" sins no more	Heb. 10:17, 18
Remembered not the Lord	Jude 8:34
Remembrance	Eccles. 1:11 + 2:16; John 14:26 + 16:13; 1 Cor. 11:23–66; Phil. 1:3–6; 2 Pet. 3:1
" lesson	John 14:26; 2 Pet. 1:12–15
" not in death	Ps. 6:5
Remind brethren	1 Tim. 4:6
Remission by blood	Heb. 9:22
" of sins	Mark 1:4; Luke 1:77 + 3:3 + 24:47; Acts 2:30, 31, 38; Rom. 3:25; Heb. 10:17, 18
" " " , only one	Heb. 9:22 + 10:10–18
" " " to be preached	Luke 24:47
Remit	John 20:23
Remnant of people	Isa. 11:11 + 37:32; Jer. 15:11 + 42:2

Remove	Gen. 8:13; Matt. 17:20; 1 Cor. 13:2
" cup	Luke 22:42
Removed	Ps. 46:2
Rend	Eccles. 3:7
Render per works	Ps. 62:12; Prov. 24:12; Matt. 22:21; Rom. 2:6
Rendering	1 Pet. 3:9
Renew	Rom. 12:2; Eph. 4:23, 24
" a right spirit	Ps. 51:10
" strength	Isa. 40:31
Renewed	Eph. 4:23, 24
Renewest face of earth	Ps. 104:30
Renewing of mind	Rom. 12:2
" " the Holy Ghost	Titus 3:5
Renounced (dishonesty)	2 Cor. 4:2
Rent	Josh. 7:6; Matt. 27:51; Luke 23:45; Acts 14:14
Repaired	1 Kings 18:30; 1 Chron. 11:8
Repay	Rom. 12:19; Philem. 1:19
Repeat history	Luke 17:26–30
Repent	Luke 13:3, 5 + 15:7; Acts 2:38–40 + 3:19 + 17:30, 31
" - change	Matt. 4:17; Mark 1:15; Acts 17:30
" - forgive	Luke 17:3, 4
" from falling	Rev. 2:5
" - one sinner	Luke 15:10
Repentance	Job 11:13–18; Luke 3:3 + 5:32 + 15:10 + 24:47; Acts 5:31; 2 Cor. 7:9, 10; 2 Pet. 3:9
" by sorrow	2 Cor. 5:9, 10
" is goodness of God	Rom. 2:4 + 11:29

Repented the Lord	Gen. 6:6
Repetitions in prayer	Matt. 6:7
Replenish	Gen. 1:28
Repliest	Rom. 9:20
Report	Prov. 18:30; 2 Cor. 6:8; Phil. 4:8
" , good - through faith	Heb. 11:39
Reproach	Ps. 39:8 + 42:10; 51:7; 57:3; Prov. 14:31, 34 + 17:5 + 18:3 + 27:11; Lam. 3:30, 61; + 5:1; 1 Tim. 4:10
" of men not to be feared	Ps. 57:1–3; Isa. 51:7, 8
Reproached for witnessing	1 Pet. 4:14
Reprobate mind	Rom. 1:28; 2 Tim. 3:8
Reprobates	2 Cor. 13:5–7
Reproof	Prov. 1:25, 30 + 6:23
Reprove	Job 6:25 + 13:10; Prov. 25:12; John 16:8; 2 Tim. 4:2
" world of sin - righteousness - judgment	John 16:7–11
Reputation	Acts 5:34; Phil. 2:7
Reputed	Job 18:3; Dan. 4:35
Request	Esther 5:3, 6–8; Rom. 1:10
Requests to be made to God	Phil. 4:6
Require	Gen. 9:5; 1 Cor. 1:22
Required	1 Sam. 12:20; Luke 12:48; 1 Cor. 4:2
Requite	Ps. 41:10; 1 Tim. 5:4
Rereward	Isa. 58:8
Rescue those unjustly sentenced to die	Prov. 24:10–12

Reserved		1 Pet. 1:4; 2 Pet. 3:7
Residue		Jer. 41:10; Acts 15:17
Resist devil		James 4:7; 1 Pet. 5:8, 9
"	not by adversaries	Luke 21:15
"	" evil	Matt. 5:39
"	" God's power	Acts 7:51; Rom. 13:1, 2
Resisted		Heb. 12:4
Resisteth		James 4:6; 1 Pet. 5:5
"	and grace	1 Pet. 5:5
Resort		Neh. 4:20
Respect		Ps. 119:15; Eph. 5:22, 23, 25; Phil. 4:11; 1 Tim. 5:1–3; James 2:3, 9
"	elderly	1 Tim. 5:1–4
"	none	Col. 3:25
"	property of the righteous	Prov. 24:15
Respected not		Lam. 4:16
Respecter		Acts 10:34
Responsibilities		Col. 3:12–24
Responsible - parents to children		2 Cor. 12:14
Rest for God's people		Exod. 33:14; Ps. 37:7; Heb. 4:1–11
"	" souls	Isa. 14:3; Jer. 6:16; Matt. 11:28, 29
"	from bondage	Isa. 14:3
"	" labours	Rev. 14:13
"	given	Matt. 11:28, 29; 2 Cor. 12:9; Heb. 4:8–11
"	in safety	Job 11:18
"	on/in the Lord	2 Chron. 14:11; Ps. 37:7
Restitution		Acts 3:21
Restore		Isa. 42:22; Jer. 30:17

"	an erring one	Gal. 6:1, 2
"	joy of salvation	Ps. 51:12
Restored		Ps. 69:4; Matt. 12:13; Mark 8:25
Restrained		Acts 14:18
Resurrection		Joel 2:31, 32; John 5:29 + 11:24, 25 + 14:6, 7; 1 Cor. 15:21–23, 41–58
"	and our behavior	Ps. 49:1–20
"	chapter	1 Cor. 15:1–58
"	, first - for the just	Luke 14:14; Rev. 20: 4–6
"	for worthy ones	Luke 20:35, 36; Rev. 3:4
"	foretold	1 Cor. 15:51, 52
"	hope	1 Pet. 1:3
"	, I am the	John 11:25
"	is Jesus	John 11:23–26; Acts 1:21; 1 Thess. 4:14
"	of dead proved	Matt. 27:53; 1 Cor. 15:12
"	" life or death	John 5:27–29; Acts 24:14, 15
"	power	Phil. 3:10
"	- two	John 5:26–29; Rev. 20:4–6
Retain		Ps. 4:4
Retained		John 20:23; Philem. 1:13
Return		Job 6:29; Ps. 90:3
"	as given	Gen. 3:19; Luke 6:38
"	good to others	Luke 6:27–38
"	of Jesus	Mal. 4:5; Matt. 24:1–51 + 25:1–46; Rev. 22:12
"	word	Isa. 55:11
Returned to Christ		1 Pet. 2:25
"	" God	Luke 17:18
Returning		Acts 8:28
Reveal by God if off course		Phil. 3:15
"	God's son	Gal. 1:16

"	the Father	Matt. 11:27
"	wicked	2 Thess. 2:8–10
Revealed		Luke 2:26 + 12:2 + 17:30; 1 Pet. 1:12
"	antichrist - Satan	2 Thess. 2:3, 4, 8–10
"	at end	1 Pet. 1:5
Revealed by God's spirit		1 Cor. 2:10
"	glory	Isa. 40:5
"	God through creation	Gen. 1:1–31; Ps. 19:1; Isa. 46:9, 10
"	Himself - God	Gen. 1:1–31 + 2:1–8, 21, 23; Ps. 19:1; Isa. 46:7, 10
"	in us - God's glory	Rom. 8:18
"	Lord Jesus	2 Thess. 1:7
"	man of sin	2 Thess. 2:3, 4
"	not by flesh & blood	Matt. 16:17
Revealeth His secrets to prophets		Dan. 2:22; Amos 3:7
Revelation		Gal. 1:12; 1 Pet. 1:13
"	book not to be altered	Rev. 22:18, 19
"	is key to book of Daniel	Dan. 2:1–49
"	of the mystery	Rom. 16:25
"	questions to Jesus	Matt. 24:3
Revenge		2 Cor. 10:6
"	forbidden	Rom. 12:17–19 + 13:4
Revenues		Prov. 16:8
Reverence - blessed to read		Rom. 16:25; Rev. 1:3
"	due God	Ps. 111:9

"	(fear) of Lord is beginning of knowledge	Prov. 1:7
"	the sanctuary	Lev. 19:30 + 26:2
"	to fathers	Heb. 12:9
"	" God	Ps. 89:7; Heb. 12:28
"	" God's name	Ps. 111:9
"	" spouse	Eph. 5:28–33
Reverend		Ps. 119:1
Revile		Matt. 5:11; 1 Pet. 2:23
Reviled		Mark 15:32; 1 Cor. 4:12; 1 Pet. 2:23
Revilest		Acts 23:4
Revival		Ezra 9:8
Revive		Ps. 138:7: Isa. 57:15; Rom. 14:9
Reward		Dan. 7:27; Isa. 55:10–13 + 64:4; Heb. 10:35; Rev. 14:12 + 20:4 + 22:12
"	by Christ	Matt. 16:27
"	" God	Ps. 31:19 + 8 4:11 + 92:13; 1 Cor. 2:9; 2 Cor. 5:10 + 6:16–18; Col. 1:9–14 + 3:23, 24
"	great	Luke 6:35
"	laborers	Isa. 32:18 + 60:18 + 65:21, 22; 1 Cor. 3:8, 9
"	, life's	Rev. 2:7, 10
"	of Christ	Rev. 22:13
"	" faith	2 Tim. 4:7, 8
"	" faithful - not beast worshippers	John 5:27–29
"	of wicked	Isa. 3:10, 11
"	per labour	Matt. 16:27; 1 Cor. 3:8, 9

"	" works	Matt. 16:27; 1 Cor. 3:8, 14; 2 Cor. 5:10; 2 John 1:8; Rev. 22:12
"	secret	Matt. 6:6
"	to God lovers	Rom. 8:28; Rev. 11:18
Rewarded per riches in	His glory	Eph. 3:17, 18
Rewarder is God		Heb. 11:6
Rib		Gen. 2:22
Rich		1 Tim. 6:9–11, 17, 19
"	and heaven	Matt. 19:24
"	" poor	Prov. 14:20; Matt. 12:21; Luke 16:20–25
"	" " tormented & comforted	Luke 16:20–25
"	fall	1 Tim. 6:9
"	follies	1 Tim. 6:8–11
"	from blessings from the Lord	Prov. 10:22
"	gets charge	1 Tim. 6:17–19
"	in good work	1 Tim. 6:18
"	made not to be afraid	Ps. 49:16
"	not to be our goal	Prov. 23:4
"	possibly not godly	Luke 12:13–21
"	saddened	Mark 10:17–23
Rich	to poverty	2 Cor. 8:9, 12
"	want more	Eccles. 5:10
Riches are the Lord's		Hag. 2:8
"	corrupted	James 5:2
"	, don't glory in	Jer. 9:23, 24
"	, greatest of kings	1 Kings 10:23
"	in Babylon	Rev. 3:11, 15–17 + 18:5–10

"	" glory	Phil. 4:19
"	" Jesus' grace	Eph. 1:7
"	, joyful	Ps. 119:14
"	judgment & ways of God	Rom. 11:33
"	not by right	Jer. 17:11
"	" important	Ps. 37:16
"	" most important	Ps. 37:16; Jer. 17:11; Mark 10:23, 24
"	of His glory	Phil. 4:19; Col. 1:27
"	- poverty	2 Cor. 8:2
"	rejected in body system	Job 20:15
"	uncertain	1 Tim. 6:17
"	vs righteousness	Mark 11:28, 31 + 12:2, 3
Richly		Col. 3:16
Riddance		Zeph. 1:18
Riddle		Jude 14:12–19; Ezek. 17:2
Rid		Ps. 144:11
Ride		Deut. 32:13; Jer. 6:23
Rider		Jer. 51:21
Right		Exod. 15:6, 12; Matt. 5:29, 30; John 18:10 + 21:6
"	hand	Ps. 16:11 + 139:10; Isa. 41:10
"	" of God - Christ	Acts 7:55; Rom. 8:34; Col. 3:1
"	way (correct)	Ps. 19:8; Prov. 14:12
Righteous		Prov. 10:30; 1 Pet. 3:12, 13; 1 John 3:7; Rev. 22:11
"	and family rewarded	Ps. 37:25
"	and wicked	Prov. 13:1–25 + 28:1–28 + 9:2–27
"	flourish	Prov. 11:28, 30, 31; Mark 2:2, 3 + 11:28, 31

"	happy	Isa. 14:7
"	inherit	Ps. 37:29
"	is Jesus Christ	1 John 1:1, 2
"	man's prayer	James 5:16
"	never to be moved	Ps. 55:22
"	, none	Rom. 3:10
"	- none under sin doeth good	Rom. 3:9–19
"	not forsaken	Ps. 1:5, 6 + 37:1–6; Rev. 13:6, 7
"	one turned to sin	Ezek. 3:20, 21
"	or unconcerned of others	Matt. 25:31–46
"	" wicked	Ps. 37:21; Prov. 10:30 + 13:1; 15:33
"	per obedience	Rom. 5:19
"	provided for	Ps. 37:16–19, 25
"	rewarded	Ps. 92:12, 13; Prov. 13:6, 7 + 14:34 + 16:12; Isa. 30:10 + 54:17; Ezek. 3:21
"	to shine	Matt. 13:43
"	vs riches	Mark 2:2, 3 + 11:28, 31
"	" wicked	Prov. 10:30 + 11:1–31 + 12:2, 3 + 13:5, 6; Rom. 12:2
Righteously, live		1 Pet. 2:24
Righteousness		Matt. 5:20 + 6:33; Rom. 10:3–6, 10; Titus 3:5
"	and wisdom vs foolish & wicked	Prov. 13:1–25
"	crown	2 Tim. 4:8
"	everlasting	Ps. 103:17; Dan. 9:24; 2 Pet. 3:13
"	for remission of sins	Rom. 3:21–25
"	fruits	2 Cor. 9:10
"	important	Matt. 5:20

"	indicated by circumcision	Rom. 4:11, 12
"	instruction	Isa. 41:10; 2 Tim. 3:16, 17
"	is new man created	Eph. 4:24
Righteousness judge		Rev. 19:11
"	- law	Rom. 3:20, 21, 28 + 10:4, 5; Gal. 2:16, 21; Titus 3:5
"	of God & believers	Rom. 3:22; 2 Pet. 1:1
"	" one	Rom. 5:17, 18
"	on earth	Ps. 36:6; Isa. 11:5–9; John 16:8, 10
"	rewarded	Isa. 54:13–17 + 59:16, 17 + 61:11; Matt. 5:6
"	vs wickedness	Prov. 10:12; 1 Pet. 3:12–17
Ring		Gen. 41:42
Riot		2 Pet. 2:13
Riotous		Luke 15:13
Ripe harvest		Joel 3:13; John 4:35
Rise false prophets		Matt. 24:11
"	if died in the earth	Dan. 12:2; Rev. 1:7
"	- third day foretold	Matt. 20:19; Luke 18:31–33 + 24:46
"	up	Mark 14:42; Luke 5:23, 24; Acts 3:2–8; 1 Thess. 4:16
Risen Lord		Mark 16:6, 19; Luke 24:6; Rom. 8:34; 1 Cor. 15:4, 5, 20
"	" announced	Matt. 26:32 + 28:5–7; Mark 14:28; Eph. 4:8
"	with Christ	Col. 2:12, 13 + 3:1–4
Rituals not acceptable		Amos 5:21–27
River		Ps. 46:4
Roar		Ps. 46:3 + 104:21; Isa. 42:13 + 59:11; Hos. 11:10
Roaring		Ps. 32:3

Roast	Exod. 12:8; Isa. 44:19
Rob not God - tithing	Mal. 3:8–10
" " the poor	Prov. 22:22, 23
Robbed	Isa. 42:22
" by not tithing	Mal. 3:8–10
Robber	John 10:1
Robbery	Phil. 2:6
" of the wicked	Prov. 21:7
Robe	Exod. 39:33–26; Matt. 27:28, 31; Luke 15:22 + 23:11; John 19:2, 5
Robes of white wearers	Rev. 7:13–17
Rock	Deut. 32:4, 37; Ps. 89:26
" , built on	Matt. 7:24, 25 + 16:18
" , my - and salvation	Ps. 18:2 + 62:2, 6, 7
Rocks	Isa. 33:16
Rod	Exod. 7:15, 17, 19, 20
" and serpent	Exod. 4:1–4
Rode	1 Sam. 30:17
Roe	Prov. 5:19 + 6:5
Roll - to eat	Ezek. 3:1–3
Rolled	Mark 15:46 + 16:4
Romankingdom will fall	Dan. 2:40 + 7:7
Romans - different customs	Acts 16:19–21
Room	Gen. 6:14; Luke 2:7; Acts 1:13
Rooster	Eccles. 12:4
Root	2 Kings 19:30; Job 14:8 + 19:28; Jer. 12:2; Matt. 3:10; Mark 4:6, 17; Luke 3:9; Rom. 11:16–18
" is love	Eph. 3:17
" of David is Jesus	Rev. 22:16
" " evil	1 Tim. 6:10

Rooted	Prov. 2:22; Eph. 3:17; Col. 2:7
Roots	Jer. 17:8; Hos. 14:5
" , our	Gen. 1:26, 27
Rose again	1 Cor. 15:4; 2 Cor. 5:15; 1 Thess. 4:14
" from the dead	Luke 16:31; Acts 10:41
" of Sharon is Jesus	Sol. 2:1
Rottenness	Prov. 14:30
Round	Exod. 29:16, 20; Num. 1:50, 53; Luke 2:9
Rouse	Gen. 49:9
Rowed	John 6:19
Royal law	James 2:8
Rubbish	Nem. 4:10
Rubies	Prov. 3:15
Rudder	Acts 27:40
Ruddy	Lam. 4:7
Rudiments of world	Col. 2:8, 20
Rue	Luke 11:42
Rule by righteous or wicked	Prov. 29:2
" by Satan - Antichrist	Rev. 13:14–18
" , carpenter's	Isa. 44:13
" , golden	Matt. 7:12; Luke 6:31
" hearts with peace	Phil. 3:16; Col. 3:15
" own house	1 Tim. 3:4, 5
" " spirit	Prov. 25:28
" them	Rev. 2:27
" , to obey	Heb. 13:17
Ruler	Mark 5:35, 36; Acts 3:17
Rulers to be observed	Heb. 13:7
Rules for living	1 Thess. 5:12–28
Ruleth	Rom. 12:8

Rumors not to trouble us	Matt. 7:17 + 24:6
" of wars	Matt. 24:6
Rump	Lev. 7:3 + 8:25
Run	1 Cor. 9:24, 26; Heb. 12:1
" to & fro	Dan. 12:4
Runnest	Prov. 4:12
Rush	Isa. 17:13 + 19:15
Rust	Matt. 6:20; James 5:3

• S •

Sabbath		Gen. 2:2, 3; Exod. 20:8–11 + 31:13–16; Num. 26:2; Deut. 5:12, 13; Isa. 58:13, 14; Jer. 17:24, 27; Mark 2:27, 28; Luke 4:16; Heb. 4:3, 4, 9, 10
"	activity	Isa. 58:13, 14; Mark 14:5
"	covenant	Lev. 24:8
"	, false	Rev. 13:16
"	, first	Gen. 2:1–3
"	lawful actions	Luke 6:9, 10
"	, Lord of	Luke 6:5
"	to be hallowed	Ezek. 20:20
"	" keep	Lev. 26:2
Sabeans		Job 1:15
Sackcloth		Isa. 37:1, 2 + 58:5; Matt. 11:21
Sacred is man		Gen. 9:6
Sacrifice		1 Cor. 10:20
"	, daily - taken away	Dan. 12:11
"	for us	Ps. 51:17; Gal. 1:4 + 2:20; Heb. 2:9–11 + 10:10–14 + 13:15, 16
"	, greatest - Jesus	John 19:1, 2, 17, 18; Heb. 10:12
"	less than justice & judgment	Prov. 21:3

" , living bodies	Rom. 12:1
" , obey	1 Sam. 15:22
Sacrifice our body to God	Rom. 12:1
Sacrifices of God	Ps. 51:17
" to please God	Heb. 13:16
" unsuccessful by humans	Heb. 10:10–14
Sad	Matt. 6:16; Luke 24:17
" - Jesus	John 1:33, 35, 38
Saddle	1 Kings 13:27
Safe with the Lord	Ps. 118:5–10
Safely	Prov. 1:38
" for those trusty in the Lord	Ps. 121:1–8
" foretold	Ezek. 38:8, 11, 14
" of godly	Ps. 121:1–8
Safety	Job 11:18; Ps. 33:17 + 91:1–16
Said	Gen. 1:1, 3, 6, 9
" Jesus	John 11:40: + 20:21
Saidst	Jer. 22:21
Sail	Isa. 33:23
Saints	Ps. 16:3; Acts 26:10; Eph. 1:18 + 4:12 + 6:18; Col. 1:1, 12, 26; Jude 1:14; Rev. 14:12
" at war	Dan. 7:21; Rev. 13:7
Saint's death precious to God	Ps. 116:15
Saints judge world	Dan. 7:22; 2 Cor. 15:3
Saint's king	Ps. 116:15; Rev. 15:3
Saints of kingdom's people	Dan. 7:27
Saint's patience	Rev. 14:12
Saints to rule world	1 Cor. 6:2
Saith	Isa. 44:6; Rev. 14:13
" Jesus "I am"	John 14:6

"	" to Satan	Matt. 4:10
Sake, elect's		Mark 13:20
"	of Christ	Matt. 10:18 + 16:25, 26; John 13:38; Rom. 4:23 + 15:30
"	" love	Philem. 1:9
Salt		Lev. 2:13; Num. 18:19; 2 Kings 2:20, 21; Matt. 5:13; Luke 14:34
"	covenant	Num. 18:19
Salutation		Mark 12:38; Luke 1:29; 1 Cor. 16:21
Salute		2 Kings 4:29; Mark 9:15; Heb. 13:24; 3 John 1:14
Salvation by believing - not seeing		1 Pet. 1:7–9
"	by Christ Jesus	1 Thess. 5:8, 9; 2 Tim. 2:10
"	" " the Lord	Ps. 35:9; Luke 2:11
"	" faith	2 Tim. 3:15; 1 Pet. 1:9
"	" free gift	Rom. 10:13
Salvation by God		Ps. 62:7; Phil. 1:28; 1 Tim. 1:1 + 2:3 + 4:10
"	" gospel	Rom. 1:16; 1 Cor. 15:1, 2, 18, 21
"	" grace	Rom. 3:23, 24; Eph. 2:8; Titus 2:11
"	" Jesus	Matt. 1:21; John 1:29 + 14:6
"	" Jesus' life	Rom. 5:10; 1 Cor. 15:17, 18; Heb. 7:25
"	" Jesus only	Acts 4:10–12; 2 Tim. 2:10
"	" repentance	Acts 3:19 + 8:22
"	" saving yourself	Acts 2:40; Phil. 2:12
"	" words	Acts 11:14; Heb. 4:12; James 1:21
"	day	2 Cor. 6:2
"	for all	Titus 2:11

"	" ever	Isa. 51:6
"	" Jews & Greeks	John 4:22; Rom. 1:16
"	by obeying God	Heb. 5:9
"	from power of God	Rom. 1:16; Rev. 7:10
"	I have seen - Luke	Isa. 51:6–8; Luke 2:30; Acts 13:47; Heb. 9:28
"	involvements	2 Cor. 5:1–7 + 6:1–10
"	is of the Lord	Exod. 15:2; Ps. 3:8 + 118:14; Isa. 45:8; Jon. 2:9; Phil. 12:11–13
"	most important	1 Cor. 5:10; Heb. 2:3
"	, my	Ps. 62:1, 2, 6, 7 + 118:14
"	of God	Isa. 12:2; Acts 28:28
"	, one's own	Phil. 2:12; 1 Pet. 1:5–11
"	revealed at end	1 Pet. 1:5
"	, shew	Ps. 96:2
"	through faith	2 Tim. 3:15
"	" one only	Acts 4:12
"	up to self	Phil. 2:12, 13
"	with heart & mouth	Rom. 10:9, 10
Same	- all to the Lord	Mark 3:34, 35; Rom. 10:12
"	, Jesus Christ always	Heb. 13:8
"	Lord - same God	1 Cor. 12:5, 6
"	since creation	2 Pet. 3:4
"	thing - mind - judgment	1 Cor. 1:10
Samson		Jude 13:24, 25 + 14:1–16 + 16:1–31
Sanctification		1 Thess. 4:3–5; 1 Pet. 1:2; 2 Pet. 1:5–10
"	prayer	Ps. 51:6–12
Sanctified		Acts 20:32 + 26:18; Rom. 15:16; Heb. 2:11 + 10:10–14

"	by Jesus' offering	Heb. 2:9–11 + 10:12–14
"	" only one	Heb. 2:9–11 + 10:10–14
"	" Jeremiah before he was born	Jer. 1:5
Sanctify		Exod. 31:13; Lev. 27:14–19, 22, 26; John 17:17; Rom. 16:15; 1 Thess. 5:23
Sanctuary		Lev. 19:30: + 26:2 + 27:25; Ps. 63:2 + 134:2
"	(earth) cleansed	Isa. 8:13, 14; Dan. 8:14
Sand		Exod. 2:12
Sandals		Acts 12:8
Sap		Ps. 104:16
Sapphire		Exod. 24:10; Job 28:6; Ezek. 1:26; Rev. 21:19
Sarah (90) with child		Gen. 17:19 + 21:1–3; Rom. 4:19; Heb. 11:11
"	died at 127 years old	Gen. 23:1
Sanding stone		Rev. 4:3
Sat		Luke 10:39
"	on right hand of God	Mark 16:19; Heb. 10:12
Satan		Rev. 12:12
"	and his people punished	Lev. 16:22
"	bound & loosed	Rev. 20:1–3
"	cast down	Rev. 12:10–13
"	deceives	Gen. 3:4, 5; 2 Cor. 11:13–15; 2 Thess. 2:9, 10
"	has power	Rev. 13:13, 14 + 16:13, 14
"	hinders	1 Thess. 2:18; 2 Thess. 2:9
"	into Judas Iscariot	Luke 22:3
"	is dragon	Rev. 12:9

Satan recognized		Luke 10:17, 18
"	to be betrayed	Dan. 11:26
"	transformed into angel	2 Cor. 11:14
Satan's end		Ezek. 28:6–8, 16–19
"	lie	Gen. 3:4
"	wrath	Mark 4:15; Rev. 12:12
Satiate		Jer. 31:14
Satisfied		Ps. 63:5
"	not - four things	Prov. 30:15, 16
Satisfieth desire		Ps. 145:16
Satisfy		Isa. 58:10, 11; Col. 2:23
"	be - with possessions	Heb. 13:5
"	Lord with my saved life	Ps. 91:15
Satyrs		Isa. 13:21
Saul - minister		Acts 26:16
"	to Paul	Acts 13:9
Save		Ps. 16:10 + 49:15; Mark 15:30, 31
"	- confess & believe	Isa. 45:22; Acts 4:12 + 16:31
"	lives by Jesus	Luke 9:62 + 19:10
"	or lose life	Matt. 10:39 + 16:25; Mark 8:35; Luke 17:32
"	people	Heb. 7:25; James 5:19, 20
"	" second time	Isa. 11:11
"	sinners	1 Tim. 1:15
"	thyself & hearers	1 Tim. 4:16
"	world	John 3:17
"	your souls	Luke 19:10 + 21:19
Saved after tribulation		Rev. 7:13–15 + 14:1–3
"	, all men to be	1 Tim. 2:3, 4
"	at last if desired	Acts 2:17–21

"	- believe & confess	Rom. 10:9
"	by baptism	Acts 2:37, 38; 1 Pet. 3:20, 21
"	" believing	Mark 16:15, 16; John 3:16; Acts 16:31; Rom. 5:9, 10
"	" " & confessing	1 John 1:7
"	by call	Rom. 10:13, 14
"	by confessing & believing	Rom. 10:9, 10
"	by enduring	Matt. 10:22; Mark 13:13
"	" faith per Jesus	Luke 7:48, 50 + 18:42; Eph. 2:8, 9
"	" grace	Eph. 2:8
"	" His matchless love	1 Tim. 1:15
"	by hope	Rom. 8:24, 25
"	" Jesus Christ only	John 14:6; Acts 4:10, 12
"	" looking to the Lord	Isa. 45:22
"	by Lord	Rom. 10:9, 13
"	" love of truth	2 Thess. 2:10
"	" mercy of God	Titus 3:5
"	" one only	Acts 2:17–21 + 4:12
"	" water	1 Pet. 3:20; 2 Pet. 2:5
"	flesh	Mark 13:20
"	from wrath to come	Rev. 5:8, 9
"	Israel	Rom. 11:26
"	Noah	1 Pet. 3:20; 2 Pet. 2:5
"	not by strength	Ps. 33:17; Rom. 10:13
"	ones must endure to end	Matt. 10:22 + 24:13; Mark 13:13
"	others	Rom. 11:14; Mark 15:31
"	through faith	Eph. 2:8
"	us before world	2 Tim. 1:9

Saving prayers & promise to God	Ps. 51:1–19
Savings	Prov. 21:20 + 30:25; Eccles. 5:13–18; Isa. 46:4
Saviour	Acts 5:23, 31; Titus 1:4 + 2:13; 1 John 4:14
"　from God	John 3:16; 1 John 4:9, 10, 14
"　- God	Titus 3:4
"　- Jesus	Acts 13:23
Saviour - Lord only	Isa. 43:11; John 4:42; Acts 5:31; Jude 1:25
"　of body	Eph. 5:23
Savour	Eph. 5:2
Savourest	Matt. 16:23
Say to churches, Spirit	Rev. 2:7, 11, 17
Saying	Rom. 4:7
"　unto me "write," voice	Rev. 14:13
Saw	Ps. 77:16
"　things	Rev. 1:1, 2
Sawest	Rev. 17:14
Scab	Lev. 14:56
Scabbed	Lev. 22:22
Scales	Acts 9:18
Scall	Lev. 13:30–37
Scapegoat	Lev. 16:22
Scarcely	1 Pet. 4:18
Scarest	Job 7:14
Scarlet	Isa. 1:18
Scatter	Dan. 12:7
Scattered	Mark 14:27; James 1:1; 1 Pet. 1:1
Scattereth	Matt. 12:30; Luke 11:23; John 10:12

Scent		Hos. 14:7
Sceptre		Ps. 45:6; Heb. 1:8
Schism		1 Cor. 12:25
Scholar		1 Chron. 25:8
Science		1 Tim. 6:20
Scoffers		2 Pet. 3:3
Scorch the ungodly		Rev. 16:8, 9
Scorched		Matt. 13:6; Mark 4:6
Scorn		Mark 5:40; Luke 9:53
Scorner		Prov. 1:22 + 21:11
Scornful		Ps. 3:1
Scorpions		2 Chron. 10:11
Scourge		Matt. 10:17 + 20:19; John 2:15 + 19:1; Heb. 12:6
Scribe		1 Chron. 27:32; Mark 12:28 + 15:31; 1 Cor. 1:20
Scripture		Mark 12:24; John 7:17, 38; Rom. 15:4; James 2:8; 2 Pet. 1:21
"	brings hope	Rom. 15:4
"	fulfilled	Mark 15:28; John 19:28, 36, 37
"	inspired by God	2 Tim. 3:16, 17
Scriptures - read under	duress	Acts 17:11
"	, search	John 5:39
Sea		Gen. 1:10, 22, 26; Ps. 46:2 + 95:5; Rev. 21:1
Seal		Sol. 8:6
"	of God	Rev. 7:2–17 + 9:4 + 22:11
"	the book	Dan. 12:4
Sealed under redemption		John 6:27; Eph. 1:13 + 4:30
Seals of Book, seven		Rev. 5:1–5, 9 + 6:1, 3, 5, 7, 9, 12 + 8:1
Seam		John 19:23

Search		Num. 14:6, 7; Ps 77:6
"	by God	1 Chron. 28:9; 2 Chron. 16:9; Ps. 44:21
"	for the Lord	Jer. 29:13
"	me	Ps. 139:23
"	the scriptures	John 5:39; Acts 17:11
Searched me & my & mine		Ps. 139:1–5
Searching - none of God's understanding		Isa. 40:28
Season		2 Tim. 4:2; Heb. 11:25
"	for everything	Eccles. 3:1–8, 17
"	of temptations	1 Pet. 1:6
Seasoned		Col. 4:6
Seasons		Gen. 8:22
"	and times changed by God	Dan. 2:21, 22 + 12:7
Seasons and times of coming known to believers		1 Thess. 5:1–5
Seat, judgment		2 Cor. 5:10
Second coming no surprise to believers		1 Thess. 5:1–5
"	coming of Christ	Jer. 23:7, 8 + 50:4–6, 19, 20
"	commandment	Matt. 22:37–40
"	death	Rev. 20:11–15 + 21:8
Secret		Ps. 139:15; Prov. 27:5; Dan. 2:19, 22; Matt. 6:17, 18
"	, nothing	Luke 8:17
"	of Lord	Ps. 25:14
"	place of Lord God	Ps. 31:20 + 91:1, 2
"	revealeth to prophets	Dan. 2:22; Amos 3:7
"	- reward	Matt. 6:6

"	things recorded	Eccles. 12:14
Secretly		Job 4:12
Secrets	- known to	
	God	Ps. 44:21
"	- none to God	Heb. 4:13
"	of men to be judged	Rom. 2:16
Secure		Jude 18:7; Job 11:18
Sedition		Luke 23:19
Seduce		Mark 13:22; 2 Tim. 3:13;
		1 John 2:26
Seducers		2 Tim. 3:13
Seducing		1 Tim. 4:1
See after being blind		John 9:25
"	and not see	John 9:39–41; 1 John 5:16
"	day approaching	Heb. 10:25
"	glory of God	John 11:40
"	in me	Ps. 139:24
"	Jesus	John 14:19
"	" coming	1 John 3:2, 3; Rev. 1:7
"	Lord - holiness	
	required	Heb. 12:14
"	Lord's qualifications	Ps. 34:8; Heb. 12:14–16
"	no man know it	Matt. 9:30
"	one - Jesus	John 12:45
"	to believe	1 John 4:20
"	ye to it	Matt. 27:24
Seed		Isa. 45:25; Rom. 4:18; 2 Tim. 2:8
"	is the good earthly	
	words parable	Luke 8:11–15
"	is the word of God	Luke 8:11–18; 2 Cor. 9:10
"	of Abraham	Rom. 9:7
"	, smallest - in earth	Mark 4:31, 32
Seeing not believing		Isa. 42:20

Seek and find		1 Chron. 28:9; Isa. 55:6; Jer. 29:11–13; Matt. 7:7; Luke 11:9
"	" search out God's own	Ezek. 34:11, 12, 16
"	- ask & knock	Matt. 7:7, 8; Luke 11:9, 10
"	death (kill)	Prov. 21:6; John 8:37
"	God early (David)	Ps. 63:1
"	him with all your soul	Deut. 4:29
"	Jesus	Matt. 28:5, 6; Mark 1:37
"	kingdom not earthly things	Matt. 6:33; Luke 12:22–24; Col. 3:1
"	Lord - rewarded	1 Chron. 28:9; 2 Chron. 7:14; Ps. 34:10
"	peace & have peace	Jer. 29:7
"	things above	Col. 3:1
Seekers of Lord not wanting		Ps. 34:10
Seeketh		Matt. 18:12; John 4:23
Seemeth		Num. 16:9; Prov. 14:12
Seen God - no one except God's son		John 1:18; Eph. 4:10
"	Jesus after risen	Acts 13:29–34; 1 Cor. 15:3–8
"	" before death	Luke 2:26–30
"	" hath seen Father	John 14:9
"	Lord's glory	Isa. 60:2
"	things & not seen	2 Cor. 4:18
Seer		1 Chron. 9:22
Seest		James 2:22
"	thou write in book	Rev. 1:11

Seeth	- Lord not as man	1 Sam. 16:7; John 14:17
"	me seeth Father	John 12:45
Seize		Ps. 55:15
Selah		Ps. 3:2, 4, 8 + 39:5–11 + 62:4, 8; Hab. 3:3, 9, 13
Self		Luke 9:23–25; Rom. 12:3 + 15:1–3; Gal. 2:20; Phil. 2:4
"	control or temperance	John 15:1, 4, 5; Gal. 5:22, 23; Rev. 3:20
"	lovers at last days	2 Tim. 3:1–5
Selfish		Eccles. 8:15
Selfsame		Exod. 12:51; Matt. 8:13; 2 Cor. 5:5
"	spirit	1 Cor. 12:11
Selfwilled		2 Pet. 2:10
Selves		James 1:22
Senators		Ps. 105:22
Send		Isa. 6:8; Matt. 21:2, 3; Luke 24:49; John 20:21
Sensual		James 3:15; Jude 1:19
Sent		John 20:21
"	Son	John 3:17 + 6:29 + 20:21; 1 John 4:9, 10, 14
"	", how	Rom. 8:3
"	word	Isa. 55:11
Sentence		Prov. 16:10; Luke 23:24; Acts 15:19
"	- longest in NT	Luke 3:23–38 (469 words)
"	- " in OT	Josh. 15:21–62 (368 words)
Separate, be		2 Cor. 6:17
"	the righteous from the uncaring	Matt. 25:31–46
"	themselves	Acts 13:2; Jude 1:18, 19

"	us from Christ & God, nothing	Rom. 8:35–39
Separated		Exod. 33:16; Gal. 1:15 + 2:12
Sepulchre		Gen. 23:6; Matt. 27:60, 61, 64, 66; Mark 16:2, 8; Luke 24:1, 2, 9, 12, 22, 24
Seraphims		Isa. 6:2, 6
Serjeants		Acts 16:38
Sermon on the mount		Matt. 5:1–7:29
Serpent		Gen. 3:2–5; Num. 21:6–9; Rev. 12:9, 14, 15
"	cursed	Gen. 3:14
"	from rod	Exod. 4:3, 4 + 7:9–12
"	or devil or Satan	Rev. 12:9, 12
"	to rod	Exod. 4:4
Serpents not hurt believers		Mark 16:18
Servant		Deut. 24:14, 15; Ps. 34:22; Prov. 30:10, 22; Matt. 20:27 + 24:45–50
"	be obedient to master	Eph 6:5–9; Col. 3:22–24; 1 Tim. 6:1, 2
"	blessed	Luke 12:37
"	for Jesus' sake	2 Cor. 4:5
"	- greatest	Matt. 23:11
"	learn from aged	Titus 2:9–11
"	obey masters	Col. 3:22
"	of Lord not to strive	2 Tim. 2:24
"	" sin	John 8:34, 35
"	reward	Rom. 6:22; Rev. 11:18
"	to God	Neh. 10:29; Rom. 6:22, 23; Acts 16:17
Servants obey		Col. 3:22
"	serve Him (God)	Amos 3:7; 1 Pet. 2:16; Rev. 22:3

Serve		Luke 16:13
"	each other	Mal. 3:18; Luke 22:26; Gal. 5:13
"	God	1 Chron. 28:9; 2 Tim. 1:3; Heb. 9:14 + 12:28; Rev. 22:3
"	" as we are His servants	Ps. 119:91
"	in newness of spirit	Rom. 7:6
"	Jesus - honor Father	John 12:26
"	Lord	Josh. 24:14, 15
"	" God - get strength	Isa. 40:31 + 41:10
Serve	Lord God only	Deut. 10:20; Josh. 22:5; Matt. 4:10; Luke 4:8; Col. 3:24
"	not other gods	Josh. 24:16
"	one only	Luke 4:8 + 16:13; Rom. 12:11
"	others	Luke 4:18; Gal. 5:13
"	the living God	Heb. 9:14
Servedst		Deut. 28:47
Serveth		Luke 22:27
Service, God's		Matt. 25:34–40
"	to God	Rom. 12:1 + 15:31
Serving		Luke 10:40; Rom. 12:11
Servitude		2 Chron. 10:4; Lam. 1:3
Set		Gen. 28:11; Eccles. 3:11; Luke 10:34; Rev. 3:21
"	affections on things above	Col. 3:2
"	some, God	1 Cor. 12:28
Setteth		James 3:6
Settle		1 Pet. 5:10
Seven		Prov. 24:16; Matt. 18:21, 22; Rev. 1:4, 11–13 + 3:1 + 16:1, 17

"	times more punishment for sins	Lev. 26:18, 21, 24, 28
Seventh day		Gen. 2:2, 3 + 8:4; Exod. 31:17; Heb. 4:4
"	" sanctified	Gen. 2:3
"	seal	Rev. 8:1, 2
Severally		1 Cor. 12: 11
Severity		Rom. 11:22
Sex		Gen. 1:27 + 2:20–23; Ruth 2:13; 1 Sam. 11:2–4 + 13:14; Prov. 6:23–26, 29; Matt. 5:27, 28; 1 Cor. 5:1–5 + 6:23–26; Mark 10:6–8
"	lust	1 John 2:16, 17
"	not materially in heaven	John 2:4
"	sins	Lev. 26:10–21; John 8:1–11; Rom. 6:12, 13
Sexual immorality		Acts 15:20
"	iniquities to the end expected	Ezek. 7:8, 9
Shackles of morality freed		Rom. 8:19–21
Shadow		Hos. 14:7; Col. 2:17; James 1:17
Shadrack & Meshack & Abednego		Dan. 3:12–30
Shake		Jude 16:20; Job 4:14; Isa. 10:32
"	earth & heaven	Heb. 12:25
"	everything	Ps. 46:3; Hag. 2:6, 7
"	nations	Hag. 2:7
Shaken		Matt. 24:29
Shall		Matt. 10:21 + 23:34, 39 + 24:2, 3, 5–7, 9–15; John 12:31 + 16:13–25, 33; Rev. 20:6–8, 10 + 21:3, 4, 7, 8, 25–27 + 22:3–5; 18, 19

" be saved	Prov. 10:30 + 11:31; Matt. 24:13; Mark 13:13
" " strengthened	Ps. 27:14
Shalt	Gen. 3:19; Matt. 4:10; John 13:7, 8; Rom. 10:9
Shambles	1 Cor. 10:25
Shame	Isa. 54:4; Mark 10:5; 1 Cor. 4:14 + 14:35; Rev. 16:15
" erring one to correction	2 Thess. 3:14, 15
Shamefacedness	1 Tim. 2:9
Shamefully	Luke 12:4; 1 Thess. 2:2
Shapen	Ps. 51:5
Share	Luke 3:11 + 12:48; Rom. 12:13; Gal. 6:10; 1 Tim. 6:17–19
Sharing	Acts 4:31–35; Rom. 12:13
Sharp	Ezek. 5:1; Acts 15:39; Rev. 2:12 + 14:14
Sharpened tongues	Ps. 140:3
Sharpeneth	Prov. 27:17
Shave	1 Chron. 19:4, 5; Job 1:20; Isa. 7:20 + 15:2; Jer. 41:5 + 48:37; Ezek. 5:1 + 44:20; Acts 21:24; 1 Cor. 11:5, 6
She	Gen. 2:23; Prov. 13:15
" ministered	Mark 1:31
Sheaf (Sheave)	Deut 24:19; Ruth 2:7, 15
Shed	Isa. 59:7; Matt. 26:28; Luke 11:50
" blood for blood	Gen. 9:6
Shed blood for remission of sin	Heb. 9:22
" love of God	Rom. 5:5; Titus 3:6

Sheep	Job 1:3, 16; Ezek. 34:1–16; Zech. 13:7; John 10:3, 7, 8, 12, 14, 16, 27, 28
" , God's	Ezek. 34:11, 12
Sheet	Acts 10:11
Shekel	1 Kings 7:1
Shelters	Matt. 17:4–7
Shepherd	John 10:11, 12, 14; Luke 2:20
" chief	1 Pet. 5:4
Sheperds of Israel failures	Ezek. 34:4
Shew	Ps. 19:1 + 51:15 + 96:2; John 16:13–15; 1 Cor. 11:26; James 2:18
Shewbread	Exod. 25:30; 2 Chron. 2:4; Luke 6:4
Shewed	Isa: 48:5, 6; Luke 24:40; John 21:1; Acts 20:35
Shewing	Titus 3:2
" self to be God	2 Thess. 2:3, 4
Shield	Gen. 15:1; 2 Chron. 32:5; Ps. 3:3 + 84:11 + 91:4; Prov. 30:5
" of faith	Eph. 6:16
Shine	Isa. 60:1; Matt. 5:16; John 1:5; Acts 12:7
Ship	Luke 5:3
Ships driven	James 3:4
Shittim wood	Exod. 25:10, 13
Shod , feet	2 Chron. 28:15; Eph. 6:15
Shoes	Matt. 3:11; Luke 15:22
Shorn	1 Cor. 11:6
Shoot	Ps. 64:3, 4
" forth	Luke 22:30
Shore	Acts 27:40

Short of God's glory	Rom. 3:23
Shortened days for elect's sake	Mark 13:20
Shortly	Phil. 2:24; 3 John 1:14
Should	Gen. 2:18; Matt. 18:33; Luke 2:1, 6; Rom. 6:4
Shoulder	Isa. 10:27
Shouldest	Prov. 5:6; John 11:40
Shout	Ps. 65:13; Isa. 12:6; 1 Thess. 4:16
Show salvation	Ps. 96:2
Shower and showers	Ezek. 34:26
Showers	Deut. 32:2; Ps. 65:9, 10
Shrank	Gen. 32:32
Shrine	Acts 19:24
Shun	2 Tim. 2:16
Shunned	Acts 20:27
Shut	Matt. 6:6; John 20:19, 26
" king's mouth	Isa. 52:15
Shutteth lips	Prov. 17:28
Shuttle	Job 7:6
Sick	Isa. 33:24; Jer. 14:18; Matt. 4:24; John 11:1–3, 6; Acts 9:37
" and sinners	Mark 2:17
" saved by prayer	James 5:14, 15
" - whole	Mark 2:17
Sickle	Joel 3:14; Mark 4:29; Rev. 14:17
Sickly	1 Cor. 11:30
Sickness	Matt. 4:23
" for glory of God	John 11:4
Side, Lord on my	Ps. 118:6
Siege	Deut. 28:53, 55, 57
Sift	Amos 9:9

Sight		Isa. 43:4; 2 Cor. 2:17 + 5:7; 1 Pet. 3:4
Sights and signs		Luke 21:11
Sign		Gen. 9:17; Matt. 12:38, 39; Acts 28:11
"	between Lord & us	Ezek. 20:12
"	of babe in manger	Luke 2:12, 34
Sign of son Immanuel		Isa. 7:14
" " "	of man in heaven	Matt. 24:30
"	to God is sabbath	Ezek. 20:20
Signet		Jer. 22:24
Signified		Acts 11:28
Signifysuffering		John 12:33; 1 Pet. 1:10, 11
Signs and sights		Luke 21:11
"	by apostles	Acts 2:43
"	in sky	Matt. 16:1–4; Luke 21:11, 21
"	of believers	Mark 16:17, 18
" "	Christ coming	Matt. 24:3–51; Mark 13:4–37; Luke 21:7–28, 33–36
" "	civilization's end	Luke 21:6–19
" "	God are great	Dan. 4:3
Silence		Ps. 32:3 + 83:1 + 115:17; 1 Tim. 2:11, 12; 1 Pet. 2:15
"	does not praise the Lord	Ps. 115:17
"	to bosom friend	Mic. 7:5
" "	the Lord	Hab. 2:20
Silk		Ezek. 16:10
Silly		Hos. 7:11; 2 Tim. 3:6
Silver		Prov. 25:4; Acts 19:24
"	and gold worthless at last days	Ezek. 7:19; Zeph. 1:18
"	lovers want more	Eccles. 5:10

Silversmith		Acts 19:24
Similarity, man & animal		Eccles. 3:19, 20
Similitude		2 Chron. 3:3; Rom. 5:14; Heb. 7:15; James 3:9
Simple - wise		Prov. 14:15 + 21:11
Simplicity		Prov. 1:22; Rom. 12:8
"	in Christ	2 Cor. 11:3
Sin		John 9:41; Rom. 3:20 + 5:12–21; 1 John 3:4–9 + 5:16–19
"	and grace	Rom. 5:21
"	- death - life	Rom. 6:2–14 + 7:4–6; 2 Cor. 5:14–18; Col. 2:20 + 3:1–4; 1 Pet. 2:24
"	- " - lust	James 1:14, 15
"	, die from	John 8:24
"	dissolved	John 1:29; 1 John 5:17
"	entered into the world	Rom. 5:12, 19
"	for us	2 Cor. 5:21
"	free	Rom. 6:22, 23; 2 Cor. 5:21
"	- incest	Lev. 20:11, 12, 17, 19, 20
"	is reproach	Prov. 14:4
"	" transgression	Prov. 14:34; 1 John 3:4
"	" unrighteousness	1 John 5:17
"	- man to be revealed	2 Thess. 2:3
"	- lust - death	James 1:14, 15
"	no more	John 8:11
"	not	Rom. 6:7, 11–13; 1 John 3:9 + 5:17, 18
"	" if in Christ	1 John 3:6, 9
"	" in body	Rom. 6:12, 13
"	" - Jesus	2 Cor. 5:21
"	of world - not believing	John 16:8, 9

"	or righteous	Prov. 14:1–35
"	, put away (Jesus' sacrifice)	Heb. 9:26
"	remission	2 Chron. 7:14; Luke 3:3
"	, servant of	John 8:34–36
"	, sex	Lev. 20:10–21; John 8:1–11; Rom. 6:12, 13
"	to not do good	James 4:17
"	- wage is death	Rom. 6:23; 1 John 5:16
Since		1 Cor. 15:21
Sincere		Phil. 1:10; 1 Pet. 2:2
Sincerity		Josh. 24:14; 1 Cor. 5:8; 2 Cor. 1:12 + 2:17; Titus 2:7
Sirred		Ps. 39:2; Isa. 64:7
Sinew		Gen. 32:32; Isa. 48:4
Sinews		Job 10:11 + 30:17 + 40:17
Sinful		Isa. 1:4; Mark 8:38; Rom. 8:3
Sing		Ps. 65:13 + 104:33; Eph. 5:19; 1 Cor. 14:15
"	and praise	Isa. 42:10
"	in heart	Eph. 5:19, 20; Col. 3:16
"	praise to the Lord	Ps. 104:33 + 147:1
Sing praises		Ps. 61:8
"	to the Lord	Ps. 33:2, 3 + 92:1 + 95:1, 2 + 96:1, 2 + 98:1 + 101:1 + 104:33 + 147:1; Eph. 5:19
Singers		2 Chron. 5:12
Singing hills		Isa. 55:12
Single		1 Cor. 7:7, 8, 34
Singleness		Acts 2:46; Eph. 6:5; Col. 3:22
Sink ship		Luke 5:7
Sinless		1 Pet. 2:22

Sinned, all have		1 Kings 8:46; John 8:7; Rom. 3:23 + 5:12–14; 1 John 8:10
Sinners and sick		Mark 2:17
Sinners called		Luke 5:32
"	consumed	Ps. 104:35
"	destroyed	Exod. 34:6, 7; Ps. 37:38 + 145:20
"	favored	Rom. 5:8
"	to be revealed	2 Thess. 2:3
"	- ungodly	Jude 1:15
Sins, confesseth or	covereth	Prov. 28:13
"	forgiven	Isa. 1:18, 19; Jer. 31:34; Mark 2:7; 1 John 1:9 + 2:1, 2, 12
"	" by a work	James 5:20
"	past	Rom. 3:25
"	recorded	Eccles. 12:14
"	, remember - no more	Heb. 10:17
"	, remission of	Luke 1:77; Heb. 10:10–19
"	, " " - to be preached	Luke 24:47
"	remitted	John 20:23
"	, sex	Lev. 20:10–21; John 8:1–11; Rom. 6:12, 13
"	, six	Isa. 5:8, 11, 18, 20–22
"	, wilful - not forgiven	Heb. 10:26
Sirs		Acts 14:15
Sister		Matt. 12:50; Mark 3:35; Luke 10:40
"	of Jesus	Matt. 12:50 + 13:56; Mark 3:35
Sit		Mic. 4:4; Rev. 3:21
Sitteth, Christ		Col. 3:1

"	on the right hand of God - Christ	Col. 3:1
Sitting	as God in temple of God	2 Thess. 2:4
"	on right hand of power	Mark 14:62; Luke 22:69
Six		Exod. 16:26 + 20:9, 11
"	hundred sixty-six	Rev. 13:11, 12, 16–18 + 14:9, 10
Sixth	day for creation	Gen. 1:31
"	to ninth hour	Mark 15:33, 34
Sixtyfold		Matt. 13:8
Skill		2 Chron. 2:8 + 34:12; Eccles. 9:11
"	in learning & wisdom	Dan. 1:17
Skin		Job 2:4 + 10:11
Skirt		Ezek. 16:8
Sky		Job 37:18; Matt. 16:2
Slack		2 Kings 4:24; 2 Pet. 3:9
Slain		Gen. 4:23; Deut. 8:6; Dan. 2:13; Rev. 5:12 + 11:13
"	of earth not lamented	Jer. 25:33
"	prophets before Jesus' birth	Acts 7:52
"	souls for word of God	Rev. 6:9–11
"	through no cause	Acts 13:28
Slander		Ps. 31:13 + 50:20 + 101:5
Slanderously		Rom. 3:8
Slaughter		Jude 15:8; 1 Sam. 4:10, 17; Acts 8:32 + 9:1; Heb. 7:1
"	weapon	Ezek. 9:2
Slay		Dan. 2:14; John 5:16; Acts 11:7

Sleep		Prov. 4:16 + 6:4, 9, 10 + 24:33, 34; Luke 22:45, 46; 1 Thess. 5:7
"	for Adam & Abram	Gen. 2:21 + 15:12
"	" laborer & rich	Eccles. 5:12
"	" earth to awake	Dan. 12:2
Sleep	for Jesus - reward	1 Thess. 4:14
"	- Lazarus	John 11:11–13
"	or work	Mark 10:5
"	- the dead until the resurrection	Job 14:10–12, 21
Slew		Acts 10:39; 1 John 3:12
Slide		Deut. 32:35
Slideth		Hos. 4:16
Slime		Gen. 11:3
Sling		1 Sam. 17:40, 50; 2 Chron. 26:14
"	accurate	Jude 20:16
Slingstone		Job 41:28; Zech. 9:15
Slip		Heb. 2:1
Slippeth		Ps. 38:16 + 94:18
Slothful	but not assurance of hope	Heb. 6:12
"	in work	Prov. 12:24 + 15:19 + 18:9; Rom. 12:11
"	man	Prov. 19:24
Slow		Ps. 145:8; James 1:19
Sluggard		Prov. 6:6, 9 + 20:4
Sluices		Isa. 19:10
Slumber		Ps. 121:3, 4; Prov. 6:4, 10; 2 Pet. 2:3
Small		Isa. 7:13; Dan. 11:23
"	thing	Num. 16:9
Smarter	were vegetarians	Dan. 1:11–20

Smell	Hos. 14:6
Smite	Ps. 121:6; Jer. 29:7; Matt. 5:39 + 24:49 + 26:31; Acts 23: 2, 3
Smiteth	Exod. 21:12–15, 20, 26, 27; Lam. 3:30
Smith (blacksmith)	Isa. 44:12
Smitten	Isa. 53:4
Smoke will be the wicked	Ps. 37:20
Smote	Job 2:7; Mark 15:19; Luke 23:48; Acts 12:7, 23
Snakes	Job 20:14, 16
Snare	Ps. 91:3; Isa. 8:14, 15 + 42:22; Luke 21:35; 1 Cor. 7:35
" of devil	2 Tim. 2:26
Sneeze	2 Kings 4:35
Snow	Job 37:6; Prov. 25:13; Eccles. 31:21; Isa. 55:10; Jer. 18:14; Rom. 19:24–26
Snuffdishes	Exod. 25:38
Snuffed	Mal. 1:13
Snuffers	2 Chron. 3:22
So	Gen. 1:7, 9, 11; Isa. 10:7 + 55:11; Jon. 1:12, 15; John 3:14, 16 + 14:2
" be it	Jer. 11:5
Sober be	1 Thess. 5:6–8; 2 Tim. 3:2, 3; Titus 2:2, 12; 1 Pet. 1:13 + 4:7 + 5:8
" "	(also see wine)
" or beside ourselves	2 Cor. 5:13
Soberly, think	Rom. 12:3
Sobriety	1 Tim. 2:9, 15
Sodom	Ezek. 16:48, 49

"	and Gomorrah	Gen. 10:19 + 13:10 + 14:8, 10, 11 + 19:24–26; Deut. 32:32; Isa. 1:9 + 13:19 + 19:1–10; Jer. 23:14 + 49:18; Matt. 10:15; Luke 10:12; 2 Pet. 2:6–8; Jude 1:7
Sodom's judgment		Matt. 11:23, 24
Soever		Mark 11:24; John 20:23; Rom. 3:19
Soft tongue		Prov. 15:1 + 25:15
Sojourn		Gen. 47:4; Lev. 19:33; 1 Pet. 1:17
Sojourner		1 Chron. 29:15; Ps. 39:12
Sold		Gen. 25:33; Acts 4:34, 37
Soldier of Jesus Christ		2 Tim. 2:3
Soldiers		Luke 3:14
Solemn		Ps. 92:3; Isa. 1:13; Zeph. 3:18
Solitary		Job 3:7; Eccles. 4:8; Lam. 1:1
"	place to pray	Matt. 6:6–8; Mark 1:35
Solomon		2 Sam. 12:24
Solomon's death		1 Kings 11:40–43
Some		Eph. 4:11
Sometimes		Eph. 2:13 + 5:8; Titus 3:3
Somewhat		Gal. 2:6; Rev. 2:4
Son and heir of God are we		Gal. 4:7
"	born to very old couple	Gen. 17:16–19 + 21:2, 3, 5; Rom. 4:16–21; Heb. 11:11
"	of	Luke 3:23–38
"	" God	Isa. 7:14 + 9:6; Mark 14:61 + 15:39; John 1:12, 34, 40 + 3:16, 17 + 8:35, 36 + 10:36; Rom. 1:4; 1 Cor. 1:9; Heb. 1:1–5

"	" " - Adam	Luke 3:38
"	" ", can be	Gal. 4:4–7; Rev. 21:7
"	" " - how God sent Him	Rom. 8:3
"	of God, Jesus	Matt. 1:18–21 + 3:17; Mark 1:11; Luke 1:31–35 + 3:21, 22; John 1:29 + 3:16, 17
"	" " - why God sent Him	1 John 4:9
"	of God's mission	1 John 3:8
"	" man	Matt. 16:13 + 24:30 + 26:64; Mark 13:24 + 14:62; Luke 5:24 + 21:27; Acts 7:56
"	" perdition	2 Thess. 2:3, 4
"	to respect father & mother	Prov. 19:26
Song	- mine of Lord	Ps. 118:14
"	, sing spiritual	Ps. 28:7; Eph. 5:19
Sons	and daughters of the Lord	Acts 2:17; 2 Cor. 6:18
"	instructions	Prov. 1:1–31:31
"	of God, made	John 1:12; Rom. 8:14; 1 John 3:1–3
Soothsayers		Dan. 2:27
Soothsaying		Acts 16:16
Sop		John 13:26, 27, 30
Sorceress		Isa. 57:3–5
Sorceries	- magic	Isa. 47:12
Sorcerer		Acts 13:6, 8
Sorcerers		Dan. 2:2
Sorcery		Acts 8:9
Sore		Job 5:18; Mark 6:51; Luke 2:9; Rev. 16:2
"	travail	Eccles. 4:8

347

Sores		Luke 16:20
Sorrow		Lam. 1:12; Phil. 2:27
"	comes with knowledge	Eccles. 1:18
"	- godly or worldly & reward	Exod. 15:14; 2 Cor. 7:10, 11
"	if not forgive	2 Cor. 2:7
"	multiplied to Adam & Eve	Gen. 3:16, 17
"	not	Jer. 31:16, 17
"	to joy	Jer. 31:10–13; John 16:20–22
Sorrowful		Luke 18:23, 24; Phil. 2:28
Sorrows beginning		Matt. 24:5–13; Mark 13:8 + 14:34
"	multiplied	Ps. 16:4
Sorry		2 Cor. 7:8–11
Sort		1 Chron. 29:14; 1 Cor. 3:13
Sought		Ps. 119:10
"	to take Jesus	John 7:30
Soul		Gen. 2:7; Prov. 6:32 + 11:25
"	can die	Ezek. 18:4, 20; Matt. 10:28
"	, living	Gen. 2:7
"	lose - world profit gain	Matt. 16:28; Mark 8:36, 37
"	need not be in hell	Acts 2:27
"	needs knowledge	Prov. 19:2
"	of believers to reign with Christ	Rev. 20:4
"	saved by patience	Luke 21:19
Soul to be saved		Luke 12:19, 20
"	wait only	Ps. 62:5–8
Souls are Lord God's		Rom. 18:4
"	, eight - saved	1 Pet. 3:19
"	of those beheaded for the witness of Jesus	Rev. 20:4

"	purified by truth & love	Acts 2:41; 1 Pet. 1:22
Soul's rest		Jer. 6:16; Matt. 11:28, 29
Sound		Josh. 6:5
"	from heaven	Acts 2:2 + 9:3; 2 Tim. 1:7; Rev. 8:6–8, 10, 12
"	heart	Prov. 14:30
"	mind from God	2 Tim. 1:7
"	one - from instruments & singers	2 Chron. 5:13
"	wisdom	Prov. 3:21
Sounded for distance		Acts 27:28
Sour		Jer. 31:29, 30
South		Job 37:9
Sovereign God		Dan. 4:35; Rom. 11:33; Eph. 4:6
Sow		Matt. 13:3; 2 Pet. 2:2
"	and reap	John 4:36–38; 2 Cor. 9:6–8; Gal. 6:7, 8
Sowed		Matt. 13:4
Sower		Matt. 13:3; Mark 4:3, 4, 14, 18; 2 Cor. 9:10
Sowest		1 Cor. 15:37
Soweth		Gal. 6:8
Sown		Mark 4:15–20; James 3:18
Space		1 Sam. 26:13; Acts 19:34
Spake		Num. 5:5; Matt. 9:33 + 13:3 + 28:18; John 12:29; 1 Cor. 13:11
Spare		Mal. 8:17
Spared not His Son & angels & world		Rom. 8:32; 2 Pet. 2:4,5
Spareth words by knowledge		Prov. 17:27

Sparingly - bountifully		2 Cor. 9:6
Sparks		Job 5:7
Sparrow		Ps. 102:7; Matt. 10:29, 31
Spat		John 9:6
Speak	against Jesus or Holy Ghost	Matt. 12:32
"	as oracles of God	John 14:10; 1 Pet. 4:11
"	, days	Job 32:7
"	face to face	3 John 1:14
"	- Holy Ghost	Mark 13:11
"	in psalms & hymns	Eph. 5:18–21
"	" tongues	Acts 2:6; 1 Cor. 14:14
"	lies at end times	1 Tim. 4:1–3
"	, Lord God will	Ps. 85:8
"	or say	Mark 2:7; John 16:4, 6, 7, 12, 13; Phil. 4:11; James 1:19
"	- the prophet	Deut. 18:21, 22 + 32:1
"	the word	Rom. 12:8
"	truth and be punished	John 8:40
"	truth helpful	1 Cor. 7:35; Eph. 4:15
"	what Jesus said	Matt. 10:27; 1 Cor. 1:10
"	" spirit of God gives you	Matt. 10:18–20
Speaketh		Heb. 12:25
"	mouth per heart	Matt. 12:34
Spear		Ps. 46:9; John 19:34
Specially		1 Cor. 5:8
Speckled		Gen. 30:32, 33, 35 + 31:8, 10
Spectacle		1 Cor. 4:9
Speech		Deut. 32:2
"	less important than gospel	1 Cor. 2:1–4

"	, wisely & godly	Ps. 19:2, 3; 2 Cor. 3:12; Col. 4:6
Speeches to be fair		Rom. 16:18
Speechless		Luke 1:20, 22, 64
Speed, God		2 John 1:10, 11
Speedily		Ps. 69:17 + 143:7; Isa. 58:8
Spent		Mark 5:26
Spices		Mark 16:1; Luke 24:1
Spider		Job 8:14; Prov. 30:28; Isa. 59:5
Spider's web		Job 8:14
Spies		Luke 20:20
Spin		Exod. 35:25, 26; Matt. 6:28; Heb. 12:27
Spirit		John 6:63 + 14:17; Rom. 8:1–16, 23, 26, 27; 1 Cor. 2:10–15; 1 John 4:1–3
"	and flesh	John 3:5, 6
"	" understanding	1 Cor. 14:14–20
"	, born of	John 3:8
"	broken - destroyeth body	Prov. 17:22 + 18:4
"	, eternal	Heb. 9:14
"	, evil	1 Sam. 16:4
"	excellent in one	Dan. 6:3
"	, false	1 John 4:1–30
"	- flesh	Gen. 6:3; John 3:5, 6; Rom. 8:1–16, 26, 27
"	found in - - -	Isa. 11:2
"	from words	John 6:63
"	given to all	1 Cor. 1:22 + 2:12 + 12:7
"	giveth life	2 Cor. 3:6
"	, God is a	John 4:23, 24
"	, God's	Gen. 1:2; Job 26:13; 1 Cor. 2:4, 11, 14–16; 2 Tim. 1:7

"	in God	John 4:24
"	" prayer	Eph. 6:18
"	" truth & witness	1 John 5:6–10
"	intercedes for us	Rom. 8:26
"	is God - Jesus	Matt. 10:20; John 4:23–26
"	" life	John 6:63
"	" Lord	2 Cor. 3:17, 18; 1 John 4:1–3
"	, Jesus to Father	Luke 23:46
"	laws	Rom. 8:1–16
"	leads	Luke 4:1
"	led	Acts 16:6, 7; Rom. 8:14
"	, live in the	Gal. 5:25
"	, Lord is that	2 Cor. 3:17, 18
"	meek and quiet	1 Pet. 3:4
"	, new	Ps. 51:10, 11; Ezek. 26:36
"	, nine gifts of	1 Cor. 12:8–10
"	- not might & power	Zech. 4:6
"	of antichrist	1 John 4:3
"	" God & man	Rom. 8:9–16; 1 Cor. 2:10–14; 1 John 4:2
"	" " in you	1 Cor. 3:16, 17
"	" " - sanctify - justify	1 Cor. 2: 9–16 + 6:11
"	of man and beast	Eccles. 3:21
"	" power - love - sound mind	2 Tim. 1:7
"	of truth to come	John 16:13, 14; 1 John 4:5
"	, one	Eph. 2:18
"	or flesh	Matt. 26:41; John 3:5, 6; Rom. 8:1–16, 26
"	, pray - sing - bless with the	1 Cor. 11:15, 16
"	quickeneth	John 6:63; Rom. 8:11

"	return to God	Eccles. 12:7
"	right	Ps. 51:10
"	ruleth	Prov. 16:32 + 18:14; Eccles. 8:8; 1 John 4:1–3
"	said	Acts 10:19, 20; Rev. 14:13
"	same	2 Cor. 4:13
"	searcheth	1 Cor. 2:10
"	to churches	Rev. 2:7, 11, 17, 29 + 3:6, 13, 22 + 4:2
"	upon Isaiah	Isa. 61:1–3
"	" Jesus	Luke 4:18; Heb. 9–14
"	vs flesh	Matt. 26:41; John 6:53; Rom. 8:8–14; Gal. 5:16, 17 + 6:8
Spirit, walk in the		Gal. 5:16, 25
"	with Christ	Col. 2:5–7, 10; Heb. 9:14
Spirit's		Num. 25:1–3; Ps. 106:28; Matt. 8:16; Mark 1:34 + 9:17–27; Luke 4:33–36; Rom. 8:16; 1 Cor. 10:20; Heb. 1:7, 14; Rev. 16:14
"	fruit	Gal. 5:22, 23 + 6:1, 8
"	gifts	1 Cor. 12:1–31; 2 Cor. 3:6
"	right	Ps. 51:10
"	witness	Rom. 8:16
Spirits are ministering	spirits	Heb. 1:13, 14
"	of world	1 John 4:1–5
"	, seven	Rev. 1:4 + 3:1 + 4:5 + 5:6
"	, try	Eph. 5:18; 1 John 4:1–3
"	, unclean	Luke 6:18
Spiritual house		1 Pet. 2:5
"	not	1 Cor. 2:14
"	sacrifices	1 Pet. 2:5
"	songs	Eph. 5:18–21

"	stages	1 John 2:11–15
"	understanding	Col. 1:9
Spiritually or carnally		
	minded	Rom. 8:6, 7
Spit on his eyes		Mark 8:23
"	upon him	Mark 15:19
Spittle		John 9:6
Spoil		Jude 2:16; Prov. 16:18 + 24:15; Isa. 33:23; Mark 3:27; Col. 2:8
Spoiled		Jude 2:16; Isa. 42:22
Spoiler		Jer. 51:56
Spoke the Lord		Jude 6:23; Col. 1:18–20; Isa. 40:5, 8 + 44:6, 8
Spoken by God		Gen. 1:28–30 + 2:16, 17 + 6:13–21 + 9:12–17; 35:10; Exod. 3:14, 15; Deut. 18:21, 22; Acts 3:21
"	" holy prophets	Acts 3:21
"	" Jesus	John 16:33
"	of	Rom. 1:8
"	, word fitly	Prov. 25:11
"	word of God	Heb. 13:7
Spoon		Num. 7:14–86 (used 14 times)
Sport		Jude 16:25
Sporting		2 Pet. 2:13
Spots		Jude 1:12
Spouse		Sol. 4:8–12
Sprang		Heb. 7:14; Mark 4:5, 8; Luke 8:7, 8
Spread		Jer. 17:8; Hos. 14:6
Spring forth		Isa. 42:9 + 43:19 + 58:8 + 62:11; Mark 4:27
"	showers	Ps. 63:9, 10
"	, wicked	Ps. 92:7

Springs in earth		Ps. 104:10–16
Springtime (winter is past)		Sol. 2:12; Isa. 61:11
Sprinkle		Exod. 29:16, 20, 21; Isa. 52:15; 1 Pet. 1:2
Sprinkled		Job 2:12; Heb. 9:19
Sprung		Matt. 13:5, 7, 26; Luke 8:6
Spue		Lev. 20:22
Spunge		Mark 15:36
Spy		Gal. 2:4
Stable		1 Chron. 16:30; Ezek. 25:5
Stablish		Rom. 16:25; 1 Thess. 3:13; 2 Thess. 2:17; James 5:8
Staff		2 Kings 4:29, 31; Ps. 23:4 + 105:16
Stanched		Luke 8:44
Stand		Phil. 14:13; Mark 11:25; Eph. 6:11, 14
"	at door - Jesus	Rev. 3:20
"	before Jesus	Luke 21:36; John 11:42
"	fast	Phil. 1:27 + 4:1; 1 Thess. 3:8; 2 Thess. 2:14–17
"	still	Job 37:14
Stand	to minister	Num. 16:9
"	up & praise	Neh. 9:5
Standard		Isa. 59:19
Standeth		Ps. 10:1; John 1:26; 2 Tim. 2:19
"	the judge	James 5:9
Standing		Acts 4:14 + 7:55, 56
"	idle	Matt. 20:3, 6
Stands forever, God's word		Isa. 40:8
Star is Jesus		Rev. 22:16
Stars, seven		Rev. 1:16, 20 + 2:1
Stature		Matt. 6:27; Luke 2:52 + 12:25 + 19:3; Eph. 4:12, 13

Statute	Lev. 24:3
Statutes of the Lord	Deut. 5:1 + 6:1, 24; Ps. 19:8 + 119:16, 33, 39, 54, 71, 72
Staves	Mark 14:48
Stay	Isa. 3:1 + 26:3 + 31:1
Stayed on thee	Isa. 26:3
Stead	Job 33:6; Philem. 1:13
Steal	Josh. 7:16–26; Prov. 30:8, 9; Zech. 5:3
" - be cursed	Zech. 5:3; Mal. 3:8, 9
" not	Deut. 5:19; Eph. 4:28
Stedfast	Dan. 6:26; 1 Cor. 15:58; Heb. 6:19; 1 Pet. 5:9
Stedfastly	Acts 1:10 + 2:42 + 6:15 + 7:55; 2 Cor. 3:7, 13
Stedfastness	Col. 2:5
Steel	Jer. 15:12
Stepped	John 5:4
Steps of Christ	1 Pet. 2:21
" " man directed	Eccles. 8:9; Jer. 10:23
Steward, faithful & wise	Luke 12:42
Stewards of God's grace	1 Cor. 4:2; 1 Pet. 4:10
" , required of	1 Cor. 4:1, 2
Stick	Ps. 38:2; Ezek. 37:16–20
Sticketh	Prov. 18:24
Stiffnecked	Exod. 32:9; Acts 7:51
Still	Exod. 15:16; Ps. 46:10; Phil. 4:13
" , be - know God	Ps. 46:10
Stilled	Num. 13:30
Stink	Gen. 34:30; Ps. 38:5
Stir up minds	Isa. 42:13; 2 Pet. 3:1
" " the gift of God	2 Tim. 1:6
Stole	Eph. 4:28

Stomach sake - wine	1 Tim. 5:23
Stone	Gen. 5:31, 45, 46; Lev. 20:27; Num. 14:10; John 8:7; 1 Pet. 2:4–8
" , corner	Ps. 118:22; Eph. 2:20; 1 Pet. 2:6, 7
" dangerous	Luke 20:18
" from Jesus' grave	Matt. 25:40
" , living	1 Pet. 2:4, 5
Stoned Jesus	John 10:31–33
" Paul	Acts 14:19
Stones	Lev. 20:27; Num. 14:10; Job 28:6, 15–19
Stony heart	Ezek. 36:26
Stood up	Luke 4:16
Stooped down	Gen. 49:9; John 8:8
Stoopeth	Isa. 46:1
Store	1 Cor. 16:2
" supplies	1 Cor. 16:2
Storehouse	Luke 12:24
" personnel to be blessed	Deut. 28:8
Stork	Ps. 104:17
Storm	Luke 8:24
Straight from crooked	Isa. 42:16; Matt. 7:14
Straightway	Matt. 3:16 + 4:20 + 14:22, 27 + 21:2; Mark 1:18 + 6:45 + 9:15, 20; Acts 9:20
Strain	Matt. 23:24
Straitened	Job 18:7 + 37:10; Prov. 4:12; 2 Cor. 6:12
Straitly	Matt. 9:30; Mark 5:43; Luke 9:21
Strake	Gen. 30:35, 37; Acts 27:17
Strange	1 Pet. 4:12

"	flesh	Ezra. 10:14; Jude 1:7
"	land	Ps. 137:4–6
"	things	Luke 5:26
"	woman's lips	Prov. 5:3
Stranger		Lev. 19:33, 34; Deut. 24:19; Ps. 119:19
"	feared by animals	John 10:4, 5
"	- Jesus	Luke 24:15–18
Strangers		1 Chron. 29:15; Ps. 146:9; Hos. 7–9; 1 Pet. 1:1
"	to be welcome	Heb. 13:1, 2
Strangling		Job 7:15
Straw		Exod. 5:16, 18
Streets		Eccles. 12:4; Matt. 6:2
Strength		1 Sam. 17:4,5; Neh. 8:10; Isa. 30:2; Phil. 4:13
"	and song	Isa. 12:2
"	from knowledge	Prov. 24:3–7
"	" weakness	2 Cor. 12:9, 10
"	great	Jude 14:5, 6 + 15:8 + 16:9, 12–14, 28–30
"	" when in the Lord	Ps. 18:29
"	less than wisdom	Eccles. 9:16
"	- mine is of the Lord	Ps. 27:1 + 46:1
"	, my	Ps. 62:6 + 118:14
"	of my heart	Ps. 73:26
"	, our - is God	Ps. 46:1, 2 + 62:7, 8 + 91:2–10 + 121:5–7
"	renewed	Isa. 40:31
"	saves not	Ps. 33:17
"	to Lord's people	Deut. 33:25; Ps. 29:11 + 33:16, 17; Isa. 40:31

" " weary	Isa. 40:29
Strengthen	Ps. 27:14; Isa. 30:2 + 41:10; Luke 22:31, 32
Strengthened	Jude 3:12; Dan. 10:18, 19
" by Christ	Phil. 4:13
" " God's power in us	2 Cor. 4:6–10; Col. 1:11
" " hope in the Lord	Ps. 31:24
Strengthenedst	Ps. 138:3
Strengtheneth	Ps. 138:3; Phil. 4:13
Stretch	Job 11:13; Matt. 12:13; Mark 3:5; Luke 6:10
Stretcheth	Ps. 104:2; Isa. 44:13
Stricken	1 Kings 1:1; Prov. 6:1; Isa. 53:4, 8
Strife	Gen. 6:3; Phil. 2:4; James 3:16
" in family	Luke 12:52:53
" to be avoided	Prov. 26:17
Strike	Deut. 21:4
Stripes	Isa. 53:5; Luke 12:48; 1 Pet. 2:24
Strive	Gen. 6:3; Prov. 25:8; Rom. 15:30; 2 Tim. 2:5, 14, 24
Striveth	1 Cor. 9:25
Striving	Phil. 1:27; Heb. 12:4
Stroke	Deut. 21:5
Strong	2 Chron. 16:9; Prov. 18:10; 2 Cor. 12:9, 10
" , be	Josh. 1:7; Hag. 2:4; 1 Cor. 16:13; Eph. 6:10
" , " - in grace	2 Tim. 2:1
" meat	Heb. 5:12, 14
" - weak	1 Cor. 4:10
Stronger than men	1 Cor. 1:25

Strongest four	Prov. 30:29, 30
" person	Jude 14:5, 6 + 16:3, 5, 28, 29
Struck Jesus	Luke 22:63, 64
Struggle	Mark 13:22
" - God's people vs Satan	Rev. 12:12–17
Stubble	Isa. 47; 14; Mal. 4:1
Stubborn	Jude 2:19
Stuck	Acts 27:41
Study	Eccles. 12:12; 2 Tim. 2:15
" - work - walk	1 Thess. 4:11, 12
Stuff	Josh. 7:11
Stumble	Prov. 24:17; Isa. 8:15 + 63:13
Stumbled & stumbling stone	Rom. 9:32, 33; 1 Pet. 2:8
Stumbleth	John 11:10
Stumbling	Isa. 8:14
" block	Ezek. 7:19; Rom. 14:13, 21; 1 Pet. 2:8; Rev. 2:14
Stump	Dan. 4:26
Subdue all things	Ps. 47:3; Phil. 3:21
" earth	Gen. 1:28
Subdued	Jude 11:33
Subject to	Rom. 8:20 + 13:1; Eph. 5:24; 1 Pet. 2:18 + 5:5
" " Jesus in heaven	1 Pet. 3:22
Subjected	Rom. 8:20
Subjection	1 Cor. 9:27; 1 Tim. 2:4
" to	Heb. 2:5 + 12:9; 1 Tim. 2:11 + 3:4; 1 Pet. 3:1, 5
Submarine suggested	Job 38:16 + 41:30–32
Submit	Eph. 5:18–22
" to God	James 4:7
" " Rulers	Heb. 13:7, 17; 1 Pet. 2:13, 14

"	yourselves	Eph. 5:21, 22; Heb. 13:17; 1 Pet. 2:13 + 5:5
"	" together	1 Cor. 16:16; Eph. 5:21
Suborned		Acts 6:11
Substance		Gen. 7:4, 23; Job 1:3; Ps. 139:15; Prov. 3:9; Heb. 11:1
Subtil		Gen. 3:1
Subtilty		Prov. 1:4; Acts 13:10; 2 Cor. 11:3
Subvert		2 Tim. 2:14; Titus 1:11 + 3:11
Success by reading Bible		Josh. 1:7, 8
Succoured		2 Cor. 6:2
Such		Mark 10:14; 1 Cor. 16:16; 2 Cor. 3:4
Suck		Isa. 60:16 + 66:10–12; Luke 23:29
Suckling		Isa. 11:8; Matt. 21:16
Suddenly		Prov. 6:15
"	a sound from heaven	Acts 2:2 + 9:3
Sue		Matt. 5:40
"	in court	Luke 12:57–59
Suffer as a Christian or	otherwise	1 Pet. 4:1, 15, 16, 19; Rev. 2:10
"	children to come	Mark 10:14
"	per Christ when others hurt	Matt. 19:14 + 25:40; Mark 7:12; 2 Tim. 2:12
"	, must the son of man	Mark 8:31
"	not your hurt	Ps. 121:3
"	persecution for the godly	Luke 21:12; 2 Tim. 7:12
"	you not - God	Ps. 55:22; 1 Cor. 10:13
Suffered		Matt. 3:15 + 19:8

"	and died for us	Heb. 9:26; 1 Pet. 2:21 + 3:18 + 4:1
"	in the flesh	1 Pet. 4:1 + 5:10
"	Jesus, not in tabernacle	Heb. 13:12
Suffering at end		Mark 13:9–11
"	of Christ foretold	Isa. 53:1–12; 2 Cor. 1:5
"	- rejoice	Rom. 5:3
Sufferings for Christ's sake		2 Cor. 12:9, 10; 1 Pet. 4:13
Suffice us, our past		1 Pet. 4:3–5
Sufficeth		John 14:8
Sufficiency, all - by God		2 Cor. 9:8
Sufficient		Prov. 25:16; Matt. 6:34; 2 Cor. 3:5
"	grace	2 Cor. 9:8 + 12:9
Suit		Job 11:19
Sum of thoughts		Ps. 139:17, 18
Summer		Prov. 10:5
Sumptuously		Luke 16:19
Sun		Gen. 1:3–5, 14–18; Josh 10:12; 1 Sam. 3:3; Ps. 84:11 + 104:19; Mark 1:32
"	of righteousness	Mal. 4:2
"	scorch people	Rev. 16:8, 9
Sunder		Ps. 41:17 + 46:9
Sundry times		Heb. 1:1
Sung		Matt. 26:30
Sup		Rev. 3:20
Superfluity		James 1:21
Superfluous		Lev. 22:23; 2 Cor. 9:1
Superscription		Matt. 22:20; Mark 15:26; Luke 23:38
Supper, Lord's		1 Cor. 11:26
Suppliants		Zeph. 3:10

Supplication	Job 8:5; Ps. 6:9 + 142:1; Eph. 6:18; Phil. 4:6
Supplications	Ps. 143:1
" heard	Ps. 28:6
Supplied	1 Cor. 16:17
Supply for theirs & yours	2 Cor. 8:14
" need according, shall	Phil. 4:19
Support the weak	Acts 20:35
Suppose	Acts 2:15 + 14:19
Supreme king	1 Pet. 2:13
Sure	Num. 32:23; Job 24:22; Ps. 19:7; Luke 10:11; Rom. 2:2
Surely	1 Sam. 16:6; Ps. 77:11 + 91:3; Isa. 45:24
Surety	Prov. 6:1 + 17:18; Acts 12:11
Suretyship	Prov. 11:15
Surfeiting	Luke 21:34
Surname	Acts 10:5, 18, 32
Sustain	Ps. 55:22; Isa. 59:16
Sustenance none	Acts 7:11
Swaddling clothes	Luke 2:7
Swaddlingband	Job 38:9
Swallow	Job 7:19; Obad. 1:16
" me up	Ps. 56:1
Swallowed up	Job 37:20; Ps. 124:4; 1 Cor. 15:54; 2 Cor. 2:7 + 5:4
Sware	Deut. 4:31; Ezek. 16:18; Heb. 3:18
Swear	Deut. 10:20; Josh. 2:12; Isa. 45:23; Matt. 23:20–22
" - be cursed	Zech. 5:3
" not	Matt. 5:34–36; Col. 3:8; James 5:12

Sweat	Gen. 3:19; Luke 22:34
Sweet	Prov. 24:13; Mark 16:1
" sleep	Eccles. 5:12
Sweetsmelling	Eph. 5:2
Swelling words	Jude 1:16
Swerved	1 Tim. 1:6
Swift	James 1:19
Swifter	Job 7:6
Swim	Ps. 6:6; Acts 27:42, 43
Swine into sea	Mark 5:11–16
Sword	Job 19:29; Jer. 45:10 + 49:37 + 50:16, 35–37; John 18:11
" fight	Rev. 2:12, 16
" , flaming	Gen. 3:24
" for wicked	Jer. 35:31
" of spirit is word of God	Eph. 6:17
" , two edged	Heb. 4:12
" user - perish with sword	Job 19:29; Ps. 37:14, 15; Matt. 26:52
Sworn	Jer. 11:5; Isa. 45:23 + 62:8; Acts 7:17
Sympathy	Rom. 8:32
Synagogue	Luke 4:16

• T •

Tabernacle	Lev. 26:11; 2 Pet. 1:13, 14
Table in kingdom	Luke 22:30
" " tabernacle	Exod. 31:8
Tablet	Luke 1:63; Jer. 31:4
Tabret	Job 17:6
Tacklings	Isa. 33:23
Take	1 Cor. 11:24
" away four things	Isa. 58:9, 10
" " sin	John 1:29
" heed	Luke 12:15 + 21:34; Acts 20:28
" own life or lay it down	John 10:17, 18
" water of life	Rev. 22:17
Taken	Luke 1:1; 2 Cor. 3:16
" by angels	Matt. 24:31
" up, Jesus	Acts 1:2
Takest	Ps. 144:3; Eccles. 9:9
Taking thought	Luke 12:25, 26
Talebearer	Prov. 18:8 + 20:19
Talents parable	Matt. 25:15–28
Talk	Ps. 77:12; Eph. 5:4; James 3:9–13
" too much	Prov. 10:19
Talked, angel	Zech. 4:1, 4–6

" , animal	Num. 22:28, 30
Tame	James 3:7, 8
Tanner	Acts 9:43
Tare	Mark 9:20
Tares	Matt. 13:40
Tarried	Acts 28:12
Tarry	Gen. 30:27; Matt. 26:38; Luke 24:39; John 21:22, 23; 1 Cor. 11:33; 1 Tim. 3:15
Taskmasters	Exod. 3:7
Taste	Job 34:3; John 8:52
" death - God	Heb. 2:9
" God's goodness	Ps. 34:8; 1 Pet. 2:3
Tasted that Lord is gracious	1 Pet. 2:3
" water (wine)	John 2:9
Tattlers, do not be	1 Tim. 5:13
Tattoo	Lev. 19:28
Taught by Jesus	Matt. 5:1; Mark 9:31; Luke 4:15
" " God the Father	Prov. 4:3, 4; John 6:45 + 8:28
Taunting	Hab. 2:6
Taverns	Acts 28:15
Teach	Ps. 32:8; Prov. 9:9; 1 Tim. 4:11–16; 1 John 1:9
" all things	John 14:26
" children per Lord	Deut. 6:1, 5–8, 24
" diligently to children	Deut. 6:7
" - exhort per Paul	Titus 2:9–15
" good & right way	1 Sam. 12:23
" gospel by Jesus	Matt. 28:18–20; Mark 6:2
" these things	1 Tim. 4:11–16; 2 Tim. 2:2
" us all things	John 14:26 + 16:13; Col. 1:28
" " by Lord	Ps. 32:8 + 119:12

Teacher absent - work	
same way	Phil. 2:12, 13
"　- Jesus	Matt. 4:23 + 5:1, 2; John 3:2
"　- Paul	Acts 28:30, 31
Teachers, false	2 Pet. 2:1
Teaching Jesus'	
commandments	Matt. 28:20
"　one another	Col. 3:16
Tears	Lam. 1:16; Ps. 25:8 + 42:3; Rev. 7:14–17 + 21:4
"　not for dead	Ezek. 24:16, 17
Teeth	Jer. 31:29, 30; Matt. 8:12; Acts 7:54
Teil tree	Isa. 6:13
Tell	Josh. 7:19; Matt. 16:17; John 4:25 + 13:19
Temper	Gen. 4:3–16; Prov. 16:32 + 20:3; Eph. 4:26, 27, 31, 32; James 1:19, 20
Temperance or self	
control	Matt. 15:1, 4, 5; Gal. 5:22, 23; Rev. 3:20
Tempered	1 Cor. 12:24
Tempest	2 Pet. 2:17
Tempestuous	Ps. 50:3
Temple	Eph. 2:21, 22; Rev. 21:22
"　defiled	John 2:19; 1 Cor. 3:16, 17
"　destroyed if defiled	1 Cor. 3:16, 17
"　is Lord God & Lamb	Rev. 21:22
"　of God - our body	1 Cor. 3:16, 17 + 6:19, 20; 2 Cor. 6:16; Eph. 4:6; Rev. 11:19
"　"　Jesus' body	John 2:19–21

Temples not made with hands	Acts 7:48
Temporal or eternal	2 Cor. 4:18
Tempt me - Jesus	Matt. 22:18
" - not by God	Matt. 22:18; 1 Cor. 10:13; James 1:13
" not Christ	1 Cor. 10:9
" " Lord thy God	Matt. 4:7; Luke 4:12
Temptation	Luke 22:39, 40, 46; Heb. 3:8; James 1:2, 3, 12–14
" - a way of escape	1 Cor. 10:13
" , endureth	James 1:2
" hour	Rev. 3:10
Temptations all common to man	Col. 10:13
" delivered from godly	2 Pet. 2:9
Temptation's seasons	1 Pet. 1:6
Tempted and way of escape	1 Cor. 10:9, 13
" , Eve	Gen. 3:1–4
" , every man can be	Heb. 3:9; James 1:13, 14
" faith of Abraham	Gen. 22:1–13
" Jesus by devil	Matt. 4:1, 3–11; Heb. 4:14, 15
" not by God	James 1:13, 14
" ones delivered	2 Pet. 2:9
" we as Jesus	Heb. 2:18
Tempter	Matt. 4:3–11
Tempting	Mark 10:2
Tempter	Matt. 4:3
Ten thousand	Jude 1:14
Tend	Prov. 21:5
" to business & walk honestly	1 Thess. 4:11, 12

Tender mercy	Ps. 25:6 + 40:11 + 51:1 + 77:9;
	James 5:11
Tenderhearted	Eph. 4:32
Tenth is for tithe	Lev. 27:30–33
Terrestrial	1 Cor. 15:40
Terrible	Ps. 47:2 + 66:3, 5; + 145:6
" pay to come	Joel 2:11, 31, 32; Zeph. 2:11
Terrified	Luke 24:37
" not by final signs	Luke 21:8, 9
Terrifiest	Job 7:14
Terrify	2 Cor. 10:9
Terror	Ps. 91:5; 2 Cor. 5:11;
	1 Pet. 3:14
Testament	Heb. 9:15–20
" , first	Heb. 9:15
" , new	Luke 22:20; Heb. 9:15
Testator	Heb. 9:16
Testified	1 Tim. 2:6
Testify	Acts 10:42; 2 Cor. 10:9;
	Eph. 4:17; 1 John 4:14;
	Rev. 22:18
Testifying	1 Pet. 5:12
Testimonies	Ps. 16:1 + 119:129
" are joyful riches	Ps. 119:14
" to be proud of	2 Tim. 1:8
Testimony	2 Tim. 1:8; Heb. 11:5;
	John 3:32, 33
" of Jesus Christ	Rev. 1:1, 2 + 12:17 + 19:10
" " Lord	Ps. 19:7
Tetrarch	Luke 3:19 + 9:7; Acts 13:1
Thank	John 11:41; Rom. 1:8;
	Philem. 1:4
Thankful be	Col. 3:15
" hearts please God	Heb. 12:28

"	to Him	Ps. 100:4
Thanks		Heb. 13:5
"	always	Eph. 5:20
"	for everything	1 Thess. 5:18
"	" gift	2 Cor. 9:15
"	" helping	
	strangers	Luke 6:31–37
"	, giving	Eph. 5:20
"	God's will	Phil. 4:4; 1 Thess. 5:16–18
"	in everything	Eph. 5:20; 1 Thess. 5:18
"	, prayer	Phil. 4:6
"	to God	1 Cor. 15:57; 2 Cor. 9:15; Col. 1:12 + 3:17
"	" the Lord	Ps. 136:1–3
"	when eat	Mark 8:6
Thanksgiving		2 Cor. 4:15; Phil. 4:6
"	to God	Ps. 50:14
"	with prayer	Phil. 4:6
Thankworthy		1 Pet. 2:19
That		John 1:8; 1 Cor. 15:37; 1 John 1:1
"	day	John 14:20–22
Thee (you)		Deut. 31:6
"	, sustain	Ps. 55:22
Them		Matt. 13:3; Eph. 2:10
Themselves		2 Chron. 7:14; Jude 1:10
Thence		Matt. 5:26
There		Ps. 139:8
Thereby		Job 22:21; 1 Pet. 2:2
Therefore		Matt. 6:2; John 8:36; Heb. 4:16; 2 Pet. 3:17
Therefore brethren		Acts 13:38; 1 Cor. 15:58
Therefrom		John 23:6

Therein	Deut. 10:14; Isa. 42:10; Rev. 10:6
Thereof	Gen. 2:19; John 6:50
Thereon	1 Cor. 3:10
Thereto	Gal. 3:15
Thereunto	Eph. 6:18; 1 Pet. 3:9
Thereupon	1 Cor. 3:10
Therewith	Prov. 25:16; 1 Tim. 6:8; James 3:9
Thick	Luke 11:29
Thief	Matt. 24:43; John 10:1–10
Thieves	Luke 10:30
Thigh	Sol. 3:8
Thine	Mic. 5:9; John 17:9
" Lord as head above all	1 Chron. 29:11, 12, 14, 16
" own	Isa. 58:7
Thing	Gen. 1:24–26, 28, 30, 31; Eccles. 3:1, 11; Isa. 1:10 + 64:6; 2 Cor. 10:5
" , make a	Isa. 43:19
" , one - to know	2 Pet. 3:8
" , small	Num. 16:9
Things	Prov. 30:15, 18, 24, 29; John 14:25, 26; Rom. 11:36; Phil., 4:8, 13; Rev. 10:4, 6
" above not on earth	Col. 3:1, 2
" , all are possible	Matt. 19:26; Mark 10:27 + 14:36
" , " - created	Gen. 1:1–31
" , " - in Christ	Luke 24:46–48; Eph. 1:10; 2 Tim. 2:10; 1 Pet. 4:28
" , " - new	2 Cor. 5:17, 18; Rev. 21:5
" , " - per Lord God	Rom. 11:36; 1 Cor. 13:7; Eph. 5:20

Things, all - to be right	Ps. 119:128; Acts 13:39; Eph. 5:20	
"	, " - under man	Ps. 8:6
"	, " - unto edifying	1 Cor. 10:23 + 14:26
"	beautiful all made by God	Eccles. 1:8–11 + 3:11; 2 Cor. 9:8
"	before & behind	Isa. 42:9; Phil. 3:13
"	command & teach	1 Tim. 4:11–16; 2 Tim. 2:2
"	God has for us	1 Cor. 2:9; Heb. 11:39, 40
"	great & mighty	Jer. 33:3
"	hidden	Isa. 48:6
"	high & low	Rom. 12:16
"	honest	Rom. 12:17
"	Jesus did	John 21:25
"	Lord hate	Prov. 6:16–19
"	marvellous	Job 5:4
"	, new things	Isa. 48:6
"	not - called as were	Rom. 4:17
"	" understood on earth	Prov. 30:15, 16, 21–31; 2 Tim. 2:7
"	old & new	Isa. 42:9; 2 Cor. 5:17, 18
"	, other's	Phil. 2:4
"	per men - good or evil	Matt. 12:35
"	seen & not seen	Matt. 6:32–34; 2 Cor. 4:18
"	, seven - Lord hate	Prov. 6:16–19
"	to come	Matt. 24:4–14; Mark 13:4; Luke 21:36
"	" enjoy	1 Tim. 6:17
"	" think about	Luke 12:15; Phil. 1:9, 10 + 2:8 + 4:8, 9
"	, whatsoever	Phil. 4:8, 9
"	with man & God	Luke 18:27

"	, wondrous	Ps. 72:18
"	, worldly - God's	
	gift	Eccles. 5:18, 19
Think		Matt. 5:17 + 26:66;
		Acts 17:29; Rom. 12:3
"	determines self	Prov. 23:7; Matt. 9:4; 2 Cor. 10:7
"	- Lord	Jer. 29:11
"	on eight virtues	Phil. 4:8
Thinkest		Acts 28:22
Thinketh		Jer. 29:11–13
"	so is he	Prov. 23:7
Third day		Matt. 20:19
Thirst		Ps. 42:2; John 17:37; + 19:28;
		Rev. 21:6
"	not with Jesus	
	Christ's water	John 4:7, 9–15 + 6:35
Thirsteth		Ps. 63:1
Thirsty		Ps. 63:1; Isa. 44:3
Thirtyfold		Matt. 13:8
This		Ps. 69:31; Matt. 3:17;
		1 John 5:20
Thistles		Gen. 3:18
Thither		Isa. 55:10; John 7:34;
		Acts 8:30 + 16:13
Thitherward		Jer. 50:5
Thorns		Sol. 2:2; Matt. 13:7; Mark 4:7;
		John 19:5; 2 Cor. 12:7
Thou		Matt. 16:16; Luke 23:3;
		John 1:49 + 11:41 + 19:11;
		1 Cor. 15:36
Though		Ps. 46:2; Acts 17:27
Thought		Luke 12:25, 26 + 19:11;
		Acts 8:20 + 10:19; Phil. 2:6
"	from God	Amos 4:13; Matt. 6:27, 28

"	, take no - for life	Matt. 6:25
Thoughtest		Ps. 50:21
Thoughts		Ps. 133:17, 18; Prov. 21:5; Isa. 55:8, 9; Jer. 29:11; Luke 24:38
"	established	Prov. 16:3
"	in heart	Luke 24:38
"	known to God	1 Chron. 28:9; Matt. 9:4
"	of Lord	Ps. 92:5; Jer. 29:11
"	perish	Ps. 146:4
"	, vain	1 Cor. 3:20
Thousand years		Rev. 20:1–7
Thousands saints		Jude 1:14
Threatened		1 Pet. 2:23
Three abideth		1 Cor. 13:13
"	days & nights	Matt. 12:38–40 + 16:21 + 17:23; Mark 8:31; Luke 24:7; Rev. 11:9–12
"	in heaven are one	1 John 5:7
Threefold		Eccles. 4:12
Threescore		Acts 7:14
Threshing floor		2 Chron. 3:1
Threshold		Ezek. 43:8
Thrice		2 Cor. 12:8
Throne -David to Jesus		Luke 1:32
"	established	Ps. 93:2; Prov. 16:12
"	heavenly	Rev. 3:21 + 4:2–6, 10 + 5:1, 7, 13
"	Lord God's	Matt. 5:34; Acts 5:49
"	of God audience	Rev. 3:21 + 7:9, 10
"	" grace	Heb. 4:16
Through		Ps. 23:4; Luke 4:14
"	faith	Eph. 2:8, 9; 1 Pet. 1:5
"	Jesus Christ	Rom. 1:8 + 5:1, 2, 11; John 1:6–9 + 3:17; Titus 3:6

"	power of Holy Ghost	Rom. 15:13
Throughly		Ps. 51:2; 2 Tim. 3:17
Throughout		Rom. 1:8
Thumb		Lev. 8:23, 24
Thunder		1 Sam. 12:17, 18; John 12:29
Thunders		Rev. 10:4
Thus		Phil. 3:15
Thy		Ps. 37:5
Thyself		1 Tim. 4:15, 16; 2 Tim. 2:15
Tidings, good		Isa. 52:7 + 61:1; Luke 2:10
Tie		Prov. 6:21
Till		Gen. 2:5; John 13:38; Acts 23:12
Tillage		Prov. 13:23
Time		Ps. 69:13; Prov. 12:24; Eph. 5:15–17
"	came for God's Son	Gal. 4:4
"	come	1 Pet. 4:17
"	for everything	Eccles. 3:1–8, 11, 17 + 8:9
"	- Jesus & them	John 7:6, 8
"	near	Mark 13:33; Rom. 13:11
"	no longer	Rev. 10:6
"	of need	Heb. 4:16
"	, old	Matt. 5:21; 2 Pet. 1:21
"	, redeeming	Eph. 5:16; Col. 4:5
"	short for devil	Rev. 12:12
"	to believe gospel & repent	Mark 1:15
"	, use - wisely	Prov. 24:32–34; Col. 3:23, 24
Times and seasons		Dan. 2:21 + 12:7; 1 Thess. 5:1–5
"	known	Luke 1:7
"	, last - advise	Luke 21:6–19; Jude 1:17–23
"	, latter	Heb. 4:1–11

"	of ignorance	Acts 17:30
"	, perilous - to come	1 Tim. 3:1, 13; Rev. 13:8
"	, troublesome	Mark 13:5–13
"	, vanity	Eccles. 3:1–22
Tinkling		1 Cor. 13:1
Tip		Luke 16:24
Tithe	- be not robber to God	Mal. 3:8–10
"	is holy unto the Lord	Lev. 27:30–33
"	lesson - put God first	Deut. 14:22, 23
"	possessions	Lev. 27:30–33; Prov. 3:9, 10; Acts 4:32–35
"	rewards	Prov. 3:9, 10; Luke 6:38
Tittle		Luke 16:17
To		Gen. 1:16–18, 29, 30
"	wit	Rom. 8:23; 2 Cor. 5:19 + 8:1
Toe		Lev. 14:14, 17, 25, 28
Together		Eccles. 4:11; John 20:24; Rom. 8:22
"	, all flesh	Isa. 40:5
Together, common things		Jer. 31:13; Acts 4:32; Rom. 15:30
"	, gathered	Ps. 133:1; Matt. 18:20; 2 Thess. 2:1
"	, work	Rom. 8:28
Toil		Matt. 6:28
Token		Gen. 9:12, 13; Josh. 2:12; Phil. 1:28; 2 Thess. 1:5
Told		Gen. 3:11; Isa. 44:8; Luke 1:45 + 2:17, 18
Tolerable		Matt. 10:15 + 11, 22, 24; Luke 10:12, 14

Tomb empty	John 20:13
" of Jesus	Matt. 27:57–60
Tomorrow	Matt. 6:34; James 4:13, 14
Tongs	Isa. 44:12
Tongue	Prov. 10–20 + 12:18, 19 + 15:1, 2 + 18:21; Jer. 23:31; James 1:26 + 3:5–10
" , bridle	Ps. 39:1; James 1:26; 1 Pet. 3:10; 3 John 1:10
" , each one hath a	1 Cor. 14:26
" - good or bad	Prov. 13:17–19 + 14:19
" is a fire	James 3:5, 6
" , lying	Prov. 21:6
" power	Prov. 18:21
" , proper	Acts 1:19
" same	Acts 2:6–11
" shall swear	Isa. 45:23
" should confess	Phil. 2:11
" , sing	Ps. 51:14
" , soft - is powerful	Prov. 25:15
" , ungodly	Ps. 52:2, 4; Isa. 59:13; Jer. 9:3; Col. 3:8, 9
" , unknown	1 Cor. 14:14, 16, 19, 27, 28, 39
" , wise - is health	Prov. 12:18
Tongues	1 Cor. 12:28 + 13:1 + 14:2, 4–6, 19, 21–23, 27, 28, 32
" , forbid not	1 Cor. 14:39
" to be interpreted	Prov. 14:13, 19, 23, 27
Too wonderful	Ps. 139:6
Took	John 11:41
Tooth - life - eye - hand - foot	Exod. 21:23, 24
Top	John 19:23
Topaz	Job 28:19

Torment, eternal	Rev. 14:8 + 17:2
" or comfort	Luke 16:19–25
" with fear	1 John 4:18
Tormented day & night	Luke 16:24; Rev. 20:10
Torn	Mark 1:26
Tossed	James 1:6
" to and fro	Prov. 21:6; Matt. 14:24
Tossings	Job 7:4
Touch not	Ps. 105:15; 1 Cor. 6:17
Touched by Jesus	Matt. 8:3, 15 + 9:25 + 20:34
" me	Dan. 10:18; Matt. 14:36
" them	Mark 10:13
Touching	Job 37:23; Acts 21:25; 2 Thess. 3:4
Tow	Isa. 43:17
Toward God & us	Acts 24:16; Rom. 11:22; 1 John 4:9
" you	2 Cor. 9:8
Tower	Gen. 11:4, 5; Ps. 144:2; Prov. 18:10; Isa. 23:13
Tradition	Matt. 15:2, 3, 6; Mark 7:8, 9, 14; Col. 2:8; 1 Pet. 1:18
Traffic as ants	Dan. 12:4
Traffick of iniquity	Ezek. 28:18
Train child	Prov. 22:6
" (cloth) of King Uzziah	Isa. 6:1
Traitors	2 Tim. 3:4
Trample	Ps. 91:13
Trance	Acts 10:10
Tranquillity	Dan. 4:27
Transferred	1 Cor. 4:6
Transfigure	Matt. 17:1, 2; Mark 9:2; Rev. 17:1, 2

Transfigured		Matt. 17:2; Mark 9:2
Transformed		Acts 26:9–23; Rom. 12:2; 2 Cor. 11:14, 15
Transgress		1 Sam. 2:24; 2 Chron. 24:30; Matt. 15:2, 3
"	against Lord	2 Chron. 26:16
"	by tradition	Matt. 15:2, 3, 6
"	, determined not to	Ps. 17:3
"	not with cause	Ps. 25:3
Transgressing		Isa. 59:13
Transgression		Ps. 32:1
"	is sin	Prov. 14:34; 1 John 3:4
"	to end	Dan. 9:24
Transgressions		Isa. 51:3
Transgressor		Gal. 2:18; James 2:9
Transgressors destroyed		Exod. 34:6, 7; Ps. 37:38 + 145:20
Translated		Col. 1:13; Heb. 11:5
"	us	Col. 1:13
Travail		Eccles. 4:4, 8; Isa. 54:1; John 16:21; 1 Thess. 5:3
Travaileth		Job 15:20; Rom. 8:22
Traveller		2 Sam. 12:4
Treacherously		Lam. 1:2
Tread		Ps. 91:13
Treadeth		1 Tim. 5:18
Treasure		Matt. 13:52; Luke 12:21
"	in God	Luke 18:22; 2 Cor. 4:7
"	is us	Matt. 13:44
"	" where heart is	Matt. 6:19–21; Luke 12:34
"	to the Lord	Exod. 19:5
Treasures in heaven or earth		Jer. 10:13; Matt. 6:19–21
Treatise		Acts 1:1

Treatment of others		Matt. 25:45; Phil. 2:4
Tree		Acts 10:39
"	of knowledge	Gen. 2:17
"	" life	Gen. 3:24; Rev. 2:7
Trees		2 Chron. 2:8; Isa. 44:14; Zech. 11:2; Luke 3:9
"	clap hands	Isa. 55:12
"	to rejoice	Ps. 96:12
Tremble		Dan. 6:26; Acts 9:6 + 24:25; Phil. 2:12, 13; James 2:19
Trench		1 Kings 18:32, 35, 38
Trespass		Matt. 18:15; Luke 17:3, 4
Trespasses		Matt. 6:14, 15 + 18:35; 2 Cor. 5:19
Trial, fiery		1 Pet. 4:12
"	of faith ends in joy	1 Pet. 1:7, 8
"	" " precious	1 Pet. 1:7
Tribe		Luke 22:30
Tribes, twelve		James 1:1
Tribulation		Dan. 7:21 + 11:32–35; Matt. 24:21, 22, 29; Rom. 5:3 + 12:12 + 14:22; 1 Thess. 3:3, 4 + 5:3; 2 Thess. 1:6; Rev. 1:9 + 2:9 + 13:5
"	advice	Deut. 4:30, 31
"	afterwards	Mark 13:24–27
"	in world	John 16:33
"	ten days	Rev. 2:10
"	to enter kingdom of God	Acts 14:22
Tributary		Lam. 1:1
Tribute		Matt. 22:17; Rom. 13:7
Trickleth		Lam. 3:49
Tried		Deut. 21:5; Ps. 12:6; Rev. 2:2

Triest	2 Chron. 29:17
" , ear	Job 34:3
Trieth	Prov. 17:3
Triumph	Exod. 15:1; Ps. 25:2 + 92:4; 2 Cor. 2:15; Col. 2:14
Trode	2 Kings 9:33; Luke 12:1
Trodden	Isa. 18:2, 7; Lam. 1:15; Heb. 10:29
Troop	Isa. 65:11
Troops	Hab. 3:16
Trouble	Ps. 37:39 + 40:1 + 46:1, 2 + 77:2; Dan. 12:1; Matt. 26:10; Mark 11:29; 1 Cor. 7:28; 2 Thess. 1:6
" not our hearts	John 14:1–4, 27
Troubled	Matt. 14:26; Luke 24:38; John 14:27
" days & keeping true	Hab. 3:17–19
" heart not for us	John 14:1
" Jesus	Matt. 11:33, 35, 38
Troubles	2 Cor. 4:8–10
Troubleth	Prov. 11:17
Trow	Luke 17:9
Trucebreakers	2 Tim. 3:3
True	John 15:1; 1 John 5:20
" holiness	Eph. 4:24
" light	John 1:9
" to Christ - Paul's example	Phil. 1:20–24
" to God per Job	Job 1:19–21
" worshippers	John 4:23, 24
Truly	Ps. 62:1; Matt. 27:54
Trump of God	1 Thess. 4:16

Trumpet to sound		Matt. 25:31; 1 Cor. 15:52; 1 Thess. 4:16
Trumpets		2 Chron. 5:12
"	, seven	Rev. 8:6
Trust in God		Isa. 12:2; Matt. 6:7, 8; Luke 12:22–24; 2 Cor. 3:4
"	" " at all times	Ps. 62:7, 8 + 91:2, 4; 1 Tim. 4:10
"	" Lord & acknowledge Him	Prov. 3:5, 6 + 16:20 + 26:4 + 30:5; John 8:23, 24
"	in Lord & reward	Ps. 37:3–5; Jer. 17:7
"	" " for path direction	Prov. 3:5, 6
"	in Lord rewarded	Ps. 34:22 + 40:4; Isa. 26:3
"	not in friend	Mic. 7:5
"	" " man or princes	Ps. 146:3; Jer. 17:5, 6
"	vs fear	Prov. 29:25
Trusty ones have shield		Prov. 30:5; Isa. 26:3, 4
Truth and deed important		1 John 3:18
"	" grace by Jesus Christ	John 1:17
"	approved by God	2 Tim. 2:15
"	, believe - for eternal life	1 John 2:23–27
"	by Jesus Christ	John 1:17
"	distorted for attention	Acts 20:30
"	doers prefer light	John 3:21
"	endureth	Ps. 100:5
"	fallen in street	Isa. 59:14
"	for ever	Ps. 100:5 + 117:2
"	free you	John 8:32:+ 14:6; 2 Cor. 3:17
"	, gospel - important	2 Thess. 2:10, 11

"	is Jesus	John 14:6
"	" Jesus' word	John 17:17
"	-life -way	John 14:6
"	of the gospel	Col. 1:5–8
"	preserve me	Ps. 40:11
"	purify souls	1 Pet. 1:22
Truth reward		John 17:17
"	spirit	John 4:23, 24; 1 Cor. 2:1–4
"	spoken helpful	Eph. 4:15, 25
"	to come	John 16:13
"	" others helpful	Eph. 4:15, 25
"	, walk in	3 John 1:3, 4
Try me		Ps. 139:23
"	spirit	1 John 4:1–3
Tumult		Matt. 27:24; Mark 5:38; 2 Cor. 6:5
Tumultuous		Isa. 13:4
Turn		2 Chron. 7:14; Prov. 1:23; Isa. 30:21; Jer. 31:13
"	body	James 3:3
"	not	Prov. 4:26, 27
"	" away speaker from heaven	Heb. 12:25
"	others to righteousness	Dan. 12:3; Acts 14:15
Turned about		Jude 2:17; James 3:4
"	to God, a king	Dan. 3:28–30 + 4:1–3
"	" " from idols	1 Thess. 1:9, 10
Turnest		Ps. 90:3
Turning him		John 21:20; Acts 9:40
"	not with God	James 1:17
Turledove		Gen. 15:9
Twain		Matt. 19:5, 6; Mark 10:8; Eph. 2:15

Twelve	1 Chron. 25:9–31
" apostles chosen by Jesus	Matt. 10:1, 2; John 6:70
Twelves for the heavenly Jerusalem	Rev. 21:10–21
Twilight	2 Kings 7:5
Twinkling	1 Cor. 15:52
Two better than one	Eccles. 4:8–12
" or more agree	Matt. 18:19, 20
Twoedged	Rev. 1:16
Twofold	Matt. 23:15

• U •

Unawares		Luke 21:34; Heb. 13:2
Unbearable, four things		Prov. 30:21–23
Unbelief		Matt. 17:20; Mark 9:24; Rom. 3:3 + 4:20; Heb. 3:19 + 4:11
Unbelievers		1 Cor. 6:6 + 14:23; 2 Cor. 6:14
Unbelieving		Acts 14:2
Unblameable		Col. 1:22
Unameably		1 Thess. 2:10
Unbraideth not		James 1:5
Uncertain riches		1 Tim. 6:17
Uncircumcised		Gen. 17:14; Acts 7:51
Uncircumcision		Gal. 2:7; Col. 2:13
Unclean		Lev. 12:2, 4, 5; Matt. 12:43; Mark 1:26 + 3:11, 30 + 6:7
"	by dead body	Hag. 2:13
"	lips	Isa. 6:5
"	spirits	Luke 6:18
"	, we as	Isa. 64:6
Uncleaness		2 Pet. 2:10
Uncomely		1 Cor. 7:36 + 12:23
Unconcern		Prov. 21:13; 1 John 3:17, 18 + 4:8
Uncorruptness		Titus 2:7
Uncovered		Lev. 20:17–21
Unction		1 John 2:20

Undefiled	Ps. 119:1; Heb. 7:26 + 13:4; James 1:27; 1 Pet. 1:4
Under	Eccles. 3:1
Undersetters	1 Kings 7:34
Understand	Isa. 6:9, 10; Dan. 10:12; Matt. 15:10; Mark 7:14, 18; Luke 24:45; Acts 28:26, 27
" and not heed	Dan. 12:3–13; Phil. 1:12
" by wise & not by wicked	Dan. 12:10
" us by Lord	1 Chron. 28:9
" - you get good information	Prov. 4:5
Understandeth	Acts 8:30; 1 Cor. 14:16
" all imaginations of thoughts	1 Chron. 28:9
" by God	Job 28:33
Understanding	Job 38:4; Ps. 119:73; Prov. 3:5 + 4:5, 7; Mark 7:18; 1 Cor. 14:14, 15
" and wisdom	Job 28:28; Ps. 49:1–20; Prov. 9:10 + 16:16 + 17:24, 27 + 17:24, 27; Dan. 1:10–20
" from peace of God	Phil. 4:7
" " Son of God	1 John 5:20
" " the Lord	Job 32:8; Prov. 2:6 + 3:6
" " word	Ps. 119:104, 130
" heart	1 Kings 3:11, 12
" in visions & dreams	Dan. 1:17
" is key to wisdom	Job 28:12–20, 28; Prov. 24:3
" , Lord's	Ps. 147:5
" , man of	2 Chron. 2:13; Prov. 15:2, 19
" of God - none	Isa. 40:28
" " Lord's words	Ps. 119:130

"	" testimonies	Ps. 119:129, 144
"	or wisdom	Prov. 19:8
"	, passeth all	Phil. 4:7
"	will of Lord	Ps. 119:34, 134, 135; Eph. 1:18 + 5:17
Understood		Matt. 26:10; Rom. 1:20; 2 Pet. 3:16
Undo		Zeph. 3:19
Undone		Isa. 6:5; Luke 11:42
Unequally		2 Cor. 6:14
Unfeigned		2 Cor. 6:6; 2 Tim. 1:5; 1 Pet. 1:22
Unfortunate to be cared for		Deut. 24:19–22
Unfruitful		Mark 4:18, 19; 1 Cor. 14:14; 2 Pet. 1:8
Ungodliness		Rom. 1:18; 2 Tim. 2:16
Ungodly		Ps. 1:1, 4–6; Rom. 5:6; Jude 1:15
"	will torment & kill	John 16:3
Unicorn		Num. 23:22 + 24:8; Deut. 33:17; Job 39:9–11; Ps. 22:21 + 29:6 + 92:10; Isa. 34:7
United in heaven & on earth		Eph. 1:10
Unity		Eph. 4:1–7, 13; Phil. 2:1–30
"	, all	Acts 4:32
"	, good	Ps. 133:1–3; Matt. 18:19
"	in Christ	1 Cor. 12:1–31 + 14:1–39; Eph. 1:10, 13 + 4:13, 25
"	" church	1 Pet. 4:8–10
"	of all in Christ - faith	Eph. 4:1–32

"	pleasant	Ps. 133:1
Unjust		Ps. 43:1; Prov. 11:7 + 28:8 + 29:27; Zeph. 3:5; Matt. 5:45
"	ones face judgment	2 Pet. 2:9, 10
"	or faithful	Luke 16:10–13
Unjustly sentenced to		
	die - be saved	Prov. 24:10–12
Unknown, four things		Prov. 30:18, 19
"	God	Acts 17:23
"	great one among	
	you	John 1:26, 27
"	tongue	1 Cor. 14:13
Unlawful		Acts 10:28
Unlearned		Acts 4:13; 2 Pet. 3:16
Unleavened bread		Exod. 12:8; Lev. 23:6; Luke 22:1, 7, 19; 1 Cor. 5:7, 8
Unloose shoes		John 1:26, 27
Unmarried more holy		1 Cor. 7:8, 11, 32, 34
Unmoveable		Acts 27:41; 1 Cor. 15:58
Unperfect		Ps. 139:16
Unprofitable		Heb. 13:17
Unquenchable fire		Matt. 3:12
Unreasonable		2 Thess. 3:2; Rom. 11:33
Unrebukeable		1 Tim. 6:14
Unreproveable		Col. 1:22
Unrighteous		Rom. 3:5; 1 Cor. 30:18, 19
"	doings in detail	1 Cor. 6:9, 10, 18
"	is lost	1 Cor. 6:9
"	or righteous	Prov. 14:1–35
Unrighteousness		Lev. 19:35; Rom. 1:18; 1 Thess. 21:10–12; 1 John 1:9
"	is sin	1 John 5:17
Unruly		Titus 1:10
Unsavoury		Job 6:6

Unsearchable		Job 5:9; Ps. 145:3; Rom. 11:33; Eph. 3:8
Unspeakable gift		2 Cor. 9:15; 1 Pet. 1:8
"	joy	1 Pet. 1:8
"	words	2 Cor. 12:3, 4
Unspotted		James 1:27
Unstable		James 1:8
"	souls	2 Pet. 2:14 + 3:16
Untaken		2 Cor. 3:14
Unthankful		Luke 6:35
Until		Jude 20:26; Isa. 6:11; Luke 1:20 + 22:16, 18; Gal. 4:2, 19
Untimely		Job 3:16
Unto		Matt. 25:14, 15, 29 + 27:53; Luke 1:77
"	all men	Titus 3:2; 1 Pet. 1:12
"	end of world	Matt. 28:20
"	God	Ps. 66:1 + 75:1 + 77:1 + 81:1; Acts 15:18
"	Him	Ps. 25:1; 1 Cor. 14:26; 2 Thess. 2:1; Rev. 1:5
"	Jesus	Matt. 25:36, 39
"	Lord, commit way	Ps. 37:5
"	" , cry	Ps. 28:1 + 120:1 + 130:1 + 142:1
"	" , give	Ps. 29:1
"	" , glory	Ps. 115:1
"	" , Joyful noise	Ps. 100:1
"	" , Lift	Ps. 28:1
"	" , sing	Ps. 95:1, 2 + 96:1 + 98:1 + 101:1 + 149:1
"	" , sware	Ps. 132:2
Unto Lord, thanks		Ps. 92:1 + 105:1 + 106:1 + 107:1 + 118:1 + 136:1

"	Me	Ps. 56:1 + 57:1; Phil. 1:12
"	other gods	2 Chron. 34:25
"	us	Ps. 67:1
"	you	Matt. 9:29; Luke 8:10; John 14:27
Untoward generation		Acts 2:40
Unusual verses		see Section UU
Unwashen hands		Matt. 15:20
Unwise		Eph. 5:17
Unworthily		1 Cor. 11:27, 29
Unworthy		Acts 13:46
Up		Acts 1:11, 13, 22; 1 Tim. 6:19
Upbraideth		James 1:5
Uphold		Ps. 51:12 + 54:4; Isa. 41:10
Upholdeth		Ps. 145:14
Upon		Ps. 51:1; 1 Cor. 16:2; Rev. 7:10 + 16:2
Upper		Mark 14:15
Upright is man made by God		Ps. 7:10 + 25:8; Prov. 2:21; Eccles. 7:29; Dan. 10:11; Acts 14:10
Uprightly		Ps. 84:11; Gal. 2:14
Uprightness		Job 33:3; Ps. 143:10
Upside down		Ps. 146:9
Upward		Hag. 2:15
"	man - downward beast	Eccles. 3:21 [[this reference is very misleading the way it is written]]
Us, for		Rom. 8:34
"	made kings & priests	1 Pet. 2:5, 9; Rev. 1:6

Use, natural - of men & women	Rom. 1:24–27
" time wisely	Eph. 5:15, 16; Col. 4:5
User, milk	Heb. 5:12, 13
Usurp	1 Tim. 2:12
Usury	Exod. 22:25; Deut. 23:19, 20; Ps. 15:5; Luke 19:23
Usward	Eph. 1:19; 2 Pet. 3:9
Utmost	Luke 11:31
Utter	Ps. 145:7; Prov. 14:5; Eccles. 1:8; Joel 2:11
Utterance	Acts 2:4; Eph. 6:19
" enriched by Him	1 Cor. 1:15
Uttereth	Prov. 1:20, 21; Jer. 10:13; Mic. 7:3
Utterly	Deut. 3:6 + 32:12; Isa. 6:11; 1 Cor. 6:7; Jer 12:17
Uttermost	Ps. 65:8 + 139:9; Matt. 5:26; Acts 1:8; Heb. 7:25

• V •

Vagabond		Gen. 4:14; Acts 19:13
Vain		Exod. 20:7; Mark 7:7; Phil. 2:16; Titus 1:10; James 2:20
"	babblings	Matt. 15:8, 9; 1 Tim. 6:20; 2 Tim. 2:16
"	, beauty is	Prov. 31:30
"	deceit	Col. 2:8
"	glory	Gal. 5:26
"	if Christ not risen	1 Cor. 15:14, 17
"	, labor not in	1 Cor. 15:10, 58; 2 Cor. 6:1; Gal. 4:11; 1 Thess. 3:5
"	regarding God's name	Deut. 5:11; Prov. 30:9
"	repetitions	Matt. 6:7
"	thoughts	1 Cor. 3:20; Gal. 3:4
Vainglory		Phil. 2:3
Vainly		Col. 2:18
Valiantly		Ps. 118:15, 16
Valley of decision		Joel 3:14
" " the mountains		Deut. 11:11; Ps. 104:8, 10; Zech. 14:5
Valour		Judg. 6:12
Value of life - Lord & man		1 Sam. 16:7

Vanish		Isa. 51:6; James 4:14
Vanished		Job 7:9; Luke 24:31
Vanities - God vs bad		Eccles. 8:14
"	, many	Eccles. 1:1–18 + 2:1–26 + 4:1–16 + 5:1–17 + 6:1–12
"	of good vs bad	Isa. 57:13
"	" life	Eccles. 1:1–7:29
Vanity		Rom. 8:20
"	cure	Eccles. 12:8, 13, 14
"	of pleasure	Eccles. 2:1 + 8:15
"	" riches	Eccles. 5:8–10
"	" times	Eccles. 3:1–22
"	" wisdom	Eccles. 1:12–18
"	words	2 Pet. 2:18
Vapour		James 4:14
Vapours		Jer. 10:13
Variableness not with		
	God	James 1:17
Variance		Matt. 10:35
Vaunteth		1 Cor. 13:4
Vegetables		Num. 11:5
Vegetarian		Dan. 1:9–20
Vehement		Jon. 4:8
Vehemently		Luke 6:49 + 11:53 + 23:10
Veil		Matt. 27:51; Luke 23:45; 2 Cor. 3:13–16; Heb. 6:19 + 10:19, 20
"	- his flesh	Heb. 10:19, 20
"	old	2 Cor. 3:14
Vengeance		Ps. 94:1; Luke 21:22; Rom. 12:19; Jude 1:7
Venomous		Acts 28:4
Ventriloquist's voice		
	(apparently)	Isa. 24:9

393

Verily	Ps. 39:5; Matt. 5:18 + 6:16 + 19:28 + 21:31; Mark 9:12 + 10:29; John 3:3, 5, 11; + 5:24, 25 + 14:2; Heb. 12:10
Verity	Ps. 111:7
Vessel	Prov. 25:4; Acts 10:11, 16; 2 Tim. 2:21; 1 Pet. 2:5
Vessels of power in God	2 Cor. 4:7
" unto honour	2 Tim. 2:20, 21
Vessels we are	2 Tim. 2:20, 21
Vesture	Matt. 27:35; Heb. 1:12; Rev. 19:13, 16
Vex	Exod. 22:21; Lev. 19:33; 2 Chron. 15:6; Ps. 2:5; Isa. 11:13; Hab. 2:7
Vexation	2 Chron. 15:5; Isa. 65:14; Eccles. 2:22 + 4:4, 6; Isa. 65:14
Vexed	Ps. 6:2, 3, 10; Matt. 15:22 + 17:15; Acts 5:16; 2 Pet. 2:7, 8
Vials of wrath	Rev. 16:1–4, 8, 10, 12, 17
Vices and virtues	Prov. 10:1–15:33
Victims - heathen's fate	Ps. 2:8, 9
Victor	Rev. 19:11, 14
Victory	2 Sam. 23:10, 12; Ps. 98:1; 1 Cor. 15:57; 1 John 5:4, 5
" for God & those who endured death	Rev. 12:11, 12
Victuals	Josh. 1:11; Neh. 13:15; Jer. 40:5; Matt. 14:15; Luke 9:12
Vigilant	1 Tim 3:2; 1 Pet. 5:8
Vile affections	Rom. 1:26, 27
" body	Phil. 3:21

" I am	Job 40:4
" person	Dan. 11:21
Village	Luke 10:38
Vine, true	John 15:1–6
Vinedressers	Isa. 61:5
Vinegar	Ps. 69:21; Luke 23:36; John 19:29, 30
Vineyards	Deut. 28: 39
Viol	Amos 6:5
Violence	Gen. 6:11, 13; Ps. 11:5; Prov. 13:2; Obad. 1:10; Luke 3:14
" of waves	Acts 27:41
Violent	Ps. 86:14 + 140:1
Viper	Acts 23:3–6
Viper's generation	Matt. 12:34; Luke 3:7
Virgin	Jer. 31:13; Luke 1:26–35
" and married woman	1 Cor. 7:28, 34–39
" man	1 Cor. 7:37
" marry molesting man	1 Cor. 7:36
" Mary	Isa. 7:14; Matt. 1:18, 20, 23, 25
" more holy	1 Cor. 7:34
" rejoice	Jer. 31:13
Virginity	Jude 11:37, 38; Ezek. 23:8
Virgins , ten	Matt. 25:1–13
Virtue	Luke 6:19; 2 Pet. 1:3, 5
" in various things	Mark 5:30; Phil. 4:8
" , moral	Prov. 13:1–25
Virtues and vices	Prov. 10:1–15:33
" , eight	Phil. 4:8
Virtuous woman	Ruth 3:11; Prov. 12:4 + 31:10–31
Virtuously	Prov. 31:29

Visage		Isa. 52:14; Dan. 3:19
Visible		Col. 1:16
Vision		2 Chron. 32:32; Prov. 29:18; Acts 10:9–17 + 16:9 + 18:9
Visions		Dan. 1:17; Acts 2:17
Visit		James 1:27
Visitation day		1 Pet. 2:11
Visitors - first for Christ child		Matt. 2:2
Visits to be short		Prov. 25:17
Vocation		Eph. 4:1–3
Voice		John 10:4, 5 + 12:30
"	from heaven	Jer. 4:31 + 16:9; Dan. 4:31; Matt. 3:17 + 17:5; Mark 1:11; John 12:28, 30; Rev. 11:12; + 14:13
"	heard by God	Ps. 55:17
"	" out of throne	Rev. 19:6 + 21:3
"	in wilderness	John 1:23
"	of bird	Job 39:26–30; Jer. 17:11
"	" God	Gen. 3:8, 9; Job 37:2–6; Ps. 46:6
" —	" Lord	Josh. 24:24; Ps. 29:3–9; Isa. 6:8; Zeph. 1:14
Void		Isa. 55:11; Acts 24:16
Voluntary		Col. 2:18
Vomit		Prov. 23:8 + 25:16; 2 Pet. 2:22
Vow		Num. 30:2; Deut. 23:21, 22; Eccles. 5:4, 5
Vows		Ps. 116:18; Prov. 20:25
"	by singing praises	Ps. 61:6
"	, God's	Ps. 56:12
"	to be paid	Job 22:27; Ps. 50:14
Voyage		Acts 27:1–44

· W ·

Wag	Zeph. 2:15
Wage due	Deut. 24:14, 15; Luke 3:14
" of sin	Rom. 6:23
Wages of wickedness	2 Pet. 2:14, 15
" " sin or gift	John 4:36; Rom. 6:23
Wagging heads	Mark 15:29
Wagon	Gen. 45:19, 21 + 46:5
Wail, all will - because of	
Jesus	Rev. 1:7
Wailing	Amos 5:16–20
Wait - be blessed	Dan. 12:8–13; 2 Thess. 3:5
" on the Lord	Ps. 27:14 + 37:34 + 62:5 +
	130:5, 6; Isa. 40:31; 1 Cor. 1:7
" - patience - patient	Rom. 8:25; 2 Thess. 3:5
" - rewarded	Isa. 64:4; Lam. 3:25, 26;
	Acts 1:4
Waiteth	Ps. 62:1
Wake up to Christ	Eph. 5:14; Luke 24:17
Waked	Zech. 4:1
Walk	Gen. 17:1; Ezek. 36:12;
	Mic. 4:5; Luke 24:17;
	Acts 3:2–8 + 14:16
" after the spirit	2 Chron. 17:3, 4; Rom. 8:4, 5;
	Gal. 5:5, 6, 16–18

"	and keep & do	Ezek. 36:27
"	as good examples	Prov. 2:20
"	" He - Jesus	Rom. 13:13; 1 John 2:6
"	" wise	Eph. 5:15, 16; Col. 4:5
"	by faith	2 Cor. 5:7
"	- evil ways	Eph. 5:14–16; Phil. 3:18, 19
"	circumspectly	Eph. 5:15
"	in Good works	Eph. 2:10
"	" His ways	Lev. 26:3; Deut. 28:1, 2, 9; Ps. 1:1, 2 + 89:15
"	" integrity	Prov. 19:1
"	" name of Lord our God	Mic. 4:5
"	newness of life	Rom. 6:4
"	in the light	John 12:35; 1 John 1:7
"	" " spirit	Gal. 5:16, 25; Eph. 4:1–6
"	" truth	3 John 1:3, 4
"	stately - four things	Prov. 30:29–31
"	- study - work	1 Thess. 4:11, 12
"	together	Amos 3:3
"	uprightly - nothing withheld	Ps. 84:11; Eph. 5:15
"	worthy	Eph. 4:1; Col. 1:10; 1 Thess. 2:12
Walked	God	Gen. 3:8
"	Jesus	John 7:1
"	through sea	Hab. 3:15
"	with God	Gen. 5:22 + 6:9
Walkest		Isa. 43:4
Walking	in own lusts	2 Pet. 3:3; Jude 1:16
"	on sea	Matt. 14:25, 26, 29; John 6:19
Wall	, David leaped over	Ps. 18:29
"	of Jerusalem	Neh. 12:27
"	or partition	Eph. 2:14

Wallow		Jer. 25:34
Wallowed		Mark 9:20; 2 Pet. 2:22
Wander		Job 12:24; Isa. 16:8; Prov. 27:8
Want		Ps. 27:14; Phil. 4:11
"	and other's abundance	2 Cor. 8:14
"	nothing if fear Lord	Ps. 34:9, 10
"	or plenteousness	Prov. 21:5
Wanton		1 Tim. 5:11; James 5:5
Wantonness		2 Pet. 2:18
War	against God	Rev. 13:16
"	, make	Rev. 13:4, 7
"	weapons less than wisdom	Eccles. 9:18
"	with saints	Dan. 7:27; Rev. 13:7
Ware		Acts 14:6
Warfare		1 Cor. 9:7
Warmth with two		Eccles. 4:11
Warn everyone		Acts 20:31; Col. 1:28
"	unruly ones	1 Thess. 5:14
Warning		John 16:1–3; Rev. 14:9, 10
"	against the evil one	2 Thess. 2:7–12
Warp		Lev. 13:48, 53, 56, 57, 59
Warreth		2 Tim. 2:4
Wars before end		Matt. 24:6
Was God & the Word		John 1:1, 14
"	, Lord	Rev. 1:8
Wash me		Ps. 51:7
"	others feet	John 13:4–17
Washed us		Rev. 1:5
Washing		Titus 3:5
Wast		Isa. 43:4; Ezek. 16:7
Waste		Isa. 58:12
Waster		Prov. 18:9

Watch		Neh. 4:9; Dan. 5:27;
		Matt. 14:25 + 25:13;
		Mark 13:5, 6, 33–37;
		Luke 21:36; 1 Cor. 16:13;
		1 Thess. 5:6; 1 Tim. 4:5;
		Rev. 3:3
"	and be worthy to escape wrath	Luke 21:36
"	for Lord to come	Matt. 24:42, 43
Watched	are all from Lord in heaven	Ps. 33:13, 14
Watches	, night	Ps. 63:6
Watching	ones rewarded	Luke 12:37–40, 43
Watchman		Isa. 21:11, 12
Water		Gen. 2:10; Num. 20:10;
		Isa. 48:21 + 55:10 + 58:11
"	and blood	1 John 5:6, 8
"	for everything	Ps. 104:10–16
"	" money	Deut. 2:28
"	from rock	Num. 20:7–11
"	, give - to drink	Matt. 10:42
"	, living	John 4:7, 10–15 + 7:38
"	of life	Rev. 21:6 + 22:17
"	to blood (first plague)	Exod. 7:14–25
Watered - watereth		Prov. 11:25
Waterflood		Ps. 69:15
Waterpot		John 2:7 + 4:28
Waters		Gen. 1:2, 6, 7, 9, 10; Ps. 77:16;
		Jer. 17:8 + 18:14
"	, cold	Prov. 25:25
"	divided	Exod. 14:16:21
"	flow	Ps. 147:18
"	from off the earth	Gen. 8:3–5

Waterspouts	Ps. 42:7
Wave offering	Lev. 9:21 + 10:14, 15
Waver	Heb. 10:23; James 1:6
Waves	Matt. 8:26
Wax	Exod. 32:10; Isa. 51:6; Jer. 6:24; Matt. 24:12
Waxed	Deut. 8:4; Ps. 32:3; Luke 1:80
Waxen	Deut. 32:15
Waxing	Phil. 1:14
Way and ways of man	Prov. 14:12; 1 Cor. 12:31
" , God's	Ps. 18:30 + 119:165
" , I am - Jesus	John 14:6
" is broad or narrow	Matt. 7:13, 14
" is only Jesus	John 14:6; Acts 4:10, 12
" , make a	Isa. 43:19
Way , mans	Jude 18:6; Ps. 18:32; Prov. 20:24
" , new & living	Heb. 10:20
" of truth	John 14:6
" " accepted godly life	Ps. 92:1, 2; Ezek. 18:5–9; Col. 1:1:18; 1 Thess. 5:11–22
" of Cain	Jude 1:11
" " Christianity is God's way of life	Deut. 30:20; Ps. 37:5; John 6:48; Acts 4:12; Gal. 2:20; Col. 3:4
" of living	Col. 3:8–17; Titus 2:11–15
" " man	Prov. 14:12 + 16:2, 9, 25; Jer. 10:23
" " " not in himself	Eccles. 8:9; Jer. 10:23
" " peace not known to some	Rom. 3:17
" righteous or ungodly	Ps. 1:6

"	, one only	Isa. 30:21; John 14:6
"	per words	Prov. 4:20–22
"	, the	John 14:6
"	through His flesh	Heb. 10:20
"	, thy	Ps. 37:5 + 77:13
"	to Father	Prov. 16:9; John 14:6
"	" life	Ps. 32:8; Matt. 7:13, 14
"	- truth - life	Isa. 30:21; John 14:6
"	we know	John 14:3, 4
Wayfaring man		2 Sam. 12:4; Isa. 35:8
Ways be established		Ps. 103:7; Prov. 4:26
"	of God's & other's	Isa. 55:8; Rom. 11:33; Rev. 15:3
"	" man	James 1:8
"	" the little	Prov. 30:24–28
We all		2 Cor. 3:18
"	are	1 Cor. 4:10
"	" given	2 Tim. 1:7
"	" His workman-ship	Eph. 2:8–10
"	are members of others	Eph. 4:25
"	changed	1 Cor. 15:52
"	- sons of God	1 John 3:2, 3
Weak gets power		Isa. 40:29
"	- strong	1 Cor. 4:10 + 9:22; 2 Cor. 13:3
"	things chosen	1 Cor. 1:27, 28
Weakness to strength		1 Cor. 1:25; 2 Cor. 12:9 + 13:4
Wealth		Deut. 8:18; Prov. 21:5; Jer. 17:7
"	by vanity shall decrease	Prov. 13:11 + 21:5
"	, God given	Deut. 8:18

"	no savior for owners	Zeph. 1:17, 18
"	not by right	Jer. 17:11
Weaned		Ps. 131:2; Isa. 11:8
Weapon against Lord God - not prosper		Isa. 54:17
Weapons		Matt. 26:47; Mark 14:48
"	for slaughter	Ezek. 9:1, 2
"	of war less than wisdom	Eccles. 9:18
Wear		Job 14:19
Wearied		Isa. 43:23, 24
"	gets strength	Matt. 11:28; John 4:6; Heb. 12:3
Weary		Ps. 69:3; Isa. 43:22 + 46:1
"	if visits too long	Prov. 25:17
"	- not God	Isa. 40:28
Weasel		Lev. 11:29
Weather		Job 37:3–22; Matt. 16:2, 3
"	, work regardless of	Prov. 20:4
Weave		Isa. 19:9
Web		Isa. 59:5, 6
"	, spider's	Job 8:14
Wedding		Matt. 22:3, 8, 10–12; Luke 12:36
Week	, first day of	1 Cor. 16:2
"	- seven days	Exod. 20:9–11; Lev. 23:16; Deut. 5:13, 14
Weep		Lam. 1:16; Jer. 31:15; Luke 23:28; John 16:20 + 20:15
"	- rejoice	Eccles. 3:22; Rom. 12:15
Weeping		Ps. 30:5; Matt. 24:51
Weighed		Dan. 5:27
Weigheth the spirit		Prov. 16:2

Weight loss	Heb. 12:11
Weights, just - etc.	Lev. 19:36; Prov. 16:11
Welfare	Deut. 14:28, 29
Well	John 4:6, 11
" doing	1 Pet. 3:17
" done	Eccles. 3:22; Matt. 25:21
" , going - four things	Prov. 30:29–31
Wellbeloved	3 John 1:1
Wellpleasing	Heb. 13:21
Wells	2 Pet. 2:17
Wellspring	Prov. 16:22 + 18:4
Welps	Ezek. 19:2, 3, 5
Went forth	Mark 16:20
Wept	Num. 14:1; Job 2:12; John 11:35; Acts 20:37
Wert	Job 8:6
Whale	Job 7:12
What	Ps. 39:4; Mark 10:3, 9, 36, 51; John 4:27; 1 John 3:1
" shall we do?	Acts 2:37, 38
Whatsoever	Lev. 27:32; Matt. 16:19 + 28:20; John 14:13, 26 + 16:23; Col. 3:17, 23
" things	Phil. 4:8, 9; 1 John 3:22
Wheat	Ruth 2:23; Matt. 13:25; Acts 27:38
Wheels	Ezek. 10:2, 6, 9, 10, 12, 13, 16, 19
Whelp	Gen. 49:9; Prov. 17:12
When	Gen. 2:4 + 3:6 + 4:8 + 7:6; Matt. 2:1, 3, 4, 9–14; Luke 1:9, 12, 22
" Christ to appear again	Heb. 9:28; 1 John 3:2

" I come - Jesus	1 Cor. 16:2
" - may believe	John 13:19
Whence	Job 1:7 + 2:2; Phil. 3:20; James 4:1
Whensoever	Mark 14:7
Where	Matt. 2:2
Whereabouts of Jesus Christ	1 Pet. 3:22
Whereby	Luke 1:78; Acts 4:12 + 11:14; 2 Pet. 3:6
Wherefore	Job 3:20; Isa. 58:3; Matt. 6:30 + 9:4; 1 Cor. 14:39; Eph. 4:8 + 6:13; Heb. 7:25
Wherein	Gen. 1:30; Jude 16:5, 6, 15 + 18:6; Rom. 5:2; Phil. 4:10; 1 Pet. 5:12
Whereinsoever	2 Cor. 11:21
Wheresoever	Mark 14:9
Whereunto	Acts 13:2; 1 Pet. 3:21
Whereupon	Acts 26:19
Wherewith	Jer. 33:16; Rom. 14:19
Wherewithal	Matt. 6:31
Whet	Ps. 7:12 + 64:3
Whether	2 Chron. 14:11; Mark 2:9; Acts 17:11; 1 Cor. 10:31
Which	Gen. 1:7, 21, 29; Ps. 118:19, 20, 22, 24 + 146:6, 7; Matt. 5:6, 10, 12, 16
While	Matt. 1:20
" , little	John 16:16–19
Whiles	Matt. 5:25
Whilst	Job 8:12; Ps. 141:10
Whip	Prov. 26:3

Whirlwind	Job 37:9; 38:1; Prov. 1:27; Jer. 25:32; Ezek. 1:4
White, make them	Dan. 11:35
" raiment	Rev. 3:4
" to harvest	John 4:35
Whiter than snow	Ps. 51:7
Whither	Ps. 139:7; John 3:8 + 14:4
Whithersoever	Josh. 1:9; Jude 2:15; James 3:4
Who	Isa. 6:8; Luke 10:22 + 12:42, 43; 1 Pet. 1:20, 21
" against us if God is for us?	Rom. 8:31
Whole	Eccles. 12:13; Matt. 12:13 + 15:28
" body	Matt. 6:22, 23
" by faith	Mark 5:34; Luke 17:19; John 5:4–15
" heart	Ps. 9:1
" - sick	Mark 2:17
Wholly	1 Thess. 5:23; 1 Tim. 4:15
Whom	Isa. 6:8; Luke 10:22 + 12:42, 43; 1 Cor. 1:9; Heb. 2:10
" say	Matt. 16:15; Mark 8:27, 29
Whomsoever	Matt. 11:27; Mark 15:6; Acts 8:19
Whore	Lev. 19:29; Prov. 6:24–28; Phil. 4:8; 1 John 21:15, 16; Rev. 17:1–6 + 19:2
Whoredom	Num. 25:1; Ezek. 23:3–19, 43; Hos. 1:2 + 2:1–13 + 4:11
Whoremongers	Eph. 5:5; Heb. 13:4
Whoring after other gods	Jude 2:17
Whose	John 20:23

Whoso		Ps. 50:23; 1 John 3:17
Whosoever		1 John 3:4, 6, 9, 10, 15;
		Matt. 5:28, 32 + 16:25;
		Mark 6:11; John 3:15, 16;
		1 John 3:4, 6, 9, 10, 15;
		Rev. 22:7
"	believeth	John 12:46
Why		Gen. 4:6 + 12:18, 19; Job 3:11,
		12, 23; Matt. 8:26 + 19:7 +
		20:6; John 4:27 + 7:45; +
		10:20; Acts 3:12
Wicked		Ps. 10:2–11 + 11:2 + 12:8;
		Prov. 18:3, 5
"	and foolish vs wise	
	& righteous	Prov. 13:1–25 + 28:1–28 +
		29:2–27
"	defined	Rev. 21:8
"	destroyed	Ps. 37:20, 38 + 145:20;
		Nah. 1:10; Rev. 20:9
"	falleth into	
	mischief	Prov. 24:16
"	goes to lake of fire	Rev. 21:8
"	no peace	Isa. 48:22 + 57:20, 21
"	" pleasure to God	Ezek. 33:11
"	not acquitted	Exod. 34:6, 7; Nah. 1:3
"	" inhabit the earth	Prov. 10:30
"	one overcome	1 John 1:14
"	" to avoid	Prov. 18:5; 1 Cor. 5:11–13
"	one's despair	Prov. 11:5; Jer. 30:6;
		Ezek. 33:7–9; Nah. 2:10
"	ones revealed	2 Thess. 2:8
"	or righteous	Ps. 37:21; Prov. 10:30 +
		13:1; 15:33

"	people	Rom. 1:21–32
"	punished	Ps. 37:14, 15; Isa. 13:9–11; Mal. 4:1; Phil. 3:18, 19; 2 Thess. 1:7–10
"	revealed	2 Thess. 2:8–12
"	reward	Ps. 37:14, 15; Prov. 1:29, 30 + 11:5; Eccles. 8:12, 13; Isa. 3:10, 11; Rom. 2:5, 6, 9
"	- righteous	Prov. 10:30; Isa. 26:10
"	saith	Job 21:14, 15
"	spring	Ps. 92:7
"	to be as ashes	Mal. 4:3
"	" " destroyed	Ps. 37:20, 38 + 92:7 + 145:20; Isa. 47:14; Mal. 4:1, 3
"	" " revealed	2 Thess. 2:8–10
"	turn - God's pleasure	Ezek. 33:11
"	understand not	Dan. 12:10
"	vs righteous	Prov. 10:30 + 12:2 + 13:5, 6 + 18:5; Rom. 12:2
"	ways even prosperity	Ps. 73:3–12
Wickedly		1 Sam. 12:25
Wickedness		Ps. 55:11,15; Eph. 6:12
"	vs righteous	Prov. 14:1–35
"	great	Gen. 6:5; 1 John 5:19
"	results	Isa. 47:10, 11 + 48:22; Mal. 4:1–3; Matt. 10:28; Rev. 20:7–15
"	wages	2 Pet. 2:14, 15
Wicked's fate		Ps. 11:6; Prov. 11:31; Isa. 9:5 + 13:11 + 34:2; Mal. 4:1
Widow		Deut. 24:19; 1 Kings 17:17–24; Acts 6:1; 1 Tim. 5:3–5, 9, 11, 16

"	not to live in pleasure	1 Tim. 5:6
Widowhood		Isa. 54:4
Widow's giving		Luke 21:1–4
"	works	1 Tim. 5:9, 10
Widows to be honored		1 Tim. 5:3–5
Wife		Gen. 2:24; Exod. 2:1; Ps. 128:3; 1 Cor. 7:33, 34; Eph. 5:23, 28, 31, 33
"	and husband duties	1 Cor. 7:1–40
"	- good thing	Prov. 18:22
"	- husband	Prov. 31:10, 11, 23; 1 Cor. 7:10–16; Eph. 5:21–23; Titus 1:6
"	-" different beliefs	1 Cor. 7:12, 13
"	, one	2 Tim. 3:12
"	rejoice	Prov. 5:18, 19
"	submit	Eph. 5:22; Col. 3:18; 1 Pet. 3:1, 2
Wild life have homes		Matt. 8:20
Wilderness		Gen. 16:7; Neh. 9:21; Matt. 4:1, 2; Luke 5:16
Wiles		Eph. 6:11
Wilful sins not forgiven		Heb. 10:26
Will do, Lord		Isa. 43:19
"	, God's	1 Thess. 5:18; 2 Thess. 5:16–18; 1 John 5:14
"	, I - God	Isa. 41:10
"	, " - Jon.	Jon. 2:9
"	I - that they	John 17:24
"	of Christ	Eph. 1:11 + 5:17
"	" Father in heaven	Matt. 7:21 + 18:14 + 26:39; John 6:38–40

"	" God	Rom. 8:27 + 12:2; Col. 1:9; 1 Thess. 5:16–18; 1 Pet. 3:17 + 4:2; 1 John 2:17 + 5:14
"	" " doer abideth ever	1 John 2:17
"	of God doer acquires knowledge	John 7:17; 1 Cor. 1:9
"	of Lord	Eph. 5:17
"	, whosoever	Rev. 22:17
Willing		Isa. 1:19; Luke 10:29 + 22:42; Rom. 9:22; 2 Cor. 5:8; 1 Tim. 6:18
"	mind	2 Cor. 8:12
Willingly		1 Chron. 29:14; 1 Cor. 9:17; 1 Pet. 5:2; 2 Pet. 3:5; Jude 5:2, 9
Wilt		Ps. 38:15; Matt. 15:28; Acts 2:27 + 9:6 + 13:10; Philem. 1:21
Wind		Job 1:19; Ps. 147:18; John 3:8; Acts 27:7 + 28:13, 14
"	, east	Exod. 10:13; Hos. 12:1 + 13:15
"	, north	Prov. 25:23; Sol. 5:16
"	, south	Luke 12:55; Acts 28:13
"	, west	Exod. 10:19
Window		2 Kings 9:32 + 13:17
Winds and waves		Matt. 8:26
"	no more	Rev. 7:1
Wine		Prov. 20:1 + 23:20, 21, 31, 32; Jer. 35:2, 5–8, 14; Hos. 4:11 + 14:7; Hab. 2:5; Acts 2:13; Eph. 5:18; Luke 10:34
"	bad & good	Prov. 31:4–7; Luke 10:34
"	- be sober	1 Thess. 5:6–8
"	for heavy heart	Prov. 31:6

"	" stomach's sake	1 Tim. 5:23
"	, much	Titus 2:3
"	not to drink if harm another	Rom. 14:21
"	regarding bishops	Titus 1:7
"	, sweet - drunken	Isa. 49:26
"	to drink	Jer. 35:2, 5, 6
"	unfermented - orginally gleukos then oinos	
Winebibber		Luke 7:34
Winepress		Lam. 1:15
Wings		Job 39:13; Ezek. 10:5, 8; Mal. 4:2
"	of Lord cover us	Ps. 91:4
Winked		Acts 17:30
Winter		Job 39:9, 10; Acts 27:12; 2 Tim. 4:21
"	is past	Sol. 2:11, 12
Wipe	tears away	Rev. 21:4
Wisdom		1 Kings 3:16–28 + 4:29; Job 28:12–28; Prov. All, especially 2:6, 7, 10 + 3:13, 19, 21; + 4:5, 7 + 8:11 + 9:1–13:25 + 24:3; Eccles. 1:12–18; Luke 21:15; Eph. 6:10; Col. 1:28; + 3:16
"	against deceivers provided by God	Luke 21:8–19
"	and understanding	Job 28:28; Ps. 49:1–20; Prov. 1:2 + 2:1–7 + 8:14 + 9:9, 10 + 14:33 + 16:16 + 17:24; Dan. 1:10–20
"	" youth	Prov. 1:4
"	beginning	Ps. 111:10 + 136:5; Prov. 3:19 + 9:10

"	better than desired things	Prov. 8:11
"	better than strength & war weapons	Eccles. 9:16, 18
"	by asking God	James 1:5
"	, earthly - is not from heaven	Ezek. 28:17; 2 Cor. 1:12; James 3:15
"	followed by grief	Eccles. 1:18
"	from above is pure	James 1:5 + 3:17
"	" applied heart	Ps. 90:12
"	" just mouth	Prov. 10:31
"	" the Lord	1 Chron. 22:12; Prov. 2:6
"	" understanding	Prov. 17:24, 27; Eccles. 2:12, 13
"	" years	Job 32:7
"	given from God	Mark 6:2; James 1:5
"	greatest for Kings	1 Kings 10:23
"	increased at end times	Dan. 12:4
"	is fear of Lord	Job 28:12–15, 23, 28; Prov. 9:10
"	, keep sound	Prov. 3:21
"	not in grave	Eccles. 9:10
"	of God not of man or world	1 Cor. 2:4–7, 12
"	" " per Christ	Matt. 11:25
"	" " " Paul	1 Cor. 1:24, 25 + 2:7–9
"	" God's Job	Job 37:1–24; Jer. 17:8; Eph. 1:17
"	" man give way to gospel	1 Cor. 2:1–5
"	or this world	1 Cor. 1:17–24 + 3:18–21
"	" understanding	Prov. 19:8
"	provided by Lord only	1 Chron. 22:12; Job 12:13, 16

"	, Satan once full of	Ezek. 28:12
"	, seek - ask God	James 1:5, 6
"	, teach - to children	Prov. 4:1–27
"	to the wise	Dan. 2:20, 21, 23
"	vs power	1 Cor. 2:5
"	, we can pray for	James 1:5, 6
Wise	and prudent	Matt. 11:25
"	" righteous vs foolish & wicked	Prov. 13:1–25
"	be	Ps. 2:10; Prov. 3:33 + 6:6–8; Eph. 5:15; James 1:5
"	, be not - in conceits	Rom. 12:16
"	but little	Prov. 30:24–31
"	- fools	1 Cor. 4:10
"	- four things	Prov. 30:24–28
"	gets wisdom	Dan. 2:20, 21, 23
"	God	1 Tim. 1:17; Jude 1:25
"	man	Prov. 1:5, 7, 8 + 24:5–7 + 27:5
"	ones waketh	Dan. 12:2, 3
"	" will heed	Matt. 7:24
"	or fool	Prov. 2:7; Eccles. 10:12–14 + 12:9–11; Mark 10:7, 8
"	shall shine	Dan. 12:3, 10
"	- simple	Prov. 21:11
"	tongue	Prov. 12:18
"	understand	Dan. 12:10
"	unto salvation	2 Tim. 3:15
"	use of time	Eph. 5:15, 16; Cor. 4:5
"	words	Eccles. 12:11–14; Prov. 27:11
Wisely walk		Eph. 5:15, 16
Wish to prosper		Isa. 58:11; 3 John 1:2
Wist		Jude 16:20; Mark 9:6; Luke 2:49
Wit		Rom. 8:23; 2 Cor. 5:19 + 8:1

Witch	Exod. 22:18
Witchcraft	1 Sam. 15:23
With and was God	John 1:2
" him, workers	2 Cor. 6:1
" Jesus, God was	Acts 10:38
" me or against me	Matt. 12:30; Luke 11:23
" thee & uphold	
thee - God	Isa. 41:10
" us, Jesus	Ps. 46:10, 11; Matt. 28:20;
	Mark 16:15
Withal	Luke 6:38; Philem. 1:22
Withdrawn from	
disorderly ones	2 Thess. 3:6–14
Withdrew	Luke 5:16; Gal. 2:12
Wither	Ps. 1:3
Withered	Matt. 13:6 + 21:19, 20
" hand	Matt. 12:10–13; Mark 3:1–5;
	Luke 6:6–10
Withereth	Ps. 90:6; 1 Pet. 1:24
Withhold	Ps. 40:11 + 84:11; Prov. 3:27;
	Mark 11:24, 26
Withholden	Job 38:15 + 42:2
Within	Gen. 6:14; Rom. 8:23; Heb. 6:19
" you	Ezek 36:26, 27; Luke 17:21
Without	Gen. 1:2 + 6:14; Isa. 55:1;
	Rom. 1:20 + 11:29;
	James 2:18, 20, 26; Heb. 7:3
Withstand	Esther 9:2; Eph. 6:13
Withstood	Gal. 2:11; 2 Tim. 3:8
Witness at end times &	
salvation offered	Matt. 24:14; 1 Pet. 1:5
" by spirit	Rom. 8:16
" , faithful or false	Prov. 14:5

"	, God's	Heb. 2:4
"	in earth & heaven	1 John 5:8–10
"	" Holy Ghost	Rom. 9:1
"	is " "	Heb. 10:5–18
"	" Jesus	Rev. 1:5
"	John	John 1:6, 7
"	not false	Deut. 5:20
"	of gospel at end	Matt. 34:14
"	" Jesus	John 1:15 + 5:31–33, 36, 37
"	" me per God	Isa. 43:10, 12
"	" " " Jesus	Acts 1:8
"	" resurrection	Acts 4:33
"	" that light	John 1:6–9, 15
"	" truth - Jesus came	John 18:37
"	true or deceitful	Prov. 14:25
Witnesses		Matt. 18:16
"	, false	Matt. 26:59, 60, 65; Acts 6:11–14
"	, my	Isa. 43:10–12 + 44:8; Acts 1:8
"	of Christ	Luke 24:46–48; Acts 1:8 + 5:32
"	" Christ's suffering	1 Pet. 5:1
"	" Jesus Christ were beheaded	Rev. 6:9 + 20:4
"	, we are	Acts 2:32
"	, " have	Heb. 12:1
Wives		Gen. 6:2, 18; Josh. 1:14; Ezra 10:14; Isa. 8:19; Eph. 5:22–25, 28; Col. 3:18, 19; 1 Pet. 3:1
Wizard		Lev. 20:27; 2 Chron. 33:6; Isa. 8:19

Woe	Isa. 5:8, 11, 18, 20–22 + 6:5; Matt. 23:13–16, 23, 25, 27, 29; Mark 14:21; Luke 6:24–26; + 11:42–47, 52; Jude 1:11; Rev. 11:14
Woes, six	Isa. 5:8, 11, 18, 20–22
Wolf	Isa. 11:6; Matt. 10:16; John 10:12
Woman	Jer. 31:22; Matt. 9:20, 22 + 15:28; Mark 5:25, 33, 34 + 10:12; John 4:7, 9, 11, 15, 17, 19, 21, 28, 42
" , adulterous	Prov. 30:20
" after man	1 Cor. 11:7–11
Woman, barren	Ps. 113:9
" behold thy son	John 19:26
" , brawling	Prov. 21:9
" created	Gen. 1:27 + 2:18, 21–23
" - man	Gen. 1:23
" - mother of Jesus	John 2:4
" to be silent	1 Tim. 2:12
" , virtuous - ideal	Ruth 3:11; Prov. 12:4 + 31:10–31
" who feareth God is praised	Prov. 31:30, 31; Rom. 8:31
Womb	Luke 1:31, 41, 44 + 2:23; Acts 14:8
Women , duties of aged	Titus 2:3–5
" , holy - adorned themselves	1 Pet. 3:3–5
" not in authority	1 Tim. 2:12
" prophets	Acts 21:9
Women's behavior	2 Tim. 2:9–13

Wonder		Acts 3:10
Wondered		Matt. 15:31
Wonderful name		Isa. 9:6
Wonderful, too		Prov. 30:18, 19
Wonders		Ps. 88:12 + 105:5; Acts 5:12
"	by apostles	Acts 2:43 + 5:12
"	foretold	Acts 2:17–21
"	, great - by beast	Rev. 13:13
"	of God are mighty	Dan. 4:2, 3
Wondrous works of God		Job 37:14, 16; Ps. 72:18 + 119:18
Wont		Dan. 3:19
Wood		Gen. 6:14; 2 Chron. 2:16; Jer. 7:18
Woof		Lev. 13:47
Wool		Dan. 7:9
Woollen		Lev. 13:47, 48, 59
Word altered		Rev. 22:18, 19
"	and action all in the name of Jesus	Col. 3:17
"	and work to be good	2 Thess. 2:17
"	brings faith	Rom. 10:8, 9, 17
"	brought gospel	1 Thess. 1:5, 6
"	confirmed	Mark 16:20
"	, famine warning	Amos 8:11, 12
"	fitly spoken	Prov. 25:11
"	for Jesus' sake	Col. 3:17
"	forever	Isa. 40:8; Luke 21:33; 1 Pet. 1:25
"	, God's	Ps. 119:11; Prov. 30:5; Jer. 1:1–3; Luke 4:4 + 21:33; John 1:1
"	, " - is forever	Isa. 40:8; 1 Pet. 1:25

"	" " " forever	1 Pet. 1:25
"	" " Pure	Ps. 119:140
"	" " prosper	Ps. 119:107; Isa. 55:11
"	" " through your mouth	Isa. 55:11
"	of Lord to Jeremiah	Jer.— most of this book
"	offend not	James 3:2
"	, our	Col. 3:17
"	power	Heb. 4:12
"	shall accomplish	Isa. 55:11
"	sown	Mark 4:14–20
"	to be effective	Isa. 55:11
"	" preach	2 Tim. 4:2
"	was God	John 1:1–4
Words		2 Cor. 12:2–4
"	after Christ Jesus' return to earth - Jesus	Matt. 28:9, 10, 18–20; Mark 16:6, 15–18; Luke 24:17, 19, 25–27, 36, 38, 39, 41, 44; John 20:15–17, 19, 21, 22, 26, 27, 29 + 21:5, 6, 10, 12, 16–19, 22, 23
"	are God's words	Deut. 23:1, 2, 14; John 14:24
"	" spirit & life	John 6:63
"	, enticing	Col. 2:4
"	, few	Eccles. 5:2
"	given by the Lord	Luke 21:15
"	" when on trial	Matt. 10:16–20
"	, hasty - less hope than of a fool	Prov. 29:20
"	, idle - judged	Matt. 12:36, 37
"	, justified - condemned	Matt. 12:36, 37
"	, malicious	Prov. 18:4, 8; 3 John 1:10

"	of Christ	Col. 3:16
"	" God pleasant	Ps. 55:21 + 119:103–105
"	" Jesus are forever	Matt. 24:35; Luke 21:33
"	" " is life	John 6:63
"	" " last before ascension	Acts 1:8, 9
"	of Jesus to be kept	John 14:21, 23
"	" life	Prov. 4:20–22; John 6:63
"	" revelation book not to be altered	Rev. 22:18, 19
"	on cross	John 19:26–28, 30
"	, pleasant	Ps. 19:14; Prov. 16:24
"	sealed until end times	Dan. 12:4, 8–13
"	to remember	2 Pet. 3:1
"	true and faithful	Rev. 21:5
"	unspeakable	2 Cor. 12:3, 4
"	used in judgment	Matt. 12:36, 37
"	, wise & fool	Eccles. 10:12–14 + 12:10, 11
Work		Exod. 18:17–23; Ps. 127:1, 2; Matt. 11:28–30; John 5:17
"	and word to be good	2 Thess. 2:17
"	, child's	Prov. 20:11
"	conscientiously	Luke 12:22–31; 1 Cor. 3:13–15
"	- every work to judgment	Eccles. 12:13, 14
"	- Father & Jesus	Eccles. 3:11; John 5:17
"	- give to needy	Eph. 4:28
"	, God's	Ps. 92:4 + 102:25; Eccles. 3:11
"	, God's - is us	Isa. 64:8; John 6:29; Phil. 1:6
"	judged	Ps. 62:12; Rev. 22:11, 12
"	or sleep	Mark 10:5

Work out own salvation		Phil. 2:12, 13
"	regardless of weather	Prov. 20:4
"	rewarded	Jer. 31:16, 17; 1 Cor. 3:12–15
"	six days	Exod. 23:12; Deut. 5:12–14
"	, slothful	Prov. 12:24 + 15:19 + 18:9
"	- study - walk	1 Thess. 4:11, 12
"	- support self regardless of weather	Prov. 20:4
"	to eat	2 Thess. 3:10, 11
"	together	Rom. 8:28
"	while it is day	John 9:4
"	with all your might while living	Eccles. 9:10; 1 Thess. 4:11
Worketh in you		Phil. 2:12, 13
"	righteous	Acts 10:35
Working body parts		Eph. 4:16
"	, Lord - with them	Mark 16:20
Workmanship of God are we		Eph. 2:8–10
Works		Prov. 16:3; John 14:12
"	are a must	James 2:14–20, 26
"	, dead	Heb. 9:14
"	dictates what consideration	Prov. 24:12
"	follow them	Rev. 14:13
"	from faith	James 2:17, 22, 24, 26 + 4:17
"	good	Eph. 2:10; 1 Tim. 6:17–19; 2 Tim. 3:17; Rev. 15:3
"	" & love	Luke 6:31–38
"	, good by widow	1 Tim. 5:10
"	, " glorify Father	Matt. 5:16

"	greater by believers	John 14:12
"	, judged by	Ps. 62:12; 2 Cor. 5:10; Rev. 20:12, 13
"	justified	James 2:14–24
"	, marvellous	Ps. 105:5
"	, not of	Eph. 2:8, 9
"	of darkness	Rom. 13:12
"	" dead & life	Rev. 20:12
'	" flesh	Gal. 5:19–21; 2 Cor. 5:19
"	" God	Job 37:14; Ps. 9:1–16
"	" " (Lord) marvellous	Ps. 92:4, 5 + 105:5 + 111:2–9
"	of man is pleasure	Eccles. 3:22
"	" widow	1 Tim. 5:9, 10
"	" yours greater than me	John 14:12
"	saves	James 2:14–24
"	to accomplish faith	James 2:20–26
"	" the Lord	Prov. 13:11; Col. 3:23
"	wondrous	Job 37:14, 16
World		John 16:21, 28, 33 + 17:5, 6, 9, 11–25
"	cleansed	Dan. 8:14
"	corruption - divine nature	2 Pet. 1:3, 4
"	created	Gen. 1:1, 6–8, 14–17
"	dictator gets power	Rev. 13:5 + 17:8
"	, do not conform to	Rom. 12:2
"	end	Matt. 13:38–50 + 28:20; Heb. 9:26
"	foundation & end	Heb. 9:26
"	friend is enemy of God	James 4:4
"	, in the	John 17:11

"	king to prosper	Dan. 11:36
"	, loveth not	1 John 2:15–17
"	may know	John 14:31
"	not known sons of God	1 John 3:1
"	or Christ	John 16:33; Col. 2:8, 9
"	overcometh	John 16:33; 1 John 5:4, 5; Rev. 3:21
"	punished for evil	Isa. 13:11
"	- saved opportunity	John 3:17; 1 John 1:1, 2
World	see Jesus no more	John 14:19
"	spirits	1 John 4:1–5
"	to be destroyed	2 Pet. 3:10; 1 John 2:17
"	- tribulation	John 16:33
"	wisdom	1 Cor. 1:17–24
Worldly	behavior	Rom. 12:1–3
"	gods	2 Cor. 4:4; 1 John 2:15–17
"	is nothing	Luke 9:25; 1 Tim. 6:7
"	pleasure prominent at end	Matt. 24:37–44
"	things	1 Cor. 7:34
"	" created & later seen	Rom. 1:20
"	things God's gifts	Eccles. 5:18, 19
"	" including sex misuse	1 John 2:15–17
"	things not most important for us	Matt. 6:25–32
"	things not of God	1 John 1:15–17
"	" " to be glorified in	Gal. 6:14
Worm		Job 7:5 + 19:26; Isa. 41:14
Worms		Job 24:20 + 25:6; Acts 12:23
Wormwood		Lam. 3:15, 19

Worry	Ps. 56:3, 4; Isa. 41:10; Jer. 29:11; Matt. 6:34; Luke 12:22–31; Phil. 4:6, 7; 1 Pet. 5:7
Worse	Matt. 12:45; John 5:14; 1 Tim. 5:8; 2 Tim. 3:13
Worship Father	John 4:21, 23
" " God	John 4:23, 24
" God	John 4:20–24; Rev. 13:8 + 14:7
" idols	1 Kings 14:15, 16; Rev. 9:20
" know not what	John 4:22
" Lord	Ps. 96:9; Isa. 66:3; Luke 4:8
" " God	Ps. 100:1–5
" " " only	Matt. 4:10; Luke 4:8
" the beast (dragon) or be killed	Rev. 13:4, 5, 8, 15 + 14:9–11
" the lamb, all creatures	Rev. 5:13, 14
Worshipped Jesus	Matt. 28:9, 17
" " after resurrection	Luke 24:51, 52
" God	Rev. 7:11
" not the beast - to reign with Christ	Rev. 20:4
Worshippers, true	John 4:23, 24
Worshipping together	Eph. 5:18–21; Col. 2:18
Worth	Lev. 27:23
Worthy	1 Tim. 5:18; Rev. 4:11 + 5:9–13
" , be	Luke 21:36
" God	Rev. 7:11
" is children of resurrection	Luke 20:35, 36; Rev. 3:4
" is lamb	Rev. 5:11, 12

"	" Lord	1 Chron. 29:11; Ps. 18:3; Rev. 4:11
"	to open book	Rev. 5:2, 5, 9
"	, walk	Eph. 4:1; Col. 1:10; 1 Thess. 2:12
"	- walk to escape wrath	Luke 21:36
Wot		Exod. 32:1; Acts 3:17 + 7:40; Phil. 1:22
Wotteth		Gen. 39:8
Would		Exod. 10:20, 27; Mark 3:2 + 16:1; John 14:2
Wouldest		John 11:40 + 21:18
Wound		Jer. 30:17; Rev. 13:3, 14
Wounded for our transgressions		Isa. 53:5; Luke 10:30
Wounds		Prov. 18:8
Woven		John 19:23
Wrap		Mic. 7:3
Wrapped in linen		Luke 23:53
Wrath - anger & envy		Prov. 15:1 + 27:4; Isa. 54:8
"	brings strife	Prov. 30:33
"	cup	1 Kings 17:17–24
"	days	Zeph. 1:14, 15; Rev. 6:12–17 + 11:18 + 16:19, 21
Wrath not for Christians		Rom. 5:9 + 12:17–19; 1 Thess. 5:9
"	" to have	Eph. 4:26, 31; 1 Tim. 2:8
"	of devil futile	Rev. 12:11–17
"	" God	Ezra 10:14; Jer. 10:10; Ezek. 7:19
"	" " to unbelievers	2 Chron. 28:13 + 30:8 + 32:25 + 34:21, 25; John 3:36; Rom. 1:18; Rev. 14:9, 10 + 16:2

"	of Lord	Ps. 2:5 + 90:7
"	" man not of God	James 1:19, 20
"	" Satan	Rev. 12:12
"	" the lamb	Rev. 6:14–17
"	punished	Job 19:29
"	to come	Rom. 5:8, 9
"	" disobedient ones	Col. 3:6
"	, vials of	Rev. 16:1
"	, who able to withstand	Rev. 6:12–17
Wrestle against		Eph. 6:11, 12
Wringing		Prov. 30:33
Wrinkles		Job 16:8
Write		1 John 2:1, 7, 8, 12, 13; Rev. 14:13 + 21:5
Writing		Prov. 30:33
"	tablet	Luke 1:63
Writings		Exod. 32:16
Written are iniquities		Isa. 65:6, 7; Gal. 6:11
"	be holy	Gal. 6:11; 1 Pet. 1:16
"	for our learning	John 20:30, 31; Rom. 15:4; 1 John 2:14, 21, 26 + 5:13
"	in book	Luke 4:17
Wrong		2 Cor. 7:12 + 12:13; Col. 3:25
Wronged		Philem. 1:18
Wrongfully		1 Pet. 2:19
Wrote		John 8:8; 3 John 1:9
Wroth		2 Chron. 28:9; Ps. 18:7 + 78:59; Isa. 54:9 + 64:5; Rev. 12:17
Wrought		Ruth 2:19; 2 Cor. 12:12; 1 Pet. 4:3
"	deeds in God	John 3:21
"	faith by his works	James 2:22

"	good to me - Daniel	Dan. 4:2
"	" work	Matt. 26:10; Mark 14:6
"	in Christ	Eph. 1:20
"	special miracles, Paul	Acts 19:11
"	us	2 Cor. 5:5
"	with labour	Neh. 6:16; 2 Thess. 3:8
Wrung out		Lev. 1:15

• Y •

Yarn		2 Chron. 1:16
Ye		Mark 14:62; John 14:28;
		1 Cor. 11:1 + 14:26; 2 Cor. 8:9
"	, all - praise	Ps. 117:1, 2
"	are - do - know	1 Cor. 4:10 + 6:2–20 + 7:1, 5, 23;
		Eph. 5:5, 7, 8
"	, be	1 Cor. 15:58
"	- body is temple	1 Cor. 3:16, 17 + 6:19, 20
"	do all to glorify God	1 Cor. 10:31
"	were - now are	Eph. 5:5, 7
"	who hope in the Lord - strengthened	Ps. 31:24
Yea		Luke 11:28; 1 Cor. 1:14, 20;
		Rev. 14:13
"	and nay	Matt. 5:37; 2 Cor. 1:17–20;
		James 5:12
Years, our		Ps. 90:10
"	teach wisdom	Job 32:7
"	, thousand - with the Lord	Rev. 20:9, 10, 12
"	, thousand with the Lord as one day	2 Pet. 3:8

Yesterday		Ps. 90:4; Heb. 13:8
Yesternight		Gen. 31:29
Yet		Prov. 9:9; John 7:39 + 14:25; Rom. 5:6–8
Yield		Matt. 27:50; Acts 5:10 + 23:21; Rom. 6:13
Yoke		Isa. 10:27 + 58:9; Lam. 3:27; Matt. 11:29, 30; Acts 15:10
"	easy with rest	Matt. 11:28–30
"	of bondage	Gal. 5:1
Yoked together		2 Cor. 6:14
Yokefellow		Phil. 4:3
Yonder		Matt. 17:20
You	- a guide light	Rom. 2:19
"	are God's	1 Cor. 6:19, 20
"	, give	Ezek. 36:26
"	- ward	2 Cor. 1:12 + 13:3; Eph. 3:2
"	with me - Jesus	John 14:3–6
"	, within	Ezek. 36:26, 27; Luke 17:21
Young get advice from		
	wise & experience	Prov. 1:1–31:31
"	men & women	Isa. 62:5; Titus 2:4–8
"	to old	John 21:18
Younger - elder		1 Pet. 5:5
Your	faith	1 Pet. 1:7, 9
"	faults	Ezek. 36:25, 26; James 5:16
"	God	Jer. 11:4
"	souls	1 Pet. 1:9
Yourselves		Josh. 23:11; Luke 12:36 + 21:34
"	, examine	2 Cor. 13:5
"	, not of	Eph. 2:8, 9
Youth		Eccles. 11:9, 10; 1 Tim. 4:12
"	bear yoke	Lam. 3:27

"	instruction	Prov. 1:2–4
"	, Jesus'	Luke 2:40, 46, 47, 52
"	shame	Isa. 54:4
"	to manhood	1 Cor. 13:11, 12
Youthful lusts		2 Tim. 2:22

• Z •

Zacharias - father of John
      the Baptist   Luke 1:5, 11–22, 59, 60, 67

Zeal   Ps. 69:9 + 119:139; John 2:17;
                              2 Cor. 9:2; Phil. 3:6

Zealous   1 Cor. 14:12; Titus 2:14;
                              Rev. 3:19

Zion   Ps. 48:11, 12

• SECTION BB •
Body of Jesus After Resurrection

Ate with Apostles	Luke 24:42, 43
" " disciples	Acts 21:9–13
Had bones and flesh	Luke 24:39,40; John 20:20
Passed through closed doors	John 20:19
Real	Luke 24:39–43
Recognizable	1 Cor. 15:44

• SECTION CC •
NOTED COVENANTS

LORD GOD WITH . . .

Abraham	Gen. 17:5, 7–14, + 21:27, 32; Lev. 26:42
Abram	Gen. 15:18, + 17:1–4
David	2 Sam. 23:5
Everlasting	Heb. 13:20
Eyes, Job's	Job 31:1
Ezekiel	Ezek. 16:8
Faithful	Ps. 103:17, 18
Flesh, all-on earth	Gen. 9:17
Hag.	Hag. 2:5
Idolatry ones	Isa. 57:8
Isaac	Lev. 26:42
Isaiah	Gen. 17:19, 21; Isa. 54:10
Israel	Deut. 4:23, + 5:2, 3; Rom. 11:26, 27
" **Children**	Exod. 31:16; Num. 18:19; Jer. 31:32
Jacob	Lev. 26:42
" **and Laban**	Gen. 31:41–53
Jeremiah	Jer. 11:1–6
Joshua - Ark of Covenant	Josh. 3:6, 8, 17, + 4:7

Judah	2 Chron. 15:12, + 34:30–32
King and his seed	Ezek. 17:12,13
Leviticus	Lev. 26:14–16
Man's	Gal. 3:15
Moses	Exod. 6:4–8, + 19:5, + 24:6–12
" - Ark of Covenant	Exod. 25:10; Num. 10:33, + 14:44
New with Israel & Judah	Heb. 8:6–13, + 9:1, + 12:24
Noah	Gen. 6:18, + 9:9–17; Isa. 54:9, 10
Perpetual	Jer. 50:5
Phineas	Num. 25:12, 13
Sabbath - children of Israel	Lev. 24:8
Saints with sacrifice	Ps. 50:5
Salt	Num. 18:19
Solomon	1 Kings 6:11–14, + 9:4–6, + 11:11
The Sanctified	Heb. 10:15–17
Them that fear [love] the Lord	Ps. 25:14; Dan. 9:4
Tribes at Jordan River area	Josh. 23:16
Zechariah	Zech. 9:11

• SECTION JJ •
Jesus' Humanity After Ascension

Jesus' humanity after ascension	Phil. 2:5–8
Appeared [stood] to many	Luke 24:36
Ate with many	Luke 24:43
Ate with two men	Luke 24:30
Blessed them [possibly in action]	Luke 24:50, 51
Came to two men	Luke 24:15
Gave food to them	Luke 24:30
Hungered	Luke 24:41
Listened to two men	Luke 24:18–24
Parted into heaven	Luke 24:51
Sat with two men	Luke 24:30
Shewed many his hands and feet	Luke 24:40
Spoke to many	Luke 24:17, 19, 25–27, 36, 38, 39, 41, 44, 46–49
Vanished out of sight	Luke 24:31
Walked with two men	Luke 24:17, 28, 29

(J. = Jesus)

Afflictions of many healed by J.	Matt. 15:30, 31
Angel slew 5,180	Isa. 37:36
Ascension, proof of	Luke 24:13–31
Axe head floats, by Elisha	2 Kings 6:6
Blind - Bartimaeus, by J.	Mark 10:46:52 (Faith)
" - Beggar, by J.	Luke 18:35–43 (Faith)
" man at Behsaida - sight restored by J.	Mark 8:22–25
" by way side - sight restored	Luke 18:35–43
" " from birth - sight restored	John 9:1, 6–9
" - many, by J.	Luke 7:21, 22
" - men, two, by J.	Matt. 9:27–30
" - " " - at roadside, by J.	Matt. 20:29–34
Blind-Saul, by Ananias	Acts 9:17, 18
" - several, " J.	Matt. 21:14
" - those, " Lord	Ps. 146:8
" (also see sight)	
Blood issue-woman, by J.	Matt. 9:20–22; Mark 5:25–34; Luke 8:43–48

Bloody flux - father of Publius, by Paul	Acts 28:8
Bones to life by Lord God per Ezekiel	Ezek. 37:1–10
Cattle saved-others died, by Lord	Exod. 9:1–7
Chains broken, by angel	Acts 12:5–7
Cripple - man, by Paul	Acts 14:8–10
Daniel spared from lions, by angels	Dan. 6:1–23
Deaf and speech impediment, by J.	Mark 7:32–37
" and dumb son of one in multitude, by J.	Mark 9:17–29
Death near - son of nobleman, by J.	John 4:46–54
" to life - daughter of ruler, by J.	Matt. 9:18, 19, 24, 25
" to life - daughter of ruler Jairus, by J.	Mark 5:22, 23, 35–43; Luke 8:41, 42, 49–56
" to life - Eutychus, by Paul	Acts 20:9–12
" to life - Lazareth, by J.	John 11:43, 44, + 12:1, 17
" to life - son of Shunammite, by Elisha	2 Kings 4:16–37
" to life - son of widow, by Elisha	1 Kings 17:17–24
" to life - son of widow, by J.	Luke 7:12–15, 22
Devil from blind & dumb man, by J.	Matt. 12:22; Luke 11:14

"	from daughter of Canaan woman, by J.	Matt. 15:22–28; Mark 7:25–30
"	from dumb man, by J.	Matt. 9:32–34
"	from dumb one, by J.	Luke 11:14
"	from man, by J.	Luke 4:33–36
"	" " -legion, by J.	Matt. 8:28–32; Mark 5:2–13; Luke 8:26–33

Devils from all, by J.   Matt. 8:16; Mark 1:32; Luke 4:40

" "	many, by Apostles	Mark 6:12, 13

Diseased healed - all in country, by J.   Matt. 14:35, 36; Mark 1:32

"	various afflictions healed - many, by J.	Matt. 15:30,31

Diseases healed - all in cities & villages, by J.   Matt. 9:35; Mark 1:32; Luke 6:17–19

"	and sicknesses healed by J.	Matt 4:23, 24
"	and evil spirits healed - in Asia, by Paul	Acts 19:11, 12
"	, divers - many, by J.	Mark 1:34
"	, others healed, by Paul	Acts 28:9

Divination spirit came out - damsel, by Paul   Acts 16:16–18

Dropsy healed - man, by J.   Luke 14:2–4

Dumb man spoke, by J.	Matt. 9:32, 33	
Dumb spirit cast out - ruler's daughter, by J.	Mark 9:17, 18, 23–25	
" to speak - many, by J.	Mark 7:37	
Ear of servant reattached [healed], by J.	Luke 22:50, 51; John 18:10	
Earth opened - rebels, by Lord	Num. 16:30–32	
Evil spirits from Jews & Greeks, by J.	Acts 19:11, 12	
" spirits from many, by J.	Luke 7:21, 22	
" spirits from son of company man, by J.	Luke 9:38–43	
" spirits from women, by J.	Luke 8:2	
Faith of man made him whole, by J.	Mark 10:52	
Fed 100, by Elisha	2 Kings 4:42–44	
" 4,000 men, women & children with seven loaves and a few fishes, by J.	Matt. 15:32–38; Mark 8:1–9, + 8:20	
" 5,000 men with five barley loaves & two fishes, by J.	John 6:7–14; Mark 6:41–44, + 8:19; Luke 9:12–17	
" 5,000 men, women, & children with five loaves & two fishes, by J.	Matt. 14:15–21	

Fever - father of publican, by Paul	Acts 28:8
Fever - Simon/Peter's wife's mother, by J.	Matt. 8:14, 15; Mark 1:30, 31; Luke 4:38, 39
Fiery furnace - three not burned, by angel	Dan. 3:20–28
Fig tree withered, by J.	Matt. 21:19, 20; Mark 11:12–14
Fire quenched, by Moses	Num. 11:2
" from heaven, by Elijah	2 Kings 1:9–12
Fishes catch, fishermen, by J.	Luke 5:2–7; John 21:1, 5–11
Flesh returned, by Ezekiel & God	Ezek. 37:10
" returned Naaman, by Elisha	2 Kings 5:10–14
Flies sent, by Lord	Exod. 8:20–24
Freed by earthquake, by Paul & Silas	Acts 16:26
" Peter, by angel	Acts 12:7
Frogs from water, by Aaron	Exod. 8:6
Girl vexed, by J.	Matt. 15:22–28
Hailstones from heaven, by Lord	Josh. 10:11
Hand dried on Jeroboam - restored by Man of God	1 Kings 13:1–6
" of man withered - restored by J.	Matt. 12:9; Mark 3:1–5; Luke 6:6–10
Handicaps, various - healed by J.	Matt. 15:31

Healed many of various diseases and sicknesses	Matt. 4:23, 24
Healing need healed - people, by J.	Luke 9:11
Illnesses, many - cured, by J.	Luke 7:21
Impotent man - made whole, by Peter & John	Acts 4:9, 14, 16, 22
" man, crippled - healed, by Paul	Acts 4:8–10
Infirmities, many, by J.	Luke 7:21, 22
Infirmity - man of thirty - eight years, by J.	John 5:5–9
" - woman + other women, by J.	Luke 8:2, + 13:11–13
Iron floats, by Elisha	2 Kings 6:6
Jonas survived being inside, by Lord	Jonah 1:17, + 2:1–10; Matt. 12:38–40
Jordan River dried up, by Joshua	Josh. 3:17
" waters divided, by Elijah	2 Kings 2:8
" waters divided, by Elisha	2 Kings 2:14
Lame healed, by J.	Matt. 21:14
" " , by Philip	Acts 8:6, 7
" walked, by Peter	Acts 3:2–16
Leprosy - healed, by J.	Matt. 8:2–4; Mark 1:40–42; Luke 5:12, 13, + 17:15–19
" of Naaman, by Elisha	2 Kings 5:1–15

" of ten men - healed, by J.	Luke 17:12–14
Lice from dust, by Aaron	Exod. 8:17
Life from bones, by Ezekiel & Lord God	Ezek. 37:1–10
Lion's mouth closed against Daniel, by angels	Dan. 6:1–23
Lunatic - son of man in multitude - healed, by J.	Matt. 17:14–20; Luke 9:38–42
Miracles and wonders for Gentiles - through Barnabas & Paul	Acts 15:12
Moon stood still, by Lord	Josh. 10:12–14
Palsy of Aeneas, by Peter	Acts 9:33, 34
" " centurion, by J.	Matt. 8:6–13; Luke 7:2, 3, 7–15
" " man, by J.	Matt. 9:2–7; Mark 2:3–12; Luke 5:18–25
" " many, by Philip	Acts 8:6, 7
" " one, by J.	Mark 2:3–12
Plagues - blood of woman, by J.	Mark 5:25–34
" - many healed, by J.	Mark 3:10; Luke 7:21
Prison - release of Peter, by angel	Acts 12:7–11
" chains loosened, by Paul & Silas	Acts 16:23–26
" doors opened, by angel	Acts 5:19, 20
Rain none, by Elias	James 5:17
" yes, by Elias	James 5:18
River Jordan divided, by Elisha	2 Kings 2:8

" Jordan dried up, by Joshua	Josh. 3:17
Rod to serpent and to rod, by Lord to Moses	Exod. 4:3, 4, + 7:9–12
Sea calmed, by J.	Mark 4:36–41
" divided, by Moses ~~Ezek~~. Exod.	14:21
Serpent for healing, by Moses	Num. 21:6–9
" from rod, by Aaron	Exod. 4:3, 4, + 7:9–12
Sick and devils,	Matt. 8:16; Mark 1:32; Luke 4:40
" - Many in cities, villages & synagogues – healed by J.	Matt. 9:35
" - Many in streets made whole by touching Jesus' garments	Mark 6:56
" - Many in multitudes healed, by J.	Matt. 14:14
" - Many were healed, by Apostles	Mark 6:13
" - Servant of centurion healed, by J.	Luke 7:2–10
" healed - son of nobleman, by J.	John 4:46–51
Sicknesses and diseases healed by J.	Matt. 4:24, 24
Sight received - Saul, by Ananias (also see blind)	Acts 9:8–18
Sins, hidden - one can convert	James 5:19, 20
" of woman forgiven, by J.	Luke 7:47–50

Soul saved from grave - David, by Lord	Ps. 30:2, 3
Speech impediment - man - spoke plain, by J.	Mark 7:32–37
Spirit, divination - in damsel - came out, by Paul	Acts 16:16–18
" , unclean - son of company man - rebuked by J.	Matt. 17:14–20; Luke 9:38–42
Spirits - deaf & dumb, healed by J.	Mark 9:17–29
" , evil - many in Asia, healed by Paul	Acts 19:18, 19
" , unclean - daughter of Greek, healed by J.	Mark 7:25–30
" , unclean - man, healed by J.	Mark 3:10, 11
" , unclean man in synagogue, rebuked by J.	Mark 1:23–28; Luke 4:33–35
" , unclean - many, healed by Apostles	Acts 5:16
" , unclean - many, healed by J.	Luke 6:18
" , unclean - many, healed by Philip	Acts 8:6, 7
Storm on lake - ceased, by J.	Matt. 8:22–26; Mark 4:37–39; Luke 8:23, 24
Sun - stand still, by Lord	John 10:12–14

Swine into sea with devils, by J.	Matt. 8:28–32; Mark 5:2–13; Luke 8:26–33
Walked on the sea, Jesus	Matt. 14:25; Mark 6:47–50; John 6:19, 20
" " water, Peter	Matt. 14:29
Water came, by Moses	Num. 20:11
" divided to dry ground, by Lord	Josh. 3:17, + 4:23
" from rock, by God	Isa. 48:21
" parted - Red Sea, by Moses	Exod. 14:21
" parted - river, by Joshua & the Lord	Josh. 3:17
Widow's son from death, by Elijah	1 Kings 17:17–24
Winds and waves rebuked, by J.	Matt. 8:26
Wine from water, by J.	John 2:3–11, + 4:46

• SECTION UU •
Unusual Word Uses

Chapter - Longest in OT,
     176 verses   Ps. 119
  "   - Longest in NT,
     eighty verses   Luke 1

Chapter - Shortest in OT,
     two verses   Ps. 117
  "   - Shortest in NT,
     ten verses each   Rom. 4 & 10

Eleven words make up four
     sentences   1 Pet. 2:17

"I" used fifty-six times in   John 14 & 15

"My" used eight times
     in one verse   Ps. 18:2

"Praise the Lord" in every
     verse   Ps. 150

Prayer - Shortest in Bible   Matt. 14:30
  "   - Longest in Bible Sol. 8:23–53
                 1 Kings

Sentence - Longest in OT, 368 words	Josh. 15:21–62
" - Longest in NT, 469 words	Luke 3:23–38
Sentence - Shortest in OT, four words	Exod. 20:13, 15
" - Shortest in NT, two words	John 11:35
Time used twenty-nine times in eight verses	Eccles. 3:1–8
Verse - Longest in OT ninety words	Esther 8:9
" - Longest in NT fifty-nine words	Rev. 17:8
Verse - Shortest in OT three verses	1 Chron. 1:24, 25, 26
" - Shortest in NT two verses	John 11:35; and 1 Thess. 5:16
" - Midway in Bible	Ps. 118:8 (anonymous)
"Whatsoever" used six times in one verse	Phil. 4:8

To order additional copies of

You Name It
The
Bible
Has It!

Have your credit card ready and call

(877) 421-READ (7323)

or send $24.95 each + $3.95* S&H to

WinePress Publishing
PO Box 428
Enumclaw, WA 98022

*add $1.00 S&H for each additional book ordered